The Gospel of Mark

BIBLICAL EXPLORATIONS

The Gospel of Mark

A Commentary

Paula Gooder

CANTERBURY
PRESS

First published in 2026 by the Canterbury Press Norwich

Editorial office
3rd Floor, Invicta House
110 Golden Lane
London EC1Y 0TG, UK
www.canterburypress.co.uk

Canterbury Press is an imprint of Hymns Ancient & Modern Ltd
(a registered charity)

Hymns Ancient & Modern

Hymns Ancient & Modern® is a registered trademark of
Hymns Ancient & Modern Ltd
13A Hellesdon Park Road, Norwich,
Norfolk NR6 5DR, UK

British Library Cataloguing in Publication data

A catalogue record for this book is available
from the British Library

ISBN: 978-1-78622-765-2

EU GPSR Authorised Representative
LOGOS EUROPE, 9 rue Nicolas Poussin, 17000, LA ROCHELLE, France
E-mail: Contact@logoseurope.eu

Typeset by Regent Typesetting
Printed and bound in Great Britain by
CPI Group (UK) Ltd

Contents

Introduction 1

Mark 1.1–15: A Title and a Prologue 15

Mark 1.1: A title 16
Mark 1.2–8: John the baptizer 20
Mark 1.9–11: The baptism of Jesus 25
Mark 1.12–13: Jesus in the wilderness 30
Mark 1.14–15: Jesus came to Galilee 31

Mark 1.16–39: A Snapshot of Jesus' Ministry 35

Mark 1.16–20: 'Come, follow me!' 36
Mark 1.21–28: Jesus revealed his authority and healed a man with an unclean spirit 41
Mark 1.29–31: Jesus healed Simon's mother-in-law 47
Mark 1.32–34: Jesus healed many at Simon's house 49
Mark 1.35–39: Prayer and proclamation 51

Mark 1.40—3.12: Jesus' Popularity Begins to Cause Problems 53

Mark 1.40–45: Jesus healed a man with leprosy 54
Mark 2.1–12: Jesus healed a man lowered through the roof 57
Mark 2.13–17: Jesus called Levi 64
Mark 2.18–22: On fasting and fitting together the new and the old 70
Mark 2.23–28: The sabbath 73
Mark 3.1–6: Jesus healed a man with a withered hand 75
Mark 3.7–12: They fell upon him 78

Mark 3.13—4.34: On Insiders and Outsiders 81

Mark 3.13–19a: The appointing of the Twelve 82
Mark 3.19b–35: 'Who is my family?' 84
Mark 4.1–20: The parable of the seed and the soil 92
Mark 4.21–32: Four short additional parables 101
Mark 4.33–34: Jesus spoke in many parables 106

Mark 4.35—8.21: Three Boats, Five Healings, Three Banquets and a Number of Responses 108

Mark 4.35–41: Boat I. 'Who then is this?' 109
Mark 5.1–20: Jesus and the man from Gerasa 114
Mark 5.21–43: A woman and a young girl were saved 123
Mark 6.1–6a: We know who he was – Jesus went home 133
Mark 6.6b–13: The next stage of the apprenticeship 137
Mark 6.14–29: The killing of John the Baptist (a birthday banquet) 140
Mark 6.30–44: A banquet for 5,000 145
Mark 6.45–52: Boat II. They did not understand about the loaves 151
Mark 6.53–56: More healings 156
Mark 7.1–23: What counted as unclean? 158
Mark 7.24–30: Jesus healed the daughter of a woman from Tyre 165
Mark 7.31–37: Jesus healed a man who was deaf 170
Mark 8.1–10: A banquet for 4,000 174
Mark 8.11–21: Boat III. 'Do you not remember?' 178

Mark 8.22—10.53: On Seeing and Not Seeing – the Challenge of Following Jesus 184

Mark 8.22–26: Jesus healed a blind man I (in Bethsaida) 185
Mark 8.27–33: 'Who do you say that I am?' And Jesus prophesied about his death the first time 188
Mark 8.34—9.1: Take up your cross 195
Mark 9.2–13: 'This is my Son' – the Transfiguration 198
Mark 9.14–29: The healing of a boy with a spirit 205
Mark 9.30–32: Jesus prophesied about his death a second time 210

Mark 9.33–37: Who is greatest? 213
Mark 9.38–41: Someone else casting out demons 216
Mark 9.42–50: On stumbling and salt 218
Mark 10.1–12: On marriage and divorce 223
Mark 10.13–16: And on children 227
Mark 10.17–31: A conversation with someone who had much to lose 230
Mark 10.32–34: Jesus prophesied about his death a third time 237
Mark 10.35–45: On being the servant of all 239
Mark 10.46–52: Jesus healed a blind man II (in Jericho) 243

Mark 11.1—16.8: On the Road to the Cross and Beyond 247

Mark 11.1–11: Jesus entered Jerusalem 248
Mark 11.12–25: Jesus cursed the fig tree and then the temple 254
Mark 11.27–33: 'By what authority are you doing these things?' 260
Mark 12.1–12: The parable of the tenants 262
Mark 12.13–17: Should we pay taxes? 265
Mark 12.18–27: Marriage and resurrection 268
Mark 12.28–34: Which Commandment is first? 271
Mark 12.35–37: Jesus posed his own question 274
Mark 12.38–44: On scribes, widows and generosity 276
Mark 13.1–2: 'Not one stone will be left' 279
Mark 13.3–37: Keep watch and know the signs 280
Mark 14.1–2: The plot to kill Jesus picked up pace 291
Mark 14.3–9: The anointing of Jesus 292
Mark 14.10–11: A betrayal planned 297
Mark 14.12–26: The Last Supper – a meal that looked backwards and forwards 298
Mark 14.26–31: A denial denied 303
Mark 14.32–42: Jesus' prayer in Gethsemane 305
Mark 14.43–51: Jesus' arrest 309
Mark 14.53–65: Jesus' first trial (before the Sanhedrin) 311
Mark 14.66–72: Peter denied Jesus (Peter's trial) 316
Mark 15.1–15: Jesus' second trial (before Pilate) and the release of Barrabas 318

Mark 15.16–32: The mocking of Jesus from the courtyard to the cross 322
Mark 15.33–39: Jesus' death … the moment of revelation 328
Mark 15.40–41: Not quite alone … the women were there 334
Mark 15.42–47: Jesus' burial 336
Mark 16.1–8: 'He has been raised; he is not here' 339

Epilogue: Alternative Endings 344

Index of Bible References 349

Introduction

Mark's Gospel is a vivid, brisk, dynamic masterpiece. From its opening, bold statement, declaring the beginning of the good news of Jesus Christ, to its oddly abrupt ending with the women at the tomb running away terrified, Mark's Gospel grasps our attention and draws us in. It's as if we have our own personal tour guide, who reaches out to us and says, 'I have someone to tell you about. Come and see what you think. Oh, and, by the way, his followers are slightly disastrous: see if you can work out who Jesus is faster than they can.'

As we read, it becomes clear that this is not just a story. It is an invitation. We are summoned to meet the most remarkable of people, Jesus. Once we have met him, and followed in his footsteps from one side of the Sea of Galilee to the other and back again, in and out of Gentile territory, and, finally, down to Jerusalem and death on a cross, we face a question: 'What will we do now? How *have* we, how *will* we respond to this person?' In Mark's Gospel, we see the beginning of the good news of Jesus Christ. The Gospel ends with a massive question mark hanging in the air. The disciples have all run away, full of terror. Even the women, who stayed far longer than the men, have now gone. What will happen next? Is it all over? The answer is – and always has been since the Gospel was first written – down to its hearers or readers. Will they … will we, pick up the threads of the story and ensure that it carries on?

Mark's Gospel is far more than 'just' a story. It will, if we let it, change our lives for ever.

Hearers or readers

I will use the word 'readers' in what follows for simplicity, since those who engage with Mark's Gospel today most often do so by reading. However, Mark's first audience were almost certainly 'hearers' not 'readers'; and some of what makes Mark's Gospel so powerful are the themes that would have been picked up by those listening to its being read out.

I would recommend listening to the Gospel all the way through at some point; it will help you to appreciate some of the threads that you might miss when you read it section by section.

The genius of Mark

I've always loved Mark's Gospel. I love its pace and dynamism. I love its passion and excitement. I love its challenge. I wanted to write a commentary on the Gospel so I could enjoy in depth what I already knew of Mark. What I wasn't ready for was its profundity and cleverness, the way themes are woven in and out of one another, dropped for a while and then picked up again. I've always loved Mark, now I am bowled over by its cleverness.

When I first studied Mark's Gospel as a student, nearly 40 years ago now, it was widely accepted to be the least theological of all the Gospels. John's Gospel was praised for its profound discourses; Matthew's for presenting Jesus as the new Moses; and Luke's for its great attention to historical detail. Mark's Gospel was seen as a somewhat rough-around-the-edges story but not much more than that.

This treatment of Mark began early in church history. The first commentary to be written on the Gospel was not written until the sixth century, far later than any other Gospel. Indeed, Augustine of Hippo (AD 354–430) thought Mark was just an abbreviation of Matthew and not to be taken particularly seriously. This attitude towards Mark continued for many years, until the rise of narrative criticism. This approach pays particular attention to how Mark's story is told and has hugely informed the way in which I read Mark. Over the years, I have come to realize that Mark's Gospel is at least as brilliant a Gospel as the others. I have even begun to wonder whether, in fact, it might have a genius that outstrips all the others.

What is profoundly clever about Mark's Gospel is that the author uses a writing technique we would now call 'show, don't tell'. Rather than setting the theology out in detail, we find stories placed next to each other that reveal theological truths. Patterns are repeated. Themes are begun early in the Gospel, only to loop around over and over again. Mark may not contain long, elaborate discourses like John's Gospel, the Sermon on the Mount or the Sermon on the Plain in Matthew and Luke's Gospels; rather, Mark's message lies in how he tells the stories about what Jesus did, how Jesus related to people and how they related to him. In particular, it lies in the order in which he tells the stories. It is no mistake that there are two feedings of thousands – first, the 5,000 (Mark 6.30–44); then the 4,000 (Mark 8.1–10) – or that the disciples argue about who is the greatest (Mark 9.33–37) one chapter before James and John then ask to sit in the most privileged positions (Mark 10.35–45). There is a reason why Jesus' two healings of blind men bookend his long journey from Bethsaida in the north (Mark 8.22–26) to Jericho in the south (Mark 10.46–52). Each story is carefully and lovingly placed in the narrative so that we can see and understand what is going on.

> ***And immediately***
>
> One of Mark's most famous techniques is his use of the word 'immediately' (*euthus*). In Matthew, the word occurs six times; in Luke, three times; and three also in John. In Mark's Gospel, it is used 41 times; 12 times in the first chapter alone. It gives a fast-paced feel to Mark's storytelling but also reminds us to look out for those times when things do not happen 'immediately'. Mark's story sets off briskly, but there are other events that happen on the next day or after a period of time. These are worth looking out for as you read.

Mark's other technique, which I have already alluded to, is that it can seem as though Mark is talking directly to us, the readers. Breaking the fourth wall is a storytelling technique, sometimes also used in plays and films, in which either a character or the author acknowledges that the play is, in fact, not an entire world, so they turn to address the audience directly: asking them questions, drawing them in, acknowledging that the audience knows things that the characters on stage do not. Long before the concept was ever developed, Mark seems to have adopted it as a technique. You can find it all the way through Mark's Gospel, beginning right at the very start, with Jesus' baptism (Mark 1.9–11). There, God speaks directly to Jesus, telling him that he is God's Son. No one else hears, only Jesus ... and us. Right from the start, we know who Jesus is: God has told us straight from heaven; but the disciples don't know, nor does anyone else. We are privy to information no one else has, as we follow the story of Jesus. As such, we watch the disciples' failure to work out who Jesus is from this privileged position, knowing something they don't, with Mark by our side seemingly rolling his eyes at their incompetence.

Throughout this commentary, my particular interest lies in *how* the story is told, as it is this that reveals to us the real genius of Mark.

Groups and individuals in Mark

Another of Mark's techniques is to present the reactions of groups that stand in stark contrast to those of individuals. There are three groups that stand out.

1. The Jewish leaders. These come in different combinations, which include the Pharisees, the scribes and the Herodians in Galilee; and then, once Jesus gets to Jerusalem, the chief priests, the Sadducees and the elders too. Every time one of these groups approaches Jesus, conflict arises. They always oppose Jesus and always find fault with him or his disciples.

In contrast, we meet two individuals who come from these groups but react very differently: the scribe who asks Jesus which is the First Commandment (12.28–34) and Joseph of Arimathea, a member of the Sanhedrin who buries Jesus (15.42–47).

2 The crowd. The crowd follows Jesus around Galilee and seems often to be amazed by him. They are voracious for his teaching and his healings and will even run around the lake to catch up with him (6.33); but their appreciation of him never seems to move beyond this to anything more meaningful.

3 The disciples. As we will see in the commentary, the disciples are presented over and over again as not understanding who Jesus is and what he has come to do. They do leave everything to follow him but then struggle to comprehend him. This is especially true between the end of chapter 4 and chapter 10, where three times in a boat their lack of comprehension is laid bare (4.35–41; 6.45–52; 8.14–21); then, in the verses that follow, they respond to Jesus' predictions of his suffering and death with questions of who is greatest and will have the best seat (9.33–37; 10.35–45).

Mark's portrayal of the disciples is apparently damning, but to us, the readers, it is encouraging. If we were tempted to imagine that we would be unable to live up to the expectations and demands of discipleship, we have before us the example of Jesus' first disciples. We may not be able to live up to the best example of discipleship, but we could never be worse than Jesus' first followers. And they, we now know, spread the good news of Jesus Christ to the ends of the earth. The bar to discipleship is set low by the disciples in Mark's Gospel; but what they did do was leave everything to follow Jesus. As the rich man discovered in 10.17–31, for some, even that low bar would be too high.

In contrast to the groups who all respond in predictable ways, individuals, throughout the Gospel, respond to Jesus wholeheartedly. They are often commended for their faith. People whose need is greatest can see who Jesus is and how he could help them. This theme becomes particularly clear in chapters 4—8, where, between three conversations in a boat with the disciples (4.35–41; 6.45–52; 8.11–21), Jesus meets, first, three individuals (the man from Gerasa in 5.1–20, and Jairus and the woman who has bled for 12 years in 5.21–43); then two (a woman from Tyre in 7.24–30, and a deaf man in 7.31–37); then one (a man who was blind in 8.22–26): all these people respond to Jesus from the heart.

Throughout the Gospel, Mark reflects on what it is that prevents people from responding to Jesus wholeheartedly. Time and time again, the answer seems to be 'need'. Those whose need is greatest are those who see Jesus for who he is.

A messianic secret?

One of the surprising themes that runs throughout Mark is Jesus' regular instruction to people not to tell anyone what he had done for them (see 1.43–45; 3.11–12; 5.43; 7.36; 8.30 and 9.9). The only exception is Jesus' healing of the man from Gerasa (5.1–20), who is explicitly told to tell people what God had done for him. This theme gave rise to something scholars called the 'messianic secret'.

The question is why Jesus was so emphatic that people should not tell anyone about him. There seem to be two answers offered to this question in Mark. The first is that when Jesus became too popular, his ministry was curtailed and opposition to him increased. On one level, his instructions seem to be pragmatic. He wanted to be able to travel around freely, proclaiming the good news as he went, and the more people were told about him, the less this was possible. The second answer is connected to the disciples' inability to understand who Jesus was. Even at Caesarea Philippi, when he announced that Jesus was the Messiah, Peter only half understood what this meant. He went on to rebuke Jesus for predicting that he would die. The angel's command to the women in 16.7 is important here. It was only after Jesus had died and risen again that the disciples had the whole story. Once they had that, they could go and tell everyone about Jesus. Until then, they were all too likely to tell them the wrong thing.

It is, however, worth balancing Jesus' commands to secrecy with the three big moments of revelation that take place in Mark's Gospel. At Jesus' baptism (1.9–11), the Transfiguration (9.2–7) and the Crucifixion (15.37–39), Jesus is revealed to be God's Son. These big revelations, sitting at the beginning, middle and end of the Gospel, point to who Jesus really is rather than the version some might have been tempted to recount of a revolutionary miracle worker. Mark makes sure that we know the truth of who Jesus is even if his contemporaries were a little unsure.

The structure of Mark's Gospel

If you consult a handful of commentaries, you will observe a wide variety of possible structures given for Mark. This variation occurs because the Gospel almost defies a structure. What is fascinating about the way in which Mark tells his story is that it seems most like a tapestry, or even a piece of music, in which threads or themes emerge, then submerge again only to re-emerge later. Reading Mark only through the lens of a single structure means that you miss a lot of his key themes. So the challenge is to recognize potential sections (as they often do help to focus a theme) while not holding so hard and fast to them that we miss the links forwards and backwards in the text.

There are even some parts of Mark that seem to fit into more than one pattern. Take, for example, the healing of the blind man at Bethsaida. As noted above, there seems to be a pattern in this part of Mark, woven around Jesus' three conversations with the disciples in the boat.

- The stilling of the storm (4.35–41), followed by three healings of individuals:
  - the man from Gerasa (5.1–20)
  - Jairus' daughter (5.21–24, 35–43)
  - the woman who was bleeding (5.25–34)
- Walking on the water (6.45–52), followed by two healings of individuals:
  - the daughter of the woman from Tyre (Syrophoenician woman, 7.24–30)
  - the man who was deaf (7.31–37)
- The yeast of the Pharisees and of Herod (8.11–21), followed by
  - the healing of the man who was blind (8.22–26).

Having said that, there are also two feeding miracles: one before the second boat scene (the 5,000 in 6.30–44) and one before the third boat scene (the 4,000 in 8.1–10).

Add on to this that Jesus' major period of teaching to the disciples about what it means to be a disciple is bookended by two healings of blind men: one, mentioned above, which took place in Bethsaida (8.22–26), and one in Jericho (10.46–52). These are wrapped around three predictions of Jesus' death (8.31–9.1; 9.30–32 and 10.32–34) in which the disciples, who are meant to 'see', really don't.

In other words, imposing a structure on to Mark can detract from his clever patterns and interweaving narratives. What I have done in this commentary, therefore, is to suggest a loose structure (since reading with a structure can help us to understand what is going on) but, alongside that, suggest patterns to look out for, and links backwards and forwards in the narrative that we should keep in mind as we go. If in your reading you notice a pattern, thread or theme that I haven't mentioned, you are almost certainly right. There are so many woven around one another in the Gospel, I wouldn't be at all surprised if I have missed some or even quite a lot.

Patterns in Mark

There are a few patterns in Mark that are worth looking out for as you read through the Gospel.

Bookends

Occasionally, Mark likes to begin and end a section with a similar story (see, for example, the two healings of blind men in 8.22–26 and 10.46–52) around Jesus' key teaching on the nature of discipleship.

Sandwiching

Mark loves to sandwich an event between the start and end of a story. In other words, a story begins, then pauses while another event is related, then concludes afterwards. For example, in chapter 3, Jesus' family came to restrain him (3.20–21 and 31–35), a story that occurs around the discussion between Jesus and the scribes about Beelzebul (3.22–30). Or there is the cursing of the fig tree (11.12–14) and the observation that it has withered (11.20–25), which appear around Jesus' cleansing of the temple (11.15–19); or when the chief priests plot to kill Jesus (14.1–2), then find a way to achieve this with Judas' proposed betrayal (14.10–11), wrapped around Jesus' anointing by a woman in Bethany (14.3–9).

Triples

There are a lot of examples of 'threes' throughout Mark. There are, to mention just a few, three boat scenes (4.35–41; 6.45–52; 8.14–21); three passion predictions (8.31–33; 9.30–32; 10.32–34); and three times the disciples fall asleep in Gethsemane (14.37, 40, 41).

Who wrote it, and where?

You will have noticed that I have called the author 'Mark' a few times so far. This is because it is how he is introduced to us. The ancient manuscripts say simply that this is the Gospel (*euangelion*) according to Mark (*kata Markon*). This is the person to whom those making the earliest copies of the Gospel attributed authorship. So I am content to call him Mark.

The question is whether we can know any more about him than this. The early Church associated Mark with the John Mark mentioned in Acts (12.12, 25; 13.5, 13; 15.37–39). The first mention of this appears in Eusebius (writing in the third century AD), who quotes Papias: a writer who flourished at the end of the first century AD, whose writings no longer exist. Papias not only identifies Mark with John Mark but also gives Mark's source as Peter. In many ways, this makes sense: only a direct link back to one of the disciples would have made someone feel so able to present the disciples in such a negative light. Mark's portrayal of the disciples, and especially Peter, does seem as though it could come from eyewitness testimony, such as Peter's.

This tradition about Mark's authorship continued in the second century AD, with both Irenaeus and Clement of Alexandria associating the Gospel's source as Peter and its location of writing as Rome. It is also worth noting that Acts 12.12 indicates that John Mark was from Judea, which would explain his tendency to slip into Aramaic at key moments in his story and, possibly, why his geography of Galilee can be a little hazy. Mark's Greek is rougher than that of either Matthew or Luke. This may well be because his first language was Aramaic, with Greek as his second language. There are certainly phrases that seem to indicate that he was thinking in Aramaic and putting it into Greek; and there are occasions where he decides to write the Aramaic word using Greek letters (see, for example, *talitha koum* (5.41), *qorban* (7.11), *ephphatha* (7.34) and *Abba* (14.36). There is no evidence, however, that Mark wrote directly into Aramaic. The Aramaisms are scattered throughout but are not so strong as to suggest that the Gospel was originally written in Aramaic and translated later.

Some scholars, however, question whether Mark knows enough about Jewish practice for us to be confident that the author was John Mark. Of this, an example often given is that Mark claims the Pharisees and all the Jews engaged in ceremonial washing (7.3–4), whereas this was not something that most Jews did. It is odd that Mark makes some of these mistakes; but, overall, the 'Aramaic feel' of the Gospel does suggest that it was written by someone who, like John Mark, came from Judea.

This leaves us with Rome as the place where Mark wrote down Peter's memories. There are some hints in the text that this could be true. Mark translates some words into Latin: see, for example, the widow's type of coin, which is *lepton* in Greek, that Mark translates as 'quadrans', a Roman coin that would have been rare in Jerusalem. Also, his description of the woman from Tyre as a Syrophoenician, which is a term that wouldn't have been used in Judea (she'd have just been a 'Phoenician'). It would, however, have been needed in Rome to differentiate her from another Phoenician group, the Liby-Phoenicians, who lived near Carthage. Others are less convinced by these arguments and view these as small details that do not shed light on where the Gospel was written.

On balance, we cannot be certain about who Mark was, where he wrote the Gospel or of the influence of Peter on his writing; but in the absence of any stronger arguments, it seems sensible to accept this ancient tradition.

When was it written?

We have no more clear evidence for the date of Mark's Gospel than we do for its authorship. The nub of the discussions about the dating of Mark focus around chapter 13, which prophesies the destruction of Jerusalem. Both Matthew and Luke contain hints that indicate they witnessed (even if from afar) the Jewish War and incorporated what they saw into the remembered words of Jesus. Mark's Gospel does not. Jesus' prophecies in chapter 13 are vague and make no reference to actual events. This suggests to many that the Gospel was therefore written before AD 70.

The early Church tradition suggests that it could have been written either before or after Peter's death.

- Before Peter's death, around the early AD 60s. According to Eusebius, who wrote about Christian history in the fourth century, Clement of Alexandria claimed that Mark wrote the Gospel before Peter's death while the apostle was still ministering in Rome. This tradition was also held by other Church Fathers, such as Origen, Epiphanius and Jerome. If Peter's martyrdom was during AD 64 under Nero's persecution, then this would give a date of the early 60s for the writing of the Gospel.
- After Peter's death but before the destruction of Jerusalem, around the late AD 60s. Another early Church Father, Irenaeus, maintained, however, that Mark was written after Paul and Peter's deaths. If this was true, then it may be that Mark wrote his Gospel shortly after Peter died, conscious that the eyewitnesses of Jesus could soon all be dead and that he had to capture what they saw before it was too late.
- After Peter's death and after the destruction of Jerusalem. Some modern scholars argue that the Gospel was written with specific knowledge of the Jewish War; and Jesus' saying, in 13.14, 'let the reader understand' referred to a specific event that his audience would have understood – but that we don't – which means that the Gospel was written either during or straight after the destruction of Jerusalem. Against this view is the fact that there are no allusions in chapter 13 that can, with certainty, be said to refer to specific events that happened during the war.

There is simply too little evidence to allow us to be confident about when Mark's Gospel was written. Given what we do have, I think it is most likely to have been written sometime in the AD 60s; but it is difficult to get closer than that with any level of certainty.

Before we leave the issue of dating, it is worth noting, briefly, the relationship between Matthew, Mark and Luke. Although Matthew and Luke are much longer than Mark, 97 per cent of Mark's Gospel can be found in Matthew and 88 per cent in Luke. Interestingly, their order is a little different, and sometimes Matthew and Luke share stories or teaching that are not found in Mark. Over the years, there has been extensive discussion about what this means concerning the sources the Gospel 'writers' (possibly more accurately editors) used in compiling their Gospels, which has become known as the 'Synoptic Problem'.

One theory that was widely held for many years was that there was an unknown document named by scholars as 'Q', which stands for the German word '*quelle*' (which means 'source'). They argued that Matthew and Luke used two sources, 'Q' and Mark, to write their Gospels (this is known as the two-source hypothesis; others, however, regard the notional existence of 'Q' to be unnecessary and argue that you can arrive at the same position if you think that Matthew used Mark as his main source, and Luke used both Mark and Matthew). There remains little agreement on this among scholars, and it does not make much difference to how you read Mark.

The only impact it has on a possible dating for Mark is if you were to take one of the views about sources that means Mark was the last Gospel written. The Griesbach hypothesis argues that Matthew was written first, Luke then used Matthew as a source, and Mark summarized both into his much shorter Gospel. If you accept this as a theory, then Mark had to have been written after both the other Gospels and so could not really have been written much before the AD 70s. This is not a widely held theory. I would argue that the lack of specific mentions of anything that happened during the Jewish War still means Mark was probably written before AD 70.

What kind of commentary is this?

The aim of this commentary is to give you what you need to read Mark's Gospel closely. I have tried to make it user-friendly. It is, inevitably, long, as looking at Mark in detail is not a short task; but I have tried to avoid technical language or extensive explorations of scholarly debates to make the commentary as accessible as possible. You may be using it to help with preparing a sermon or for a Bible study on a particular passage; or you may (and I hope there will be quite a few people like this) want to read Mark slowly and thoughtfully, with a guide to help you on the way. I absolutely love Mark's Gospel. I sincerely hope that others who feel similarly might be tempted to read through it with the aid of this commentary.

There are, I think, three features that particularly help with a deeper reading of the text, and I have focused on them: historical and scriptural context; patterns and themes in the Gospel; and insight into the Greek text.

Historical and scriptural context

One of the challenges for reading any book in the New Testament is the gap we find between our own world and that of first-century Galilee and Judea. I have attempted throughout the commentary to provide information, either in the body of the text or in additional boxes that explain details such as who the Pharisees were or what a first-century fishing boat might have been like. I've also to picked out some of the resonances with Old Testament passages that help to shed light on individual passages.

Boxes

You will notice that, throughout the commentary, there are boxes containing extra information about, say, who the Pharisees were or the significance of a historical event. The aim is to give you background to help you to understand the context a little better.

Patterns and themes in the Gospel

As noted already, one of the key features of Mark is the way in which he establishes patterns and threads that weave backwards and forwards through the Gospel. I try to point out as many of these as I can so that you can see how these threads are woven together to form the Gospel and to show the theology that Mark is attempting to convey.

Insights into what the Greek text says

One of the most interesting features of reading a book from the New Testament is digging into what it meant in Greek; doing so helps to cast more light on what the English translation might mean. For people who have never had the chance to learn Greek, or for whom it is rusty, many modern commentaries can be bemusing and off-putting, since they plunge into technical descriptions using the original Greek to make their point. What I have tried to do in this commentary is pull out 'interesting words'. Each section begins with a list of what I think are the most interesting words because they can be translated in different ways or they are often used by Mark. You won't want to read them all, but you might find a few in each section that catch your attention. I will inevitably have missed something that you wish I had mentioned, for which apologies in advance. Deciding what to include and what to exclude was not easy.

Some people won't be interested in this at all; so please feel free to skip this section if it doesn't interest you.

You can follow the text in whichever English translation is your favourite. I have used the NRSV as the base English text throughout; and, when commenting on the Greek, I compare it with the NRSV translation. It might, therefore, be helpful to use a different translation alongside to enrich your understanding of what is going on in the text.

'Interesting words' sections

In each 'Interesting words' section, I have pulled out particular Greek words that may help you to understand the text a little more. I have put them into English characters (transliterated them) for those who don't know the Greek alphabet well.

If you want to try to pronounce them, note that

- The letters 'ch' are a transliteration of the Greek letter *chi*. They are therefore not pronounced 'ch' as in English (for example, 'church') but with a slightly aspirated 'c' sound (as with 'Bach'). Most people often just use a 'c' sound (as in 'Christ'), which is easier to pronounce. The hard 'c' or 'k' sound comes from the Greek letter *kappa*, which is transliterated as 'k'.
- In Greek, there are two 'o' sounds (*omicron* and *ōmega*) and two 'e' sounds (*epsilon* and *ēta*). When o and e and marked as ō and ē, they indicate the long vowels *ōmega* and *ēta* respectively:
  - *epsilon* is pronounced with a short 'e', like 'egg';
  - *ēta* is pronounced with a long 'e', like 'see';
  - *omicron* is pronounced with a short 'o', like 'dog';
  - *ōmega* is pronounced with a long 'o', like 'bone'.
- When you see the letters 'ng' this represents a double *gamma* (gg), which is pronounced 'ng', as in 'anger'. So, *aggelos* is, of course, pronounced *angelos*.

For those who do know Greek and are looking at the words in the text as we go, when referring to a verb, I have put it into the first person singular present tense and when referring to a noun or adjective I have it in the nominative, singular. These are 'base' forms of each word in Greek, and do not require any knowledge of how words change in different grammatical constructions. I have used only the form given in the text when that particular form is important, when it appears in a phrase or when the verb is so irregular that you would not be able to find it in the text without knowing the form in which it appears.

Mark's message

All of this brings us to Mark's message. As I have indicated, Mark is a clever, thoughtful Gospel, which has many themes woven together; but there are two main themes that run throughout the Gospel.

The first is the question of who Jesus is. From the moment of Jesus' baptism – with God's voice ringing in our ears that Jesus is God's beloved Son in whom God is well pleased – the scene is set for us to ask what this will mean in his ministry. As the story unfolds, we see the disciples wrestling with the question of who Jesus is. This question reaches its climax in 4.41, when full of fear they ask: 'Who then is this, that even the wind and the sea obey him?' As they encounter more of Jesus, this question rumbles along, until, at last, Peter can find the words to say that Jesus is the Messiah (8.29), only to be horrified at the thought that Jesus would think he should suffer and die. The rest of the Gospel frames what it means for Jesus to live in the shadow of the cross as he travels towards Jerusalem, ends up in inevitable conflict with the Sanhedrin and is eventually handed over to die.

A second question runs alongside this first one, which is what this means for those who follow Jesus. At first, the question focuses around their, and our, ability to recognize the deep nature of Jesus from what he says and what he does; but in the middle of the Gospel it shifts to what difference this makes to the lives of Jesus' disciples: what it means for the way in which they live their lives in this upside-down kingdom of God in which the first are last and the last first. Not only will it mean that they should be prepared for Jesus to die and rise again; it will also mean that they need to be prepared to take up their own crosses and follow in Jesus' footsteps.

Right at the start of the Gospel, Jesus proclaims, 'The time is fulfilled, and the kingdom of God has come near; repent, and believe in the good news' (1.15). That word 'repent' means a complete reorientation: away from the old way of being into a completely new life, shaped by the values of the kingdom and by following in the footsteps of Jesus Christ, Son of God. What does this reorientation look like? Mark's Gospel, from beginning to end, carefully and painstakingly tells us the answer.

These two questions:

- Who is this?

and

- What difference will knowing who he is make to my life?

lie at the very heart of Mark's story.

They are the simplest of questions, but the answers we give to them will change our lives for ever.

For further reading

If you would like to consult other commentaries, especially for more detail on scholarly discussions, in my opinion the best are those listed here.

Technical commentaries

France, R. T., 2002, *The Gospel of Mark*, New International Greek Testament Commentary, Grand Rapids, MI: Eerdmans. This is a technical commentary but contains some really helpful discussion of key issues.

Keener, C., 2026, *Mark*, International Critical Commentary, London: T&T Clark. This commentary is in seven volumes and is extremely technical and full; but if you want a deep and full commentary, this is excellent (at the time of writing it hasn't all been published yet).

Strauss, M. L., 2014, *Mark*, Zondervan Exegetical Commentary on the New Testament, Grand Rapids, MI: Zondervan Academic.

Yarbro Collins, A., 2007, *Mark*, Hermeneia, Minneapolis, MN: Fortress Press. This commentary draws on a lot of contemporary historical detail, including texts written around this period.

Mid-range commentaries (slightly less technical but still academic)

Healy, M., 2008, *The Gospel of Mark*, Catholic Commentary on Sacred Scripture, Ada, MI: Baker Academic. If you are interested in a commentary that represents well a more Catholic view of Mark, this would be an excellent choice.

Hooker, M., 1992, *The Gospel According to Saint Mark*, Blacks Commentary Series, Peabody, MA: Hendrickson Publishers. This is quite old now but the emphasis on what Mark wants his readers to understand remains as helpful as it ever was.

Witherington III, Ben, 2001, *The Gospel of Mark: A Socio-Rhetorical Commentary*, Grand Rapids, MI: Eerdmans. Although this commentary sometimes skims over bits of detail, its insights into the social history of the time are very helpful.

Accessible commentaries

McKnight, S., 2023, *Mark: The Way of Jesus-Shaped Discipleship*, New Testament Everyday Bible Study Series, Nashville, TN: HarperChristian Resources. This is excellent and its focus on discipleship is especially helpful.

Wright, N. T., 2001, *Mark for Everyone*, London: SPCK. As with all volumes in this series, this one is an easy-to-read and very helpful commentary for applying Mark to everyday life.

A note about ancient sources

For sake of ease in the commentary, when I have cited a quotation from an ancient source, I have given the name of the source in full. The only exceptions to this are quotations from the Mishnah or Talmud. When I cite something from the Mishnah, you will see *m.*, followed by the name of the relevant tractate or book; when I cite from the Talmud, you will see *b.*, followed by the name of the relevant tractate or book, or *j.*, followed by the name of the relevant tractate or book, if it is from the Babylonian or Jerusalem Talmud respectively. Most of the texts I cite are available online if you are tempted to look them up.

Mark 1.1–15: A Title and a Prologue

Beginnings are important. The start of a book, no matter what kind it is, sets the tone, establishes the scene and hints at how the reader is to understand what follows. Paying close attention to the way a book begins gives a sense of how to read what follows.

Over the years, a lot of attention has been paid to the opening verses of the other three Gospels. The prologue of John's Gospel and the birth narratives of Matthew and Luke's Gospels are clearly stylized and carefully crafted 'beginnings'. Much less attention has been paid to the start of Mark's Gospel. This is partly because most of the opening verses of Mark focus on John the Baptist, who, in Matthew and Luke's Gospels, appears well after the opening verses (in Matt. 3.1–23 and Luke 3.1–20) in what is really the main body of the narrative. Their treatment of John the Baptist suggests that stories about him are to be seen as part of the main gospel story. The obvious exception to this, however, is the prologue to John's Gospel, which does include John the Baptist.

In fact, if you place the opening verses of Mark's Gospel alongside John's prologue, a number of overlapping themes emerge. These range from the use of the word 'beginning' (in Greek, *archē*) to the introduction of John the Baptist as a character; and, most importantly, to the fact that the person speaking appears to be a narrator with a 'God's-eye' view of what is going on. Mark's prologue, though much less famous or indeed poetic than John's, does deserve close attention because it sets up the Gospel for us in a very similar way to the beginnings of the other Gospels. It draws out themes and gives us a guide by which to understand what comes next.

Patterns to look out for in 1.1–15

- There are three opening scenes in Mark's Gospel:
  - the arrival of John the Baptist – looking backwards to the prophets;
  - the baptism of Jesus – looking upwards to heaven;
  - the proclamation of Jesus' good news – looking forwards to the rest of his ministry.

- Verses 2–15 have a pattern (see pp. 19–20 for more on this):
  - the good news of Jesus Christ (v. 1);
    - John the Baptist in the wilderness;
      - John baptizing in the Jordan (vv. 2–8);
      - Jesus being baptized in the Jordan (vv. 9–11);
    - Jesus in the wilderness (vv. 12–13);
  - the good news of God (vv. 14–15).

Mark 1.1: A title

It is widely accepted that the first verse of Mark's Gospel is a title. It would be hard to categorize it as anything else. Mark declares boldly that this is 'the beginning of the good news of Jesus Christ'.

The question is, to what is it a title? Here are the two main options.

1 To the prologue of Mark's Gospel (which may end in v. 8, v. 13 or v. 15).
2 To the whole Gospel.

The answer you give affects how you read the rest of the Gospel.

Interesting words ...

- v. 1: *beginning*. Although always translated as 'the beginning', the Greek word (*archē*), which begins the Gospel, has no definite article ('the'). It is tempting to suggest that this is similar to John's prologue, which again begins without the 'the'. Literally, it reads 'In beginning'; but the beginning Mark is talking about is different from John's. When John says, 'In beginning', it is clear he has in mind the dawn of time itself (similar to the beginning in Genesis 1.1), whereas Mark has in mind the start of Jesus' ministry. A much closer parallel is Hosea 1.2, which, if translated literally, reads 'Beginning of the word of the LORD through Hosea', again without a 'the'.
- v. 1: *gospel*. The word 'gospel' is the Old English equivalent of the Greek word *euaggelion*; both mean 'good news'.
- v. 1: *the good news of Jesus Christ*. This can mean either 'the good news that Jesus proclaimed' (what he said) or 'the good news about Jesus Christ' (his whole life and ministry and why that was such good news). Some commentators choose one or the other; others argue that the Greek is ambiguous and might deliberately mean both. Mark's Gospel certainly both contains Jesus' teaching and tells us about Jesus Christ, who he was and what he did.
- v. 1: *Son of God*. The phrase 'Son of God' (*ho huios tou theou*) is present in some ancient manuscripts but not others. Significantly, it has been clearly added

in, in a different hand, to the Codex Sinaiticus, one of the oldest and most important manuscripts of the Greek Bible. This may suggest the words are a later addition by a scribe who, knowing that God declares Jesus to be his Son, is keen to ensure that this is stated in the opening verse.

What kind of title?

The question is so important of what kind of title this is that it is worth looking at each type in turn.

A title to the opening verses of the Gospel

If Mark 1.1 is seen as a title to the opening verses of the Gospel, then it is really saying 'the good news of Jesus Christ began like this'; then our attention is focused fully and clearly on Isaiah's prophecy, John the Baptist and the start of Jesus' ministry in Galilee. If we understand it in this way, the good news of Jesus Christ began with John the Baptist and, most importantly, with Jesus' baptism, followed closely by his teaching and healing ministry.

A title to the whole Gospel

The other option ties the beginning of Mark's Gospel to its ending. We will look in more detail at the ending when we get there; but in the earliest manuscripts, Mark's Gospel finishes simply with the women hearing about Jesus' Resurrection and running away, saying nothing to anyone because they were afraid. If that ending is the original, it is at first glance odd but then, on further reflection, becomes much more interesting. As we noted in the Introduction, Mark's focus is on being a disciple of Jesus: understanding who he really was and taking up our cross to follow him. Jesus' original disciples do not give the best example of how to do this. They often misunderstood who Jesus was. They regularly asked the wrong questions, at the wrong times. The male disciples ran away when Jesus was arrested; and the women, who stayed throughout the Crucifixion, ran away when instructed to announce the news of Jesus' Resurrection to the others. They were not, to put it mildly, shining examples of discipleship.

If Mark 16.8 – 'they went out and fled from the tomb, for terror and amazement had seized them; and they said nothing to anyone, for they were afraid' – was indeed the original ending of the Gospel, the obvious questions are 'What next? How will the good news of Jesus Christ survive if there is no one to tell anyone about it?'

This brings us to the other possible meaning of 1.1, which is that the whole of the Gospel, Mark 1.1—16.8, serves as the beginning of the good news of Jesus Christ. In other words, the story of Jesus' ministry and life (his calling of the first disciples, his teaching and the miracles he did, his death and Resurrection) all fall under the title 'the beginning of the good news'. This raises the question of what will happen next. Will anyone pick up the message and start proclaiming it?

Mark and Mark's readers

We are only one verse into Mark and twice already there have been questions, each with two possible answers:

- Was the good news of Jesus Christ good news about Jesus or the good news he proclaimed?
- Was the title intended to introduce the start of Jesus' ministry ('Jesus' ministry began like this')? Alternatively, was it to introduce the whole ministry, with the question remaining at the end of the Gospel about how the good news, which had begun with the life of Jesus, would continue?

These possibilities alert us to something about the way Mark writes. It is easy to assume, because of his dynamic, immediate style, that Mark lacks nuance. I would argue that the opposite is the case. In my view, Mark writes with one eye constantly on us, the readers, asking, 'What do you think? What sense do you make of this? And most importantly of all, how will you respond? Will you run away like Jesus' original disciples did, or will you take up your cross, no matter what the consequences, and follow him? And what of the good news of Jesus Christ – the message he proclaimed and the good news about him – will you share it and continue what he started?'

Mark's Gospel, more than any other of the Gospels, includes us – the readers – among its list of characters, inviting us into the story he is telling and asking what part we will play in the good news of Jesus Christ, the Son of God.

We know, of course, 2,000 years later, that people did pick up the message; but if we take Mark 1.1 as a title to the whole book, then the Gospel challenges us, the readers, directly. If this is the beginning of the good news, what will we do to ensure that the good news of Jesus Christ continues and never ends?

Mark's prologue?

One of the points of disagreement among commentators on the Gospel is whether the prologue finishes at verse 8, verse 13 or verse 15. The different options shape the opening in slightly different ways:

- If the prologue ends at verse 8, it focuses almost entirely on John the Baptist as the forerunner to Jesus, making the main ministry of Jesus begin with Jesus' baptism. This reading emphasizes the strong connection between the beginning of Mark and the end of Malachi. Malachi is the final book of the Hebrew Scriptures and ends: 'Lo, I will send you the prophet Elijah before the great and terrible day of the LORD comes. He will turn the hearts of parents to their children and the hearts of children to their parents, so that I will not come and strike the land with a curse' (Malachi 4.5–6).

  Verses 2–8, focusing as they do on John the Baptist, draw attention to him as an Elijah-type figure who came to turn the hearts of God's people before the coming of the day of the Lord. The significance of this is that we are invited to imagine that Jesus' ministry is simply the next stage in the story of God's people. The story merely paused at the end of Malachi. We turn the page (or indeed open the next scroll) and continue reading to encounter the one Malachi prophesied about; we discover him to be John the Baptist, who has come to turn the heart of God's people.

  The Gospel proper then begins with the arrival of Jesus and his baptism by John.
- If the prologue ends at verse 13, the focus is much more on the preparation for Jesus' ministry: a preparation that takes place in the wilderness.

  In this scenario, the Gospel opens with a quote from the prophets (for more on this, see pp. 20–1) and introduces John the Baptist in the wilderness, where he baptizes Jesus, who is then himself driven out into the wilderness.

  The impact of this is that the wilderness becomes the focus of the Gospel's prologue, with all its accompanying significance of being the location where God will do a new thing (see the box, 'Wilderness', on p. 24, as a symbolic theme in the Bible).

  The main narrative of the Gospel then begins in Galilee after Jesus has returned from the wilderness.
- If the prologue is seen to end at verse 15, then it may have a criss-crossed (chiastic) structure:
  - The good news of Jesus Christ (v. 1);
    - John the Baptist in the wilderness;
      - John baptizing in the Jordan (vv. 2–8);
      - Jesus being baptized in the Jordan (vv. 9–11);
    - Jesus in the wilderness (vv. 12–13);
  - The good news of God (vv. 14–15).

With this structure, Jesus' ministry begins in verse 16, when he calls the first disciples, and the prologue focuses attention on the nature of the good news that is being proclaimed.

The challenge of these different scenarios is that they all have merit, and all add to the understanding of the opening of Mark. The first focuses our attention on the continuation of the story about God's people, which pauses at the end of Malachi and begins again with the arrival of John the Baptist, for whom they waited; the second emphasizes the importance of the wilderness as the place where God does a new thing; and the third highlights the fact that Jesus' ministry is integrally linked with the proclamation of the best of all good news.

Given that Mark likes threes (see the Introduction, p. 7), I would be tempted to keep them all in play as helpful explanations of the opening of the Gospel: three openings that provide three helpful lenses for understanding it. Each one provides a shaping that gives insight into what follows. Each has value, though you may find you favour one over another.

Mark 1.2–8: John the baptizer

If we take off the title, Mark's Gospel begins with a quotation from the Old Testament. This gives the sense of the story being a continuation. As Malachi says at the end of his book, that for which we have been waiting has now arrived. We can read on to find out what happens next.

Links backwards

- Mark links backwards to the prophets in general and to Malachi in particular (it is worth reading the last chapter of Malachi before starting Mark).

Links forwards

- John's baptism points us to Jesus' baptism, which follows in the next section (1.9–11).
- The presence of John also points forwards to the story of his beheading (6.14–29), which sets up a pattern that encourages us to think of Jesus' own death in 15.33–41.

Interesting words ...

- v. 2: *messenger*. The Greek word *angelos* is sometimes translated as 'messenger' and sometimes 'angel'.
- v. 4: *John the Baptist*. Although John is called 'the Baptist' elsewhere in the Gospel, here and in John 6.14 the phrase contains a participle, which makes it more dynamic: 'John the one baptizing' or simply 'John the baptizer'.
- v. 4: *repentance*. 'Repentance' is the translation of the word *metanoia*. For more on its significance, see the box, 'Metanoia', on p. 23.
- v. 5: *confess*. *Exomologeō* can also be translated as 'to admit' or 'acknowledge'. The key element is that the people who came to John acknowledged their sins and, one assumes, the consequences of them.

As it is written ...

The earliest manuscripts of the Greek text nearly all say that the 'quotation' in verse 2 was 'written in the prophet Isaiah'; just two say 'in the prophets'. This was picked up in Byzantine manuscripts for obvious reasons: the quote is not, or at least is not solely, from Isaiah. It consists of a combination of

- Malachi 3.1: *See, I am sending my messenger to prepare the way before me, and the Lord whom you seek will suddenly come to his temple.*
- Exodus 23.20: *I am going to send an angel in front of you, to guard you on the way and to bring you to the place that I have prepared.*
- Isaiah 40.3: *A voice cries out: 'In the wilderness prepare the way of the LORD, make straight in the desert a highway for our God.'*

What this suggests is that these verses were combined in popular memory, when looking forward to the coming of a Messiah, and attributed to Isaiah. Similar 'memories' happen today, even when copies of the Bible are readily available to read. Possibly the best example of this is that people regularly cite a vision of the end time involving a lion lying down with a lamb, drawn from Isaiah 11.6. In reality, what the text says is: 'The wolf shall live with the lamb, the leopard shall lie down with the kid, the calf and the lion and the fatling together, and a little child shall lead them.' It is a phrase drawn from the text but not an actual quote.

The combination of Exodus 23.20 (which is talking about an angel guiding God's people through the wilderness) and Isaiah 40.3 (which looks forward to the return from exile through the wilderness), and the omission of 'temple' from the Malachi quote locates the action – and hence John the Baptist – firmly in the wilderness. It is worth noting in passing, though, that in the Hebrew of Isaiah 40.3, the verse reads: 'A voice cries out: "In the wilderness prepare the way of the LORD"' (in other words, it is the preparation, not the voice crying out, that is in the wilderness). It was only in the Greek translation of the Hebrew that the voice was located in the wilderness too: 'A voice cries in the wilderness, prepare the way of the LORD.'

A God's-eye view

The combined quote, which begins 'See I am sending my messenger', means that Mark's Gospel, like John's Gospel, begins with a God's-eye view. Verses 2 and 3 of the Gospel lay out that God has sent the messenger to begin the whole chain of events that will ultimately lead to Jesus' death and Resurrection. The good news of Jesus Christ is part of God's plan for the world and is introduced by this composite quote.

We begin the Gospel by seeing the world and the plan as God sees them. God sends a messenger to prepare the way. Then, the messenger sent to proclaim the good news picks up the story.

A baptism of repentance

Mark summarizes John's whole ministry with the simple phrase 'proclaiming a baptism of repentance for the forgiveness of sins' (v. 4).

One of the major points of discussion among scholars is precisely what the 'baptism of repentance' was. There is plenty of evidence in contemporary Jewish sources (not least those from the Qumran community) that ritual cleansing was well known in this period. People would cleanse themselves regularly to purify themselves for worship. The key element here, however, is that this was self-administered – you would cleanse yourself. John's baptism, as with the baptisms that took place in the early Christian communities, was done by one person to another. It was also public. This seems to differentiate it from a private self-cleansing ritual.

Another comparison made with John's baptism is the act of cleansing undertaken by a Gentile proselyte on becoming Jewish. The problem with this, however, is that there is no evidence of this taking place as early as the first century.

This seems to point to John's baptism as something that had roots in earlier Jewish purification rituals, but which had genuinely new elements: it was done publicly, not privately, and was administered by someone, not self-administered. It was then picked up and adapted into the rite of baptism referred to elsewhere in the New Testament. One key issue, which remains unclear, is how *often* John expected people to be baptized for the 'forgiveness of sins'. If John's baptism is seen as the forerunner of Christian initiation, it would be obvious to imagine that it happened just once; if it was more of an adaptation of the ritual cleansing ceremonies and a means of acknowledging sin, then it could have happened more than once. The only hint in the New Testament that might push us in in one particular direction can be found in Acts 19.4, which mentions Paul's encounter with 'some disciples' in Ephesus. These individuals reported that they had not received the Holy Spirit when they became believers because they were baptized into 'John's baptism'. They were then baptized by Paul into the Lord Jesus (19.5). This implies that the baptism of John was a one-off but could be superseded by baptism into Christ.

Metanoia

The word *metanoia*, normally translated as 'repentance', is a hugely significant one in the Christian tradition. It is interesting, however, to notice that, although what it conveys is central to the Christian faith, the word itself doesn't occur very often in the New Testament. The noun *metanoia* occurs only 22 times in the New Testament and only once in Mark; the verb, *metanoeō*, appears 34 times in 32 individual verses, but only twice in Mark. Intriguingly, the idea that it expresses runs throughout the Gospel even if the word itself does not.

The English translation 'repentance' captures only a small fraction of the full meaning of *metanoia*, which has a resonance of not just changing one's mind but reorienting yourself so that your thoughts, dispositions and actions are realigned. In other words, it doesn't just focus on what you turn from, but on what you turn to. There isn't a single word that fully works for this: 'a baptism of reorientation for the forgiveness of sins' simply doesn't sound right. It is probably one of those words that will always need additional explanation in English.

This is one of those places where the importance of the prologue becomes clear. The beginning of Mark provides 'reading notes' for the rest of the Gospel. Just as with 'good news', we are to read the Gospel with *metanoia* in mind. We are also to note where it occurs and where it does not; and (of course, because this is Mark's Gospel) to ask ourselves how and where we need *metanoia* in our life of faith.

The whole Judean countryside

It is quite important to note that Galilee and Judea, though loosely joined in this period, had been quite separate. Judea was the area of the historic southern two tribes, Judah and Benjamin. Galilee was the tribal area of Naphtali and Zebulun. After the fall of the northern kingdom and the resettlement into the area of numerous Assyrians, Galilee remained separate from Judea until the time of the Hasmoneans (the descendants of Judas Maccabaeus), around 112–110 BC. It was conquered by the Maccabean army and reannexed to Judea. At the time of Jesus, the population of Galilee was largely Jewish.

It is, nevertheless, striking that Jesus' baptism, the start of his ministry, took place in Judea, where his life ended, rather than in Galilee. The vast majority of Jesus' ministry took place in Galilee; but John was sent as a messenger to the Judean region where Jesus' ministry began.

Wilderness

In biblical tradition, the wilderness was the place where new beginnings emerged: the people of God wandered for 40 years in the wilderness; under Joshua's leadership, God's people entered the Promised Land from the wilderness; Elijah fled to the wilderness after his battle with the prophets of Ba'al and there encountered God; Isaiah 40 identifies the wilderness as the place where a highway should be prepared for God and so on. Many Messiah-type figures took their followers into the wilderness because they expected God to arrive from that direction.

It is probably worth noting that, while God appeared in various wildernesses, the wilderness with the most theological significance was the patch of land on the other side of the Jordan from Israel. It was from there that the people of God entered the Promised Land, making it the obvious setting both for John's ministry and for the opening scenes of Jesus' ministry. If you were expecting God to do a new thing, the wilderness east of the River Jordan was the most obvious place to look.

The wilderness continued to be resonant in early Christianity as evidenced by, among others, the Desert Fathers and Mothers. It is interesting, therefore, to reflect on where that tradition might be found, or rediscovered, today. We naturally avoid wilderness places or, indeed, experiences because they are wild and bleak, uncontrolled and uncontrollable. They sit right on the edges of what we know and are comfortable with. Yet it was in the wilderness where, time and time again, people would meet God and be transformed. Some, like Hagar or Elijah, were driven into the wilderness without a choice; others, like John the Baptist, chose the wilderness as the place in which to proclaim their message. However we get there, it is worth remembering that God was often encountered in the bleakest of places and at the most despairing of times.

It was in the wilderness that new life and new hope were found, so much so that people would go out to the wilderness in search of them.

Clothed with camel hair

The description of John as clothed in camel hair, with a leather belt around his waist, and as one who had a diet of locusts and wild honey, firmly identifies him as a prophet. Elijah in 2 Kings 1.8 is described as wearing a garment of hair (which is sometimes translated as his being 'a hairy man'), with a leather belt around his waist. His diet of locusts and honey would be expected for someone who subsisted by foraging. Such a lifestyle did exist at the time of John. The first-century historian Josephus described Bannus, a Jewish ascetic who lived in the desert and with whom Josephus had trained for three years before deciding to become a Pharisee. He 'wore [only] what could be grown on trees and only ate what grew of its own accord' (*The Life* 11). Both John's appearance and his diet clearly marked him out in this tradition as a 'holy man'.

The one coming after me

In verse 4, Mark provides a summary of John's ministry; but he goes on, in verses 7–8, to ensure that the focus is then turned firmly and clearly towards Jesus. Jesus is described as 'more powerful' than John; but the much more vivid description is of John's not being worthy to untie the thong of Jesus' sandal. Taking off sandals was a menial task normally reserved for slaves. The Jewish Talmud was clear that a disciple should not demean themselves so far as to take off their master's shoe (Rabbi Joshua ben Levi said that a disciple should render every service that a slave would render their master, except for taking off their shoes (*b. Kethuboth* 96a). While John is evidently exaggerating here, his point is clear. He saw Jesus as of far more significance than himself and used a vivid image to illustrate his point.

Before leaving this section, it is worth pausing for a moment over John's statement that Jesus would baptize with fire (Mark 1.8). While it is now clear to us, after the sending of the Holy Spirit at Pentecost, what Jesus' baptizing with the Holy Spirit means, it is much more difficult to work out what John's original hearers would have made of it. It is possible that it would have brought to mind the prophecy from Joel 2.28 that God would pour out his spirit on all flesh and prepare them for God's breaking into their world in a dramatic way. In terms of Mark's Gospel itself, the reference focuses attention on the very next passage in which Jesus is baptized by John: a baptism that features the appearance of the Holy Spirit.

Mark 1.9–11: The baptism of Jesus

Jesus' baptism in Mark's Gospel is short and personal. The voice that speaks from heaven speaks directly to Jesus ('You are my Son'). It isn't clear whether those who were there heard God's voice, but we, the readers, certainly do. Once the action gets going in the next few chapters, the focus is more on the characters and their action; but, in these early passages, it seems as though Mark is drawing his readers in, giving us information that is not shared with people such as the disciples.

Links forwards

Two passages pick up the announcement of Jesus' identity in Mark:

- The Transfiguration, where God says, 'This is my Son, the Beloved; listen to him' (Mark 9.7).
- The Crucifixion, where an unnamed centurion says, 'Truly this man was God's Son' (15.39).

Interesting words …

- v. 9: *in those days*. Mark adopts a Hebrew turn of phrase here to note the significance of Jesus' arrival. It reads literally, '(A)nd it happened in those days that Jesus came'. In Hebrew, this was used to indicate the start of a new episode. Mark has borrowed it here to show the importance of Jesus' arrival.
- v. 10: *just as*. Anyone who knows anything about Mark's Gospel will talk about Mark's love of dynamic immediacy: he rushes from one episode to another with apparent urgency. He does this via the use of the Greek word *euthus*, which means 'immediately', 'at once' or 'right away'; although, unusually, it is translated as 'just as' here. The start of verse 10 is the first time it appears in the Gospel.
- v. 10: in this verse, there is a play on words in Greek. Jesus came out of the water (*anabainō*); and the Spirit came down from heaven (*katabainō*). As one came up, the other came down.
- v. 10: *torn apart*. The power of the word that Mark uses for 'torn apart' (*schizō*) is striking. It means to split or cleave in two. This is not a gentle parting but a ripping apart; it sets up an idea that we will see again when the curtain in the temple is torn in two.
- v. 10: *dove*. The word *peristera*, used here, can mean 'dove' but could also mean 'pigeon', a much less glamorous bird.
- v. 10: *on him*. Although most English translations say that the Spirit descended on him, the Greek uses the word *eis*, the meaning of which is much closer to 'into'. The implication of this is that the Spirit came and stayed, inspiring Jesus throughout his life, not just resting on him for a while.

Why was Jesus baptized?

The baptism of Jesus has caused more heated debate than almost any other passage in the Gospels. The key question is this: if baptism marked the repentance of sins and Jesus was sinless, why was he baptized? Historically, scholars have suggested that the purpose of Jesus' baptism was either so that he could clearly and definitively identify with those he came to save or that, by accepting John's baptism, he was associating himself with John's message.

There is, I think, another possibility. Baptism is linked closely, in John's message, with reorientation (*metanoia*). As mentioned above, although it is about turning away from sin, it is also about turning towards something. Reorientation is about a new beginning. This is something you would expect in the wilderness: going out into the wilderness allows you to come back with a new vision, purpose or allegiance. If the baptism symbolizes a new beginning, then this would make perfect sense of Jesus' baptism here. It was the beginning of Jesus' ministry. A symbolic act to mark this beginning would be entirely natural. If the emphasis in baptism is placed on reorientation, then Jesus' baptism makes much more sense. His reorientation was away from his previous private existence and towards public ministry; ours is away from sin and towards following him. Both are marked by baptism.

Jesus came from Nazareth of Galilee

One of the questions unanswered in any of the Gospels is *why* Jesus travelled all the way from Nazareth to the River Jordan, a journey of around 85–90 miles, which would have taken about five days on foot. The most obvious explanation was that word of John's baptisms had reached Nazareth and that Jesus was drawn to come to see them for himself. We are left to surmise what Jesus understood about himself at this point. Did he know who he was and what his ministry would be? Was he simply waiting for John's ministry so that he could begin? Or was he unaware of all that lay before him but was drawn by what he heard about John, and then realized his calling when he heard John's message or when he was baptized? Or a combination of the two: he knew a little and had it confirmed at baptism? The question of why is one for which no answer is offered in the Gospels. It is nevertheless interesting and well worth reflecting on, as it also affects the temptation narrative that follows this account.

He saw ...

Whereas in the other Gospels the tearing apart of the heavens and the voice from heaven was seen and heard by others present, in Mark's Gospel only Jesus saw and heard what happened. This seems to fit in with Mark's theme that, although we, the readers, know who Jesus was from the start, his identity was revealed very slowly to those around him, and was understood even more slowly by the disciples. Even in these earliest chapters, Mark is looking in our direction and asking, 'Do you understand yet?'

The heavens opened

The biblical writers all thought that heaven was located directly above the earth and separated from it by a firmament that was permeable. This permeability allowed human beings to ascend into heaven and angels to descend from heaven; and, very occasionally, heaven could be opened so that people on earth could see what was going on up there. As noted in the 'Interesting words' section, the language used to describe heaven opening here is violent and implies something being torn apart. What is unclear is why the heavens needed to be torn apart. Since angels could descend from heaven, it wasn't necessary to rend it to allow the Holy Spirit to descend. Nor was it needed to allow God's voice to be heard: God's voice was often heard without the heavens being torn apart.

This therefore pushes us to realize that, when Jesus came out of the water, three things happened: the heavens opened, the Holy Spirit descended and God spoke. In other words, the tearing apart of the heavens was symbolic in its own right: heaven was now open to earth. The tearing open of the heavens indicated that God's long-awaited intervention in the world had begun, and heaven and earth were now united. God was on the loose, though at this point in the Gospel, only Jesus knew this to be the case.

The Spirit descended like a dove

The second symbolic action was the descending of the Spirit. This coheres with Isaiah's various prophecies about the one who was coming.

- Isaiah 11.2: *The spirit of the LORD shall rest on him, the spirit of wisdom and understanding, the spirit of counsel and might, the spirit of knowledge and the fear of the LORD.*
- Isaiah 42.1: *Here is my servant, whom I uphold, my chosen, in whom my soul delights; I have put my spirit upon him; he will bring forth justice to the nations.*
- Isaiah 61.1: *The spirit of the Lord GOD is upon me, because the LORD has anointed me; he has sent me to bring good news to the oppressed, to bind up the broken-hearted, to proclaim liberty to the captives, and release to the prisoners.*

If the tearing open of the heavens indicated that the barrier between heaven and earth had been opened, the Spirit descending meant that Jesus was the long-awaited Messiah who had come to save his people.

One of the major areas of discussion concerning this passage is whether, when the Spirit descended 'as a dove', it looked like a dove or just descended like a dove (with a fluttering of wings). The art world has certainly taken it to mean 'looking like a dove' and, without that, there would be few other ways of depicting the Holy Spirit in art. Since Mark is clear that Jesus saw something and does not provide any other evidence of what he saw, the most likely explanation was that the Spirit did indeed look dove-like.

A voice came from heaven

The third and final element that completes the picture was the voice that came from heaven. As with other passages in Mark, there are strong Old Testament allusions in the phrase: 'You are my Son, the Beloved; with you I am well pleased' (1.11). These include:

- Psalm 2.7: *He said to me, 'You are my son; today I have begotten you.'* This psalm celebrates the enthronement of a king, probably David, who rules the earth in God's stead.
- Isaiah 42.1: *Here is my servant, whom I uphold, my chosen, in whom my soul delights.*
  Here in Isaiah, God introduces his servant who will bring justice with compassion and gentleness.
- Genesis 22.2: *He said, 'Take your son, your only son Isaac, whom you love.'* (The Greek translation of the Hebrew here reads literally, 'Take your beloved son whom you love.')
  The story of Abraham and Sarah's yearning for a child leaves us in no doubt of how beloved he was. The resonance here gives an added depth of love to God's statement from heaven.

Mark 1.11 is, clearly, not a direct quotation from any of them; but the combination of all the allusions gives us a sense of Jesus' particular identity and role: as King, Messiah and beloved Son.

Three strands, therefore, declare to Jesus and to us, the readers, that what we are observing marks the dramatic intervention of God in the world – the tearing apart of the heavens, the descent of the Spirit on God's chosen one and the declaration of his identity as 'beloved Son'.

Son of God

The title 'Son of God' for Jesus stands alongside 'Son of Man' (see p. 61) as one of the key titles for Jesus. But what does it mean?

Throughout the Old Testament, 'Son of God' is used to refer to God's people (Ex. 4.22), but most often to judges (Ps. 82.6: 'You are gods, children [in Hebrew, 'sons'] of the Most High') and kings (Ps. 89.26–28). The most important psalm is Psalm 2, which is thought to relate the enthronement of a king, and includes the line: 'I will tell of the decree of the LORD: He said to me, "You are my son; today I have begotten you"' (Ps. 2.7).

Somewhat counterintuitively, then, the title 'Son of God' is not necessarily a divine title. It refers to someone who has a special relationship with God and who is doing God's will.

The language here is reminiscent of Psalm 2.7, with one important difference. Jesus is declared by God to be his Son, as in the psalm, but is not declared to be begotten (for obvious reasons). Instead, God is well pleased with him here and, in Mark 9.7, is beloved.

As the story of Jesus unfolds, we, the readers, now know who he has been sent to be; the question is, will anyone else know this?

Mark 1.12–13: Jesus in the wilderness

One of the fascinating features of Mark's temptation narrative is that it is not so much a narrative as a moment. Where Matthew and Luke have more extensive accounts, Mark's is brief to the point of brusqueness. Far more important in Mark's temptation narrative is the theme of wilderness.

Links forwards

- Satan is mentioned in the discussion about Beelzebul (Mark 3.23, 26), in the parable of the sower (4.15) and when Peter is rebuked by Jesus, after Peter tries to say Jesus should not die (8.33).
- Right at the end of Mark (15.41), the women who had followed Jesus from Galilee, and who watched the Crucifixion at a distance, were said to have ministered to Jesus (using the same verb that describes the angels' actions here).

Interesting words ...

- v. 12: *drove*. The word *ekballō* is more violent than 'drove'. It means 'to expel' or 'throw out'.
- v. 13: *Satan*. There are various names for the devil in the New Testament. The two most common are 'devil' (*diabolos*) used in Matthew and Luke's versions of the temptations and 'satan', used in Mark. The second word comes from Hebrew, meaning 'the accuser', and is always used in Mark rather than 'devil'.
- v. 13: *waited on*. The word translated in the NRSV as 'waited on' is *diakoneō*, which is usually interpreted as 'ministered'.

Deep into the wilderness

It is interesting that this passage says that the Spirit drove Jesus into the wilderness: only a few verses earlier, we established that Jesus was already in the wilderness. In reality, however, there are gradations of wilderness. The land around the Jordan, though very definitely wilderness, is not as bleak or as barren as land further away from the river. This is probably what is meant here. If Jesus went from the wilderness into the wilderness, the idea is that he was driven deep into the wilderness, far from human habitation.

Tempted in the wilderness

Mark's account of Jesus' temptation in the wilderness is brief in the extreme. Not so much a 'narrative of temptation' as a passing reference to it. This indicates that the temptation itself is not the most important feature for Mark. There is the merest hint, however, that Mark suggests that Peter's rebuke of Jesus at Caesarea Philippi, where Jesus called him Satan, was a sort of temptation, similar to what he experienced in the wilderness.

Much more striking in Mark is that, as well as being tempted while he was in the wilderness, Jesus was with the wild animals and angels ministered to him. Jesus being with the wild animals is reminiscent of the story of the Garden of Eden, where Adam and Eve were with the wild animals and named them. The angels ministering to Jesus also further emphasizes the tearing apart of the barrier between heaven and earth that was established in the baptism narrative. Mark's account thus joins Jesus' temptation much more firmly with the story of his baptism than do any of the other Gospels. Mark is showing us in another way that the new age has begun with Jesus' ministry on earth, a new age in which Eden is reconstituted and heaven and earth are reunited.

Mark 1.14–15: Jesus came to Galilee

As Mark does not have a birth narrative, this is the first mention of Jesus' being in Galilee so far in the Gospel. Mark does not explain why Jesus came to Galilee or, indeed, where in Galilee he came to. The announcement of his arrival, though, along with the accompanying content of his message, makes it clear that a gear-change has taken place. Wherever you think the prologue ends, we can be in no doubt that the main action is about to begin.

Links backwards

- The last time we saw Jesus, he was in the wilderness in Judea (Mark 1.9–13); this change of location indicates one of Mark's 'beginnings'.

Links forwards

- Jesus stayed in Galilee until, in 10.1, he started his journey to Jerusalem.

Patterns in Mark

Another pattern to see in Mark relates to his geography. It is possible to split the Gospel into a few simple acts governed by geographical location:

- Act one: before Galilee (1.2–13)
- Act two: in Galilee and its environs (1.14—9.50)
- Act three: towards Jerusalem and Judea (10.1—16.8 or 16.1–8 can be an epilogue pointing back to Galilee).

Interesting words ...

- v. 14: *arrested*. The Greek word *paradidōmi* is best translated as 'handed over'. This word is the one also used of Jesus' arrest and betrayal at the end of his life.
- v. 14: the phrase 'the good news of God' occurs a few times in Paul's letters (in Rom. 1.1; 15.16; 2 Cor. 11.7; 1 Thess. 2.2, 2.8, 2.9) and in 1 Peter 4.17, but only here in any of the Gospels.
- v. 15: Mark often introduces direct speech with the small word *hoti*; since Greek has no punctuation marks, this word serves as speech marks do in English.
- v. 15: *has come near*. One of the biggest discussions over this verse is about the meaning of the phrase 'has come near'. The verb is in the perfect tense. In Greek, the perfect tense refers to something that has happened and therefore affects the present. So this verb could mean either 'the kingdom has come near, and therefore its arrival is imminent' or 'the kingdom has come near and now is here'. For more on this, see p. 34.

Jesus came to Galilee

Although in John's Gospel the ministries of John the Baptist and Jesus overlap so that John's disciples can ask questions about who Jesus is, in Mark, John and Jesus' ministries are sequential, with John's ending as Jesus' begins. Mark introduces details of John's beheading later as a flashback. For now, the detail about his arrest is all that is mentioned.

Mark offers no explanation as to why Jesus returned to Galilee. Indeed, his passing description of John's arrest by Herod Antipas makes less, rather than more, sense of Jesus' return to Galilee, into Herod Antipas' territory. Jesus' life was fully in danger when he finally travelled to Jerusalem at the end of the Gospel; but here, even at the start, a shadow hung over him. He returned to the place where John was only recently arrested. It may be that this detail, early on in the Gospel, hints at the shadow of the cross that looms over the Gospel evermore insistently as it unfolds.

It is also worth noting that Jesus' Galilean ministry focused on Capernaum, which is on the northern tip of the sea of Galilee. None of the Gospel writers explains why he moved from his home town of Nazareth to Capernaum. However, it would have made sense to do so. Nazareth was a small village (with an estimated population of around 300) with little passing trade. Few people would have visited Nazareth. Capernaum, on the other hand, was a bustling trading city on the Via Maris (the trade route that ran along the coast down to Egypt and up to Syria and Mesopotamia) and had an estimated population of around 1,000–1,500. It was also on the border between Herod Antipas and Philip's territories, hence the need for tax collectors to sit in booths to collect taxes from traders travelling through the region.

The Herods

Herod the Great ruled as king until 4 BC. At his death, the kingdom was split between three of his sons: Herod Archelaus ruled Judea (but he was deposed, at the request of the Judeans, in AD 6 to be replaced by a Roman governor known as a Pontius); Herod Antipas ruled over Galilee and the land on the opposite side of the Jordan from 4 BC to AD 38 (for more on Herod Antipas, see p. 143); and Philip ruled to the north and east of Galilee and the Jordan from 4 BC to AD 34.

By the start of Jesus' ministry, Pontius Pilate was the Roman governor of Judea and Herod Antipas was the ruler of Galilee and the Transjordan area. The Herod mentioned during Jesus' adult life in the Gospels was always Herod Antipas. He had no authority in Jerusalem; but he did have a palace there, which he would visit from time to time.

The Herod mentioned in Acts 12 was Herod Agrippa, the son of Aristobulus IV and Berenice. Agrippa was the grandson of Herod the Great. Agrippa's father, Aristobulus IV, had been executed by Herod the Great in 7 BC on charges of treason. For more on the Herodians, see pp. 77–8, and on the Herod family, see p. 143.

The good news of God

As noted above, if the prologue stretches as far as verse 15, then it begins and ends with good news. In verse 1, the good news is described somewhat vaguely and could refer either to good news about Jesus or the good news he proclaimed (or both). Here, in verse 15, the good news is defined.

The phrase 'the time is fulfilled' does not appear in Matthew's equivalent verse (Matt. 4.17); it fits well with the theme that Mark has been painting here in the Gospel: the tearing open of the heavens, the return to Eden with the animals and the angels pointing to the time being fulfilled – the moment when God would intervene in the world to bring salvation and hope. To avoid any doubt at all, Jesus now proclaims it as the content of the good news he has come to bring.

The kingdom of God

The phrase 'the kingdom of God' is one of the most important in Jesus' teachings. The question is what it refers to. It is possible to make the kingdom of God complex and convoluted, or very straightforward. I favour simple, though I would want to stress that it is a simple idea on the surface but much more complex beneath.

The kingdom points to God's rule and therefore refers to any time, any place or any event in which God's rule is present – seen or unseen. It is marked by steadfast love, justice, peace, harmony, joy, and so on; and, most of all, by a context in which God is recognized and worshipped for who God is.

God's rule in heaven is eternal and constant. The point about the tearing open of the heavens at Jesus' baptism is that God's rule on earth has begun, as in heaven. The question is not whether God rules; the question is whether God's rule is recognized and acknowledged for what it is. Hence the need for the extra words in Jesus' proclamation: 'repent' (or 'reorientate yourself') and 'believe'. The kingdom has come near and, with the start of Jesus' ministry, has broken into our world. As with so much of this Gospel, the question mark lies over how the world, and particularly the readers of Mark, will respond.

These opening verses of Mark set the scene for the start of Jesus' ministry. The long-awaited time has come: God has broken into the world – the question is, what will happen next?

Mark 1.16–39: A Snapshot of Jesus' Ministry

The first thing that happened next was that Jesus called Simon, Andrew, James and John. The importance of this cannot be underestimated. In a world that focuses almost exclusively on sole leaders and their significance, it is noteworthy that Jesus' first act, after the world-changing events of the previous stories, was to call people to join him. His was not a solo mission: the people around him were essential.

After that, the following few episodes in Mark – the healings of the man in the synagogue, of Simon's mother-in-law and of those brought to Jesus at sundown – all apparently took place in a single day. The next day, first thing in the morning, Jesus got up early to pray and then travelled through the towns around Capernaum, proclaiming 'the message'.

This concentrated depiction of Jesus' early ministry serves to give a sense of what the rest of it would be like: calling people to follow him, healings, the casting out of demons and proclaiming the good news of God. These were the hallmarks of who he was and what he came to do, with proclamation sitting at the heart of everything else.

Patterns to look out for in 1.16–39

These verses contain examples Jesus' teaching and actions that summarize what his ministry would look like for the rest of the Gospel.

- Calling followers (1.16–20; found later in 2.14; 8.34; 10.21).
- Healing individuals (1.29–31; found later in 1.40–45; 2.1–12; 3.1–6; 5.25–34; 5.35–43; 7.31–37; 8.22–26; 10.46–52).
- Healing large numbers of people (1.32–34; found later in 3.7–12; 5.24–34; 6.53–56).
- Exorcisms (1.21–28 and 1.39; found later in 3.11; 5.1–20; 7.24–30; 9.14–29).

- Teaching and proclaiming the good news (1.35–39; found later in 2.13; 4.1–2; 6.34; 7.17; 8.31—9.1; and then in increasing quantity on the way to Jerusalem and in the temple in chapters 9—13).
- Conflict with Jewish leaders (1.26–28 contains just amazement; this becomes conflict a few verses later, in 2.1–11; 2.23–28; 3.1–6; 7.1–23; 11.27–33; 12.1–12; 12.13–24; 14.53–65).

Mark 1.16–20: 'Come, follow me!'

It is striking that the very first thing that Jesus did in his ministry was to call people to follow him. There were different circles of people around Jesus: the inner group of Peter, James and John; the Twelve; the wider group of disciples; and then the crowd who followed more distantly. It is right, therefore, that the first to be called were Simon (Peter), Andrew, James and John.

Links forwards

- Jesus' call to people to follow him continues throughout the Gospel: when he calls Levi in Mark 2.14; when he talks about what this will mean (take up your cross and follow me) in 8.33–34; and when he invited the rich man to follow him in 10.21. As the Gospel progresses, it becomes clearer what following Jesus means; for now, it simply means the disciples' leaving their nets behind and joining him.

Interesting words ...

- v. 16: *the Sea of Galilee*. When talking of Galilee, Mark's language mimics Hebrew terminology, in which it is also called a 'sea'. It is really a lake, which is what Luke calls it.
- v. 16: *casting a net*. The word used for 'casting a net' (*amphiballō*) means 'to throw around' and indicates that the net involved was a circular net, either thrown out from the boat or placed in the lake by someone wading into the water.
- v. 17: *follow me*. Jesus' call to the four is recorded in the Greek without a verb and means literally, 'Here! Behind me!'
- v. 17: the play on words that is beloved of some English translations ('I will make you fishers of men') is not present in the Greek, which reads literally, 'I will make you become fishermen *(alieis)* of people (*anthrōpos*)'.

- v. 18: *immediately*. The word immediately (*euthus*) is normally used in Mark to start a new scene and keep the action coming thick and fast. Here, it is used differently. The four immediately left their nets. The scene has not changed but their response is instant. Given the word's use throughout the Gospel, their instant response is even more remarkable here.
- v. 20: *followed him*. The word (*aperchomai*) is more dramatic in Greek. The verb means 'departed', which, added to the adverb 'behind' (*opisō*, the same word used in Jesus' call of the Four), lends a sense of finality about their action. They departed behind Jesus.

Simon and Andrew

In Mark 3.16, we are told that Simon was also given the name Peter. Between this point in Mark and that one, he is called Simon (Mark 1.29, 30, 36). After 3.16, he is called Peter, with one exception: when Jesus addressed him in the Garden of Gethsemane (14.37). There, he is called Peter by Mark but addressed as Simon by Jesus ('he said to Peter, "Simon, are you asleep?"').

Although John's Gospel gives Bethsaida as the place where Simon and Andrew came from (John 1.44), it is clear from Matthew, Mark and Luke that, at the start of his ministry, Jesus lived in Capernaum (see the healing of Simon's mother-in-law in Mark 1.29–31). Christian tradition locates the house right next to the synagogue and identifies the spot as one of the largest houses in Capernaum. If the tradition is correct, and there is no reason to think it is not, then this indicates that Simon and Andrew were relatively wealthy. This would fit in with what is known of the fishing industry in the first century, which suggests that it was a thriving business and the source of a good level of income for those involved in it.

'Here! Behind me'

Jesus' command appears brusque but is probably better understood as being a dynamic call to action. It is clear from elsewhere in the Gospels that Jesus' invitation to follow is expected to be accepted right away, as it was here.

As far as Mark's narrative is concerned, the disciples saw Jesus for the first time when he called them. They accepted his invitation and responded immediately. This stands in considerable contrast to John's Gospel where Jesus was seen around Galilee; he invited people to 'Come and see' (John 1.39) and, after they had done so, the disciples of John (one of whom is said to be Andrew, Simon's brother) followed him. The two different models fit the style of each Gospel: immediacy in Mark and after greater reflection in John. Whether straight away or after due consideration, the key feature in both Gospels is that the disciples do follow. As becomes clear, at least in

Mark's Gospel, the disciples had a way to go before they truly understood who Jesus was; but their first instinct was right, which was to follow him.

There is considerable discussion among scholars about whether Jesus' disciples were in fact following the rabbi/disciple model that existed elsewhere in the first century. Some argue that the differences are too great between the two. One of the biggest differences is that, in the usual rabbi/disciple relationship, a young male individual, approximately between the ages of 13 and 15, would seek out a rabbi and ask to study with him. He would then spend the next few years learning from him, as Paul did with Rabbi Gamaliel (Acts 22.3).

The relationship between Jesus and his disciples was strikingly different. Although the text does not reveal how old the disciples were when they heard Jesus' call, the implication is that they were older than 12 (it would certainly change our mental picture and much of Christian art if the disciples were all teenagers). Much more important, however, is that Jesus chose *them*, not the other way around. Mark also makes clear that Jesus did not invite Simon and Andrew to follow him so that they could learn from him, but so that they could 'fish for people'. Some argue, therefore, that Jesus should be seen as more of a charismatic prophet than a rabbi.

I'm not convinced that this distinction is necessary. There are certainly overlaps between Jesus' role and that of a charismatic prophet such as Elijah. Nevertheless, although the relationship between Jesus and his disciples was not exactly 'usual', it is important to note that the followers of Jesus are called disciples in the Gospels; and Mary's addressing the risen Jesus as *Rabbouni* (the Aramaic for 'rabbi'), in John 20.16, suggests that they were accustomed to calling him 'Rabbi'. It seems, therefore, that the rabbi/disciple relationship can be seen as the jumping-off point for understanding how Jesus related to those that followed him, even if we then add to this his similarity to numerous other characters from the Old Testament, such as Elijah and Moses, which adds depth. As so often with Jesus, he far exceeded the hopes, dreams and expectations of those around him. He was indeed a rabbi to his disciples, both then and now, but he was also much more than that too.

In this, it is important to notice that one of the key features of the learning that took place between rabbis and disciples was that the disciples of a rabbi were not seeking the transfer of knowledge; rather, they hoped to see the world as their rabbi saw it. In other words, their goal was to comprehend their rabbi's world view. This fits well with what we see of the disciples in the Gospels. Jesus' teaching, his miracles and healings all showed those who followed him how he saw the world: a world view that turned norms and expectations on their head; one in which the last would be first and the first last, the mighty would be brought down from their thrones, and the humble and meek would be exalted. Jesus was not so much teaching the disciples what he knew as how to live in the world and how to view those around them.

The word 'disciple' is as important today as it was then, but it is easy to forget its significance. When asked what the word 'disciple' means, many people might well answer that a disciple is someone who follows Jesus. While they would be right, it isn't all that being a disciple means. Literally, 'disciple' means 'a learner'. The Greek word *mathētēs* and the Latin word *discipulus* (from which our word 'disciple' comes) both mean 'someone who learns'. A disciple of Jesus, therefore, is learning day by day to see the world as Jesus saw it. Following him is *how* we learn; but if all we do as disciples is follow, then we are missing out on a life-transforming experience. Being a disciple is not just about following Jesus; it is also about learning to see the world as he saw it and to react to it as he did.

Disciples/apostles/the Twelve

It is easy to conflate three key terms in the Gospels: 'disciples', 'the Twelve' and 'apostles'. Although these terms overlap, it is worth observing that they do not refer to the same groups. 'Disciples' is used for a wider group of those who followed Jesus, which includes more than just 12. Luke's Gospel contains an account of Jesus sending out 70 or 72 (the precise number differs in different manuscripts) in Luke 10.1; but, clearly, the term 'disciple' also includes more people than the Twelve in Mark as well. Just before the Last Supper, Jesus sent two disciples to prepare everything and then Jesus and the Twelve arrived later.

In the Gospels, 'the Twelve' refers to the 12 disciples closest to Jesus. 'Apostles' refers to those sent out by Jesus, both during his ministry and after the Resurrection. Since Paul was counted as an apostle, as indeed were Andronicus and Junia in Romans 16.7, it seems that 'apostle' refers to a wider group than just the original 12.

Keeping these three different categories clear in our minds is important, not least because it is obvious from the Gospels that, while the Twelve was made up solely of men, disciples and apostles included women as well.

'I will make you fish for people'

Jesus' famous metaphor is one that is great on the surface and best not thought about in too much detail. While fishing is great for those who will subsequently eat the fish, it isn't so good for the fish themselves. You could hardly conclude that a fishing boat was good news for the fish in the Sea of Galilee. So the metaphor both plays with an idea and extends it. Andrew, Simon, James and John leave behind their old methods of fishing for a new method, in which not only are different subjects caught (people not fish) but the catching is something that is good news for those 'caught'.

James, John and Zebedee

The calling of James and John is very similar to that of Simon and Andrew. Two differences, however, stand out.

1 While Simon and Andrew were actually in the process of fishing, casting their net into the lake, James and John had finished fishing and were mending, folding and cleaning their nets, ready for the next day's work. This detail is small but lends a vivid reality to the scene.
2 This difference is more poignant. We are told that all Simon and Andrew left behind to follow Jesus were their nets (though only a few verses later we discover that Simon had a mother-in-law and so also a wife; maybe even children too), whereas what James and John left behind was their father, Zebedee (and the hired hands in the boats). Although Mark is not ready yet to talk about the cost of discipleship (this comes much later in the Gospel), the first seeds of that cost are indicated here for those who have eyes to see.

As we will see in the next chapter or so, Mark works hard to sow seeds in this opening that will, later in the Gospel, grow into significant themes. A careful reading of these opening chapters gives us a glimpse of what is to come.

Peter, James and John

Although Peter, James and John are never given an official title (such as 'the Three') they form around Jesus the inner circle who are selected when others are left behind. At the healing of Jarius' daughter (5.37), the Transfiguration (9.2) and the Garden of Gethsemane (14.33), they are taken aside by Jesus and seem to be trusted more than the others.

It rather begs the question about what happened to Andrew. Later on in Mark, Andrew reappears a couple of times but not nearly as often as Peter, James and John.

Mark 1.21–28: Jesus revealed his authority and healed a man with an unclean spirit

Jesus' first miracle encapsulates some of the most important features of his ministry: teaching with authority, casting out a demon and healing on the sabbath. It is worth noting that whereas, later, Jesus' similar healings caused opposition, this one did not. There was simple amazement and nothing more. This first miracle establishes who Jesus was in such a way that it sets up categories for us to look for in subsequent stories.

Links backwards

- While we, the readers, know that Jesus' identity (and authority) were revealed at his baptism (Mark 1.9–11), this is the first time his authority is revealed to those around him.

Links forwards

- This story draws together themes that run throughout the Gospel, especially exorcism and the recognition of Jesus by demons; the question of Jesus' authority; healing on the sabbath; and conflict with Jewish leaders (for references throughout the Gospel, see the patterns listed on p. 36).

Interesting words ...

- v. 21: although the NRSV does not contain the word 'into', this verse, in the Greek, has two uses of the preposition 'into'. First, Jesus and the disciples went 'into' Capernaum (*eisporeuō*). Second, Mark applies the slightly clunky phrase 'he taught into the synagogue', which has the idea of going in and then teaching.
- v. 22: *taught*. Mark uses the words for 'teach', 'teaching' and 'teacher' (*didaskō*) more often than any other Gospel writer, indicating that Jesus' teaching ministry lay right at the heart of who he was and what he did.
- v. 22: *authority*. *Exousia* is used nine times in Mark to refer to Jesus' recognized ability/authority. It is therefore not surprising, in this opening story, for Jesus' authority to be the first thing recognized by the crowd.
- vv. 22 and 27: *astounded; amazed*. One of the regular reactions of the crowd to Jesus was one of astonishment. Mark uses different words to express this: *ekkplēssō* ('amaze', 'astound' or 'spellbound') in 1.22; 6.2; 7.37; 10.26; 11.18; *thambeō* ('astound', 'amaze' or 'perplex') in 1.27; 10.24 (the word *ekthambeō*, which means 'to be overwhelmed', 'to be flabbergasted', 'to be distressed', 'to be agitated' or 'to be alarmed', is also used in 9.15; 14.33; 16.5–6);

10.32; *thaumazō* ('wonder' or 'marvel at') in 5.20; 6.6; 15.5; 15.44; *existēmi* ('astonish', 'astound' or 'gone out of his mind') in 2.12; 3.21; 5.42; 6.51. See pp. 46–7 for a chart of the different uses of these words.

- v. 23: *unclean spirit*. Mark uses the awkward phrase 'a man in an unclean spirit' to refer to the man whom Jesus healed. The word used for 'unclean' refers to something that is ritually or morally impure. The opposite of this kind of spirit is the Holy Spirit. Following so close after Jesus' baptism, the contrast with Jesus who is 'in the Holy Spirit' is strong.
- v. 24: *what have you to do with us*. Literally, the question the spirit asked Jesus was 'What to you and to us?' (see more below).
- v. 24: *Jesus of Nazareth*. In Mark, and twice in Luke (4.34 and 24.19), Jesus is described as Jesus of Nazareth (in Greek, *Nazarēnos*); by contrast, Matthew, John and the rest of the time in Luke, Jesus is termed *Nazōraios*, which can simply mean 'from Nazareth' but might have a wider meaning and point to an early description of followers of the Way – the Nazarenes.
- v. 25: *be silent*. The word here means 'to silence something with a muzzle'.
- v. 28: *fame*. Although the word *akoē* can mean 'fame', it more literally means 'what people hear', hence 'a rumour'. This seems a good translation here: 'the rumour of him spread throughout Galilee'.

They went to Capernaum

The opening to this story hints that when Jesus first called Simon, Andrew, James and John, they were not in Capernaum and only went there later in the company of Jesus. However, as Simon's mother-in-law was healed in a house in Capernaum, it seems natural to assume that this was where Simon lived. It is possible that the boats were kept a little way outside Capernaum or, indeed, in Bethsaida (around five miles away) as John implies (1.44).

Synagogues

For many years, scholars assumed that there were no synagogues before the destruction of the temple in Jerusalem in AD 70, on the grounds that worship was focused on the temple and not in local gathering places. Both archaeological evidence (which indicates that there were around 50 synagogues in Galilee at the time of Jesus) and evidence from the Gospels themselves, however, reveal that this assumption was wrong. While sacrifice took place within the temple, synagogues were, as their name implies (the Greek word means literally 'a bringing together'), important places of gathering, reading Torah, discussion, teaching and prayer.

The remains of the synagogue that can be visited in Capernaum today are of a fourth-century synagogue. Underneath these remains, however, is evidence of a much earlier synagogue, from the first century AD.

As one having authority

It is tempting to think that Jesus was believed because of the miracles that he performed. Mark makes clear, in this very first story about Jesus, that this was not the case. The crowd was already astounded by Jesus' authority *before* he healed the man with the unclean spirit. Jesus taught with an innate authority that caused people to follow him. His healings flowed out of who he was; but they were not, first and foremost, designed to make people believe him. His teaching did that by itself. Intriguingly, the healing of the man was seen as evidence of the authority already observed by the crowd. They were not alone in seeing him as authoritative: unclean spirits did too.

The scribes

Jesus' teaching is contrasted here with that of the scribes. The question is who they were. We know a lot about the various groups that Jesus met during his ministry, particularly the priests (and the high priest), the Pharisees, the Sadducees and the Herodians. These groups will be introduced as they appear in Mark. Possibly the hardest group to identify, even though they pop up at regular intervals in the Gospel, is the scribes. There was no formal grouping in the first century known as 'scribes'.

However, it is clear from their description that they were literate (hence being scribes) and had extensive knowledge of the law. In a largely illiterate society, their role would have been significant. They would have been the prime interpreters and handers-on of the law, as well as those able to write down and communicate messages with people in other towns. One possibility is that the scribes were off-duty priests.

Priests were literate because they needed to know the law in order to interpret it during their duties in the temple. However, priests were only on duty for around two weeks per year. This begs the question of what they did for the other weeks of the year. A natural explanation would be that they acted as scribes, interpreting the law and writing for those who could not write.

The scribes may not only have been priests, but it certainly makes sense to imagine that at least some priests were scribes when not on duty in the temple.

Exorcisms in Mark's Gospel

Jesus' casting out of demons is something that is presented as commonplace in Mark's Gospel. This first occasion sets up a pattern that we will see repeated regularly. A few chapters later, in Mark 3.11, we learn that 'whenever the unclean sprits saw him, they fell down before him', implying that this was something that happened habitually. Following that, in Mark 5.1–20, Jesus casts out 'Legion' from the man from Gerasa, then an unclean spirit from the daughter of a woman from Tyre (7.24–30) and finally an unclean spirit from a boy (9.14–29).

It is also worth noting that the conflict between Jesus and the scribes from Jerusalem in 3.22 is centred around the fact that Jesus cast out demons and that the disciples were given authority to cast out demons, both in chapter 3 and chapter 6 (3.15; 6.7, 13).

All this paints a picture in which the casting out of demons is a central pillar of Jesus' ministry; and accounts of him doing so are spread evenly throughout the Gospel (chapters 1, 3, 5, 7 and 9). In our modern world, where we struggle to make sense of casting out demons, it is tempting either to ignore the accounts or to attempt to translate them into medical conditions that do make sense in the twenty-first century. The problem is that they occur too regularly to ignore and are not accompanied with sufficient detail to allow a modern diagnosis. Even more importantly, the stories are told from the perspective of Mark's own world and, as a result, are communicating something that is lost if we attempt a contemporary medical diagnosis. It is best to receive them as stories that made sense in Jesus' day and to Mark's own audience without attempting to translate them into a modern context. When we do, these passages begin to make a lot more sense. Demons, who encountered matters on a spiritual level, saw and understood who Jesus was far more readily than most others.

Demons

Although there are very few references to demons in the Old Testament, they became much more frequent in later texts, such as Tobit (3.8). Belief in them may have originated in Persian religion rather than Hebrew thinking.

They were regarded as bringers of harm who would overwhelm and take control of a person, causing dumbness, blindness, epilepsy, fever and mania (as here). Most importantly, they were part of the natural world. The Essene community was particularly interested in demons; various scrolls contain detailed descriptions of incantations and magical ceremonies that had to be used to combat and defeat them.

What is vital to recognize is that demons were regarded as being subject to God. This is why casting them out was such an important part of Jesus' ministry. Over and over again, Jesus is shown to use no elaborate ceremonies or complex magical rituals to defeat demons. He commanded and they obeyed, just as they obeyed God. In a world where fear of uncontrollable demons (who might creep up on some unsuspecting person, overwhelm them and take control) was rife, Jesus' absolute command over them was key, revealing something important about who he was.

'What have you to do with us?'

The question the unclean spirit asked Jesus is strikingly like the question that Jesus asked his mother in John 2.4: a question that often evokes comment. In John 2.4, when Mary told Jesus that the wine at the wedding at Cana had run out, Jesus replied 'Woman, what concern is that to you and to me?' The Greek, however, says, 'Woman, what to you and to me?' Here in Mark, the unclean spirit said, 'What to you and to us?' It suggests that the real question in both instances is what connection is there between us?

At the end of Jesus' baptism, a question that hangs in the air is who would be the first to recognize who Jesus really was. We do not have to wait long to find out. The first to recognize Jesus and to declare him to be 'the Holy One of God' was an unclean spirit. Given the way that Mark's Gospel begins, this is unsurprising. The story starts with a 'God's-eye view': God sending his messenger to announce the good news. It is therefore predictable that those who recognized Jesus first would also come from non-earthly realms, even if they were, as here, unclean spirits. This sets up a theme that will run throughout the Gospel – that of recognition and response. We, the readers, know who Jesus was; the demons and unclean spirits knew it too. The question is, who else would recognize him to be who he was?

Jesus' response to the spirit equally establishes a thread that will run through Mark: one that has provoked a lot of discussion over the years. That thread is Jesus' muzzling of a spirit, so that it couldn't reveal Jesus' identity more widely (for more on this theme in Mark, see the Introduction, pp. 1–14). I would argue that Jesus' refusal to allow the demon to speak existed for a reason: Jesus' life, ministry, teaching and healings, as well as his death and Resurrection, provided the whole picture of who Jesus was and what he came to do. Any premature proclamation of who he was risked providing a partial picture. Jesus prevented anyone from declaring who he was until they could proclaim the whole story, including his death and Resurrection. It was at that point that the angel said to the women at the tomb, 'Go, tell'; the problem was that they ran away instead.

There is a strong contrast between what happened here (as far as we know, the man with the unclean spirit obeyed Jesus' command) and what happened at the end of chapter 1. There, the man with leprosy was also commanded not to tell anyone what had happened; but he took no notice and reported it widely. The consequence of this was that Jesus was no longer able to travel about openly.

Amazed/astounded/astonished/flabbergasted

- Mark uses a number of words with similar meanings to refer to people being astonished in his Gospel. It is interesting to see them all laid out together, to give a flavour of how he uses them. In the translation, I have italicized the English words equivalent to the relevant Greek words. For the exact phrases used, see 'Interesting words', the notes on 1.22 and 27, on pp. 41–2.

Greek word used	Who was amazed?	Verse
ekplessō	The crowd	'They were *astounded* at his teaching' (1.22)
thambeō	The same crowd as in 1.22	'They were all *amazed*, and they kept on asking one another' (1.27)
existēmi	The crowd	'they were all *amazed* and glorified God' (2.12)
existēmi	Jesus (or his family thought he was)	'When his family heard it, they went out to restrain him, for people were saying, "He has *gone out of his mind*"' (3.21)
thaumazō	The people to whom the man from Gerasa spoke	'and everyone was *amazed*' (5.20)
existēmi	The small crowd in Jairus' house	'At this they were overcome with *amazement*' (5.42)
ekplessō	Many	'many who heard him were *astounded*' (6.2)
thaumazō	Jesus	'And he was *amazed* at their unbelief' (6.6)
existēmi	Disciples	'And they were utterly *astounded*' (6.51)
ekplessō	A crowd in the Decapolis	'They were *astounded* beyond measure' (7.37)
ekthambeō	The crowd	'When the whole crowd saw him, they were immediately *overcome with awe*' (9.15)
thambeō	Disciples	'And the disciples were *perplexed* at these words' (10.24)
ekplessō	Disciples	'They were greatly *astounded* and said to one another, "Then who can be saved?"' (10.26)
ekplessō	The whole crowd	'the whole crowd was *spellbound* by his teaching' 11.18)

Greek word used	Who was amazed?	Verse
ekthambeō	Jesus	'He took with him Peter and James and John, and began to be *distressed* and agitated' (14.33)
thaumazō	Pilate	'so that Pilate was *amazed*' (15.5)
thaumazō	Pilate	'Then Pilate *wondered* if he were already dead' (15.44)
ekthambeō	The women at the tomb	'they were *alarmed*. But he said to them, "Do not be *alarmed*"' (16.5–6)

Mark 1.29–31: Jesus healed Simon's mother-in-law

Mark's fast-paced narrative moves immediately from the synagogue to Simon's house, which, if archaeological tradition is to be believed, lay right next door. It would have taken no more than a minute to get from one to the other.

Links backwards

- This story fits firmly in Mark's opening narrative (1.16–39), which serves as an introduction to Jesus.

Links forwards

- This healing points forwards to the many other healings of individuals that we will encounter in Mark (1.40–45; 2.1–12; 3.1–6; 5.25–34; 5.35–43; 7.31–37; 8.22–26; 10.46–52).

Interesting words ...

- v. 30: *fever*. The word is pleasingly literal. *Puressō* ('to be feverish') is connected to the verb *pureuō* ('to light a fire').
- v. 31: *serve*. The verb is *diakoneō*, which can mean generic serving; but it is also the verb translated as 'minister', which was what the angels did to Jesus in the wilderness.

And immediately ...

The impact of Jesus' going directly from the synagogue to Simon and Andrew's house is that Jesus healed Simon's mother-in-law on the sabbath. The controversy around healing someone on the sabbath emerges in chapter 3 (3.1–6); but it is worth noting that Jesus did it here too. The crowd waited until it was no longer the sabbath before they asked Jesus to heal their sick (in verse 30, they brought the sick to Jesus at sundown, which was the start of the next day in the Jewish calendar); but in the privacy of Simon's home, where there was no one to object, he healed Simon's mother-in-law on the sabbath too. This is important. Some see Jesus' action as being deliberately provocative. This healing, right at the start of his ministry, reveals this to be untrue. He was simply acting out of compassion, no matter when people needed him and who was present.

The house of Simon and Andrew

None of the Gospels tells us why Jesus moved from Nazareth to Capernaum. We are left to surmise that it was due to Capernaum's being a more vibrant 'hub' than Nazareth. The question of where Jesus lived is also left unanswered. Some assume that he lived in Simon and Andrew's house, though passages such as Matthew 8.20 and Luke 9.58 ('Foxes have holes, and birds of the air have nests; but the Son of Man has nowhere to lay his head'), suggest that he had no permanent home.

Simon's mother-in-law

One of the intriguing features of the stories about Jesus is that they make very little mention of the families of those who followed him. The easy assumption to make, therefore, is that the disciples didn't have families. This encounter, early on, reveals this to be untrue. If Simon had a mother-in-law, he had a wife and possibly children. What becomes clear here in Mark is that the themes of Jesus' ministry are being set up gently and subtly. In these opening scenes, we encounter the recognition of Jesus by unclean spirits and the command not to reveal his identity, healing on the sabbath, and the dismantling of family units – all of which become explicit later in Jesus' ministry. For now, they are simply introduced so gently that it is easy to miss them.

The healing of Simon's mother-in-law is a story full of emotion and yet Mark tells it in a sparse, stripped-back manner. In the space of three verses, we learn that the mother of one of Jesus' first followers was burning up with a fever (with the implication that she might die from it); on hearing of this, Jesus went to heal her. She then got up and served him and his disciples. The telling of the event is very matter of fact; as with much of Mark's Gospel, the emotion lies beneath the surface.

Mark 1.32–34: Jesus healed many at Simon's house

It is unusual in Mark to have three healings so close together. The effect of this is that we get a sense of the three key types of healing that Jesus did:

1 Casting out of demons.
2 Healing individuals in need of compassion.
3 Healing large numbers of people.

These three types of healing run through Mark, with the most common being the healing of individuals in need of compassion.

Links backwards

- Like the previous two stories, this fits firmly in Mark's opening narrative (1.16–39).

Links forwards

- It points forwards to other stories where Jesus heals crowds (3.7–12; 6.53–56).

Interesting words ...

- v. 32: *sick*. The word for 'sick' is *kakōs*. The adverb from *kakos*, meaning 'bad' or 'evil', is akin to the English idiom 'badly' ('So and so is doing badly'), which, in some English dialects, means 'poorly'.
- v. 32: Mark differentiates the two categories he has just introduced by adding the word *daimonizomai*, 'possessed by a demon'. Having healed an individual possessed by a spirit and having healed one person who was ill, Jesus was then presented with many people who fell into either category.
- v. 34: *many*. The 'many' is stressed in this account: he healed 'many' (*polus*) with a 'variety' (*poikilos*, literally 'many-spotted' or 'coloured') of diseases (here, the word changes from *kakōs* to *nosos*, a more specific word for 'diseases' or 'plagues') and cast out 'many' (*polus*) demons.
- v. 34: *cured*. For more on the different words for 'healing', see the box, 'Words for "heal" in Mark's Gospel', on p. 50. Here, the word is *therapeuō*.

From the one to the many

One of the key features of Mark's account of Jesus' ministry is his switch from the particular to the general and back again. The story of Jesus is told through the lens of his ministering to individuals; but the account constantly pans outwards to show that this also includes encounters with large crowds before zooming back in again to show the impact Jesus had on specific individuals. This occasion is one where two individuals are identified (though not named) – the man with the unclean spirit and Simon's mother-in-law – and healed, followed by similar healings for the crowd who came to Jesus.

Words for 'heal' in Mark's Gospel

There are three different words for 'heal' in Mark: *therapeuō* (which means 'to cure' or 'heal'), *iaomai* ('heal', often in a miraculous way) and *sōzō* (most usually translated as 'save'; but it can also mean 'heal'; the examples given below are only the ones that refer to healing). The table shows the use of the words in different parts of Mark.

Word	Verse
therapeuō	'And he *cured* many who were sick with various diseases' (1.34)
therapeuō	'They watched him to see whether he would *cure* him on the sabbath' (3.2)
therapeuō	'for he had *cured* many, so that all who had diseases pressed upon him to touch him' (3.10)
sōzō	'Come and lay your hands on her, so that she may be *made well*, and live' (5.23)
sōzō	'If I but touch his clothes, I will be *made well*' (5.28)
iaomai	'she felt in her body that she *was healed* of her disease' (5.29)
sōzō	'your faith has *made you well*; go in peace, and be healed of your disease' (5.34)
therapeuō	'he laid his hands on a few sick people and *cured* them' (6.5)
therapeuō	'[the Twelve] cast out many demons, and anointed with oil many who were sick and *cured* them' (6.13)
sōzō	'they laid the sick in the marketplaces, and begged him that they might touch even the fringe of his cloak; and all who touched it *were healed*' (6.56)
sōzō	'Jesus said to him, "Go; your faith has *made you well*"'(10.52)

Mark 1.35–39: Prayer and proclamation

This sample section of Jesus' ministry ends, as the opening verses have done (in 1.12–13 and 1.14–15), with a focus first on Jesus' spending time alone and then proclaiming his message of good news. Although healings and exorcisms were what drew attention to Jesus' ministry, a summary of his ministry would not be complete without his withdrawing by himself to pray and travelling throughout Galilee, proclaiming his message of good news.

Links backwards

- Jesus' prayer, followed by proclamation, mimicked exactly Mark 1.12–15, with Jesus spending time by himself in the wilderness, followed by travelling to proclaim his message of good news.

Links forwards

- This passage looks forward to 6.30–33, where Jesus had an abortive attempt at taking the disciples away by themselves to a wilderness place. The crowd saw that they were going and followed, which led to the feeding of the 5,000 (where Jesus taught until evening). Jesus eventually was able to spend time alone praying in 6.46. Jesus also withdrew to pray in Gethsemane (14.32–42).

Interesting words …

- v. 35: *in the morning*. The phrase for 'early in the morning' is clunky. Literally, it reads 'early in the morning' (*prōi*), 'by night' (*ennuchos*), 'very' (*lian*). The phrase doesn't easily make sense, but the gist is clear. Jesus got up before daybreak.
- v. 35: *deserted place*. The idea of the Greek word is that the wilderness is not just a 'location' but also a place without anyone or anything in it. We might say the 'middle of nowhere'.
- v. 36: *hunted for him*. The word used for 'hunted' is usually used in a hostile way. Here, it is probably not hostile but nevertheless communicates the focus of Simon and the other disciples, and their eagerness to find Jesus.
- v. 38: *neighbouring towns*. The place that Jesus suggests that they go is 'elsewhere to the next village-towns'. The word for 'village-town' is made up of the word *kōmē* (village without a wall) and the word *polis* (city): it is quite a specific description – a place that was larger than just a 'village' but smaller and of less significance than a 'city'. In 1.33, Mark describes Capernaum as a city, so the places are settlements smaller than Capernaum but presumably bigger than Nazareth.

- vv. 38–39: *proclaim the message.* The phrase rendered in the NRSV as 'proclaim the message' is a translation of a simple verb, *kērussō*, which means 'proclaim'. That verb, and the noun that comes from it (*kērygma*, 'proclamation') lies right at the heart of Mark's presentation of Jesus. The NRSV adds 'the message' to indicate that Jesus wasn't just saying any old words: he had come to proclaim something very particular – the good news referred to right at the start of the Gospel. The fact that Mark does not say what the message was indicates it was so well known that it was not necessary to do so.

Proclamation

In this summary section at the start of Jesus' ministry, Mark ensures that it is clear what Jesus had come to do. It was Jesus' healings and casting out of demons that drew attention, but that was not why he had come. He had come to proclaim the good news of God that, as reported in 1.15, the 'time is fulfilled, and the kingdom of God has come near; repent, and believe in the good news'. This was the content of Jesus' proclamation; and it helps to make sense of Jesus message in the chapters that follow:

- The time was fulfilled. This affected how people should act. They should wait expectantly, like slaves waiting for the return of their master.
- The kingdom of God had come near; and Jesus told parables to explain the nature of the kingdom.
- The key was, therefore, how people would respond to this message by repenting and believing.

In their synagogues

In Matthew's Gospel, the addition of 'their' to 'synagogues' has been understood to indicate that there was animosity between the early Christian community and the Jewish community. Its use here, however, suggests that this may not be entirely correct. There is very little to indicate animosity here. Instead, it suggests that in each 'village-town' that Jesus visited, the most obvious place to begin his proclamation was in the synagogue of each place: it was where the people would gather to talk, worship and listen to the reading of the law. It also suggests that there were a lot of synagogues in even the smaller village-towns.

Mark 1.40—3.12: Jesus' Popularity Begins to Cause Problems

The previous passage marks the closing of the first episode of Jesus' ministry. As it draws to an end, we get a sense of who Jesus was and what he had come to do. The scene is set for what will come next.

The first mentions of Jesus' ministry have no accompanying criticism. Jesus called disciples, healed the sick (even on the sabbath), cast out demons and proclaimed the good news of God, first in Capernaum and then in the surrounding village-towns, with no reported opposition. From the end of chapter 1, this begins to change. As Jesus' notoriety grew so did the animosity to his actions and his message. The next section of Mark's Gospel, from 1.40 to 3.12, is marked by increased and increasing opposition; this theme reaches its peak in 3.12, when the Pharisees were so incensed by Jesus that they overcame their animosity to the Herodians to plot his destruction. Although some think the section ends there, it seems more likely that it continues for another six verses to 3.12, where the crowd was so besotted with Jesus that the people fell on him in their eagerness to touch him.

The theme of Jesus' notoriety, and the opposition it evoked, began with someone spreading the news of what Jesus had done for him. This raises a tantalizing question of whether notoriety lies at the heart of a lot of opposition, whether to Jesus or anyone else. Perhaps it is not so much what people do but how popular or well known they are that draws disapproval? It certainly seemed to be the case here.

Patterns in 1.40—3.6

This section begins and ends with Jesus' popularity. It begins with the healed leper telling everyone what Jesus had done (despite being told not to in 1.40–45) and ends with a crowd so desperate to be healed that Jesus had to take to a boat to avoid being crushed (3.7–12). Mark does like to bookend or frame themes to focus them and provide food for thought. Here, five controversy stories are framed, beginning and end, with stories of Jesus' popularity; the two appear to go together.

In between the two popularity stories, we see Jesus doing what he had done in the previous section, but this time it caused conflict:

- Declaring the paralytic man's sins to be forgiven (2.1–12).
- Calling another disciple, but this time a tax collector (2.13–17).
- Not fasting when others did (2.18–22).
- Plucking grain on the sabbath (2.23–28).
- Healing a man in the synagogue on the sabbath (3.1–6).

These twin motifs – of growing popularity and of being exactly who he was (but their leading to conflict) – are intertwined in this section. Mark's narrative here hints at Jesus' inevitable future. Jesus was simply being who he was, but it brought both notoriety and condemnation.

Mark 1.40–45: Jesus healed a man with leprosy

As we move towards the end of the first chapter of Mark, the story changes very slightly. Until now, Jesus had been doing exactly what he came to do, with no adverse effects: people followed him, others were healed, his message was being proclaimed, and demons had scattered before him. From this story onwards, the storm clouds, though still small at present, begin to gather. Jesus begins to draw attention to himself whether he wants to or not.

Links backwards

- The healings so far have happened without incident. Even when the crowd gathered to be healed, the report implies it was calm (Mark 1.32–34); it all changes with this healing.

Links forwards

- Jesus instructs people not to tell anyone about him in 3.12; 5.43; 7.36 and 8.30. This story is the first time it happens in Mark; and in it, we see some of the reasons why.

Interesting words ...

- v. 40: *leper*. The word for 'leper' is not a technical one. *Lepros* refers simply to scabby, scaly or rough skin. The adjective is used here in place of a noun (something known as a nominalized adjective) and means a person with 'scaly skin'.
- v. 41: *moved with pity*. In many of the stories about Jesus' healing people, Jesus is described as feeling compassion (*splangchnizomai*, a word that refers to a feeling in the gut). This is not the word used here. A better translation of this word (*orgizō*) would be 'feeling angry'.
- v. 41: *be made clean*. It is significant that Jesus' words of healing here are 'be made clean' (from *katharizō* – to make clean – from which the English word 'cathartic' comes). This highlights the ritual impurity that lies behind the text – healing a person with leprosy meant making them clean.
- v. 45: *began to proclaim it freely*. In the light of the importance of Jesus' 'proclamation', which was highlighted in the previous story, it is interesting to note that the man who was healed also proclaimed (*kērussō*) a lot (*polla*).

Feeling angry

The word for 'feeling angry' is not in all ancient manuscripts of Mark's Gospel. Its use is so surprising, however, that scholars are agreed that Mark probably did use the word here, but that scribes later changed it to the more acceptable 'was moved by compassion'.

The key question is, what was Jesus angry about? It could be that the man's words caused the anger. The formulation 'if you want to' or 'if you choose' might imply that he recognized Jesus' ability but questioned whether he had the will to help. The implication that Jesus might choose not to help could have sparked anger. On the other hand, it could simply have indicated a polite opener to his request: something along the lines of 'if you wouldn't mind'.

The other option is that Jesus' anger was caused by the suffering of the man. Someone cast out from society, spurned by those he loved and left to make the best of his life alone outside his village-town would be in a woeful condition. It could be that Jesus was angry about the isolation and exclusion of the man with leprosy. The problem is that Mark does not tell us.

Whatever the reason for Jesus' anger, it is worth noting that it is reported here. This is a far cry from the 'gentle Jesus, meek and mild' of Charles Wesley's hymn. This was a Jesus moved to deep emotion, even if the gospel accounts do not report the reason for it. Again, so early in the Gospel, this sets up a theme that will emerge over and over again. Jesus felt deeply about the people he met and these emotions were what shaped his relationships with those around him.

Leprosy

As noted above, the word *lepros* is not used technically in the Gospels. It refers to any kind of disfiguring skin complaint. The man who spoke to Jesus may have had 'leprosy proper' (known these days as Hansen's disease) but he might equally have had any kind of skin condition, such as severe psoriasis or eczema. The problem was that in a culture that had limited diagnostic tools, and a deep fear of leprosy, people with all kinds of diseases were termed 'lepers'.

The social impact of this designation was devastating. In both Hebrew and Greek, someone designated *ṣāra* (Hebrew) or *lepros* (Greek) was considered ritually unclean and unable to enter the temple for worship. They would be admitted only if designated clean by a temple official. Not only that, they were also social outcasts, unable to live in normal society because of the fear of contagion. One of the tragic ironies of leper colonies was that people with non-contagious skin conditions often caught Hansen's disease as a result of being banished to them.

The story doesn't tell us where Jesus met the man with leprosy; but the implication is that he was travelling from place to place and therefore he met him outside one of the village-towns that he was passing through, not in any kind of community. This would make sense. Someone banished from a community would most likely be found wandering outside a town.

The key feature of this story is that Jesus touched the man. This would have risked not only contagion but being rendered 'unclean' himself. Someone declared leprous would probably not have been touched by anyone for a long time. Here again, we encounter a seam of deep and affecting emotion but signalled in a simple, stripped-back way.

'Say nothing to anyone'

From this moment on, the theme of Jesus' asking people not to tell others what he had done began to grow. An explanation for this is offered here: as a result of the man's proclamation, Jesus could no longer travel openly. This was clearly a factor in Jesus' requesting people not to tell others about what he had done; but, as noted above, it was not the only factor.

Mark 2.1–12: Jesus healed a man lowered through the roof

This story describes Jesus' first 'run-in' with the scribes. It is worth noting that their opposition began quietly: they questioned in their hearts and were unsure whether Jesus was blaspheming or not. This illustrates the way in which opposition often begins: it starts small, with uncertainty, and then grows into something much bigger.

Jesus' statement to the man on the mat, that his sins were forgiven, was what caused this uncertainty in the scribes. It also reveals to us that Jesus was much more than a 'mere' miracle worker. His proclamation of the word would cause at best uncertainty and sometimes downright opposition, but he would proclaim it anyway.

Links backwards

- This story continues the theme of Jesus' proclamation, which began in Mark 1.15. The occasion of the healing was his 'speaking the word'.

Links forwards

- From this moment onwards, Jesus' conflict with Jewish leaders begins to emerge and can be found in 2.23–28; 3.1–6; 7.1–23; 11.27–33; 12.1–12, 13–24; and 14.53–65.
- This story begins a series of five controversy stories focusing on Jesus' right to forgive sins (2.1–12); eat with sinners and tax collectors (2.13–17); let his disciples not fast (2.18–22) or let them eat grain on the sabbath (2.23–28); and heal on the sabbath (3.1–6).

Interesting words ...

- v. 1: *after some days*. Mark's Gospel is known for its use of *euthus* ('right away' or 'immediately'); a contrasting phrase is used here. *Di'hēmerōn* means, literally, 'after days' and hence 'sometime later'. Its vague time frame is unusual in Mark and worth noting.
- v. 2: *speaking the word*. When referring to Jesus' teaching, Mark usually uses the verb *didaskō* ('teach'); but here he uses *laleō ho logos*, 'speak the word'. Although *logos* ('word') isn't used by Mark as John uses it, the phrase implies that Jesus wasn't speaking any old word but announcing the message referred to in 1.14.
- v. 3: *a paralysed man*. Just as the man with leprosy was described with a nominalized adjective, *lepros*, the man in this story is described with the adjective *paralutikos* ('paralytic'). The choice of words indicates the ancient

belief that the entirety of a person could be described using the illness that they experienced. Today, we would recognize that people comprise much more than one element of their lives.

- v. 5: *faith*. When Mark uses the word 'faith' or 'belief' (*pistis*), it usually refers to a response to something miraculous. In this instance, the faith was of the four friends, more than that of the man on the mat. The implication of Mark's account is that miracles are what allowed people to see who Jesus really was and it is this that evoked faith.
- v. 5: *son*. The Greek word is actually *teknon* or 'child' and was usually used of people who were either family members or who were minors. Jesus' use of it here seemed affectionate and softened what he said next: 'your sins are forgiven'.
- vv. 4 and 12: *mat*. The Greek word *krabatton* can mean 'couch' or 'bed'; but the fact that the four were able to carry it to the house and that the man was able to pick it up and walk off at the end suggests that 'pallet' or 'mat' is what is meant here.
- vv. 5, 9 and 10: *forgiven; forgive*. The word used for 'forgive' is a common, everyday word (*aphiēmi*), which means simply 'to let go', 'to loose', 'to set free' or 'to send away'. It can be used to describe letting anything go and only means 'forgive' in the context of sin.
- vv. 6 and 8: *questioning*. This is the translation of *dialogizomai*, which means 'debate', 'reason' or 'discuss'. What is interesting here is that, at this point, the scribes debating is internal ('in their hearts'). It has yet to become full-blown opposition: they are asking themselves the questions.
- v. 6: *it is blasphemy*. The questions the scribes asked were two longer ones, with the simple verb 'he blasphemes' in the middle. The first question was 'Why is he speaking like this?' and the second, 'Who is able to forgive sins except God?' The verb (*blasphēmeō*) in the middle can be translated as 'it is blasphemy', as in the NRSV, or 'Is it blasphemy?' This second option seems to make more sense. They were listening and asking questions. It seems logical to assume that they were wondering whether Jesus was blaspheming or not.
- v. 8: *perceived*. *Epiginōskō* refers to possessing knowledge or perceiving something. Here, Jesus perceived in his spirit. It isn't clear whether we are meant to understand this as 'he had a sense of intuition' or whether he gained the knowledge directly from God.
- vv. 9 and 11: *stand up*. The word *egeirō* means 'to rise' and so can mean 'get up', 'stand up' or 'rise from the dead', depending on the context.
- v. 12: *amazed*. For more on Mark's use of 'amaze', see above p. 41. Here, the word used is *existēmi* ('astonish' or 'astound').

So many gathered …

It is interesting to observe how Mark turns up the tension gradually at this point in the Gospel. Following the opening scenes in Jesus' ministry where he healed the sick, proclaimed the good news of God and cast out demons with no opposition at all, the story now focuses on the problems Jesus faced. In the previous story, the healed man spread the news about Jesus to the extent that Jesus could no longer go about openly. In this story, the crowd is so intense that there isn't even room by the front door. The feeling is one of Jesus' being besieged by the large number of people present. The scene is set for confrontation.

'Your sins are forgiven'

Jesus' response to the man on the mat is surprising to a modern audience. It would have been much less startling to the original audience. It is clear, throughout the Gospels, that people believed that sin and illness were integrally connected. Take, for example, the story of the man born blind in John 9, where the disciples asked Jesus directly whether it was the man's own sin or that of his parents that caused his blindness. Throughout the Bible, the question of the connection between sin and illness is explored. Sometimes the biblical writers make a direct correlation between sin and suffering (for example, 'As for me, I said, "O Lord, be gracious to me; heal me, for I have sinned against you"' (Ps. 41.4) or 'For all who eat and drink without discerning the body, eat and drink judgement against themselves. For this reason many of you are weak and ill, and some have died' (1 Cor. 11.29–30)). At other times, the link is expressly denied (for example, throughout the book of Job and in John 9.3, when Jesus said clearly, 'Neither this man nor his parents sinned; he was born blind so that God's works might be revealed in him').

The question of the connection between sin and illness was a live one in the ancient world and continues to be asked today. At the heart of the issue lies the question of 'fault'. If misfortune or illness can be chalked up to doing something wrong, then it suggests that it may be possible to avoid such misfortune. If we make sure we do nothing wrong, then perhaps calamity will pass us by. While this is a question that was asked more explicitly in the ancient world, it is one that is surprisingly tenacious even today. It is often expressed through the lens of Eastern religions, such as Hinduism or Buddhism, and the concept of 'karma': the view that 'we get what we deserve'.

It is important to note that this was not what Jesus meant here. Although Jesus declared the man's sins to be forgiven, he did not draw a direct connection between the man's physical state and his sin. The point being made was around Jesus' authority. In other words, the connection between sin and illness lay in Jesus, not in the man being healed. The man's sin did not cause his paralysis. Jesus' authority to forgive sins was connected to his authority to heal. Jesus' ability to heal revealed his ability to forgive sins: that was where the connection between sin and illness was to be found, not in the person being healed.

Questioning in their hearts

For more on the scribes, see the box on p. 43.

It is interesting to see that the opposition to Jesus was something that grew gradually. The scribes, we discover, were there in the house already. The press of people around the door suggests that the scribes had arrived early and had not come solely to criticize. They appear to have been drawn, as had the crowd, by a curiosity about what Jesus was teaching. This impression is reinforced by the fact that, on this occasion, they questioned in their hearts. It was only later that they joined other groups in opposition to Jesus. Indeed, it does seem to be this incident that hardened their opposition to him.

A particularly interesting feature of this story is that Jesus knew what they were thinking without their saying it out loud. There is no commentary in the story itself that explains this detail. So it is impossible to know whether the scribes had a particularly pained look on their faces or whether knowing what people thought was something at which Jesus was adept. Since the opposition to Jesus became more overt as time went on, it is not something that it is easy to tell from the Gospels themselves. If we compare this episode, however, to Luke's Gospel, it resonates with Simeon's observation in Luke 2.34–35 that Jesus was 'a sign that will be opposed so that the inner thoughts of many will be revealed'. This does suggest that knowing what people really thought and revealing it was part of what Jesus came to do.

Was this blasphemy?

The issue at the heart of the scribes' concern appears to be focused on their anxiety about blasphemy. The third question the scribes asked themselves is important here: 'Who can forgive sins but God alone?' (2.7). They were wrestling with whether what Jesus was claiming to do was what only God could do. This would be worth a debate about how close to blasphemy that brought him.

What lies at the heart of the controversy is whether Jesus was declaring that God had forgiven the man's sins or whether he was forgiving them himself. To put himself in the place of God would indeed have been blasphemy. New Testament scholars have, over the years, spent a long time discussing whether Jesus considered himself to be God or not. Some said that he did; others that he didn't. This story seems to me to be significant in this discussion. If we think that Jesus actually did declare the man's sins to be forgiven – and considered them forgiven by him and him alone – then it seems likely that he did see himself as having divine authority.

Son of Man

New Testament scholars have spent a long time discussing the relative significance of the different titles for Jesus: key among them are 'Son of Man' and 'Son of God'. 'Son of Man' occurs here and later in this same chapter (2.28); then not again until 8.31, where it begins to be used regularly.

The question is the significance of the title. The Greek phrase, 'Son of Man' (*ho huios tou anthrōpou*), is the translation of the Hebrew *ben-'ādām* and the Aramaic *bar-'enash*. These mean simply 'a human being'. It is certainly used this way in the book of Ezekiel, when it appears more than 90 times as a form of address for Ezekiel the prophet.

The problem is that it could mean very little or a huge amount. Sometimes the title seems to be simply another word for 'I'. At other times, it seems to draw on a significant use of Old Testament Scripture, such as Daniel 7, where the Son of Man approached the throne of the Ancient of Days and received from him 'dominion and glory and kingship' (7.14).

However, in the book of Daniel the phrase is used differently. Daniel 7.13–14 reads: 'As I watched in the night visions, I saw one like a human being [Son of Man] coming with the clouds of heaven. And he came to the Ancient One and was presented before him. To him was given dominion and glory and kingship.' This clearly indicates someone who is much more than just a human being. What is important here is that the 'Son of Man' was in the form of a human being and represented humanity, yet was given authority and power by God to rule.

When the title is used to refer to 'coming with the clouds', there seems to be little doubt that Jesus (and Mark) have Daniel 7 in mind. In this chapter, it is tempting to imagine that Jesus meant simply 'I' until you recognize that he is talking about whether he has authority to forgive sins or not. As Daniel 7 is so clear that the Son of Man was given dominion or authority from the Ancient of Days, its use here suddenly makes more sense. The Son of Man does indeed have the authority to forgive sins because he has received it directly from God, who is sitting on the throne.

Later in Mark, where 'Son of Man' refers to Jesus' dying and rising, it again brings to mind Daniel 7 and the authority given to Jesus as a result of his death and Resurrection.

Discussions about exactly what 'Son of Man' means will continue among scholars; but these are the key elements of the term and the identifying of the Son of Man as a human being who receives God's authority.

They were all amazed ...

We noted previously (on p. 41) the importance of the variety of Greek words used for 'amazed' in Mark's Gospel; and in the Introduction (on pp. 3–4), we saw the dual roles of the crowd, who were amazed at what Jesus did, and the authorities, who (as a group) were opposed to him.

This story is the story in which Mark really draws our attention to the opposition of the scribes and the amazement of the crowd. In a narrative that draws full attention to how two key groups felt – the scribes, who were perplexed, and the crowd, who were amazed – the lack of mention of how the man who was healed felt, stands out. All of this points to what Mark is doing in his account. There are, at least, three audiences at play in any story that Mark tells.

1 The individuals whom Jesus met, taught and healed form the key substance of the story. Sometimes their responses to Jesus are recorded and sometimes not; though, when noted, their responses were universally positive.
2 The groups of people who encountered Jesus responded in differing ways. Three key groups included the authorities, which varyingly were made up of some of the scribes, the Pharisees, the Sadducees, the Herodians and the high priests, who always responded negatively; the crowd, unnamed and largely undescribed, which responded with amazement but not much else; and the disciples, whom we expect to comprehend who Jesus was, but often didn't.
3 The readers of the Gospel (us), who are presented with the key Markan question woven through every story: 'This is how these people responded. How will you respond?'

Using this technique, Mark helps us to see our own responses to Jesus in the context: not just of how the individuals Jesus met responded to him, but also of how groups of people responded. From astonishment to opposition, Mark's story, even from the opening chapters, reminds us that the shadow of the cross fell over Jesus' ministry from the outset and that its shadow would grow darker and more threatening as the story unfolds.

Glorified God

The phrase translated as 'glorified God', though common elsewhere in the Bible, is found only here in Mark (in contrast to Luke's Gospel, where it occurs eight times). The question is what it means. It is hard to imagine that there is anything a human being can do to add to God's glory.

In order to understand this phrase, it is worth looking at the word 'glory' itself. Glory is notoriously difficult to define. The Hebrew word *kabod* comes from the verb *kabed* ('to be heavy') and seems therefore to develop into referring to the weightiness of a person or their reputation. Thus, the word is often used in the Old Testament, when describing people, to refer to what makes them important. Intriguingly enough this, in its turn, seems to become wealth (by which you can evaluate the worth of a person). So in Genesis 13.2, Abraham is described as being 'rich (*kabod*) in livestock, in silver, and in gold'. It is easy to see how this connects to God and God's glory. If *kabod* is one's weightiness or reputation, then God's *kabod* is his weightiness, or impressiveness, in the world.

The Greek word is similar. In Hellenistic Greek, the word *doxa* (coming from the verb *dokeō*, 'to seem') means what people think about you, their opinion or view, but with an added resonance of something that is shiny. So when glory is described, it has the appearance of something with a gleaming, shining, splendorous, fire-like substance. This, of course, becomes important when we reach the story of the Transfiguration in chapter 9, where Jesus' nature is revealed and he is seen in dazzling white.

All of this helps us to understand what glorifying or giving glory to God means. It does not mean that anything is added to God, but that God's impressiveness is recognized for what it is and proclaimed. It means to acknowledge who God really is, in a world that cannot see this truth.

In the context of this passage, this idea makes a lot of sense. The crowd were amazed and recognized who God was, talking about that to their neighbours. The question is what they would go on to do with this knowledge. In his usual subtle way, Mark is laying out the options for responses to Jesus: opposition (as with the scribes) and amazement and recognition (as with the crowd); but there is room for more. The scene is set for us to see what that 'more' looks like.

It also nudges us to reflect on how we respond differently when by ourselves and when in a group. The bystander effect is a well-known phenomenon: it is one in which the more people there are present, the less likely it is that someone will intervene to help someone in need. Being in a group affects our behaviour in more ways than one: from a group's willingness to block a pavement (individuals would politely move out of the way) to a group's unwillingness to intervene when a crisis emerges in front of them. In the same way, how we think and come to decisions changes depending on whether we are alone or in a group. Mark's account highlights this dynamic in a fascinating way, and it is worth paying attention to it throughout the Gospel. His emphasis on this is particularly interesting in a context that functioned much more corporately than individually (in contrast to our own society, which is the other way around).

Mark 2.13–17: Jesus called Levi

As so often in the Gospel, Mark poses a question and then immediately tells a story that suggests an answer to it. Here, we see what the 'more' response, beyond simple amazement, could look like. In this next story, Jesus called someone else to follow him and, without hesitation, Levi did. In contrast to the astonishment of the crowd and the questioning of the scribes, Levi heard and responded right away. However, who this person was, raises a new challenge. It was harder to object to Jesus' calling fishermen; but tax collectors were another matter altogether.

Links backwards and forwards

- The call of Peter, Andrew, James and John lies behind this story (Mark 1.16–20). Just as Jesus' healings became more complicated when he announced forgiveness, so now whom he chose to call to follow him begins to cause conflict.
- Unlike in the other Gospels, a tax collector appears only here in Mark, but Jesus goes on to mix with other 'unclean' people, such as Gentiles and people with illnesses (including the woman who had bled for 12 years).
- This story is the second in a series of five controversy stories focusing on Jesus' right to forgive sins (2.1–12), eat with sinners and tax collectors (2.13–17), let his disciples not fast (2.18–22) or eat grain on the sabbath (2.23–28), and heal on the sabbath (3.1–6).

Interesting words ...

- v. 13: it is worth noting the lack of a timescale here, Mark often associates narratives in terms of time; but here, the connection is with location (by the sea) and people (the crowd). We are given no sense of when this happened in relation to the previous account.
- v. 14: *walking along*. This is a translation of *paragō*, which means 'to lead by' or 'passed' a place. The implication is that Jesus was walking and talking, leading the crowd with him.
- v. 14: *tax booth*. The word for 'tax collector' is *telōnēs* and for 'tax booth' *telōnion*. The translation 'tax booth' gives a slightly inaccurate mental image of what Levi was doing. This has resulted in many inaccurate depictions of Levi sitting in what looks like a ticket office in the middle of the road. For more on taxation, see the box, 'Taxation in Roman Judea and Galilee', on p. 65.
- v. 14: *follow me*. When Jesus called Simon and Andrew, he used the slightly unusual phrase 'here, after me'; when he called Levi, we find the more expected

verb *akoloutheō* ('follow' or 'go after' someone), which then becomes the word most often used for those who followed Jesus.

- v. 15: *sat at dinner*. Jesus would not have sat to eat, nor does the Greek say that he did. The word *katakeimai* means 'to recline' or 'to lie down'. This was how people in the Ancient Roman world ate. Later in the same verse, Mark says that the tax collectors and sinners reclined with him *(sunanakeimai)*.
- vv. 15–16: *sinners*. A sinner (*hamartolos*) was someone who had committed so much sin (*hamartia*) that they were deemed permanently in the category of 'sinner'.

As he was walking along ...

As noted above, the verb for walking along implies leading. So we are invited to imagine a large crowd behind Jesus as he called Levi to follow him. This is a significant detail. Whereas when Jesus first called Simon, Andrew, James and John, he did so alone; but now, ever since the healing of the man with leprosy, a large crowd surrounded and followed him. In this story, he was teaching as he walked along the seashore. We are left to imagine the tuts, murmurings and gasps of horror that the calling of a tax collector would have evoked.

Levi

Matthew's Gospel tells a very similar account of the calling of a tax collector. There, however, the name of the tax collector is given as Matthew, not Levi. Later in Matthew's Gospel, Matthew is listed as one of the Twelve (Matt. 10.2–4) and called a tax collector. In Mark's list of the Twelve (3.16–19), the name Matthew is also listed but without the description of his being a tax collector. Most interpreters assume that Matthew/Levi has two names, as was common in the period; but it is also possible that Levi became a general disciple (that is not one of the Twelve) and that Matthew was similarly called but became one of the Twelve: the close disciples of Jesus. Given the reference in Mark 2.15 to 'many tax collectors ... for there were many who followed him', both are options.

Taxation in Roman Judea and Galilee

Taxation in Roman Judea and Galilee was complex. The Gospels record there being tax collectors in both Capernaum and Jericho.

There were various forms of tax that a tax collector in Capernaum would *not* have collected. Chief among them were the temple tax and the poll tax.

The temple tax

The temple tax, at a rate of a silver half-shekel (also called a Tyrian shekel, since the silver shekels were originally minted in Tyre) per adult male, was paid directly to the temple. The usual coinage (Roman denarii) had to be changed into the Tyrian shekel for payment, which was why there were money changers in the temple.

The poll tax

The Roman poll tax (for which a census was often carried out to establish how many people should pay it) only applied in territories directly ruled by the Romans. So the people of Judea, who were governed directly by Rome through a governor, were liable to pay the poll tax; but Galileans, who were ruled directly by Herod Antipas, would have paid taxes to him instead.

Taxes collected by tax collectors

Other taxes may well have been collected by tax collectors, especially the land tax (which took a proportion of the crop-yield) and the customs tax (often called *portoria*), usually around 2.5 per cent, which was levied on goods brought in or taken out of a city. Capernaum was on a trade route (the Via Maris) and was close to the border between Herod Antipas and Philip's territory. As a result, there would have been a number of tax collectors present in Capernaum to collect the *portoria* for goods travelling in and out of Capernaum, along the Via Maris.

In some instances, it may be misleading to translate the word *telōnion* as 'tax booth'. It implies something like a ticketing booth, with a single occupant. There would certainly have been a customs house in Capernaum, accommodating a number of tax collectors. We certainly know that there were many tax collectors there, because verses 15–17 talk about a lot of them dining with Levi at his house. However, the details of the story do suggest a tax booth because it would have been unlikely that Levi was, in this account, collecting *portoria*. Instead, he was probably receiving land tax. Fish, just like crops, were taxed in kind; and sources suggest that fishermen would be expected to pay between 25 and 40 per cent of their catch. For those who like to imagine the scene, Levi would, therefore, have been surrounded by baskets of fish surrendered by the fishermen at the lake.

This brings us to the question of tax collectors' unpopularity. It is often said that tax collectors were very unpopular because they engaged in tax farming. This was a system in which they would buy the franchise to enable them to tax a region and then extort much higher prices from the inhabitants to make money. This system originated in Persia and was widespread in the Greek empire. The problem is that it was outlawed by the Emperor Augustus and was therefore no longer formally in place by the time of Jesus.

> The question, then, is why tax collectors were so hated. Some suggest that it was because they were seen as Roman collaborators; others propose that the taxation system was so onerous and disparate (including temple tax, Herodian tax, Roman land tax and *portoria*/customs tax) that they were loathed as representatives of a hated system. The answer may well lie somewhere between these two. There is ample evidence that the tax burden on ordinary people in Galilee had become so great that it was driving them away from their homes to live as bandits in the hill country. So excessive taxation would certainly have stirred up resentment of those who represented the imposition of this burden.

Sitting at dinner

As we previously noted, Jesus and his dinner guests would not have been 'seated' but would have been reclining around a table. The more interesting question is in whose house they were. The Greek simply says, 'and it happened as he reclined in his house'. The most obvious conclusion from this is that Jesus was in his own house but, as there is no mention of such a house anywhere else in the Gospels, it is usually taken to mean Levi's house.

Sinners

At dinner, there were both tax collectors and sinners. One of the fascinating, but often unquestioned, categories in the Gospels is that of 'sinners'. It is made even more intriguing by the fact that 'sinners' are often introduced alongside 'tax collectors', implying that 'sinner' describes some kind of role in the way that 'tax collector' does. A sinner, therefore, was not someone who committed the odd sin, but one whose lifestyle and choices systematically put them outside the law. It is interesting that, in this passage, Jesus contrasts 'sinners' with 'the righteous'. The righteous were those who, as a matter of course, kept as much of the law as they could. At the opposite end of the spectrum were those who did not try to keep it at all. Unfortunately for us, neither Jesus nor the Gospel writers saw fit to say exactly which practices (or lack of them) it was that plunged someone into the category of sinner; but not tithing, sacrificing or observing the rites of purity at all would be likely 'sins'.

It is also possible that sinners – or at least some of them – would have been wealthy. Luke's Gospel suggests that Zaccheaus was wealthy; and tax collectors who had a steady income (as opposed to day labourers who had to go out every day to find work) would have been among the higher earners of a largely peasant society. One possibility, then, is that an isolated community formed of those who sought wealth above keeping the law and, as a result, were forced to the outskirts of society.

The scribes of the Pharisees

For more on the scribes, see the box on p. 43.

This particular group, however, were not 'just' scribes but scribes of the Pharisees. In other words, people who were experts in the law and literate, and who subscribed to the principles of Pharisaism (see the box, 'Pharisees', below). The phrase is unusual and used only here in the Gospels. Here, it is probably intended to draw our attention to the precise nature of their objection. A particular Pharisaic concern was purity: by eating with tax collectors and sinners, Jesus was knowingly becoming ritually impure, just as he did when he healed the man with leprosy.

Pharisees

The word 'Pharisee' has passed into English as a profoundly pejorative term. If you look up the word in almost any dictionary, the first definition given will say that a Pharisee was a member of an Ancient Jewish sect; the second will be that it means 'a self-righteous or hypocritical person'. This kind of definition comes from passages such as the current one, in which Jesus warned his disciples against becoming hypocritical like the Pharisees. Indeed, Jesus clashed with them so often during his lifetime that generations of Christians have assumed that there was nothing more to them than being a nit-picking, holier-than-thou, duplicitous group of religious zealots, loitering around in wheat fields, waiting to catch out unsuspecting passers-by as they broke tiny details of the law.

If you look outside the New Testament, however, you realize that the Pharisees were somewhat different. In the first century, much (though not all) of the practice of the Jewish faith was formal and distant. Most people would go to the temple only three times a year for the major festivals: Passover, Pentecost and Tabernacles. For the rest of the year, they got on with their lives. By contrast, the Pharisees, driven by their devotion to God, wanted to embed worship in daily life. They were passionate and devout, sincerely wanting to find ways to make faith in God alive and relevant to their everyday lives.

The Pharisees were a party committed to a strict understanding of Levitical law. They were opposed to the Sadducees (for more on the Sadducees, see p. 269), whom they considered to be insufficiently devout and interested only in defending the temple. The Pharisees were a group devoted to the law, both written and oral, and to learning. They were particularly attentive to understanding how the law should be applied to daily life. They also believed in resurrection, unlike the Sadducees. The Pharisees' regular clashes with Jesus emerged out of their passionate devotion. It may sound odd to us, but their theology came from a genuine love for God. For them, everyday faithfulness was measured by the careful observation of rules that governed how they ate, whom they ate with, what they wore, and so on. Jesus came proclaiming a very different expression of devotion to God, and that is where the source of conflict lay.

For more on the oral law, see p. 161.

'Those who are well ...'

Jesus' response to the scribes of the Pharisees consisted of a proverb and a statement. The proverb was one that can be found, in a slightly different form, in Greek literature. A particularly interesting version of the proverb is in the writings of Plutarch (*Apophthegmata laconica* 230f), who records that King Pausanias of Sparta (408–394 BC) was exiled but then spoke very well of the Spartans he had left behind. Someone asked him, 'Why did you not stay in Sparta instead of going into exile?' And he said, 'Because physicians, too, are wont to spend their time, not among the healthy, but where the sick are.' It is possible, then, that Jesus was quoting a saying that his audience would have recognized immediately (though whether a proverb used in Greek philosophy would have been known in rural Galilee is distinctly questionable).

The key part of what Jesus said comes next: 'I have come to call not the righteous but sinners.' The question this raises is allied to the question of who the 'sinners' were: who were the righteous? First-century Judaism understood righteousness to refer to living according to the law; and, as far as the Pharisees were concerned, this included both the written law and the oral law. Conversely, those who did not live according to the law were considered to be sinners. This explains a lot of Paul's discussion in Romans, which culminates in Romans 3.23: 'all have sinned and fall short of the glory of God'. In other words, these two categories simply do not exist – or if they do, one (sinners) is full and the other (the righteous) is completely empty.

Jesus' interactions with the scribes throughout his ministry suggest that the categories 'righteous' and 'sinner' were not ones with which he agreed at all, and certainly not ones that he allowed to dictate whom he spent time with. We might, therefore, consider it wiser to put both words in inverted commas, since he was citing categories used by others.

Mark 2.18–22: On fasting and fitting together the new and the old

Mark placed the stories in his account very carefully and it is important to notice why each story is put where it is. The conversation about fasting falls under the overall umbrella of 'controversy'; but it occurs here because it is the companion to the feasting story of the previous passage. Matthew's Gospel (11.18–19) has a passage in which Jesus condemned the crowds because 'John came neither eating nor drinking, and they say, "He has a demon"; the Son of Man came eating and drinking, and they say, "Look, a glutton and a drunkard, a friend of tax collectors and sinners!"' Mark's Gospel, which prefers to 'show, not tell', does not have a comparable passage; but placing the two stories about fasting and newness next to each other has the same effect.

Links backwards and forwards

- This passage sits in the middle of five controversial stories focusing on Jesus' right to forgive sins (Mark 2.1–12), eat with sinners and tax collectors (2.13–17), let his disciples not fast (2.18–22) or eat grain on the sabbath (2.23–28), and heal on the sabbath (3.1–6).

Interesting words …

- v. 18: The construction of the sentence makes it clear that it is not John's disciples and the Pharisees themselves who came to ask Jesus about fasting, but an unknown 'they': people who observed all the different groups and their practices and wanted to ask why Jesus' disciples didn't do the same thing as other groups.
- v. 19: *wedding guests*. The Greek for 'wedding guests' is, literally, 'the sons of the wedding chamber'. In modern parlance, this would be translated as 'groomsmen'.
- v. 21 *patch*. The word for 'patch' changes in this short parable. The first time it appears, it is translated as 'piece' in the NRSV; it is the word *epiblēma*, which means to 'throw over' and hence is more likely to mean 'a covering'. The next time, it is the word *plērōma* that is used, which literally means 'that which fills': in other words, something that complements what is there. If translated more literally, the verse reads: 'No one sews a patch of unfulled cloth on a garment, lest the filling takes something from it, the new from the old.'
- v. 21: *unshrunk cloth*. The word for 'cloth' (*rakos*) can mean something ragged or tattered, or a strip of cloth. The key word is the next one (*agnaphos*). *Gnaphos* or *gnaptos* means 'fulled' so *agnaphos* means 'not fulled'. This is

a technical term referring to the process of finishing woollen material in this period (see p. 72).

- v. 22: *wineskin*. The word *askos* refers to an animal-hide container.

John's disciples

Mark mentions John's disciples only twice. Here and in Mark 6.29 when, after John's death, his disciples came to bury his body. What is interesting is the reference to both John's disciples and the Pharisees. They are clearly listed here as groups comparable to Jesus' disciples.

The presence of John's disciples in Galilee suggests that Jesus was not the only person to travel from Galilee to Judea and the banks of the River Jordan to hear John's preaching. The implication of their presence in this story is that, after having been baptized by John, they returned home to Galilee and attempted to live out their everyday lives in the light of his teaching.

Fasting

One aspect of John's teaching seems to have aligned with that of Pharisaic practice – fasting. The Torah dictated only one day of fasting a year, on the Day of Atonement; but later texts added additional days for communal fasting (see Zechariah 8.19 and Esther 9.31). The Pharisees, however, expanded that practice to regular personal fasting, which Luke's Gospel (18.12) characterizes as occurring twice a week. It is unsurprising that a movement inspired by John the Baptist should adopt similar ascetic practices.

Jesus' reply to the question about fasting drew on the analogy of a wedding banquet. It is important to note that he was fully supportive of the practice of fasting, but indicated that there were times for fasting and times not to fast. This coheres with elements of Jesus' teaching that we find elsewhere. These aspects can be boiled down to an understanding that although rules about fasting, the sabbath or other devotional practices are important, they should not be followed to the exclusion of all other considerations. Over and over again, Jesus made it clear that human well-being, compassion, and times and seasons should always be considered alongside what rules dictate. He did not advocate abandoning rules altogether; he simply argued that other factors should be brought into play before deciding when and how to follow them.

New and old

There are three short parables in these five short verses, the first parables in Mark's Gospel: the parable about fasting and the bridegroom in verses 19–20; and the parable of the patch in verse 21 and of the wineskin in verse 22. All three are examples of the shortest of Jesus' parables; they are little more than brief analogies.

What is interesting about them is that the first parable points to a slightly different overall message from the other two. The first one indicates that time and circumstance affect action: you wouldn't fast at a wedding banquet, but you would afterwards. The second two point to the problem of incorporating something new into something old. The first one suggests that there will come a time when it would be appropriate for Jesus' followers to fast; the second two that fasting might not fit into the 'new' of following Jesus. The disjunction between these two suggests that, although verses 18–22 are normally seen as a single passage, they should be seen as two separate passages: one about fasting and the other about the radical newness of the kingdom of God.

The fulling process

Jesus' parable about 'unfulled' cloth would have resonated strongly with his first-century hearers. Fulling was a finishing process for woollen cloth. After it had been woven on a loom, the cloth was removed and washed to remove the lanolin and dirt that would have been present in the raw sheep's wool. The cloth was beaten to ensure that the fibres matted together, and urine was often used for the ammonia it contained: it degreased and bleached the fabric being treated. 'Unfulled' cloth was unstable and would still stretch or shrink with use or when wet, whereas 'fulled' cloth was matted, thicker and much more stable. It is hard to imagine why anyone would have even a strip of unfulled cloth; but, as with a number of Jesus' parables, it is the absurdity of the proposition that makes the point.

Wineskins

The next parable also refers to a process that would have been well known to Jesus' hearers. The first stage of fermentation was carried out in a vat. After pressing (often by people, with their feet), wine would begin to ferment in a vat, subsequently helped by the natural yeast found in the wineskins. It would then be strained and placed in jars or leather wineskins to complete the fermentation process. New leather was supple and would be able to stretch as the wine fermented; but old leather tended to be brittle and would burst if used at this stage of the process.

Jesus' teaching here should probably be understood to refer to much more than fasting, especially since the first parable implies that there would come a time when it would be appropriate for Jesus' disciples to fast. This is a much wider note of caution against automatically attempting to enforce upon something new practices that worked well with something old.

Mark 2.23–28: The sabbath

The controversies between Jesus and various questioners continue with another objection directed at Jesus' disciples. In verses 18–20, the objection was to what they did not do (fast); in this passage, the objection was to what they did do (pluck grains on the sabbath). The implication of both stories is that Jesus, as the rabbi, was responsible for what his disciples did and did not do.

Links backwards and forwards

- This story is the fourth in a series of five controversy stories focusing on Jesus' right to forgive sins (Mark 2.1–12), eat with sinners and tax collectors (2.13–17), let his disciples not fast (2.18–22) or eat grain on the sabbath (2.23–28), and heal on the sabbath (3.1–6).

Interesting words …

- v. 23: the sentence structure of this verse in the original Greek is clunky. It reads something like: 'And it happened that, as he was going through the cornfields one sabbath, his disciples began to make a way, picking the corn.' The sense is clear, but the structure is awkward.
- v. 23: *cornfield*. The word *sporimos* refers to corn or barley and can mean either 'grain ready for sowing' or 'fields full of ripe corn' or 'fields full of ripe barley'. The meaning can only be known from the context.
- v. 23: *pluck*. The verb *tillō* means 'to pull' or 'to pluck'. It is used for plucking the strings of a harp or lyre and pulling on hair as a sign of grief, as well as for picking corn.
- v. 24: *look*. The small word *ide* is used often in the Gospels. It means 'to look' or 'to behold'. It does not necessarily imply that someone is pointing at something; but here it probably means that the Pharisees are pointing at Jesus' disciples.
- vv. 24 and 26: *lawful*. The verb *exestin* means 'permitted' or 'lawful' but, when used in Mark, means specifically 'permitted by God's law' (Mark 2.24, 26; 3.4; 6.18; 10.2; 12.14).
- v. 24: *read*. *Anaginōskō* means not just 'read' but 'read out loud', as this was the only form of reading known in this period. Reading silently became common only in the medieval period (though St Augustine did comment on

St Ambrose's unusual technique of reading quietly in the fourth century). The specific reference here, then, is to the reading out loud of the Scriptures, probably in the synagogue.

- v. 26: *Abiathar*. Although the priest is named as Abiathar, 1 Samuel 21.1–9 gives the name of the priest as Ahimelech (Abiathar's father).

Corn plucking

The reference to the disciples plucking ripe grain can locate this story within a certain month or so of the year. Barley ripened in late April or early May and corn a few weeks later. However, since no other details are given in surrounding stories to indicate when in the year events happened, this seems to be an incidental detail, not a significant one.

The objection of the Pharisees was not to the disciples plucking ripe corn or barley; provision for this was given in the law (see, for example, Deuteronomy 23.25: 'If you go into your neighbour's standing grain, you may pluck the ears with your hand, but you shall not put a sickle to your neighbour's standing grain'). In other words, there was a 'fair usage' law for plucking grain that grew in a field owned by someone else. The issue, here, was that they did it on the sabbath. There is no doubt that the Pharisees were correct to chastise the disciples for 'harvesting' on the sabbath. Exodus 34.21 declares that God's people should rest on the seventh day: 'even in ploughing time and in harvest time you shall rest'.

David and the bread of the tabernacle

The challenge of the example that Jesus gave here is that it is not immediately, obviously relevant to the situation of Jesus and his disciples. It is not said that David went into the tabernacle on the sabbath (though some argue that the 'holy bread' was replaced on the sabbath). What David took was holy bread, not corn or barley from a field; and David conversed with a priest (Ahimelech), not the equivalent of the Pharisees. Nevertheless, Jesus clearly thought that the underlying principles were the same, which are that flexibility in interpreting the law should be allowed and should be matched to human need.

The heart of Jesus' point is an important one. God instituted sabbath rest for the benefit of human beings, and the following of the law should reflect this. The law should not be used to enact the opposite of this. It is interesting to observe how easily 'rules' that are designed to be beneficial become burdensome, particularly when the focus is on doing them for the sake of doing them rather than on the good they are meant to achieve.

Mark 3.1–6: Jesus healed a man with a withered hand

The last of this short series of controversy stories features a healing on the sabbath. Here, the focus on the conflict between following rules and bringing life and hope is at its greatest. The rules dictated that Jesus should not have healed the man with the withered hand; compassion dictated that he should. As we have seen so far in Mark, Jesus' care for the man trumped all other considerations.

> ***Links backwards***
>
> - The only other occasion, in Mark, where Jesus healed on the sabbath was in chapter 1, where the healing caused no controversy (Mark 1.29–34).
> - This story is the final of a series of five controversy stories focusing on Jesus' right to forgive sins (2.1–12), eat with sinners and tax collectors (2.13–17), let his disciples not fast (2.18–22) or eat grain on the sabbath (2.23–28), and heal on the sabbath (3.1–6).

Interesting words ...

- v. 1: *withered.* It is possible that this story came to Mark's mind because of the Greek word for 'withered' and its connection to the previous story. The word for 'wither' (*xērainō*) means 'ripe' and hence, in the passive form (as here), 'to become dry' or 'to become parched'. As the previous story is about the disciples plucking ripe grain, Mark may have connected them in his mind.
- v. 2: *watch.* Mark does not say who was watching closely. As the previous passage featured the Pharisees, it seems natural to assume it was still them. The Greek word for 'watch closely' is *paratereō*, a compound of *tereō* ('to guard' or 'to observe') and *para.* The addition of *para* gives greater emphasis to 'guard'.
- v. 2: *cure.* There is a range of different words for 'heal' in Greek. This one, *therapeuō*, is a commonly used word meaning 'to take care of' and by extension 'to heal'. For more on the words for 'heal', see the box, 'Words for "heal" in Mark's Gospel', on p. 50.
- v. 3: *come forward.* Literally, 'Arise (*egeirō*) into the middle (*mesos*)'. The importance of this is that Jesus could have chosen to do this quietly on the outskirts of the synagogue; instead, he summoned the man into the middle of the gathering.
- v. 4: *lawful.* The word *exestin* means 'permitted' or 'lawful'; but, when used in Mark, means 'specifically permitted by God's law' (Mark 2.24, 26; 3.4; 6.18; 10.2; 12.14).
- v. 4: *to do good or to do harm.* The verbs here are *agathopoieō* (*agathos* means 'good') and *kakopoieō* (*kakos* means 'evil').

- v. 5: *anger*. The word for 'anger' (*orgē*) is the noun connected to the verb (*orgizō*), which was used in 1.41 and translated as 'moved with pity' but means 'was angry'. On both occasions, Jesus is reported to be angry.
- v. 5: *grieved*. The only time the verb *sullupeomai* occurs in the New Testament is here. The verb has a range of meanings from 'sympathize' to 'be hurt'. The key feature of the word is that Jesus was gripped with emotion.
- v. 5: *restored*. *Apokathistēmi* means 'to rebuild', 'to restore' or 'to return'. Hence, the idea is that the hand was restored to its former condition.
- v. 6: *conspired*. Literally, the Greek says that they 'gave counsel' (*sumboulion*, 'counsel', and *didōmi*, 'give') with the Herodians against him.
- v. 6: *destroy*. At this stage, it is not clear precisely how the Herodians and the Pharisees planned to destroy Jesus. The verb *apollumi* can mean 'to kill' but more often means 'to ruin' or 'to destroy'. It seems likely that the decision at this point was to undermine him and ruin his credibility.

Another sabbath incident

The timing of this encounter is different in Luke, and Matthew and Mark. Luke indicates that it happened on 'another' sabbath day. Both Matthew and Mark imply that the two events happened on the same day. If it was the same day, it makes more sense of Mark's not saying who 'they' were who were watching Jesus. The implication is that having observed the disciples breaking the sabbath law, they then watched Jesus to see whether he would flout it too. All of this resonates with what we all know about suspicion. Once a person is identified as someone who raises concerns, then they are watched to see what they will do next. The narrative hints that Jesus knew that and behaved as he did anyway.

Healing on the sabbath was discussed in oral law: the verdict was that when there was uncertainty about a threat to life, then healing could be done on the sabbath. Mishnah *Yoma* 8 discusses the issue at length and concludes that interventions can be made only in the case of risk to life. This example of a man with a withered hand was clear-cut. It was obviously a long-term condition and there was no threat to life (unlike with Simon's mother-in-law in 1.29–31).

In Matthew (12.11–12) and Luke (13.15 and 14.5), when Jesus was arguing this point, he began by citing a Pharisaic law that permitted someone to save an animal on the sabbath. As noted above, however, this was not a strong argument in this instance, as there was no hint that the man's life was saved. A much more general case is made here that the sabbath is for doing good and that was what Jesus was doing. In other words, Jesus reframed the entire discussion. In oral law, it is characterized as articulating what does and does not count as 'law'; Jesus framed it as using the sabbath to do good.

He looked at them with anger

This is the second time that Jesus' anger has been described in the context of a healing. The first time, Jesus was angered when the man with leprosy said, 'If you choose, you can make me clean' (1.40); here, he was angered by the hardness of heart of those present. It is worth noting that the heart, in Hebrew thought, was where decisions were made, so hardness of heart reflects an unwillingness to see things in a new light.

From popularity to the decision to destroy Jesus

It is worth remembering that this section, which stretches back to 1.16, comes immediately after 1.15 in which Jesus was declared to have come proclaiming the good news of God. This whole section demonstrates how he proclaimed it – in word and in deed. The things he said, the healings he did (and when he did them), the people he called and those he mixed with were all proclamations of the good news of God. In this section, which comes to its climax in this passage, Mark is laying out clearly that the good news of God was genuinely good news, but not for everyone.

The story Mark tells in this section is that of the slow growth of opposition from being too popular (1.40–45). We see the misgivings about Jesus progress from wondering what he was talking about and asking whether it was quite right (2.1–12) to criticism of his mixing with the wrong crowd (2.13–17); to questions about Jesus' followers (2.18–28); and, finally, to opposition to Jesus himself (3.1–6). This is how suspicion grows in any of us. There are very few occasions on which we turn against someone at the first meeting. Much more common is beginning with a sense of unease, then watching the person more acutely, then raising questions about how they behave, before finally coming to a view and deciding to do something about it.

Herodians

The Herodians appear in Mark 12.13–17 (and it's parallel in Matt. 22.15–22; the similar passage in Luke 20.20–26 does not name them).

Their name (*Herōdianoi*) comes from a common Roman usage to describe the followers of a certain person. The *Augustianoi* were the followers of the Roman emperor and the *Pompeianoi* the followers of Pompey the Great. It is also possible that 'Christians' (in Greek, *Christianoi*) was similarly coined to describe the followers of Christ. Josephus uses a similar word (*Herōdeioi*) to refer to the followers of Herod the Great. As Herod the Great died in 4 BC, this term clearly refers to the followers of Herod Antipas, the ruler of Galilee during the time of Jesus.

What is less clear is what they stood for, other than following Herod Antipas. Some suggest that they advocated for instating a Herodian dynasty but, since Herod Antipas and his brothers Philip and Herod Archelaus had been appointed to rule after their father, this does not seem entirely plausible. What is most likely is that they were people whose primary loyalty was to Herod as opposed to the Romans or the Sadducees, or another party.

One intriguing theory about them is that they were part of the family of Boethus. The Herod family controlled the appointment of high priests before AD 6 and after AD 37; and, when they did, they appointed people solely from the family of Boethus. When the Romans appointed high priests, they appointed Sadducees. There would be a strong argument, therefore, for the Herodians being members of the family of Boethus (Boethusians) keen to restore their familial claim to the role of high priest (for more on the high priests, see the box on p. 258).

The surprising feature of their mention here, and in chapter 12, is that they had formed an alliance with the Pharisees. This was a very unlikely coalition. As noted above, the Pharisees were focused on the following of the law as devotion to God; the Herod family was known for being morally disreputable (for more on this, see p. 143). If the Herodians were in fact the Boethusians, then their coalition was even more unlikely as they were denounced by a leading Pharisee for being a wicked and sinful family (*b. Pesachim* 57a). In a way this makes the point even more strongly: Jesus' and the good news he proclaimed upset them so much that they were even prepared to form an alliance with their enemies against him.

Mark 3.7–12: They fell upon him

This story brings this section of Mark's Gospel (1.40–3.12) to a close. It began, in 1.40, with the man healed from leprosy telling everyone about Jesus and ends with this passage, which indicates that Jesus' popularity has grown so great that a large crowd fell upon him.

Between these two accounts, we read of growing opposition to Jesus. The overall impression is of the danger Jesus faced, both from those among whom he was popular and from those who disapproved of him and his message.

Links backwards

- This passage seems to be closely linked with Mark 1.40–45, where the leper ignored Jesus' command and told everyone about him.

Links forwards

- **This theme continues throughout Mark. Interestingly, it particularly returns when Jesus is in Tyre (7.24–25; the word about him had even spread to another country).**

Interesting words ...

- v. 7: *departed*. The Greek word *anachōreō* means, literally, 'to walk backwards' or 'to withdraw'. It can mean 'to withdraw from battle'. The implication here is that, since the controversy with the Pharisees had just reached fever pitch, Jesus decided to withdraw to the sea.
- v. 7: *multitude*. Throughout Mark's Gospel the word 'crowd' (*ochlos*) is used regularly. He uses the word *plēthos* ('mass' or 'multitude') here and in the next verse (but nowhere else), with *polu* ('many'). This emphasizes the vastness of the crowd.
- v. 9: *boat*. *Ploiarion* is the diminutive of *ploion* ('boat'), sometimes translated as 'skiff', though there is a disagreement about whether this actually refers to the smallness of the boat or whether Mark is simply using a diminutive here, as he likes to do and does on a number of other occasions.
- vv. 9–11: *crush; pressed*. Two different words are used here for the crush of the crowd. The first, *thlibō* (v. 9), means 'to squeeze', 'to compress' or 'pressure'; the second, *epipiptō* (v. 10), has more of a sense of 'to fall upon' or 'to assail'. In a slight play on words, the large number of people who had diseases fell upon Jesus (*epipiptō*); whereas the unclean spirits fell down before him (*prospiptō*) (v. 11).
- v. 10: *cured*. There are a range of different words for 'heal' in Greek. This one, *therapeuō* is a commonly used word meaning 'to take care of' and, by extension, 'to heal'. For more on the words for 'heal', see the box, 'Words for "heal" in Mark's Gospel', on p. 50.
- v. 12: *sternly ordered*. Literally, the Greek says, 'he warned (*epitimaō*) them a lot (*polla*)'.

A summary

This short passage functions as a summary, very similar to the summary in 1.32–34. As we noticed above, Mark's technique is one of zooming in to explore the particular dynamics of Jesus' relationship with one or more people, followed by zooming out to set his ministry in a broader context. In other words, while the opposition to him grew and grew in some quarters, his popularity among others grew in similar proportion.

Geographical area

Mark stresses Jesus' great popularity not only by using an unusual word for a great mass of people (*polu plēthos*), but also by mentioning the geographical spread from which they came. The region mentioned stretches for around 100 miles south of Galilee, to Judea and Jerusalem; south-east and east to Idumea and across the Jordan (sometimes known as Transjordan, again around 100 miles) and then north to Tyre and Sidon (around 50 miles). It would have taken people at least a week to travel that far; longer, for those with illnesses and infirmities.

Fell upon him

The final element in this story, which communicates the near frenzy of the crowd, are the two words 'crush' and 'press'. As noted above, these two words together give the idea of the crowd's compressing Jesus, falling upon him in a frenzy of hope.

Mark then adds another element to this depiction: the crowd believed that simply touching Jesus would heal them. Although Mark does not say whether it worked for them, it is clear that it did happen because of the story of the woman with the haemorrhage in Mark 5.24–34: she simply touched Jesus' robe and was healed. The whole picture is one that suggests that Jesus could have been torn to pieces by the crowd's desperation to draw close to him.

Mark 3.13—4.34: On Insiders and Outsiders

Mark's narrative now focuses on an intriguing theme: that of insiders and outsiders. The first story in this section describes the appointing of the Twelve; and the final one features a conversation between Jesus and his disciples about parables and their purpose: a discussion that explicitly points to the categories of insiders and outsiders. In between these two, Jesus' family come to take him home – by force if they need to; and Jesus redefines his 'family' as being anyone who does the will of his Father. Lurking behind this section is the question of what defines an insider and an outsider. It is an idea that becomes even more important in the following section.

In some ways, this short section could be the prologue to the next one: 4.35—8.21. It sets out the motif of insiders and outsiders (and boats), which is then picked up and turned on its head in that section. For the culmination of this theme, see the box, 'Insiders and outsiders', on p. 182.

Patterns in 3.13—4.34

There is an intriguing pattern that emerges here.

- Jesus calls and names a small group of 'insiders' (3.13–19).
  - Jesus' family come to restrain him (3.20–21).
    - Scribes from Jerusalem accuse him of having Beelzebul (3.22–30).
  - Jesus' family is redefined as those who do the will of God (3.31–35).
- Jesus tells the parable of the sower, in which he says those outside will look and not perceive, and so on (4.1–20).

The section ends with some additional parables.

Mark seems to be setting up a definition of insider and outside here. The ultimate outsiders are the scribes who accuse Jesus of having Beelzebul.

Mark 3.13–19a: The appointing of the Twelve

The importance of Jesus' calling of the Twelve becomes clear between this account and the end of chapter 4. As we have already seen, Mark makes much of the crowd, who follow Jesus around, amazed at what he does, and from time to time 'falling upon him' in their enthusiasm. While that level of response is better than the opposition of the amorphous opposition groups – variously made up of the scribes, the scribes of the Pharisees, the Pharisees and the Herodians (the Sadducees are later mentioned in this category too) – Jesus expects much more. This next stage of the story begins to highlight those who did more than follow him around, amazed.

The disciples of Jesus fall into two groups in Mark's Gospel (for more on this, see p. 238): the wider group, which includes women and probably also children, are largely not named (with the exception of a few key women – such as Mary Magdalene, Mary the mother of James and Joses, and Salome – who are named and identified as those who provided for Jesus in Galilee, Mark 15.40–41); and the Twelve who are called here, some of whom appear throughout the story (especially Peter, James and John). As a result, there are two circles of 'insiders': the general disciples, who count as 'insiders'; and the Twelve, who are 'inside insiders', a closer group identified and sent out by Jesus to proclaim the message (vv. 14–15).

Links backwards

- Thus far Jesus has called Peter, James, John and Andrew (Mark 1.16–20), and Levi (2.13–17). These are included in Jesus' wider calling and commissioning of a group of 12 mentioned here but rarely later in the Gospel.

Links forwards

- The Twelve are explicitly mentioned in 4.10; 6.7; 9.35; 10.32; 11.11; 14.17 – most commonly in connection with specific teaching that Jesus gave to them.

Interesting words …

- v. 13: *called to him*. Mark often uses the verb *proskaleō* when Jesus is about to do or say something important. This is the first time Mark uses it; and it introduces Jesus' calling of the Twelve.
- v. 13: *up the mountain*. The Greek has slightly odd phrasing here: 'Jesus went up into the mountain' (*eis to horos*). Although the word for 'mountain' is clearly singular, what is meant is that Jesus went into the hill country.

- v. 14: *appointed*. 'He made (*poieō*) 12.' (For more on the Twelve and their significance, see p. 39).
- v. 14: *proclaim the message*. The Greek simply says that Jesus sent the Twelve 'to proclaim' (*kērussō*). 'The message' is clearly implied but not stated.
- v. 15: *authority*. The word for 'authority' (*exousia*) means the ability or power to do something.
- v. 17: *Boanērges*. Although it is not entirely clear where this word comes from, it is thought that this is a (poor) attempt to put a Hebrew or Aramaic phrase into Greek. *B'ne regesh* would mean something such as 'sons of commotion'; or *b'ne rogez*, 'sons of agitation'.

The names of the Twelve

When we look at the list of the names of the Twelve, it becomes clear that while there are two formal circles of disciples (general disciples and the Twelve), there is a third informal, even smaller, circle that includes Simon, James and John. The list of the Twelve begins with these three, who all have nicknames. Simon's is Peter (which in Mark is not explained); James and John share Boanērges, which is said to mean 'the sons of thunder' (see 'Interesting words', v. 17, above, for why Boanērges might mean this). Although Andrew was called first, along with Simon Peter, he is relegated in the list to fourth position and is not mentioned alongside the other three at the healing of Jairus' daughter (5.37), the Transfiguration (9.2–3) or at the Garden of Gethsemane (14.32); he does reappear in 13.3, when Simon, Andrew, James and John ask Jesus about the sign that 'all these things are about to be accomplished'.

After this opening naming of the Twelve, the only other disciple to be mentioned again by name in Mark's account is Judas Iscariot.

He sent them out

One of the first things that Jesus did in his ministry was to gather disciples around him (Mark 1.16–20; 2.13–17). This story takes the calling of disciples one stage further. Here, Jesus shared his ministry with the Twelve and sent them out. So far in the account of Jesus' ministry, there have been three key elements: proclaiming the good news of God, casting out demons and healing. It is, therefore, surprising that, when Jesus commissioned the Twelve, he commissioned them to do two out of these three: proclaiming and casting out demons but not healing. Matthew's equivalent account (10.1, 8) has proclaiming, casting out of demons, healing and raising the dead, so it is reasonable to assume the healing is implied if not directly stated.

By contrast, Luke has the naming of the Twelve (6.12–16); but when

Jesus sent people out, he sent out 70 or 72 disciples (different manuscripts have different numbers; see 10.1–23).

Mark 3.19b–35: 'Who is my family?'

As Mark begins to explore the theme of insiders and outsiders, that of family is obviously important. We might naturally assume that the real 'insiders' were Jesus' family, beyond which lay the Twelve, then the general disciples, and so on. In what is some of the most uncomfortable of Jesus' teachings, he made it clear that this was not the case. Jesus' family consisted not of blood relations but of those who did the will of God.

Verses 19b–30 and 31–35 are often presented as two separate sections. However, verses 19b–21 and 31–35 appear to focus on Jesus' family, so it seems more natural to join the two together (see the longer discussion on p. 86). This is an example of Mark's 'sandwich' technique, in which he splits a passage in two to insert another in the middle.

No links

- Given the way that Mark links his stories backwards and forwards throughout the Gospel, it is striking that this is the only time Jesus' family is mentioned at all in the Gospel.

Links backwards and forwards

- Satan is mentioned four times in Mark: at the temptation (1.12–13); here; in the parable of the sower (4.15); and when Jesus rebukes Peter (8.33, which makes the nature of this last rebuke even more shocking).

Interesting words …

- v. 19b: *he went home*. Literally in Greek, 'he went into a house (*oikos*)', though the implication is that it is his home.
- v. 20: *to eat*. The word used for what Jesus and his disciples ate indicates a simple meal. *Artos* can refer just to bread (usually a loaf) or to wheat porridge. The point is that this was not an elaborate feast but staple food; and the press of the crowd was so great that it precluded consuming even the simplest of meals.
- v. 21: *his family*. The phrase usually translated 'his family' is problematic. The text simply says, 'those around him' or 'those close to him' (*hoi par' autou*). The best explanation is that this is a colloquial phrase for 'family'.

- v. 21: *restrain him*. The verb *krateō* means 'to rule', 'to control', 'to master' or 'to lay hold of'. The idea was that they went out to rule over Jesus, thereby demonstrating how little they understood him.
- v. 21: *he has gone out of his mind*. For more on Mark's different words that can mean 'amaze', see the notes on 1.22 and 27 (pp. 41–2). The verb *existēmi* here clearly means something slightly different: 'He is so amazed or astounded that he is out of his senses.'
- v. 22: *Beelzebul*. The name seems to come from *Ba'al zebub* ('Baal (Lord) of the Flies', in 2 Kings 1.2–6, 16). The Greek translation of the Old Testament, known as the Septuagint, translates this name as 'Beelzebub'. Mark clearly thinks that the name equates to the 'ruler of demons' (see the box, 'Beelzebul', on p. 87).
- v. 23: *he called them to him*. In verse 13, Jesus called the disciples to him in order to identify the Twelve. Here, ten verses later, he called the scribes to him (the verb is *proskaleō*, which can also mean 'to summon'). In Mark's Gospel, this verb indicates Jesus was about to do something significant. Here, he confronted the scribes for their nonsensical and libellous assumption that he was working with Beelzebul to cast out demons.
- v. 23: *in parables*. The word *parabolē* is the usual word for 'parable'. Even though this is not a normal parable, it is the first time that something is described using *parabolē* in the Gospel.
- v. 23: *Satan*. The character of Satan occurs throughout the Old Testament to refer to an accuser figure. In places such as the book of Job, the accuser was part of the heavenly court; he suggested to God a course of action (cursing Job to test his piety) that God accepted. In other words, Satan was not always evil. His role was simply to question or accuse.

  The fact that Jesus used Satan as another word for Beelzebul indicates that, by the first century, figures that personified evil (the devil, Satan, Beelzebul, and so on) had begun to be drawn together and associated with a single malevolent being.
- v. 28: *Truly I tell you*. This is one of the most characteristic openings to a saying by Jesus. It occurs in all four Gospels (though in John it is emphasized by the repetition of 'truly', *amēn*). It has the force of alerting the hearers that what follows is particularly important and should be listened to with care. It is translated from the Greek phrase *amēn legō humin. Amēn* has been transliterated into Greek letters from Hebrew, where it means a strong affirmation either at the start (as here) or the end of something (hence its use at the end of prayers today). It appears only here, early in Mark's Gospel, but then returns with frequent usage from 8.12 onwards as Jesus' teaching becomes more urgent and focused (3.28; 8.12; 9.1, 41; 10.15, 29; 11.23; 12.43; 13.30; 14.18, 25, 30).
- v. 29. This verse is slightly tricky to translate. Literally, it reads: 'does not have forgiveness into the age, but is guilty of (or liable for) eternal sin'.
  - 'Age/eternal': 'age' is translated from the noun *aiōn* and 'eternal' is the adjective derived from the same noun (*aiōnios*). 'The age' often refers to 'the age to come'. So not having forgiveness into the age implies a lack of forgiveness both in this age and the age to come, hence it is eternal (for more on 'the age', see the box, 'The age/eternal', on p. 90).

- 'Sin': the word for 'sin' is unusual here. *Hamartēma* is used instead of the more common *hamartia*.

- v. 31: *mother and brothers*. The words used here are the usual words for 'mother' (*mētēr*) and 'brother' (*adelphos*). Mark's account gives no indication that he is talking about anyone other than a strictly biological family.
- v. 35: *sister*. Up until verse 35, Jesus has been speaking of mother and brothers; but when he refers to who is a member of his newly constituted family, he uses the word that specifically means 'sister' (*adelphē*) alongside the word that means 'brother' (*adelphos*). This is significant. He could have continued in the plural, since a masculine plural includes both men and women within it; but the choice to refer specifically to brother and sister makes a clear point about inclusivity. Jesus' family includes men and women; we are not left to infer that women are included (as often happens elsewhere). The explicit inclusion of the word of 'sister' means that Jesus expected to find women playing a key part in the newly established community of the kingdom.

He went home

The question of Jesus' 'home' has come up a few times in Mark so far. The only house that has been mentioned is that of Simon Peter (1.29–31). The remark that the crowd came together 'again' implies that this was something that had happened already (see 1.32). What is curious here is the mention of 'home or 'house' with Jesus' family, though there is no hint in the story that they lived there with him.

Jesus' family

Mark 3.20–21 and 3.31–35 are often presented in English translations as two separate stories. If verses 20–21 are understood to refer to Jesus' family, however, then their mention in those verses and 31–35 suggests that they form a 'sandwich' around the discussion of Beelzebul and a divided house.

The phrase *hoi par' autou* ('those around him' or 'those close to him') would usually refer to Jesus' associates; but that the disciples in general, or indeed the Twelve, just named, should suddenly decide that he was out of his mind seems unlikely. As a result, the mention of the family, nine verses on, who stood outside and called to him, seems to be the most likely group to be associated with those around or close to him; it would make sense if they were the people worried that Jesus had lost his mind. It is, nevertheless, odd that if this is the first mention of them in the whole gospel, it is done in such an opaque way.

The effect of the 'sandwich' around the Beelzebul discussion is to introduce those who should be insiders but aren't (Jesus' family) alongside those who have already been established to be outsiders (the scribes). The presence of the scribes' accusation makes the family's accusation tame by comparison – having lost your mind is surely preferable to being possessed by the prince of demons.

The scribes from Jerusalem

For more on the scribes, see the box on p. 43.

This is the first time that Mark says the scribes had come down from Jerusalem. It could mean that they had come en masse deliberately to question Jesus or that this group had recently been on duty in the temple, where no doubt Jesus had been discussed; and now, having returned home, they were keen to question him further.

It is slightly curious that the scribes attributed Jesus' power over demons to his having Beelzebul. As Jesus pointed out in his response to them, this is not the first, nor the most obvious, conclusion to draw from his ability to cast out demons. In fact, the scribes' response is a classic example of drawing the worst conclusion about someone, even if it makes little sense. This is a tendency that is still prevalent today, even if we no longer attribute motivations to demons. When things happen that are out of the ordinary, we still tend to assume malicious intent or incompetence rather than something good. The way in which Mark tells his story – a technique that focuses so intently on how people respond to Jesus – draws attention to this innate human tendency. The scribes could have concluded that Jesus was moved by compassion for the people he met, who were possessed by demons, and healed them out of love; but they preferred a negative interpretation even though it made little sense.

Beelzebul

The name Beelzebul, or Beelzebub as it is sometimes spelled, seems to come from the account in 2 Kings 1, where Ahaziah, then king of the northern kingdom of Israel, was so seriously injured by a fall that he wanted to find out if he would recover. He sent messengers to the Philistine city of Ekron to enquire of the god Baal-zebub (which means 'Lord of the Flies') whether he would survive or not. He was punished for this action by God, who sent the prophet Elijah to tell him that because he had done so, he would definitely die.

There is very little evidence of the name being used in texts between 2 Kings and the Gospel of Mark, though its shift in meaning suggests that it was used, possibly popularly, to refer to the prince or ruler of demons. Christian texts picked this up and various forms of the name are used in texts written after the New Testament period.

> The most notable occurrence of the name Beelzebul can be found in the *Testament of Solomon*, a text written in Greek, probably of Jewish origin but with significant Christian additions. Scholars are divided on when it might have been composed (with options stretching from the end of the first century AD all the way to the High Middle Ages).
>
> The story of the *Testament of Solomon* involves Solomon gaining control over Beelzebul, the prince of demons (and consequently the rest of the demons), by using a ring given to him by the archangel Michael. Solomon then harnesses the demons to help to build the temple.

He spoke in parables

Parables are notoriously difficult to define. The use of the word here to describe what Jesus goes on to say does not help in the task. This is an unusual form of a parable (neither a narrative nor a short aphorism) but does, like most other parables, cause the hearer to think in a different way about what is being said.

As noted above, Jesus pointed out to the scribes that what they were saying was nonsensical: they were assuming that Jesus' power over the demons came from an alliance with Beelzebul, the prince of demons, which made no sense. If one assumes that the desire of demons is to spread their influence by possessing people, when Jesus cast them out, he thwarted them. It, therefore, lacked sense to assume that he was one of them.

This is the first parable Jesus tells in Mark's Gospel, but it is rather unusual. Nevertheless, it prepares us for the fact that subsequent parables that Jesus would tell would be equally taxing to understand and require reflection to understand.

> ### *Parables*
>
> The parables of Jesus are, arguably, the most characteristic feature of his teaching. This is not to say that he spoke only in parables (he clearly taught in a wide variety of ways, including with actions as well as words), nor that no one else ever used parables (there are examples of parables in nearly every ancient culture in the world). What is striking, however, is the variety and range of Jesus' parables. There are about 50 parables across all the Gospels, and they are in a range of styles: both longer and shorter narratives, short clear aphorisms, and sayings that are hard to comprehend. They are, with a few exceptions, like the one about the banquet of a king, based in everyday rural life. Some of them are interpreted allegorically (that is, a connection is made between each detail of the parable and characters or features of life, such as

the parable of the sower in the next chapter), while other parables defy any attempt to identify recognizable characters, least of all God.

The one thing that holds true for parables is that what can be said of one parable cannot be said of all of them. Since I wrote a book called *The Parables* (Canterbury Press, 2020), it has been suggested to me that the one thing that applies to all parables is that they challenge us to think more deeply and widely than we did before. Although the truth of this may vary, it is nevertheless a good place from which to begin to read the parables.

'How can Satan cast out Satan?'

On the surface, what Jesus says about Satan here is simply a philosophical rejection of the accusation the scribes have made against Jesus. Their claim, Jesus argues, is nonsensical: Satan would not weaken his kingdom from within. As is often the case with parables, however, a further unwritten implication hangs in the air. If it is obvious and logical that Satan's kingdom is not under attack from within, the suggestion remains that it is under attack – but from the outside, not the inside. In other words, Jesus' casting out of demons is motivated not just by his care for the people he meets, but by an intention to wage war on Satan's kingdom. If the kingdom of God is at hand, it cannot and will not cohabit with Satan's kingdom. Satan's house may not be divided but his end has nevertheless come.

As is often the case in Mark's Gospel, much more lies beneath the surface of the action than initially meets the eye.

A strong man's house

Although Jesus calls only his first saying a parable, his second saying, tucked behind the first, is equally parabolic; and, if anything, it is more recognizably so than the saying about Satan.

It is a saying found also in a parallel passage in Matthew's Gospel (12.22–32), in which Jesus was criticized by the Pharisees (not, as here, the scribes) after healing a 'demoniac who was blind and mute'. The two parables are linked there as here. This short parable about binding the strong man can also be found as a stand-alone saying in the *Gospel of Thomas* 35.

The linking of the two in both Mark and Matthew sets up an intriguing interpretation. Most parables of Jesus cannot be read allegorically: that is, in a way that clearly pinpoints the identity of each of the characters in the parable. This is especially true of parables in Luke's Gospel where, for example, the parable of the dishonest steward in 16.1–9 defies any attempts to work out who the individual characters should represent. What we have here is something very unusual in Jesus' parables: a parable that is best understood through an allegorical interpretation of a parable immediately before it. In other words, the first parable introduces Satan; and this second parable is best understood as also referring to Satan, whose house has been plundered because he has been tied up and rendered powerless.

Blaspheming against the Holy Spirit

The verse that probably causes more concern among readers than any other is the reference to a sin that can never be forgiven. The verse occurs in Mark, in a parallel passage in Matthew (12.31–32) and in Luke 12.8–10. Each context provides a slightly different emphasis to the saying; but here, in Mark, the reference is tied clearly to the accusation from the scribes. Jesus had been casting out demons by the power of the Spirit; the scribes misattributed this power to Beelzebul. In Mark's Gospel (note that the verse has a different context and therefore meaning in both Matthew and Luke), the blasphemy against the Holy Spirit was simply calling the action of the Holy Spirit demonic. They said that Jesus had an unclean spirit (Mark 3.30) and, therefore, blasphemed against the Holy Spirit, who is the very opposite of unclean.

The age/eternal

Mark uses the noun *aiōn* ('the age') and the adjective *aiōnios*, pertaining to the age (and hence often 'eternal') only occasionally (*aiōn* occurs here, in Mark 3.29 – 'can never (i.e. 'into the age') have forgiveness' – and in 4.19, 10.30 and 11.14 – 'may no one eat fruit from you again (i.e. 'into the age')'; and *aiōnios* can be found here in 3.29, in 10.17 and in 10.30. It is also found in the additional shorter ending to Mark, which I do not consider to be part of the original Gospel).

It is a tricky word to translate because we need to work out which age is being referred to. Sometimes this is clear: for example, in Jesus' talks about the age to come (literally, 'the age the one coming'), and then in 10.17 and 10.30 to talk about life pertaining to the age (in other words, eternal life). This is easy to understand and translate. In 3.29 and 11.14, *aiōn* is used with the preposition *eis* ('into'), so again its meaning is clear: 'into the age'; in other words, from this age to the next or for ever.

The use that stands out is in 4.19, which talks about the cares or anxieties of the age, which Jesus goes on to make clear are 'the lure of wealth and the desire for other things'. In other words, the age he is talking about is clearly this age. Hence, the translation 'cares of the world'.

It is useful to understand that whenever 'age' is used in the New Testament, it is drawing on the Old Testament idea that there are two ages: this age and the age to come. The age to come is marked by the full reign of God and will never end; this age is marked by oppression and sorrow but will come to an end. There is, however, an overlap between this age and the age to come; and in this overlap, the kingdom of God is present, if only in part, giving us a glimpse of the age to come.

Although 'world' is often an obvious translation of the Greek for 'age', there is a problem with it. It is common in Christian circles to contrast the 'church' with the 'world', with the world being understood to be negative and the church positive. While a negative view of the world can be found in John's Gospel, it is not in the other Gospels (nor indeed in the writings of Paul). There the contrast is between this age and the age to come. This distinction is important. With the exception of John's Gospel, it is not the world that is regarded negatively so much as this age, which will come to an end. The key thing is not to place our faith in something that will end but rather in something that will last eternally.

'Who are my mother and brothers?'

This passage presents Jesus' family in an *inclusio* (sandwich). In verse 21, they set out to restrain Jesus when they heard about his notoriety; in verse 31, they came and stood outside the house where he was. The account suggests that he was still in the house where he had been when they set out, which implies that they had not come far (in other words, they had not travelled from Nazareth). No background is offered to us, however, to explain why Jesus was not 'at home' with his family, rather than in another house, which was apparently close by.

Jesus' brusque attitude to his family is profoundly discomfiting. The implication is that the crowd was so packed in that he was unable to move; nevertheless, it seemed rude of him not to attempt to push his way out to them. One of Jesus' most difficult teachings is his apparent dismantling of the family unit and parallel insistence that 'family' consists of those who do God's will. Mark is apparently content to leave Jesus' relationship with his family here, with a brusque dismissal of their importance. Unlike in the other three Gospels where Mary reappears from time to time, she gets no obvious, further mention in Mark's Gospel. It is even unclear, in Mark, whether Mary is present at the Crucifixion. Mary Magdalene is mentioned by name (15.47) as is Mary the mother of Joses (15.47). The name Joses can be seen as a variant of Jesus (and has often been understood to refer to Jesus' mother); but it seems as though Mark is reluctant to give any limelight to Mary in the way that other Gospels do.

There can be no doubt that the metaphor of family was one of the most important in the early Christian community: Paul used 'brothers and sisters' most often to refer to members of the community; and in the Lord's Prayer, in Galatians 4.6 and in Romans 8.15, we are encouraged to call

God *Abba* or 'Father'. How this relates to relationships within Christian communities today is a question that needs further reflection. It is arguable that contemporary churches struggle with both aspects of this difficult teaching: families remain vitally important for many of us while, at the same time, the experience of being part of a Christian community falls a long way short of feeling like family.

There are no easy answers to engaging with this teaching of Jesus. It is nevertheless important to acknowledge its existence right at the heart of Jesus' teaching, and the difficulty we have in following it, if nothing else.

As we look at this passage as a whole, however, we see a key dynamic taking shape. Those we expect to be 'insiders' (Jesus' own family) are bracketed with the clear outsiders (the scribes). The impact of this *inclusio* is that a very clear line has been drawn between those on the inside (those who do the will of God) and those on the outside (those who struggle to comprehend and accept who Jesus is). The implication is clear: if Jesus' own family can be relegated to outsider status, it can happen to anyone.

Mark 4.1–20: The parable of the seed and the soil

This parable opens a chapter focused on the teaching of Jesus, which consists almost entirely of parables. So far in Mark's Gospel, Jesus' teaching has been kept to a minimum.

At the start of the Gospel, he declared the message he came to proclaim: 'The time is fulfilled, and the kingdom of God has come near; repent, and believe in the good news' (1.15). But most of the other teaching he did was in response to questions from those around him: even the parable of Satan and the strong man in the previous chapter was told to counteract what the scribes had just said. Chapter 4 contains the largest amount of concentrated teaching thus far and is presented as coming directly from him, not in response to questions or opposition.

The first parable in this chapter is universally known as the 'parable of the sower'. Jesus calls it that in the parallel account in Matthew (13.18), when Jesus explains its meaning. The reality is, however, that the sower has, at best, a bit-part in the story: he sows the seed and then disappears from the action. So much so, in fact, that the sower is not identified in the interpretation of the parable in Mark 4.14.

Mark 4.1–20 usually is split into two or three parts: either into verses 1–9 (the parable), 10–13 (a discussion about the mystery of the kingdom) and 14–20 (the interpretation of the parable); or into verses 1–9 and 10–20, including the discussion about the mystery of the kingdom in the interpretation. I prefer to keep it as a single passage to understand the whole.

Links backwards and forwards

- Other than John's Gospel, Mark is the Gospel with the fewest parables. The first is the strange parable interpreted by another parable in 3.23–27. The rest of Mark's parables are either in the latter part of chapter 4 (21–32) or in chapters 12 (1–9) and 13 (28–31).
- Jesus tells the parable of the sower while in a boat because of the crowd: in chapters 4—8, Jesus talks to his disciples three more times in a boat (4.35–41; 6.45–52; 8.11–21). As will become clear in the commentary on those passages, the themes established in 4.11 become crucially important in Jesus' three conversations in boats with his disciples.

Interesting words …

- v. 1: *again*. Intriguingly, Mark says that Jesus began teaching 'again' (*palin*) beside the sea. So far in Mark, we haven't yet seen Jesus do extensive teaching – at least, not what we would consider teaching. See the box, 'Jesus' teaching', on p. 96 for a reflection on what constitutes Jesus' teaching.
- v. 1: *crowd*. The crowd (*ochlos*) in Mark is important. Here, the crowd is so great that Jesus has to teach from a boat. What is striking to note is that there is no hint of response from them. The crowd follow Jesus around, hemming him in when he is indoors, gathering around him by the sea; but, as a multitude, no response from them is recorded.
- v. 3: Listen! The verb *akouō*, which means 'to hear', 'to understand' or 'to listen', is the clue to this whole section of Jesus' teaching. As becomes clear throughout this chapter, the key is not just that people hear what Jesus says but that they listen, understand and change what they do accordingly. This is repeated in verse 9, with added emphasis: 'Let anyone with ears to hear, listen.'
- vv. 4–8: *seed*. What is not clear in the English translation is that Jesus is talking about six or more seeds here. The first three are mentioned using *ho men … kai allo … kai allo*. This means 'on the one hand one … and another … and another'. In other words, Jesus is talking in each case about one particular seed. In verse 8, the word *allo* ('another') becomes plural, *alla*: 'and others fell on good soil'. As three different amounts of seed produced are mentioned, it may indicate that verse 8 refers to three seeds or indeed to more than three. So there were at least six seeds if not more than that: three that produced nothing and three or more that grew well and produced ample grain.
- v. 4: *path*. The word *hodos* can refer to a path, road or way.
- v. 5: *rocky ground*. The word *petrōdēs*, connected to *petros* ('rock'), means 'like rock' or 'stony'.
- v. 7: *thorns*. *Akantha* is a generic word and is used to refer to any thorny or prickly plant; and, indeed, it can also be used of fish to describe the prickly backbone.

- v. 10: *those who were around him*. The start of verse 10 locates Jesus by himself; but then we discover that he isn't all that alone, since not only are the Twelve present but also 'those who were around him' (*hoi peri auton*). The contrast seems to be with the crowd of verses 1–2, comprising outsiders. Here, we have a select few (even if the few were quite many) who are around Jesus: general disciples as well as the Twelve.
- v. 11: *secret*. The word *mustērion* can mean both 'secret' and 'mystery'. 'Mystery' is potentially a better translation here. A secret is something that is intended to be kept as such; whereas a mystery is something that can be understood in the right circumstances, complex though it may be. Once understood, it can be shared freely. This seems to be closer to what is meant here. Jesus' message is not to be kept a secret; rather, it is a mystery that requires careful listening, thoughtful attention and then action.
- v. 11: *outside*. The word *exō* means 'outside' ('those outside') and is the same word used to describe where Jesus' family stand when they come to find him. Mark is making explicit here the inside/outside dynamic.
- v. 11: *comes*. The word translated as 'comes' is *gignomai*, which means 'takes place', 'happens', 'comes into being'. So this could be translated as 'for those outside, everything happens in parables'.
- v. 12: *look; perceive; listen; understand*. The words chosen here are used to explain the paradox of what is lacking when some look and listen.
  - 'Look' is translated from *blepō*, which is the simple word for 'looking at'.
  - 'Perceive' is translated from *idōsin*, which is a very irregular verb that comes from *horaō* and can mean 'look' or 'behold'; but it also has the added meaning of 'perceive', 'examine' or 'investigate'.
  - 'Listen' is translated from *akouō*, the word Jesus used at the beginning and end of the parable he just told; although it can mean 'understand', another word is added here to make this point.
  - 'Understand' is translated from *suniēmi*, which means 'bring together' and so 'comprehend' or 'understand'.

  Note also that the Greek says, 'looking they might look and not perceive, hearing they might hear and not understand'. In English, the translation includes the word 'indeed'.
- v. 12: *turn again*. The Hebrew Scriptures place a lot of emphasis on 'turning' as an image of repentance and restoration. The idea is that humanity turns away from God and God in response turns away from them. The way to restore relationship once more is for humanity to 'turn again' so that God then turns to them. The Greek word *epistrephō* captures this idea beautifully.
- v. 13: *understand*. As there is a play on words connected to 'understand' going on in this passage, it is worth noticing that there are two more words for 'understand' in this verse. So far, we have had *akouō* ('hear', 'listen' and hence 'understand' in vv. 1, 9 and 12); *suniēmi* ('bring together' and hence 'understand', v. 12). The use of the word 'understand', which comes at the start of verse 13, is a translation of *oida*, which means 'to comprehend' or 'to understand'; at the end of the sentence, it is translated from *ginōskō*, which means 'to have pieces of knowledge' and, therefore, be in a position to make a judgement.

- v. 15: *Satan*. The same word is used here as in 3.23, where Jesus argues with the scribes about whether he can drive out demons because he 'has Beelzebul'.
- v. 17: *endure only for a while*. The word *proskairos* means 'occasional' or 'temporary'. Literally, the Greek reads, 'they do not have a root, but they are temporary'.
- v. 17: *fall away*. *Skandalizō* can be translated as 'to cause to stumble' or 'to give offence'. Here, it would mean 'they are made to stumble' or 'they are given offence'. In this context, the first option seems most likely.
- v. 19: *cares of the world*. The Greek word *mermimna* is 'worry', 'care' or 'anxiety'; in short, it is something that occupies the mind. The anxiety is laden with concerns that come from this age (*aiōn*; for more on *aiōn*, see p. 90).
- v. 19: *lure of wealth, and the desire for other things*. This is the first time that money is mentioned in Mark's Gospel. The phrase here effectively talks about everything in this age that distracts attention.
  - 'Lure of wealth': *apatē*, translated as 'lure' in the NRSV, more often has the connotation of 'trick' or 'deceit': the promise of something that can't be delivered. The word for 'wealth' or 'riches' is *ploutos*.
  - 'Desire for other things': *epithumia* refers to yearning or desire in general and also to lust; *loipos* means 'the rest'. In other words, wealth is specifically identified as being deceitful; but the desire for anything that isn't wealth is also in view here.
- v. 20: *accept it and bear fruit*. This phrase makes it clear what Jesus expects of people who 'hear' (*akouō*: the word that has run through this whole passage). *Paradechomai* doesn't just mean 'accept' (in a grudging manner) but 'receive and welcome'; it is this that will allow the person to 'bear fruit' (*karpopherō*).

The Sermon in a Boat

It will become clear, as we continue into Mark 4.35—8.30, that boats are important in this Gospel. Whenever something significant is about to happen, it often happens in a boat. It is possible, therefore, that Mark 4 is, in some ways, parallel to Matthew's Sermon on the Mount and Luke's Sermon on the Plain. In each one, the location is a motif in the Gospel that shows the readers that something particularly important is about to happen.

This effect is heightened by Jesus' first word – 'Listen!' or 'Hear!' – which brings the opening of the Shema to mind (the Hebrew word *shema* means 'hear'): 'Hear, O Israel: The LORD is our God, the LORD alone. You shall love the LORD your God with all your heart, and with all your soul, and with all your might' (Deut. 6.4–5).

Sowing seed

If we read the parable of the sower as it is usually translated, with some seed falling on a path, some on rocky ground, some on thorny ground and some on good soil, it makes it sound as though there is a 1 in 4 chance of hearing, receiving the word and bearing fruit. The way in which the parable is told here means that there is a 50/50 chance of productivity or, indeed, one that is much greater. As there are three seeds that do not thrive and three or more that do (see 'Interesting words', vv. 4–8, on p. 93), this realization changes the feel of the passage quite significantly.

The parable assumes that we understand how seeds were sown in the Ancient Middle East. Without this knowledge, the sower simply seems wasteful: someone throwing seed around on a whim. In the Ancient Middle East, the ground was ploughed after the seed was sown, not before as in modern farming practice. The seed would be sown and then the earth ploughed incorporating the seed into the soil. We should not imagine an immaculately ploughed field, but a plot of earth through which a path wound its way; spots in which rocks existed just below the surface, unseen until the earth was ploughed; and areas where there were a lot of weeds that would also be ploughed into the soil. After sowing, a path or road would be too compacted to plough up properly; a rocky patch would defeat the plough, meaning there was not much depth of soil; and a ploughed-in weedy patch would mean the weeds would grow with the seed and choke the crop.

This would have been a familiar scene for Jesus' hearers; and they would have understood immediately what he was talking about.

Jesus' teaching

Two features pop out in this chapter.

The first is that Mark says that Jesus began teaching 'again' by the sea, when we haven't yet been introduced to a significant block of Jesus' teaching.

The second is that Mark has spent the first three chapters introducing us to who Jesus was. He has done so, however, without yet including any significant chunks of teaching, other than responses to various people's questions or opposition. What we have seen is Jesus' calling the disciples, healing people and casting out demons.

All of this suggests that Jesus' teaching is seen by Mark not just as the words that Jesus said but everything that he was and did. This requires quite a shift for us: we tend to think about teaching in terms of words said (often leaning towards the quantity of words said). If this observation about Mark's understanding of Jesus' teaching is correct, it fits in with the rabbi/disciple model discussed on p. 38. Jesus' teaching should be understood to include who he was, how he related to those around him and what he did, as well as what he said. Unless we include all of this, Jesus' teaching in Mark's Gospel, in particular, becomes quite thin.

It also prompts us to reflect on our own teaching. We all know the adage that only 7 per cent of first impressions are shaped by what we say, with 38 per cent coming from our tone of voice and 55 per cent from what we look like, including our body language. It is nice to think that words alone can convey what we want to say but experience suggests that this is not true. Mark's Gospel challenges us, therefore, to reflect on the whole of who we are and what we do, and to ask ourselves what that tells people about the God we worship. A question that cannot be ignored is, what are we teaching people about Jesus by how we live rather than just what we say?

Asked him about the parables

In some ways, it seems as though this question should not appear here and that it fits better at verses 33–34. So far in Mark, we have had three parables: the parable of a divided house (3.23–26); the parable of binding the strong man (3.27); and this one, the parable of the seed and the soil (4.1–9). This would not provoke those around Jesus to 'ask him about the parables' as happens here. It would make much more sense for this to happen at verse 33, after five parables; but then it would be even more clear that there was an interpretation for one parable but not the other four.

It does seem likely that this section, verses 10–13, has been misplaced – deliberately – so that the interpretation can then be given much greater significance.

'To you has been given the secret of the kingdom of God'

One of the passages that people wrestle with most in the Gospels is here, in verses 10–12. Jesus appears to be saying that it is his intention to prevent those on the outside from understanding by speaking in parables to keep them in the dark. While this might be what the passage appears to be saying, there is much more going on here, which is worth unpicking.

One of the key elements to notice is how Mark is playing with the categories of insiders and outsiders. To ensure that we don't miss this, he even makes a clear reference to 'those outside' ('for those outside, everything comes in parables' (v. 11)). If we have been reading our way through Mark's Gospel in order, our minds go back immediately to Jesus' family who stood outside (*exō*) the house where Jesus was, just ten verses before. This verse reminds us how shocking this episode is. Jesus' family should have been the archetypal insiders, but their actions demonstrated them to be outsiders. Not only did they stand outside but they were so shocked by Jesus that they had come to control him. If Jesus' own family fell into the category of being outside, we are left with the question of who else will fall into this category?

The answer is those who don't look and don't perceive, who don't hear and don't understand. By contrast, insiders are those who respond to Jesus, who hear his message and understand it. And to ensure we do not overlook the importance of understanding, we find four different words for 'understanding' in this passage (see 'Interesting words', v. 13, on p. 94).

Mark reassures us, though, that at least the Twelve and those others around Jesus had received the mystery of the kingdom. Mark returns to this point again in 4.34, which is always a sign in the Gospel that he is hammering a point home so that we will remember it later in his story. In 4.34, Mark says that Jesus spoke only in parables but that he explained everything in secret to his disciples. Verse 34 seems to bring this part of Mark to a close; we leave it with the assurance ringing in our ears that at least the disciples understand what is going on because it is being explained to them in private.

The next four chapters contain key episodes that reveal to us quite how much the disciples do understand, and the answer is ... not very much. In 8.21, this theme comes to a head when Jesus asks the disciples, 'Do you not yet understand?' And we realize that even these insiders are not as much inside as we had thought, because they don't understand either.

In other words, these verses reveal something vitally important about Mark's message. At its heart lies the importance of response to Jesus: the response is what identifies insiders or outsiders. While we expect the scribes to define themselves as outsiders, when Jesus' family and even the Twelve fall into this category, it calls for reflection. The point seems to be that it doesn't matter who we are, where we come from or even the status that we might imagine ourselves to have, the questions are the same for everyone: 'Do you understand yet? And having understood, what will you do?'

One point of reassurance, though, also comes from this theme. The boundaries that mark insider from outsider are porous and flexible. We know that the Twelve, not to mention the wider group of disciples, did eventually understand and respond. Outsiders can become insiders at any moment. Those who rest on the laurels of certain connections or established status may find themselves, with Jesus' own family, on the outside; but those who hear, understand and respond are welcomed in immediately. Once in, they may find themselves surprised to discover who else is there.

One aspect that hovers around for me concerning this episode is the constancy of Jesus' question: 'Do you understand? And now? And now?' The mystery of the kingdom of God may have been given to us, who follow Jesus, but it remains mysterious, shifting and changing, in such a way that constantly challenges our comprehension. The parables act as a kaleidoscope in this task: the kingdom of God is like a seed, a lamp, a woman baking, a fig tree or a vineyard owner; our task is to allow the shapes and colours to fall afresh each time and maybe, just maybe, to catch a deeper glimpse of the mystery of God's kingdom.

Isaiah 6.9–10

Mark 4.12 comes from Isaiah 6.9–10 and presents almost as complex a challenge as Jesus' statement here. These verses come at the end of Isaiah's call narrative, in which Isaiah sees the Lord in the temple and responds to God's call, 'Whom shall I send, and who will go for us?' with the well-known and well-loved, 'Here am I; send me.'

This passage – beloved of those choosing readings for commissionings, licensings and ordinations across Christian denominations – is often cut off at verse 8, with the resounding, 'Here am I; send me.' The problem is that the passage does not end here. It goes on and, as it does, God gives to Isaiah his task, which appears to cause the people of Israel not to believe lest they turn and are forgiven. Subsequent interpreters of Isaiah 6.9–10 have softened the language of the command. Instead of the prophet's seeming to deliver a message that causes the people's lack of understanding, the translation allows for the possibility that they won't believe.

This seems to be a good way to understand what is going on and might be called a counsel of realism. We have, after all, to acknowledge that no matter how well-crafted our message, no matter how passionately delivered, there will always be people who do not and apparently cannot hear it and respond. In Isaiah, the reassurance given seems to be that even people's lack of understanding falls within God's plan.

The ones by the path, the rocky ground and the thorny ground

The interpretation of the parable makes clear that its focus is the different kinds of soil.

The image of the various types of soil develops slowly.

- We begin with the soil by the path. It is so compacted that the word does not penetrate at all and is lost.
- The next type is soil with stones on or below the surface. Here, the word does penetrate, and it is received with joy. The reason why this reaction is temporary is the heat of the sun. The heat of the sun is commonplace in Galilee, both then and now. So what causes the seed not to thrive is something ordinary that affects its reception.
- The third type, thorny soil, has more particular problems. Here, as with

stony soil, there is an initial reception but then anxieties, pressures and persecution choke the growth of the plant. In other words, thorny soil represents events that will nevertheless affect everyone from time to time.

- The fourth type, the good soil, is productive, though varyingly so. This is an important feature of the interpretation of the parable. The seeds grow in good soil, and the good soil produces copious grain; but even then, some soil produces more grain than others.

This final verse points to the overwhelming generosity of the kingdom. It would have been expected, at the time of Jesus, that an increase in yield would be somewhere between 5:1 and, at best, 15:1. In this parable, even the least productive of the seeds that fell on good soil yielded an increase of 30:1, and the others 60:1 and 100:1 respectively. The outcome is abundant. This points us early in the Gospel to an understanding of the economy of the kingdom: an economy that might appear wasteful but that is, in reality, profoundly generous.

One of the questions that has often been raised by interpreters of this passage is whether this interpretation came from Jesus originally or whether it was added by a later community to explain why faith stuck with some people but not others. It would be very difficult to decide which might be true: there is little evidence to tie it to either the time of Jesus or a later context. One way of deciding could be whether the interpretation is in line with, or shifts away from, the original meaning of the parable. In this case, the interpretation seems sufficiently close to the original parable to suggest that it might have come from Jesus himself.

A potentially much more hard-hitting question is whether all four types of soil could be identified in one person at different times. If we are to have ears to hear and if we can recognize that the boundary between insider and outsider is so porous, should we be asking ourselves whether there are times in our lives when the word cannot penetrate? Perhaps there are seasons when it grows quickly but fails owing to lack of depth or is choked out by the anxieties of the age we live in? If that is the case, the question then is what makes the good soil good? In other words, what is it that allows the word to land, be received and grow to produce grain? As is often the case with the most provocative of parables, there may not be an easy answer, but the question is worth reflection.

Mark 4.21–32: Four short additional parables

Following the parable of the sower, Mark presents us with four short parables (or two sayings and two parables, depending on whether you think those about the lamp and measure are parables). The first two of these begin with 'and he said to them' (*kai legen autois*) and the second two with 'and he said' (*kai legen*). This formula indicates that we are to read all four together.

> ***Links backwards***
>
> - The links in these passages are mostly to the parable of the sower. These themes connect back to this passage:
>   - 'Secret' (vv. 11 and 22), though the words are all different: *musterion* (v. 11), *kruptos* (v. 22) and *apokruphos* (v. 22).
>   - 'Pay attention' (v. 24), connected to v. 12 through the words *blepō* ('see') and *akouō* ('hear').
>   - 'Kingdom of God' (vv. 26 and 30), connected to v. 11 (and also backwards to 1.15).
>
> A few other times in Mark, additional sayings are added to the end of a passage that seem to be connected via trigger words or catchphrases (see 9.42–50).

The lamp on a lampstand

This parable has a different meaning in Matthew's Gospel from that in Mark and Luke, alerting us to the fact that Jesus' parables were probably told more than once, with slightly different emphases, depending on context. In Matthew, the focus of the parable is the disciples ('you'), who are to shine before others. In Mark and Luke, the focus seems to be on parables more generally: they may appear to be confusing but in fact are what shine light into even the darkest corners.

Interesting words …

- v. 21: *Is a lamp …?* In Greek, unlike in English, you can add a word to a sentence to indicate whether you expect the answer to be 'yes' or 'no'. *Ou/ouk* expects the answer 'yes' and *mē/mēti* expects 'no'. This question begins with *mēti* and very clearly expects an emphatic 'no'.
- v. 21: *lamp*. A lamp (*luchnos*) was a clay lamp filled with oil. It would have been lit and hung on a lampstand (*luchnia*) to ensure that its light shone as far as possible.

- v. 21: *bushel basket*. A *modios* was a measure for dry material (such as wheat) of around 7.5 litres or 2 gallons in capacity (about the size of a large pot that you might use in the kitchen to make stock today). It would have been a large basket, and most houses would have had something like it.
- v. 21: *bed*. A *klinē* was either a bed used for sleeping or a couch upon which you might recline to eat.
- v. 22: *hidden/secret*. The two halves of this verse are parallel to each other. The first word is *kruptos* and means 'something that is hidden or secret'; the second word is *apokruphos* and is, indeed, connected to *kruptos*. It can mean 'something that is hidden or secret' or 'something that is hard to understand'. In some contexts, *apokruphos* has the meaning of 'deliberately hidden knowledge' (esoteric knowledge), hence some books outside of the Bible are called the 'Apocryphon of …' to show that they contain hidden knowledge.
- v. 22: *disclosed/come to light*. In the same way, the words for 'what will happen to what is hidden' are also parallel. The first word in Greek is the verb *phaneroō* and the second the noun *phaneron*. The verb has the sense of making known or making clear; the noun means 'visible' or 'easily seen'; both have a hint of 'shining'.

What is hidden will be revealed

It is important to read this parable with verses 10–12 above, as they make clear that it is not the intention of God that the mysteries will remain a mystery. The intention is that they will be brought to light and revealed. It is not apparent when this 'revelation' will take place; but the idea seems to be that the parables are to be held in full vision, because they, like lamps on a lampstand, will shine light into dark corners and reveal what might currently be hidden.

Indeed, a double meaning seems to be functioning here. Not only will the meaning of the current confusing parables be made plain; but the parables themselves also function as light, revealing secrets and things that have been hidden.

It is often said in teaching that the learning you work out for yourself is the learning that has the most transformational effect on your life. This seems very similar to what Jesus is saying here about parables. They are hard to understand, not because Jesus doesn't want people to understand them; it is because once you have wrestled with them and understood, even if only in part, this understanding will shed a greater light on much else in your life. I would certainly agree with this. After many years of working on the parables, it is their slipperiness – the fact that you have to work so hard to understand them – that provides a key to comprehending what is going on in the world.

Giving and receiving a measure

This is a parable that seems as though it is not really a parable because the imagery it contains has passed thoroughly into regular use. The context that lies behind it is bartering and the measuring out of commodities.

Interesting words …

- v. 24: *Pay attention to what you hear*. The opening of verse 24 is a reminder of the theme that began in v. 1 and that is woven throughout the whole chapter. It is difficult to put into English in a way that indicates this. Literally, the phrase reads: 'See (or look at) what you hear.' The words *blepō* and *akouō* are repeated from verse 12 (and elsewhere in this chapter). A paraphrase of this might be: 'Don't forget, we are paying close attention to listening so that we understand.'
- v. 24: *measure*. The noun *metron* refers to anything that you measure with and the verb *metreō* refers to the act of measuring. The verse revolves around the root of the same word. A more literal translation might read: 'In which measure you measure, it will be measured for you and added to.'
- v. 25: *to those who have*. The Greek phrasing here is sparse and hard to put well into English. Literally, it reads something such as, 'For who has, it will be given to them. And who does not have, what they have will be removed from them.'

You get what you give

In Luke's Gospel, this short parable is used to encourage people towards generous giving: 'give, and it will be given to you … for the measure you give will be the measure you get back' (Luke 6.38). But here the parable is focused on listening; and we are reminded of this at the start of Mark 4.24: 'See what you are listening to!' It is somewhat intriguing, that more than 1,900 years before the first use of the term 'active listening' (the concept first began to be discussed around 1957), Jesus was recommending a similar concept to his disciples. The point of this parable, in Mark, seems to be that those who listen with close attention to what Jesus is saying, will receive their reward in what they gain from it. Paying close attention so that we can understand will reap great rewards.

This short parable leads on to a proverb that, again, is used differently from the way it is in the other Gospels. Here, Mark adds it to the idea of focused, active listening: those who have the focus and ability to listen carefully to what Jesus is talking about will receive more understanding; those who do not have that capacity, however, will have even the little comprehension they do possess stripped away.

The use of this proverb here is very different from that of Matthew and Luke, where it is used in the parable of the talents and seems to refer to money rather than attention.

The growing seed

This parable and the one that follows it (the parable of the mustard seed) are the first parables that include images of the kingdom of God. So far in Mark, the kingdom of God has been mentioned twice: once in 1.15, where Jesus proclaims that the kingdom of God has drawn near; and once in 4.11, where Jesus says that the mystery of the kingdom has been given to the Twelve and those others around him. This, therefore, is the first time that any definition of the kingdom has been offered.

This is possibly the most ordinary and most simple of all the parables: a man sows seed and watches it grow.

Interesting words ...

- vv. 26–27: the verbs in verses 26–27 are all in the subjunctive, which gives a conditional air to the whole parable: 'The kingdom of God is as if a man were to throw seed on the ground, and were to sleep ...'
- v. 26: *scatter*. The word here is different from the one used at the beginning of chapter 4. There, the sower 'sowed' seed; here, the man threw, cast or scattered the seed (*balō*). The effect is the same, just the word is different.
- v. 27: *sprout and grow*. The growth cycle of wheat is explained in two simple words: *blastanō* ('to bud', 'to sprout' or 'to propagate') and *mēkunō* ('to lengthen' or 'to grow long').
- v. 27: *know*. The verb for 'know' is *oida*, 'to comprehend' or 'to understand'. The point is that the man has no idea how the seed grows, but this does not stop it growing.
- v. 28: *of itself*. The Greek adjective is *automatos*. It is the origin of our word 'automatic' and means 'self-acting' or 'spontaneous'.
- v. 28: *first the stalk, then the head, then the full grain in the head*.
  - 'Stalk': the word *chortos* refers to any green crop or pasturage.
  - 'Head': *stachus* this is the word that was used to describe what the disciples plucked and ate on the sabbath in 2.23. It means 'the head of the grain'.
  - 'Full grain in the head': this is a close translation of *plērēs* ('full'), *siton* ('grain') and *en tō stachui* ('in the head').
- v. 29: *goes in*. The verb *apostellō*, connected to the noun 'apostle', means 'to send'. This raises the question about whether the man harvests the grain himself or sends servants to do so.

The simplicity of this parable belies the profundity of its point. Just like the hypothetical man in the parable who has no idea how the seed grows (it just does), so the kingdom of God is the same. Just as it is in the nature of a seed to grow, it is in the nature of the kingdom to grow. There will come a time, as with the seed in the parable, that the kingdom reaches its harvest. In the meantime, however, we simply have to trust in the growing of the kingdom: we sleep, we get up and the kingdom grows. That is the nature of the kingdom; and, like the farmer, we simply have to trust that it will grow.

The mustard seed

This is one of the most well known of all the parables: so much so that there is more than one interpretation of it. One of the big debates about this parable is which kind of seed the generic word used is referring to. Two main options include *Brassica nigra* and *Salvadora persica*. For the implications of each option, see below.

Interesting words ...

- v. 30: *with what can we compare, or what parable will we use for it?* The phrase used here is a little clunky. *Pōs homoisōmen* means 'how (*pōs*) might we liken (*homoisōmen*), or in which parable (*parabolē*) might we present (*thōmen*) it?'
- v. 30: *mustard seed.* A mustard (*sinapi*) seed (*kokkos*) is a relatively generic word and does not help to identify exactly which plant Jesus has in mind here.
- v. 32: *shrubs. Lachanon* is more specifically a cultivated plant as opposed to a wild weed.
- v. 32: *make nests.* The importance of the word *kataskēnoō* is that it implies permanence: the birds come and make their homes in the shrub's branches.

Which seed was it?

As noted above, there are two main options for understanding this parable.

1 The first is that the seed Jesus refers to is *Brassica nigra* or black mustard. This plant was grown widely in the Ancient Near East and was popular for its pungent flavour. The plant does grow very rapidly, can reach a height of 10–12 feet in the right conditions and has many branches. The problem is that it couldn't by any stretch of imagination be considered to have 'branches' that are sufficiently robust to bear the weight of many birds, and certainly not a bird's nest.

If black mustard is what Jesus had in mind, the focus of the parable is very similar to the previous one, with a slight extension: it is in the nature of the kingdom of God to grow; and when it grows, it grows rapidly.

2 The second option is that the seed is that of *Salvadora persica*, a tree that is native to the Middle East. The *Salvadora persica* has a pungent

flavour, like mustard, and does grow swiftly into a large tree. Pliny the Elder (a Roman naturalist and historian) said of the plant that it was

> extremely beneficial for the health. It grows entirely wild, though it is improved by being transplanted: but on the other hand when it has once been sown it is scarcely possible to get the place free of it, as the seed when it falls germinates at once. (*Natural History* 19:170)

The challenge of this plant is that it can grow wild and therefore may not qualify for the label of *lachanon* (see v. 32 above, in 'Interesting words'). Pliny does observe, though, that it can be transplanted and, at that point, it would be a cultivated plant.

If this is what Jesus meant by a mustard seed, then the meaning of the parable becomes quite different. It is not just a parable of growth. If the kingdom is like *Salvadora persica*, it is a plant that, in growing, can quickly take over a whole plot of land. In this case, the kingdom is compared to an invasive plant that attracts, to its branches, birds that could eat and destroy an entire wheat crop. This interpretation portrays the kingdom as a disruptive and unsettling force that cannot be eradicated, no matter how hard you try. It also attracts outsiders to its branches, which disrupts neat plans.

We cannot be certain which seed Jesus had in mind: the word used is too vague to be sure. This second interpretation rings true, however, from what we have seen of Jesus' ministry so far: a ministry that focuses on outsiders and those not wanted in the neat structures of an ordered society.

Those who were listening, in the way that Jesus required, might by now be making connections about the nature of the kingdom. It grows and grows beyond any expectation you might have; and, as it grows, it brings in its wake disruption and conflict.

Mark 4.33–34: Jesus spoke in many parables

With this small passage, we reach the end of this section of Jesus' teaching and, indeed, the first section of the Gospel. As noted above, the next four chapters focus on Jesus' encounters with a range of different people. Jesus also has some key discussions with his own disciples, who (we discover as the chapters unfold) do not understand Jesus as much as we might have expected, despite the private teaching they receive.

Links backwards

- Jesus speaking in many parables links backwards strongly to Mark 3.23–27 and then to the whole of chapter 4.

Links forwards

- The key link is Jesus' conversations with the disciples. We discover here that while for outsiders 'everything comes in parables' (4.11), he explains everything to them in private. We are primed, therefore, to expect that 'outsiders' will not understand, whereas they, the insiders, will (see 4.35–41; 6.45–52; 8.11–21).

Interesting words ...

- v. 33: *hear*. The word 'hear' (*akouō*) is used again here. Jesus speaks in parables as much as they are able to hear and understand.
- v. 34: *in private*. The Greek makes an emphasis here that English cannot. Jesus explains everything privately (*kat'idian*) to his own (*idios*) disciples. Something that is one's own is by its nature private. We don't have a word that makes quite this emphasis.

Mark makes clear that he is not recording anything even close to all the parables of Jesus. His phrase here – 'many such parables' – indicates that there were a large number of them that were not captured in the Gospels.

The next phrase seems to be a sweeping generalization: 'he did not speak to them except in parables'. Nevertheless, it draws attention to the fact that the Jesus of Mark's Gospel did very little teaching (speaking to them) in the pages of the Gospel. It would be hard to argue that he spoke only in parables; but it is certainly true that the majority of Jesus' spoken teaching in Mark was in parables.

Verse 34 sets up a theme that runs throughout the next chapter of this commentary, until it is picked up again in 8.11–21. Jesus spoke in parables to 'the outsiders' but explained everything in secret to the disciples: 'the insiders'. The question is whether the disciples will understand and respond to him. (For more on this, see the box, 'Insiders and outsiders', on p. 182.)

Mark 4.35—8.21: Three Boats, Five Healings, Three Banquets and a Number of Responses

Although the structure of Mark can be laid out in various ways, one of the intriguing features of this section of Mark is the number of repetitions and patterns that it seems to contain.

Patterns in 4.35—8.21

There are three events that take place in a boat (4.35–41; 6.45–52; 8.11–21). The boat scenes are spread relatively evenly throughout these four chapters; one might reasonably expect that the disciples' understanding of Jesus, in response to their question 'Who then is this?' in the first story, might develop as the section unfolds. I do not think I am providing too many spoilers when I say that their understanding does not develop. The final boat scene ends with Jesus asking, 'Do you still not understand?'

Between these three boat scenes, there are two feedings of large crowds (first, 5,000 people in 6.30–44; then 4,000 people in 8.1–10). As well as this, Jesus meets and heals three people between the first and second boat scenes (the man from Gerasa, who is full of demons (5.1–20); a woman with a long-term haemorrhage (5.24–34); and a young girl, whom the crowd believes to be dead (5.21–24, 35–43). Between the second and the third boat scenes, Jesus meets and heals two people: a woman from Tyre whose daughter is ill (7.24–30) and a man in the Decapolis who is deaf (7.31–37). After the third boat scene, Jesus meets and heals one person: a blind man, who at first sees people as 'trees, walking' but then is fully healed (8.22–26).

These patterns can be missed because around these stories are other accounts, such as the beheading of John the Baptist (6.14–29) or the discussion with the elders about tradition (7.1–23). It is only when reading the Gospel in a single sitting that the patterns begin to emerge.

Overall, three themes materialize from this section of Mark.

1 Jesus revealed who he really was through a series of healings and miracles.
2 The disciples, whom we were assured in 4.34 were told everything in private, continued not to understand who Jesus really was or what he had come to do.
3 Individuals who had the least to lose, because they were outsiders of one kind or another, recognized and understood Jesus most easily. People in groups, however, continued to dispute with him or fail to comprehend who he really was.

For the culmination of the theme of insiders and outsiders, see the box on p. 182.

Mark 4.35–41: Boat I. 'Who then is this?'

The first of the 'boat scenes' in this section ends with the question that both stretches back to the start of the Gospel and underpins and informs everything that follows: 'Who then is this, that even the wind and the sea obey him?' The questions of who Jesus is and who people think he is lie right at the heart of Mark's Gospel.

Links backwards

- We, the readers, know who Jesus is – God revealed this to Jesus (and us) at his baptism (Mark 1.9–11). Until now, Jesus has been showing who he is by his words and deeds.

Links forwards

- The question of Jesus' identity is picked back up again at Caesarea Philippi (8.27–30), at the Transfiguration (9.2–7) and at the Crucifixion (15.39).
- Jesus' conversations with the disciples in the boats at 6.45–52 and 8.11–21 continue the theme of how much they understand who Jesus is.

Interesting words ...

- v. 35: *and he said to them*. Although the English changes the order, in Greek this sentence begins: 'And he said to them, on that day when evening had come'. This connects this passage with the four short additional parables earlier in the chapter, which all begin 'and he said' or 'and he said to them' (4.21, 24, 26, 30). It also suggests that the 'they' in the boats with him were those who were around him, along with the Twelve, who had been mentioned in 4.10 (hence the need for the other boats mentioned in 4.36).

- v. 35: *to the other side. Eis to peran* (meaning precisely 'to the other side') is a short, unremarkable phrase that becomes significant, in this section of Mark, as Jesus goes from one side of the Sea of Galilee to another (see the box, 'To the other side', on p. 111, for more on this).
- v. 37: *a great windstorm.* A *lailaps* is very specifically a windstorm or hurricane, such as those that can abruptly arise on the Sea of Galilee. Surrounded as it is by hills, rapid eddies of wind can swirl around the lake, causing sudden and unforeseen windstorms. To ensure that we are clear about the nature of the storm, the Greek reads 'a great windstorm of wind' (*amenos*).
- v. 38: *cushion. Proskephalion* (literally, 'for the head') might imply that 'pillow' was a better translation here; but the word was used far more generally to mean any kind of padded fabric, hence a cushion.
- v. 38: *perishing.* The verb *apollumi* can mean 'perish', 'die' or 'destroy entirely'. It has the sense of being entirely wiped out by something.
- v. 38: *rebuked.* The word *epitimaō* most often means 'to censure', 'to blame' or 'to rebuke', though in a few instances it means 'to honour'.
- v. 39: *peace, be still.* Jesus uses commands derived from two verbs here: *siōpaō* ('to be still or silent') and *phimoō* ('to muzzle' or 'to cause to shut up'); so literally, 'be still and muzzled'. The use of 'muzzle' indicates that the sea isn't just falling quiet but is contained by Jesus.
- v. 39: *calm. Galēnē* refers specifically to the stillness of the sea. In Mark and Matthew's versions of this account, they add *megalē* ('great'), to mean 'great stillness'.
- v. 40: *afraid.* The usual word for 'afraid' is *phobos*; throughout the New Testament, it is the word most often used when people are instructed by angels not to be afraid. This is not the word used here. What Jesus says is, 'Why are you *deilos* ('cowardly')?' This makes much more sense of the question (see 'Why are you afraid?', p. 113).
- v. 41: *filled with great awe.* The word *phobos* occurs here, one verse later. The Greek reads literally, 'and they feared a great fear' (*ephobēthēsan phobon megan*), using the verb *phobeō* with the noun *phobos*.
- v. 42: *obey.* The verb *hupakouō* means 'to listen to' (archaically, 'to hearken') and hence 'to obey'.

The first of three boat scenes

The stilling of the storm, the first of the boat scenes that we find in Mark's Gospel, is probably the most famous. The second scene (6.45–52) is reminiscent of the first. There is still a boat in a heavy wind but this time Jesus is walking towards them on the water, rather than sleeping in the boat. The third boat scene (8.11–21) contains no dramatic revelation of the nature of Jesus, just the disciples' continuing lack of ability to understand.

To the other side

The small phrase 'to the other side' occurs five times in Mark: here (4.35); then in 5.1, when they had arrived 'to the other side' in the Decapolis;* in 5.21, when they came back again; in 6.45, when they got into the boat ahead of arriving at Bethsaida; and in 8.13, just before Jesus discussed the leaven of the Pharisees.

In other words, Mark uses the phrase three times in this first boat scene, and twice more (once each) in the two other scenes. The phrase does not occur anywhere else in Mark.

While the Decapolis can easily be seen as 'the other side' from Capernaum (Capernaum is at the north-west corner of the Sea of Galilee and the Decapolis – if that is where Mark means – is south-east), the trip from Bethsaida (Mark 6.45) to Gennesaret (6.53) cannot really be said to be to the other side of anything. Both are located on the north side of the Sea of Galilee and would not be far to walk.

The aim of this small phrase, however, is to point out that something 'horizon-changing' was about to happen, which would, ideally, have prepared the disciples for a change of perspective.

*For more on the Decapolis, see p. 121.

A fishing boat

In 1986, a fishing boat was discovered on the shores of Galilee, during a drought when the water level had dropped. Carbon dating of the remains identified it as coming from a period between the first century BC and the first century AD, hence it's popular name 'the Jesus boat'. The design of the boat casts light on this story. It is about eight metres long and two metres wide. Originally, it was sturdy and flat-bottomed; its style was ideal for fishing, leaving lots of room to contain a catch of fish. The boat was also well adapted to the vagaries of the weather on the Sea of Galilee, the location of which means that the wind can suddenly turn and whip up a storm. In such conditions, a flat-bottomed boat would be less easy to overturn in a sudden squall. The downside of its wide, flat-bottomed style was that waves could easily break into it, filling it with water and causing it to sink, as here.

One detail about the boat's design that fits with Mark's description is that of Jesus sleeping in the stern. The boat that was found had a raised section at one end: it would have provided the only protection in a vessel that was otherwise entirely open to the elements. If anyone were to sleep in such a boat, this is where they would do so.

Jesus was asleep in the boat

The mention of Jesus sleeping during a storm in a boat is reminiscent of the story of Jonah, who likewise sleeps through a storm; both are awoken by their terrified companions. The key difference, of course, is that, while Jonah is then thrown into the sea to be swallowed by a large fish, Jesus calms the storm. Since, in the book of Jonah, the storm is caused by God, Jesus' command of the wind and sea indicates that he has the same control over the natural world. The implication of the story is that the disciples should have been able to work out for themselves the answer to the question they pose in verse 41: 'Who then is this?' The evidence of who Jesus is has been laid out for them through his actions; the question is whether they can work out what it all means.

This theme is one that recurs a number of times over the next few chapters, until it reaches a climax at the end of chapter 8 and the beginning of chapter 9.

'Do you not care?'

The contrast between what the disciples say to Jesus in Mark's account and in Matthew's is stark. In Matthew's version, the disciples rouse Jesus and say, 'Lord, save us! We are perishing!' (Matt. 8.25). In other words, they go to Jesus with the expectation that he will be able to save them. In Mark's Gospel, their question is rawer: 'Teacher, don't you care that we are dying?' It's also interesting to notice that, in Matthew, they address him as 'Lord' (that is, as someone with the power to act), whereas, in Mark, it is as 'Teacher' (as someone who has been teaching parables but not necessarily with more power than that).

In Matthew's Gospel, Jesus woke up, reprimanded the disciples and then calmed the sea; in Mark's Gospel, he woke up, calmed the sea and then reprimanded the disciples. Jesus' actions matched the greater desperation of the disciples in this account.

'Peace! Be still!'

It is striking that the words Jesus used to calm the storm appear to be anthropomorphic. The last time the terms 'rebuked' and 'be silent' (or 'be still') were used in Mark was in 1.25, when Jesus drove out the demon from the man in the synagogue in Capernaum. The use of these words here suggests that the storm is to be regarded similarly to the demons. Just as the demons were a frightening and uncontrollable feature of the world in which people lived, so too were storms. Jesus had power over both, to muzzle and banish them.

'Why are you afraid?'

Jesus' question, as commonly translated, seems unusually harsh. It seems quite clear why the disciples are afraid: they are in a boat that is taking on water in the middle of a storm and think they are going to die. Those would be sufficient grounds for fear in anyone. In reality, as noted above in 'Interesting words', this isn't quite what Jesus asks them. What Jesus asks is 'Why are you so timid or cowardly or liable to fear?' In other words, 'Why are you the kinds of people whose first response is fear?' This is coupled with the second question: 'Have you still no faith?' or 'Do you not yet have faith?' This seems to pose a very interesting opposition. People often claim that doubt is the opposite of faith; but, here, Jesus gives 'tendency to fear' as faith's opposite. The implication is that if they had faith, they would not be the kind of people whose first response in a crisis is terror. Knowledge of God and of the nature of God, and trust in that God, leads not to fear but to confidence, and Jesus expects the disciples to know this.

They were filled with great awe

It is somewhat ironic that the disciples' response to Jesus' question 'Why are you so timid?' is to 'fear a great fear' (see 'Interesting words', v. 40, on p. 110). What is clear is that Mark is making a point here; he is playing with the idea of what fear is. There is fear ... and fear (see the box, 'Fear', below): the fear that prevents us from seeing anything but the danger right before our eyes; and the fear that lifts our eyes higher, to see the very edges of the nature of God, who holds the whole world in his hands, in the knowledge that he is God and we are not. The first one leads to paralysis; the second to worship.

The disciples' lack of faith made them timid and unable to see anything about who Jesus really was; but then, after the stilling of the storm, for a fleeting moment, they encountered in his actions the very nature of God. For the first time in this Gospel, the disciples ended up asking the right question about Jesus. The question that remained unresolved, at this point in Mark, was whether they would be able to provide a similarly good answer.

Fear

The word 'fear' is such an important one in biblical tradition that it is worth pausing with it here for a moment. In modern usage, fear is a purely negative emotion and is connected with terror, horror and fright. Throughout the Bible, however, fear (in Hebrew, *yirah*, and in Greek, *phobos*) is both positive and negative and can just as easily be translated as 'awe', as it is in verse 41 in most English translations.

The connection is that a sense of awe, or holy fear, is evoked by the presence of God. This comes from the belief that God's very nature is so pure and holy that it is far beyond anything that we can comprehend or touch. Indeed, there are stories dotted throughout the Bible of people who are physically affected by their experience of God, whether it be Uzzah, in 2 Samuel 6.1–23, who reaches out to steady the Ark of the Covenant on the ox cart and dies, or Zechariah, in Luke 1.5–25, who is struck dumb after seeing an angel in the sanctuary of the temple.

The stilling of the storm is a beautifully worked example of the nature of fear, both negative and positive. When they thought they were going to die, the disciples were so paralysed with terror that they could think and do nothing outside of their panic; when Jesus stilled the storm, they were filled with awe and a curiosity to understand more of who Jesus was.

Fear (*phobos*) is not in and of itself wrong – it is often absolutely right and proper to feel fear – the question is what that fear causes us to do and think. If we remain locked in paralysis, then fear remains solely negative; if it causes us to learn more about the nature of God, it is positive.

It strikes me that Jesus' questions – 'Why are you so timid? Do you not yet have faith?' – are as relevant today as they were for the first disciples. They are questions that resonate both personally and institutionally. Why are we as people so likely to assume the worst and to jump to panic as our first response to events? But also, why do our institutions do the same? What would things be like if fear were not such a common factor in our lives?

Mark 5.1–20: Jesus and the man from Gerasa

After the dramatic events of the stilling of the storm, Jesus and his disciples arrived on 'the other side', a phrase that we saw first being used a few verses earlier, in 4.35. The end of chapter 4 has left us with the disciples' question ringing in our ears: 'Who then is this, that even the wind and the sea obey him?' On 'the other side', we might hope that the disciples would begin to find an answer to their question; instead, they barely feature in this story at all. The way in which the disciples fade into the background indicates that this question will not be answered right away. They, like us the readers, must watch what Jesus says and does and, from that, piece together an answer to their crucial question.

In the context of this, Jesus' command over 'Legion' is designed to reveal something fundamental about who he is: something that the demons could recognize (just like the wind and the sea did) even if the disciples do not.

Links backwards and forwards

- Legion recognizes Jesus in this story, just as the wind and sea did in Mark 4.35–41.
- A theme that runs all the way through Mark is Jesus' power over demons (and that they immediately recognize who he is). See 1.21–28 and 9.14–29. (Jesus also casts a demon out of the daughter of the woman from Tyre (7.24–30); but as the girl is not present, there is no hint of recognition.)

Interesting words ...

- v. 1: *Gerasenes.* Although the place on the other side, where Jesus went, is identified as Gerasa, it is unlikely that this is where he went, as the man approached him as soon as he left the boat; and Gerasa lies about 35 miles from Galilee (see the box, 'Timings in Mark's Gospel', on p. 117).
- v. 1: *the other side.* For the significance of the other side, see the box, 'To the other side', on p. 111.
- v. 2: *met.* The Greek equivalent of this verb is relatively unusual and appears only here in Mark's Gospel. Elsewhere, it occurs twice in Matthew's Gospel (in the parallel account to this one in 8.28; and in 28.9, where Jesus meets the women outside the empty tomb) and twice in Luke's Gospel (again, in the parallel account to this one in 8.27; and in 14.31, in the parable of the king counting his troops before going into battle). *Hupotanō* has the meaning of 'going out to meet' or 'to encounter'.
- v. 2: *tombs. Mnēmeion* is connected to the verb 'to remember' and refers to anything that is a memorial, remembrance or record of someone or something. In the ancient world, tombs were always located outside a village, town or city.
- v. 2: *unclean spirit.* Mark uses the same awkward phrase, 'man in an unclean spirit', here as he did in 1.23.
- v. 3: *lived.* Literally, the Greek says he had a 'dwelling' or a 'settlement' (*katoikēsin*) among the tombs.
- v. 3: *no one could restrain him.* The dire situation the man found himself in is communicated in Greek by the number of negatives that are stacked up in this half sentence, reading literally, 'and not even in a chain no longer no one was able to bind him' (*oude ... ouketi oudeis*).
- v. 4: *shackles and chains.* The word for 'shackle' (*pedē*) suggests that the man's ankles were bound. But it may be used to describe restraining both his wrists and ankles, with *alusis* (a more general word for 'chain') referring to chains around his body.
- v. 4: *wrenched apart; broke in pieces.* The first verb (*diaspaō*) refers to breaking by tearing apart and the second (*suntribō*) to breaking by shattering or crushing.
- v. 5: *bruising.* Although this verb, *katakoptō*, can mean 'to bruise', it more commonly means 'to cut' or 'to cut into pieces'. It seems likely that the man was lacerating himself with the stones he found lying around.

- v. 6: *bowed down before*. The verb *proskuneō* can refer either to physical posture (bow down) or to internal attitude (worship), or indeed both. The challenge of translating the verb when it is used in the Gospel is to decide whether the person involved is merely bowing out of respect or offering worship. I would suggest the man is worshipping here, given the conversation that then ensues.
- v. 7: *What have you to do with me?* This man asked a similar question ('What to me and to you?') to the man in the synagogue in 1.24. For more on the significance of this question, see 'What have you to do with us?', on p. 45. What is intriguing, however, is that, in 1.24, the question is posed as 'What to us and to you?'; whereas here, where the large number of demons possessing the man is stressed, he asks the question in the singular: 'What to me and to you?'
- v. 7: *adjure*. This is a very rare word in the New Testament, used only here and in Acts 19.13, and means 'to make someone swear an oath'. The word would be more usually used by an exorcist who would bind a demon with an oath. It seems that by using Jesus' name and by attempting to bind him with an oath, Legion was trying to gain authority over Jesus.
- v. 7: *torment*. The verb *basanizō* means not just 'to torment' but also 'to put to the test', 'to investigate scientifically' or 'to question by applying torture'. It begs the question of what kind of torture demons might expect at the hands of Jesus; not only that, it also indicates that Jesus' treatment, even of demons, was compassionate.
- v. 9: *Legion*. This is a Latin word referring to a Roman legion that would have been made up of around 6,000 troops. It is unlikely that the exact number is significant here, the name probably should be taken to mean simply 'lots'.
- v. 11: *herd*. The word *agelē* can be used of a group of any kind of animal, from horses to pigs to fish.
- v. 13: *steep bank*. The pigs ran down a steep bank (*krēmenos*) or over a cliff. Given the geography of the area, a steep bank is most likely.
- v. 14: *swineherds*. Literally, 'the ones feeding or tending' them. The word is the participle that comes from the verb *boskō*. It is a general word and can be used for any animal, though rarely of sheep. The word for shepherd is usually *poimēn*. It is likely that the 'herders' did not own the 2,000-strong drove of pigs, but that they cared for them for the townspeople. This may explain the townspeople's response to Jesus.
- v. 15: *they saw the demoniac sitting there, clothed and in his right mind*. The word for 'demoniac' remains the same here – 'the one being possessed by a demon' (*daimonizomai*) – which is technically incorrect as he was no longer possessed by the demon. This point is demonstrated by the following three participles: he was sitting (*kathēmai*), clothed (passive form of *himatizō*) and of sound mind (*sōphroneō*). This last verb is especially interesting as it means 'to be sensible', 'to be temperate', 'to be moderate' and 'to be able to show self-control'.
- v. 15: *they were afraid*. The response of the townspeople was the same as that of the disciples, even down to the grammatical construction (*ephobēthēsan*). This is hidden, though, in the NRSV, in which the first is translated as 'filled with great awe' and the second as 'were afraid'.

- v. 17: *neighbourhood*. The word *horion* refers to boundaries and hence to the whole territory. In other words, they begged Jesus to leave their entire area, not just the place where he was then.
- v. 20: *amazed*. For more on Mark's use of different words for 'amaze', see the notes on 1.22 and 27 (p. 41). The verb used here is *thaumazō* ('to wonder' or 'to marvel at').
- v. 20: *proclaim*. The verb describing what the man did (*kērussō*) is the same one that described Jesus' proclamation at the start of his ministry.

Timings in Mark's Gospel

One of the odd features of Mark's Gospel is the timings described. The quick pace of the Gospel implies that events tumble over each other, one after another; but, as here, sometimes the timings don't tie up. The previous story had Jesus stilling the storm 'when evening had come', yet he appeared to arrive in Gerasa during the day. The journey by boat across the Sea of Galilee would have taken only a few hours, even in a storm. We are left, then, to guess what happened between the stilling of the storm and Jesus and his disciples' arrival on 'the other side'.

This seems to illustrate what might be called the theological ordering of Mark's Gospel. In other words, Mark says events happened one after another because they are theologically connected and should therefore be read together, not necessarily because the timing worked exactly as described.

The key is to pay attention to the events that are strung together and to reflect on why they are held together so closely. Here, the connection seems to be that, while the disciples find it difficult to work out who Jesus is, the wind and the sea, as well as a vast hoard of demons, all recognize him immediately.

Another point worth noting is that it isn't very clear why they went to 'the other side' in the first place. The purpose of the trip seems to be to heal the man possessed by Legion; but Mark does not say whether Jesus knew of his existence before setting off or not.

Exorcism and power

This is another of Jesus' exorcisms, which, as we noted before, are a central feature of his ministry. Mark makes much of this story: it is more than four times as long as the parallel account in Matthew's Gospel (Matt. 8.28—9.1).

For more on the significance of exorcisms and demons, see the discussion of 1.21–28 (pp. 41–2).

Although much of this story is a repeat of earlier exorcisms, the scale and the drama of this account sets it apart from previous ones: Jesus has power over many demons just as he has power over one. The way in which Mark recounts this story emphasizes over and over again the theme of authority and control. While there is never any doubt that the demons would ultimately be defeated, the content of the conversation between Jesus and Legion underlines a subtle but distinct wrestling for power.

- Mark tells us that Jesus commanded Legion to leave the man; but Legion attempted to strike a bargain instead (vv. 7–8), using Jesus' name.
- The word used by Legion to ask Jesus not to torment them (translated as 'adjure' in the NRSV) is a word that implies making someone swear an oath. The word was often used by magicians/exorcists to 'bind' a demon, to allow them to have authority over it. Here, however, the demons attempted, unsuccessfully, to bind Jesus.
- Jesus then asked them for their name. There is a strong tradition, throughout the Bible that knowing the name of someone allowed you to know their identity and character, and hence gave you power over them. Legion's attempt to bind Jesus with an oath and the use of his name, two verses before, suggests that, at that point, Legion thought they might gain power over Jesus; when Legion was forced to reveal their name, however, the battle was lost.
- Despite this, Legion continued to bargain for their future. While apparently accepting defeat, Legion nevertheless requested where to go. There is even the merest hint of their asking Jesus to be compassionate: begging him neither to torment them nor to send them out of the region.

While, in this account, there is never any doubt about who will win, it is fascinating to observe that Jesus allowed Legion so much say in how they would be cast out of the man.

Gerasa

As noted in 'Interesting words', it is widely thought that Gerasa is a scribal error made by someone who did not know the area. Gerasa is around 35 miles from the Sea of Galilee and therefore would not realistically have had control over land next to the lake. Matthew's version of this story locates it at Gadara, which was about six miles south-east of the Sea of Galilee.

A later tradition locates the story in Gergesa, which is thought to be associated with El Kursi, where there is a steep bank running down to the lake.

What does come out of the vagueness of the naming of the place in Mark and Matthew is a sense that, for them, this story happened on 'the other side': in other words, 'over there'; and that was sufficient for the location, as far as they were concerned.

'Do not torment me'

When Legion begged Jesus not to torture them, it isn't entirely clear what is meant. Matthew's parallel account offers a possible clarification: 'Have you come here to torment us before the time?' (Matt. 8.29). 'Time' is the translation of the word *kairos*, the key or critical time, often used in the New Testament to refer to God's time, especially the Day of Judgement. This would make much more sense of the question. Legion accepts that, at the 'right time', their fate would be eternal torture; they ask whether Jesus has arrived to begin that torture before the Day of Judgement. If this is correct, it is a direct acceptance by Legion of Jesus' divine nature.

Impurity I

One of the themes that emerges in this story (and continues onwards into the healing of the woman with a haemorrhage and Jairus' daughter) is that of impurity. The man was possessed by unclean spirits; he lived among tombs that were impure and the pigs into whom the unclean spirits were sent were also, by their nature, impure.

This becomes important in the bargain that is struck between Jesus and the demons. Presumably, if Jesus had just cast them out without sending them somewhere, they would have had to exist fully in the presence of Jesus, which would, indeed, have been a torment for unclean spirits. Going from an unclean area (the tombs) into unclean animals (pigs) meant that they did not remain fully in Jesus' presence, but found a location as equally impure as the tombs had been.

The request not to send them out of the region implies a tradition that demons associated themselves with particular places. This is also suggested in Tobit 8.3. In that story, Tobit and Raphael, the archangel, travel to a place where Tobit meets his future wife. The problem is that she is possessed by a demon who killed all seven of her former husbands. Tobit is advised by Raphael to drive off the demon by burning fish liver and heart on an incense burner. The demon is so overwhelmed by the smell that it leaves the region where it lived and flees to the remotest parts of Egypt, where Raphael pursues it and binds it hand and foot. Here, the subjugation of the demon involves driving it away from its territory.

For a second reflection on impurity, see 'Impurity II', on p. 132.

The drowning of Legion

In an otherwise very detailed account, Mark does not explain what happened to Legion after the pigs had drowned. This implies that Mark's audience would have understood the significance of the event. The most likely explanation is not that Legion died – especially since they begged so hard to be able to relocate to the pigs – but that demons were particularly associated with water, which was chaotic and dangerous (as had just been established by the stilling of the storm). For example, in the Talmud (*b. Pesachim* 112a and *b. Avodah Zarah* 12b) there was a warning against drinking water at night lest a water-demon enter the drinker and possess them. When the pigs rushed into the water, therefore, Legion went back to living in the dark waters of chaos. There may even have been a hint, here, that there was a connection between the storm that Jesus stilled and demons that lived in the water.

The drowning of 2,000 pigs provides yet another dramatic flourish to this already dramatic story. Then, as now, 2,000 pigs would have been worth a lot of money, and their loss would have been felt by their owners.

The responses to Jesus

The townspeople reacted to the miracle exactly as the disciples had done in the boat (see 'Interesting words', v. 15, on p. 116): they were afraid. There was, however, one key difference. The disciples continued to follow Jesus; whereas the townspeople begged him to leave. This raises an important point in defence of the disciples. Even though they didn't really understand what was going on, nor who Jesus really was, they still followed him. The fear of the townspeople had the opposite effect on them; they did everything in their power to make sure that Jesus went away from them. This puts another layer on to the issue raised by the disciples in the previous story. It isn't just enough to catch a glimpse of the majesty of Jesus' character and to feel awe as a result. The real question is, having caught that glimpse, what people then do.

In contrast to the townspeople who couldn't get Jesus away from them quickly enough, the man who had been possessed by Legion begged to be allowed to go with him. The fact that Jesus declined tells us something crucial both about discipleship and about vocation. We might be tempted to imagine that Jesus would be delighted for anyone to follow him who wished to. The fact that he turned this man away and sent him to proclaim 'how much the Lord has done for you, and what mercy he has shown you' is important. The vocation of the man from Gerasa was not to follow Jesus as one of the Twelve, but to go and proclaim what had happened in the place where he lived. It is so easy to slip into assuming that everyone who hears Jesus' call on their lives will hear it in the same way and be called to do the same thing. Even at this very early stage, it is clear that being called does not mean being called in the same way as others. The Twelve were called to accompany Jesus in his life and ministry; but this man was to be faithful not by following but by staying where he was.

The Decapolis

The Decapolis was a group of ten independent Greek cities east of the River Jordan. The people around them came from a variety of backgrounds; but the ten cities were bound together by a common language and formed an alliance against the peoples who surrounded them (though there is a debate about whether this alliance was ever formalized). The Roman naturalist and historian Pliny the Elder named the ten cities in his book *Natural History* as Philadelphia, Gerasa, Gadara, Pella, Dion, Raphana, Scythopolis, Hippos, Canatha and Damascus.

These ten cities traced their influence back to the invasion of Galilee and Judea by the Romans in 63 BC. When Pompey, the Roman General, conquered the land, he was welcomed warmly by the cities in which Greek was spoken. By way of thanks for the warmth of their welcome, Pompey granted to the ten cities autonomy under Roman protection. In other words, the inhabitants were free to live as they chose, and their freedom was protected by Rome.

As the Greek language was such an important part of the identity of these ten cities, it is intriguing to wonder whether Jesus spoke to them in Aramaic, the common language of the Ancient Near East, or in their own language, Greek.

Given the stress on territory throughout this passage, it is interesting that the man declared what had happened to him throughout the whole of the Decapolis. Jesus simply told him to tell his friends; but he took this much further and spread the 'good news' throughout the whole region, from as far north as Damascus, all the way down to Philadelphia (which was just a little north of the Dead Sea, on the east side of the Jordan).

'Tell them how much the Lord has done for you'

One of the most striking features of this passage is that, with the exception of Mark 16.7 after the Resurrection, this is the only time that anyone is instructed to tell what has happened to them. This episode stands out in a Gospel that, time and time again, stresses that people are not to tell anyone about Jesus (for example, see 1.44–45, where the man healed of leprosy was explicitly told not to tell anyone what had happened to him – a command he ignored – which meant that Jesus was no longer able to go into town openly). The obvious question is why the former demoniac from Gerasa was allowed to tell others about what had happened, whereas everyone else was not.

The answer seems to be that, in his own territory, Jesus wanted to be able to define his ministry in his own way and in his own time. When the man healed of leprosy told everyone what had happened, Jesus was no longer able to travel openly; when Peter, in 8.29, declared that Jesus was the Messiah, he then went on to attempt to prescribe what this meant for Jesus. The Gospel of Mark tells a story of how people partially understood who Jesus was and what he had come to do; as a result, they constricted (or attempted to constrict) what he did and where he went. The man from Gerasa would have had no such impact on Jesus' ministry and so could tell others freely what had happened to him. (It is interesting to note, though, that the deaf man who was healed in 7.36 was also from the Decapolis; he was told not to tell anyone anything: perhaps by then, Jesus' fame had become cumbersome even in the Decapolis.)

Before we leave this passage, it is worth contrasting the sending out of the Twelve in 3.14 with what Jesus told the man to say. The Twelve, when sent out, were 'to proclaim the message'; the man from Gerasa was told: 'Go home to your friends, and tell them how much the Lord has done for you, and what mercy he has shown you.' There are a few interesting points to draw out from this:

- *Go home to your friends.* The man has been living alone and isolated among the tombs for as long as he had been possessed by the demons. Jesus' first command to him was to go back to his community and find connection once more. So many of Jesus' miracles, which convey the good news he has come to proclaim, involve reintegrating people into homes, families and community networks.
- *Tell them how much the Lord has done for you.* Whereas the Twelve were in a position to relay 'the message' that Jesus had come to proclaim, because they heard him doing so regularly, this man was not. All he could do was tell his own story of what God had done for him. This is the very best place for anyone who wants to start sharing the good news. 'The message' contains more than this (the kingdom of God, repentance and reorientation, and the call to belief: see 1.15); but the ability to declare it begins with the knowledge of what God has done for us.
- *What mercy he has shown.* The word mercy is closely associated with compassion. The man is to go and tell those he loves about the love that was shown to him.

The man doesn't quite do what he was told to do: he far exceeded the instructions he was given.

- He didn't just go home: he travelled throughout the whole of the Decapolis telling people what had happened.
- He didn't just 'tell' what had happened: he proclaimed it. Mark applies to his action the same word (*kērussō*) used to describe Jesus' proclamation of the message.
- Probably most fascinating of all is that he was told to tell people what the Lord had done for him. In this context, it is clear that this means what God had done. Instead, he told people what Jesus did. We are not told what to make of this; but the hint is that, as far as he was concerned, the two were the same.

Mark 5.21–43: A woman and a young girl were saved

The next episode contains two intertwined healing stories, using Mark's 'sandwich' technique: that is, embedding one story in the middle of another. The passage begins and ends with an unnamed daughter of a leader of the synagogue. In between these bookends, we find the story of a woman who had had a haemorrhage for as long as the leader's daughter had been alive. All three stories (these two and the previous one) explore the theme of impurity: the man with the unclean spirits lived among (unclean) tombs before the demons were cast into (unclean) pigs; the woman had been bleeding, making her unclean for 12 years; and Jairus' daughter was thought to be dead, rendering her unclean.

Links backwards and forwards

- The previous female individual healed by Jesus was Simon Peter's mother-in-law (Mark 1.29–31). After the two stories here, the only other one was the daughter of the woman from Tyre (7.24–30).
- The theme of being an outsider runs strongly through this section of Mark. All the people healed (the man from Gerasa, the woman who was bleeding, the woman from Tyre's daughter, the deaf man and the blind man) were all on the outskirts of society. The only exception was Jairus' daughter; though, since she was thought to have died, she had become an outsider of another kind.

Interesting words ...

- v. 21: *the other side*. Mark uses a familiar phrase here to imply another change of perspective. For more on this, see the box, 'To the other side', on p. 111. It is not clear exactly which synagogue Jairus led, but most assume it was Capernaum.
- v. 22: *one of the leaders of the synagogue*. For more on the role of a leader of the synagogue (*archisunagōgos*), see the box, 'Leader of the synagogue', on p. 126. The lack of clarity about exactly what this role entailed means that this phrase can be translated variously as 'one of the leaders', 'a certain synagogue leader' or 'a leader of one of the synagogues'.
- v. 22: *fell at his feet*. The word *piptō* ('fall') was used of the demons who fell down before Jesus in 3.11.
- v. 22: *little daughter*. The Greek word *thugatrion* specifically means 'little daughter', as opposed to *thugatēr*: a daughter of any age. Words for minors are nearly always neuter (that is, neither masculine nor feminine) and this is, ironically, no different.

- v. 22: *at the point of death.* The phrase used here is colloquial and hard to put into English. It means literally 'has finally' or 'has exceedingly' and hence means *in extremis.*
- vv. 23, 28–29 and 34: *made well.* The word (*sōzō*) 'saved' is used throughout this passage to refer to healing. The word means much more than simply 'healed' (see the box, 'Healing and salvation', on p. 129). For more on the different words for heal, see the box, 'Words for "heal" in Mark's Gospel', on p. 50. In verse 29, the word used is *iaomai* ('healed', possibly by a miracle).
- v. 24: *pressed in on him.* In 3.9, Mark drew attention to the crush of the crowd with the word *thlibō*. He uses this word again here in a slightly different form: *sunthlibō* means 'to press together' or 'to compress'.
- vv. 25 and 29: *suffering from haemorrhages.* The Greek is both more vague and more descriptive than this English translation and reads 'with flowing (*rusis*) blood (*haima*)'. The second occurrence is also vivid, though the phrase is slightly different: 'the fountain or spring (*pēgē*) of blood (*haima*)'.
- v. 26: *endured. Paschō* is the verb from which we get our English word 'passion'. It can mean 'endure' or 'suffer'. Here, I think 'suffer' might be closer to the woman's reality.
- v. 26: *physicians.* An *iatros* in the ancient world was a general word for someone who healed others. Professional physicians generally lived in urban areas; in rural locations, healers were more often without formal training. The existence of trained doctors can be verified from passages such as Sirach (Ecclesiasticus) 38, which praises the role of doctors: 'Honour physicians for their services, for the Lord created them' (38.1).
- v. 27: *spent.* The verb *dapanaō* has the sense of 'to consume' or 'to use up'.
- v. 27: *no better.* A close translation of this might be 'she in no way benefited (*ōpheleō*) but rather returned worse'.
- vv. 27–28: *cloak; clothes. Himation* refers to the outer garment, made up of a rectangular piece of cloth draped over the shoulders. The same word is used for both 'cloak' and 'clothes' in these two verses.
- vv. 29 and 34: *disease.* A *mastix* was literally a whip; but the word was often used figuratively to refer to something that was a scourge or a torment.
- v. 30: *power.* The word *dunamis* (from which we get a range of words, such as 'dynamite' and 'dynamic') is used here.
- v. 33: *fear and trembling.* The usual word for 'fear' (*phobeō*) appears here along with *tremō*, which means 'to shake' or 'to quake from fear'.
- v. 33: *truth.* The word *alētheia* ('truth') occurs regularly in John's Gospel but only three times in Mark: here and twice in chapter 12 (vv. 14 and 32).
- v. 34: *daughter.* In the introduction to this story, Jairus referred to his daughter in the diminutive (*thugatrion*); here, the usual word *thugatēr* is used.
- v. 34: *go in peace.* Literally, 'go into (*eis*) peace (*eirēnē*)'.
- v. 34: *be healed.* The word *hugiēs* has the sense of wholeness: that is, 'be whole or complete'.
- v. 35: *dead. Apothnēskō*, used here, is the common word for 'die'.
- v. 36: *overhearing. Parakouō* ('to hear alongside') can mean 'to hear accidentally' or 'to hear carelessly'; in other words, 'to take no notice of'. Either could be meant here.
- v. 38: *commotion.* A *thorubos* is a noise of a confused assembly and hence

'tumult' or 'clamour'. It is interesting that Jesus is said to 'see' the *thorubos*: you would usually hear one.

- v. 38: *weeping and wailing*. The two words (*klaiō* and *alalazō*) often go together and mean similar things. *Klaiō* refers to crying, however, and *alalazō* to the noise made when grieving.
- v. 39: *sleeping*. *Katheudō* refers to lying down to sleep rather than just napping.
- vv. 40–42: *took; get up; got up*. The same set of words is used here as for the boy healed of the mute spirit in 9.27: 'took' (*krazō*), 'get up' (*egeirō*) and 'got up' (*anistēmi*, which can also mean 'rise' as in 'resurrection').
- v. 41: *Talitha cum*. Very occasionally, Aramaic words are transliterated into Greek in the Gospels. This is one of those occasions where Greek lettering is used for an Aramaic phrase.
- v. 41: *little girl*. When translated into a Greek word, *korasion* is used. Like *thugatrion*, it is a diminutive and is neuter.
- v. 42: *overcome with amazement*. For more on Mark's different words for amazement, see the notes on 1.22 and 27 (pp. 41–2). Here, the word used is *existēmi* ('astonish' or 'astound'), with the words *euthus* ('immediately'), *ekstasis* (the noun from *existēmi*: 'amazement') and *megas* ('great'). The phrase is one of Mark's Aramaisms: 'they were immediately amazed with great amazement'.
- v. 43: *strictly ordered*. The verb *diastellō* means 'to give precise instructions about'.

Jairus

The only characters in a healing narrative who are named in Mark's Gospel are Jairus (here) and Bartimaeus (10.46). Just as with Simon of Cyrene, who is identified by the names of his two sons (Alexander and Rufus) in 15.20, it is most likely that Jairus is named here because he was well known in the early Christian community. It would therefore help to locate him for the readers.

Both the fact that he is named and has a title communicates Jairus' importance; given this, his desperation is also highlighted by his willingness to fall at Jesus' feet. As noted above, the same word is used for both Jairus and demons falling at Jesus' feet.

The theme that begins to emerge from this story onwards is that those who recognized Jesus were those driven by desperation, which included Jairus here and the woman in a few verses' time. Although they came from very different backgrounds and had very different experiences, both had nothing to lose. They reacted very differently from those with the most to lose (the scribes, Pharisees and other religious leaders) or those, like the disciples, who didn't have much to lose but were not desperate like Jairus and the woman who was bleeding.

One of the most significant features of the culture of Jesus' day was an honour/shame dynamic. It was key for people to maintain their honour in all circumstances; and the more important they were, the more key their honour was to them. Jairus' willingness to fall down at Jesus' feet was a sign that he had abandoned his 'honour' because he was driven by his love for his daughter and his fear that she would die. Mark begins to point to the correlation between how much someone had to lose and how they responded to Jesus.

As this Gospel is speaking as much to the reader as describing what happened, this question lands for each one of us. Is our response to Jesus similarly connected to how much we have to lose or how desperate we are?

Leader of the synagogue

The role of 'leader of the synagogue' can mean different things (and probably varied from synagogue to synagogue). Most commonly, the leader of the synagogue was someone who acted as an administrator, looking after the building and organizing services. There is no hint that synagogue leaders were priests or Levites, or indeed scribes.

In some places, there appears to have been more than one synagogue leader. For example, in Acts 13.15, there is a reference to '*hoi archisunagōgoi*', which is in the plural. The phrase used here – 'one of the leaders of the synagogue' – might suggest that a similar set-up was in place, with more than one 'leader'. Alternatively, it could be translated as 'a certain leader of the synagogue' or 'a leader of one of the synagogues'.

The key point about the description is that Jairus was important within his community.

Twelve years

Although Luke introduces the fact that the little girl who had died was 12 – the same number of years that the woman had been bleeding – at the start of his story, Mark keeps this detail until the end (v. 42). The joy brought to Jairus by his daughter for 12 years versus the torment of the continuous fountain of blood suffered by the unnamed woman makes the contrast even more poignant, and the desperation of each even more vivid.

It is hard to tell whether 12 years is to be taken as symbolically important or not. Certainly, the number of the tribes of Israel and of those called to follow Jesus most closely is 12. The age at which a boy, in those days, was deemed to be 'grown up' was 12 years, which was the age of Jesus when he was 'lost' in the temple. In this context, however, I suspect its significance is simply that the woman's pain had gone on for a 'lifetime' – the young girl's lifetime.

Flowing/fountain of blood

The conditions that would cause flowing blood (v. 25) or the even more evocative fountain or spring of blood (v. 29) are, sadly, many: they could range from endometriosis to fibroids and from non-cancerous polyps to cancer. Most commentators concentrate on the social isolation that such a condition would bring. Jewish purity laws dictated that a woman was impure – and would render all those who touched her similarly unclean – during the time of menstrual bleeding. A woman who was bleeding permanently would, therefore, be permanently impure and would not be able to risk touching others in case she made them unclean. As a result, she would have been lonely, cut off and isolated.

This is an important consideration; but it is important to note that most of the conditions that would cause a continuous flow of blood would also bring debilitating pain, fatigue and weakness because of anaemia. The woman's desperation did not just proceed from loneliness but also from a condition that affected nearly every aspect of her life. This poor woman was desperate beyond words; and only that level of desperation would have driven her to do what she did.

Doctors in the ancient world

The reference to the woman using up all the money she had on doctors raises the question of what doctors existed at the time of Jesus. As noted above, there were two main types of 'healers': so-called professionals (who largely lived in urban areas) and local 'healers' who healed using knowledge passed down through the generations. The reference to the woman using up all her money in going to physicians suggests that she had seen professional healers as well as local ones.

Physicians existed across the ancient world (and indeed Luke is described as 'the beloved physician' in Colossians 4.14). Ancient Egypt was particularly well known for medicine and its doctors' skill in curing disease. The first known physician is thought to have been Imhotep, who lived around 2500 BC. Assyria and Babylon also had famous healers; their work is referred to in the Code of Hammurabi.

In the Roman world, most medical knowledge came from people of Greek heritage who practised surgery and pharmacology as well as other areas of medicine. Intriguingly (although born later than the context for this story), there was a famous physician called Soranus of Ephesus (AD 98–138), who wrote a treatise on gynaecology. It was rediscovered and republished in the nineteenth century.

Touched his clothes

Iconic paintings of this scene all have the woman who was bleeding touching Jesus' cloak near the ground: the hem of his garment. This detail comes from Matthew (9.21, which refers to the hem or tassel, *kraspedon* – probably the tassel (*tzitzit* in Hebrew) required by Jewish law); but it's not from Mark, where the woman is described as simply touching his outer garment.

This episode emphasizes the significance of touch in the healing experience, something that the woman understood. Many of the healing narratives describe Jesus touching the person about to be healed (see Mark 3.10 and 6.56). In the modern world, touch is complicated and has been made even more so by the accounts of survivors of abuse, with whom touch has been appallingly misused. Nevertheless, touch remains significant in well-being and healing; and it is important to acknowledge its impact in contexts where it is used appropriately to bring life and hope. The fact that the woman had been isolated, due to her condition, for 12 years adds emotion to this story. She might have touched only Jesus' cloak but that could have been the most contact with another she had encountered in more than a decade.

Who touched me?

The farcical nature of Jesus' question in the midst of the press of the crowd is emphasized by the disciples' response: 'Who touched you? Well, everyone. You're in a crowd that is pressing around you.'

What it does, however, is tell us something that we do not get from any other story. When Jesus healed people, it affected him. The story doesn't tell us whether he felt the effects physically, emotionally or spiritually (or indeed in all those ways); we are told simply that 'power had gone forth from him'. In other words, healing people was a draining experience. This probably explains why Jesus needed to take time alone to recuperate (see Mark 1.35 and 3.13). It is often said that, if Jesus took time to recuperate, we should follow his model and do the same. Stories like this remind us of why it is so important. Encounters or experiences that drain us don't mean that we should avoid them; but, having experienced them, we need to take time to rest and recuperate.

'Daughter, your faith has made you well; go in peace, and be healed'

The only person addressed as 'daughter' by Jesus in Mark's Gospel was this woman; and the fact that he does so here is significant. We began the story with a man who cared so deeply for his daughter that he was prepared to sacrifice his dignity to save her. The subtle hints of this story tell us that this woman had no one who cared for her in this way. In terms of connection, the most she could hope for was a glancing brush of her hand against Jesus' cloak. Jesus' first response to her was to establish a connection as deep and loving as that between Jairus and his daughter.

Mark also makes clear that Jesus' healing was not a magical transaction providing healing to anyone who happened to brush by him. There were not hundreds of accidentally healed people who had happened to touch him in the crush. The woman was healed because of her faith. She believed that Jesus could save her and that was enough. As with the man from Gerasa, who was told to tell people what God had done for him, the woman's faith was not a systematic, fully worked out vision of who Jesus was, what he had come to do and what difference that would make in the world. This exchange makes a little more sense of what Jesus said to the disciples in the boat after the stilling of the storm: 'Why are you timid? Have you still no faith?' In other words, in the middle of the storm, they had asked Jesus the wrong question. Instead of asking why he didn't care that they were perishing, they should have asked him to save them.

Healing and salvation

Three times in this passage, as well as in other passages too (see 6.56 and 10.52), the word *sōzō* ('save') is used and translated as 'healed'. There is nothing wrong with this as a translation. *Sōzō* can, properly, be translated as 'heal'; but it means much more. In addition to 'heal', *sōzō* can mean 'to preserve', 'to keep safe', 'to save from death', 'to save from sickness' and 'to make complete'.

With the word 'save' there are always two movements: one away from something and one towards something else. For example, when the apostle Paul discusses salvation he is talking about being saved from sin and for a new life in Christ. In this passage, the woman was saved from 12 tormenting years of ill health and isolation for a life of wholeness and reintegration. This twofold dynamic is made evident by what Jesus said to the woman after he confirmed her healing: 'Your faith has made you well [saved you]; go in peace, and be healed of [whole from] your disease.'

The word 'peace' in Hebrew (*shalom*) means perfect wholeness/completeness. Jesus stressed this here when he used the Greek words for 'peace' (*eirēnē*) and for 'whole' or 'sound' (*hugiēs*). The woman was healed when she touched Jesus, but she then faced the lifelong task of living out that wholeness. The impact of her disease would not have disappeared overnight. Jesus' command reminded her, and us, of the importance of living into a new way of being, marked by peace and wholeness. It was something that she had to embrace consciously and intentionally. She had already been healed; Jesus then commanded her to go and 'be whole'.

'Your daughter is dead'

The stories in this part of Mark demonstrate Jesus' utter control of the situation he found himself in. The wind and the sea obeyed him; Legion was subjugated to him; and, here, time was under his control.

Arguably, the woman who had been ill for 12 years could have waited a few more minutes while he went to heal the young girl at death's door. It is not clear from the text whether, had Jesus hurried, he would have arrived before she had died. It is, in any case, an academic question because she was healed anyway. What is striking is that Jesus put the needs of the woman who was bleeding (someone, as far as we know, unimportant and not about to die) above the pleas of Jairus, the wealthy leader of a synagogue. In a Gospel that stresses that things happened 'immediately', Jesus spent time with the woman and didn't hurry her on his way to Jairus' house.

It is impossible to know whether the girl had, in fact, died or whether she was just sleeping, as Jesus declared. Matthew's account certainly suggests that everyone thought she was dead since Jairus, when he made his initial request, told Jesus that she had died (Matt. 9.18). Also, Luke adds the detail that her spirit returned to her (Luke 8.55). It is clear that the family believed her to have died, not least because the house was full of mourners when Jesus arrived and because they laughed when Jesus said she was not dead. The impact of the story does not change much if the girl was in a deep coma or had actually died. She was saved either way.

The importance lies in what it says about Jesus' relationship to death. In the ancient world, before the advent modern medicine, the pronouncement of death was closer to an art than a science. Someone could be in a deep coma but still pronounced dead. This is why three days was a significant time: after three days there was no doubt that someone was dead. Jesus' Resurrection after three days was significant, as it proved to the satisfaction of an ancient audience that he really had been dead, not just in a coma. Likewise, Lazarus whom Jesus raised from the dead had been in the tomb for four days. Jairus' daughter had only just died and so didn't count as 'all dead'. Nevertheless, whether all dead or just dead, Jesus' power over death remained the same. Whether he faced wind and storm, myriad demons or death itself, nothing could stand in the way of Jesus' ability to bring peace, hope and life.

Professional mourners

The hiring of professional mourners was common in the ancient world. The mourners were usually women and their role was to lead the family in weeping over the death of the one who had died. There are frequent references to the practice of mourning in the Old Testament; see for example, Jeremiah 9.17–18: 'Thus says the Lord of hosts: Consider, and call for the mourning-women to come; send for the skilled women to come; let them quickly raise a dirge over us, so that our eyes may run down with tears, and our eyelids flow with water.'

It seems rather quick for the mourners to have arrived in the space between Jairus' asking for Jesus to come and his arrival. Matthew's account therefore makes more sense if Jairus and his family already believed her to be dead before he went to seek Jesus.

'Do not fear, only believe'

The theme that has been circling since the stilling of the storm (Mark 4.40–41) reappears here. It was touched on in the previous story of the man from Gerasa, when, at the end, the townspeople were afraid and the man was sent to proclaim his story. It is also in this account, when the woman who had suffered 12 years of bleeding was commended for her faith. Now it resurfaces in full focus. What can't be reflected in English is that both commands (not to fear and to believe) are in the present tense. In Greek, present imperatives (commands) are continuous: Jairus is encouraged by Jesus not to continue fearing but, instead, to continue believing. Both fear and belief exist, for Jairus, side by side (of course they did, considering the circumstances); but Jesus urged him to abandon the fear and, instead, believe even more strongly than before.

Faith and belief

It is worth noting briefly that the words 'faith' and 'belief' are translations of the same Greek word, *pistis*. We are left with two overlapping words in the English language because of the way English developed. 'Faith' has Anglo-Saxon roots and 'belief' has Norman-French origins. Whereas 'belief' has a verb connected to it – 'to believe' – faith does not (we say 'to have faith' to compensate for the lack of a verb).

Over time, 'faith' and 'belief' have developed very slightly different nuances; but in the New Testament they are translations of the same word. So when Jesus asked the disciples if they still had no faith (*pistis*) and when he told Jairus to believe (*pisteuō*), there is a much stronger connection in Greek than is apparent in English translations.

'Little girl, get up!'

As noted above, the question of whether Jairus' daughter really had died or not was moot. Jesus would have been able to raise her either way. Here though, his language to the girl is noteworthy.

First, this is one of the few occasions when original Aramaic words have been preserved and simply transcribed using Greek lettering (other occasions include the healing of the deaf man in Mark 7.34; Jesus' prayer in Gethsemane, where he addressed God as *Abba* in 14.36; and his cry from the cross in 15.34). It is hard to tell why these few phrases were kept when others were not. In the case of the two healing miracles, one interesting feature is that the words in both cases are prosaic. A theory I find attractive is that they are kept to demonstrate that Jesus did not use magical formulae or exotic incantations to perform miracles. He simply said, 'Get up!' That was all he needed.

A second point of note is the tenderness of his phrase. It mimics the tone both of Jairus' initial request ('my little daughter') and of Jesus' address to the woman with the bleeding ('daughter'). The rest of Jesus' interaction in this passage feels so matter of fact as to be almost brusque; but this exchange reverses all of that. In the moment when it mattered, he spoke directly and tenderly to the young girl, with words as simple those uttered by parents across the ages every morning: 'Little girl, get up!'

Impurity II

One of the themes that Mark explores in this chapter is the theme of impurity. As noted above, the healing of the man from Gerasa, the healing of the woman who was bleeding, and the healing of Jairus' daughter all introduce different elements of the theme of impurity. Tombs, pigs, menstrual bleeding and death all introduce uncleanness in different ways. In the middle of this Jesus is, himself, unafraid and urges those around him to be similarly lacking in fear. None of these objects of terror in the first century concern him at all, nor is he affected by the fear of others. Instead, he encourages and applauds faith, wherever he sees it, most notably here in the woman who has bled for 12 years.

What comes out of these stories is an assurance that we should not fear those things that everyone around us, for whatever reason, is telling us to fear. The opposite of fear in these stories is faith: faith in the one who has power over storms, illness and even death itself. Jesus' words to Jairus cannot help but ring in our ears: 'Do not fear, only believe.' If we find this problematic, Mark at least comforts us with the knowledge that the first disciples did too. It is, nevertheless, held up as a goal to those who follow Jesus – to lay aside fear and believe instead.

Mark 6.1–6a: We know who he was – Jesus went home

The disciples' question in 4.41 – 'Who then is this?' – is answered in a different way in this short passage; it also adds another layer to Mark's reflections. The issue posed is the evidence that people draw on to answer the question of who Jesus was. The people of Nazareth turned to what they knew about his family. This left them with a very partial picture of who they imagined Jesus to be and to reject who Jesus really was.

Links backwards

- This story links backwards to Mark 3.20–35 in which Jesus' own family came out to restrain him. Here, we find a similar reaction from the people in his home town.

Links forwards

- As with all stories exploring the theme of Jesus' identity, this passage looks forward to 8.27–30 and Peter's declaration of who Jesus is, to the Transfiguration (9.2–7) and to the Crucifixion (15.39).

Interesting words ...

- v. 1 and 4: *home town*. The Greek word *patrida* is connected to the word for 'father' (*patēr*), so the land is connected to one's father.
- v. 2: *astounded*. For the different words used throughout Mark to mean 'astounded' or 'astonished', see the notes on 1.22 and 27 (pp. 41–2). The word used here is *ekplēssō*.
- v. 3: *where did this man ... given to him?* These two phrases are slightly clunky and depend on the repetition of *toutōi* ('in this person' or 'to this person'), and, in the Greek, read something similar to 'From where (*pōthen*) are these things in this person. And what is the wisdom (*sōphia*) that was given (*dotheisa*) to this person?' The repetition of 'this person' implies a questioning of how he knew all this.
- vv. 2 and 5: *deeds of power*. *Dunamis* can mean either 'power' itself or 'the deed of power'. It is used in the plural in verse 2 and the singular in verse 5.
- v. 3: *carpenter*. A *tektōn* could be a carpenter or joiner; but the word also refers to any type of craftsman or artisan. See the box, 'Carpenter', on p. 135, for more on this.
- v. 3: *brother, sisters*. The usual words for 'sibling' *adelphos* (masculine, hence 'brother') and *adelphē* (feminine, hence 'sister') are used here. As in chapter 3, there is nothing in the words used to suggest that those mentioned are anything other than a normal brother and sisters.

- v. 4: *took offence*. The verb *skandalizō* means 'to cause to stumble', 'to give offence' or 'scandalize'. In the passive voice, as here, it means 'to be scandalized'.
- v. 4: *without honour*. The word *atimos* means 'unhonoured' or 'dishonoured'. In a culture where honour was prized highly, being *atimos* was to be avoided if at all possible.
- v. 4: *kin; house*. *Sungenēs* refers to one's family tree and those biologically related even if quite distantly. The usual word for 'house', *oikia*, is used.
- v. 5: *sick people*. The unusual word, *arrōstos*, refers to people who are weak or sickly.
- v. 5: *cured*. There are a range of different words for 'heal' in Greek. This one, *therapeuō*, is a commonly used word meaning 'to take care of' and, by extension, 'to heal'. For more on the words for 'heal', see the box, 'Words for "heal" in Mark's Gospel', on p. 50.
- v. 6: *amazed*. See the notes on 1.22 and 27 (pp. 41–2) for the different words used for 'amazed' or 'astounded' in Mark. Here, it was Jesus' turn to be amazed (*thaumazō*) at their unbelief.
- v. 6: *unbelief*. *Apistia* means 'unbelief' or 'distrust'.

He went to his home town

None of the Gospels explains why Jesus moved from Nazareth to Capernaum. Of all the Gospels, the timescale of Luke's account makes the most sense. Jesus was baptized by John in the Jordan in Judea (Luke 3.21–22); he was then tempted in the wilderness (also presumably in Judea; Luke 4.1–13). From there, he went back home to Nazareth and taught in the synagogue (Luke 4.14–30); and then moved on to Capernaum, where his ministry proper began (Luke 4.31 onwards). Mark's account is much more disjointed and has Jesus fully settled in Capernaum before going back to his home town, where he taught in the synagogue. It is impossible to know if the event featured here, in Mark 6.1–6a, is the same one mentioned by Luke (4.14–30) at the start of Jesus' ministry, since the content of Jesus' teaching in the synagogue is not mentioned in Mark's account. What does suggest that the two accounts are referring to the same event, however, is the negative reaction of the people of Nazareth to Jesus' teaching. In Luke, they were angered by what he said; while, in Mark, they were annoyed because they thought they knew who he was.

His disciples followed him

Mark's addition, noting the presence of the disciples, seems a little like an afterthought. It is, however, important to Mark's unfolding narrative. The disciples have asked the most significant question about who Jesus is, one that he will challenge them to answer for themselves in Caesarea Philippi in chapter 8. Between these two points, they are with him in everything that happens: they are there when Jesus casts out demons and heals people; they are there when he enters into conflict with people in different ways; they are there for the feeding of the 5,000 and then the 4,000; they are there in two more boats when their understanding is tested. The point is that the Twelve are there and see everything. The question that Mark poses is what they will make of what they see; just as his allied question to us, the readers, remains: what will we make of what we see?

They were astounded ... Jesus was amazed

Until this point in the Gospel, we have observed the crowd being amazed/astounded/astonished at what Jesus has said and done. We have been left thus far to assume that amazement is a good thing. The crowd notices what Jesus says and does and is moved. This account raises, for the first time, the hint that amazement is not enough. The key question is what happens next. In Nazareth, the amazement turns quickly to dismissal. In the chapters that follow, the shadow of the cross begins to loom more and more; this is one occasion, quite early on in Mark, where we see its shadow, if only dimly. We know that the Pharisees and Herodians have resolved to destroy Jesus (3.6); now we see how quickly a group of people can move from amazement to rejection. A nice flourish at the end of this story is that Jesus himself is amazed at the unbelief of the crowd in Nazareth. He is as astounded by them, as they are by him.

Carpenter

Almost anyone who knows anything about the Gospels will tell you that Jesus was the son of a carpenter and a carpenter himself. The problem is that the word usually translated carpenter, *tekton*, is much less precise than this ascription suggests. A *tekton* was someone who worked in wood, metal or stone. A town the size of Nazareth in the first century (estimated to comprise between 100 and 400 people) would be unlikely to support a specialized carpenter. Having said that, Herod Antipas rebuilt Sepphoris (about 25 miles from Nazareth), a large, wealthy trading town, in the early first century; Joseph could have found employment there.

The tradition of Joseph and Jesus being carpenters is a strong one, but the word it is based on is much vaguer. All we can know for certain is that they were skilled artisans; 'builder' would be a more likely description.

Son of Mary

It is unusual for Jesus to be called the 'son of Mary'; a person was more often known by their father's name. Indeed, in both Luke 4.22 and John 1.45, Jesus is referred to as 'Joseph's son' and 'son of Joseph' respectively. Some people think that he is called the son of Mary here because of local speculation about his illegitimacy. However, nothing more in what the people of Nazareth say suggests that this is an objection to the validity of Jesus' ministry. It is therefore more likely that 'son of Mary' simply refers to the fact that Joseph has died, and the family is now known by the name of the remaining parent.

Very little is known of Jesus' siblings in the New Testament. Four brothers are named here and in the parallel passage of Matthew 13.55:

1 James or Jacob (in Greek, the name is Iacobus). In later Christian tradition, he was called James the Just. In Galatians 1.19, James is identified as the leader of the Church in Jerusalem.
2 Joses or Joseph.
3 Simon.
4 Jude or Judas. Traditionally, the New Testament letter that bears the name Jude has been associated with this brother of Jesus.

The only other reference to Jesus' brothers in the New Testament (beyond the account in 3.20–35) can be found in a vague reference in 1 Corinthians 9.5, which implies that they are all married: 'Do we not have the right to be accompanied by a believing wife, as do the other apostles and the brothers of the Lord and Cephas?'

The sisters of Jesus are never named in the New Testament.

'Prophets are not without honour ...'

In response to his reception in Nazareth, Jesus quotes what we can only assume is a well-known proverb. The exact wording does not exist in other literature, though the sentiment is common in Old Testament prophecy. There, for example, God warns Jeremiah that even his own family has dealt treacherously with him (Jer. 12.6). The theme is also present in Greek philosophy: Apollonius of Tyana, a first-century philosopher from Cappadocia, complained to his brother: 'Other men regard me as the equal of the gods, and some of them even as a god, but until now my own country alone ignores me' (*Epistle 44*); and Dio Chrysostom, a first-century orator from Turkey, stated: 'It was the opinion of all the philosophers that life in their own native land was hard' (*Discourse* 47.6).

No deed of power

The emphasis of the previous few chapters comes to the fore in a short phrase at the end of this passage. We are told that Jesus was not able to do any 'deeds of power' among the citizens of Nazareth, apart from a few healings. This may seem somewhat incongruous: surely healing counts as a deed of power? In this context in Mark, it is clear that, by 'deeds of power', Mark means stilling a storm, casting out a legion of demons and raising people from the dead. In a sense, the enormity of who Jesus was is emphasized by the fact that a few healings don't really count. This was such a part of who he was that they were as normal as his teaching.

Mark 6.6b–13: The next stage of the apprenticeship

The famous medical education model 'see one, do one, teach one' seems to underlie Jesus' own discipleship method. Thus far, as we have seen, the disciples have been in the 'seeing phase'. Now they are sent out to proclaim, cast out demons and heal the sick. From the vantage point of the reader, it is tempting to ask Jesus whether this is a good idea. The Twelve have not yet shown any indication that they fully understand who Jesus is and what he has come to do. The fact that this is not, apparently, a factor in Jesus' decision suggests that we might have to think again about discipleship: perhaps it is not necessary to understand everything before people become proclaimers of the good news.

Links backwards

- This story reminds us first of the callings to discipleship (Mark 1.16–20 and 2.13–17) and then of Jesus choosing the Twelve (3.13–20). This passage relates the next stage in this calling process – sending.

Links forwards

- While Jesus is away with Peter, James and John during his Transfiguration, the disciples attempt to cast out a demon unsuccessfully (9.14–29). Their activity reminds us that Jesus' commission of them remained live after this particular sending out.

Interesting words …

- v. 6: *he went about*. Two words are used here to describe Jesus' movements: he went about (*periagō*) in a circle (*kuklōi*). This implies he didn't just go through villages on his way back to Capernaum, but deliberately went around visiting them all.

- v. 6: *villages. Kōmē* refers to an unwalled village as opposed to a fortified town or city. Someone living in a village would need to retreat to a town or city if enemies invaded.
- v. 7: *two by two*. Simply, *duo duo*.
- v. 7: *authority. Exousia* is the authority or licence to do something.
- vv. 7 and 13: *unclean spirits; demons*. As elsewhere in the Gospel, Mark slips between 'unclean spirit' (*pneuma akathartos*) and 'demons' (*daimonion*).
- v. 8: *staff. Rabdon* is a word for any kind of stick: a fishing rod, a magic wand, a limed twig, a hunting spear, a rod for beating someone with or a shepherd's crook.
- v. 8: *bag. Pēra* was specifically a leather pouch for carrying food; it might also have referred to a beggar's bag that was used to beg for food.
- v. 8: *money. Chalkon* means 'copper', 'brass' or 'bronze', and hence became used for any kind of money.
- v. 12: *proclaimed that all should repent*. The Greek phrase is simply that they proclaimed (*kērussō*) into (*eis*) repentance (*metanoia*). For more on *metanoia* and its importance, see the box, 'Metanoia', on p. 23.
- v. 13: *cured*. There are a range of different words for 'heal' in Greek. This one, *therapeuō*, is a commonly used word meaning 'to take care of' and by extension 'to heal'. For more on the words for 'heal', see the box, 'Words for "heal" in Mark's Gospel, on p. 50.
- v. 13: *oil. Elaion* is the usual word for olive oil.

He went around about; he sent them out

The specific context of Jesus' travelling around in a circle through all the villages seems to lie behind his commissioning of the Twelve. If he were to go to every village by himself, it would take far too long. So he commissions the Twelve to help.

The significance of the disciples' going out in pairs may be nothing more than for companionship and protection. It is possible, however, that it also relates to the Old Testament injunction that two (male) witnesses were needed to give testimony in court (Deut. 17.6; 19.15).

Intriguingly at this point, only exorcism is cited as what the disciples are to do; later on, though, it is clear that they also proclaim and heal the sick. It may be that it is specifically the authority to cast out demons that Jesus has to give them. Proclamation and healing were expected of a disciple, whereas the handing on of authority over demons might have been particularly needed. Alternatively, perhaps Mark sees authority over demons as incorporating all three elements: proclamation, healing and exorcism.

Take nothing ... except ...

In Mark, all that the Twelve were permitted to take with them was sandals, a single tunic and a stick. At the time of Jesus, a tunic was made from two rectangular pieces of fabric sewn together at the sides and shoulders. A man would wear a knee-length tunic and a woman an ankle-length one. One possible explanation for the ban on a second tunic was that it could be used as a covering for someone sleeping out in the countryside. The point of the venture was, first, to proclaim the good news and, second, to rely on hospitality. Having only one tunic each would ensure that the disciples sought shelter in someone's home.

As noted above, a *rabdon* was a multipurpose stick used for walking and, possibly, for protection (for example, beating off bandits or wild animals). One of the challenging features of the parallels to this story is that both Matthew and Luke relate that Jesus also forbade taking sandals and a stick (Matt. 10.10; Luke 9.3). There seems to be no explanation for this beyond a different memory of the occasion.

'Shake off the dust that is on your feet'

This command from Jesus was predicated on Ancient Near Eastern rules of hospitality. The assumption was that people would welcome the disciples in line with the demands of hospitality; and similarly in line with this custom, the disciples were to accept the first offer they received and not move on to a better offer. There is an interesting parallel description of the Essenes by Josephus, the first-century Jewish historian, who said:

> They have no one certain city, but many of them dwell in every city; and if any of their sect come from other places, what they have lies open for them ... For which reason they carry nothing at all with them when they travel into remote parts, though still they take their weapons with them, for fear of thieves. (*Jewish War* 2.124–126)

The other notable command was that if someone did not receive them, then they should shake the dust off their sandals. This seems to be similar to the expectation that a travelling rabbi would shake the dust of Gentile territory off his feet when he returned to Galilee or Judea (*b. Shabbat* 14b). This might suggest that Jesus was saying that if the disciples were not welcomed, they should treat the household as though it were Gentile.

If we take them together, the implication seems to be that the disciples were to treat everyone as though they were one of them; but if rejected, they were to treat them as they would a Gentile. Underlying this is the experience that Jesus had just had in Nazareth: they were to expect rejection as well as welcome; but, when that happened, they were not to waste time trying to change the householders' minds but instead were to move on to another place.

It is worth noting that all of this would have taken a considerable amount of time. Mark tells his story at such a pace (and many of the events that he records took place in a single day) that it is easy to lose track of the length of time. At the very least, these few verses refer to weeks, if not months, of time.

Mark 6.14–29: The killing of John the Baptist (a birthday banquet)

Every now and then, in the earlier chapters of the Gospel, the shadow of the cross can be felt in the story. Once we reach chapter 9, that shadow looms evermore darkly over the story; but for now, Mark reminds us, from time to time, of the opposition to Jesus and what it will lead to. This is one of those occasions that points subtly but clearly to how the story will end. One of the striking features of the passage is how long it is (16 verses) as opposed to Matthew's 12 verses and Luke's three.

Links backwards

- John the Baptist bursts into the story in Mark 1.2–8.
- This event was hinted at in 1.14, where it speaks of John's arrest.

Links forwards

- Mark's placing of this story before the feeding of the 5,000 strikingly contrasts two banquets of very different kinds.
- The words used for John's disciples taking John's body to be buried ('they came and took his body, and laid it in a tomb' (6.29)), are reminiscent of Joseph of Arimathea taking Jesus' body and placing it in a tomb (15.46).

Interesting words …

- v. 14: *Herod.* The Herod in this story is Herod Antipas. For more on his family relationships, see the box, 'The Herods', on p. 33.
- v. 14: *king.* Technically, Antipas was not a king. After Herod the Great died, his kingdom was split between his three sons: half was given to Herod

Archelaus (see p. 167); the other half was divided between the remaining two sons, Philip (see pp. 186–7) and Antipas. So Antipas' title was tetrarch ('ruler of a quarter'). By the time of Antipas, this meant someone, generally, a little less important than a king. He was acknowledged as a tetrarch by the Emperor Augustus.

- vv. 14 and 16: *raised*. The verb *egeirō* means 'to rouse', 'to awaken' or 'to raise up' and is also used of Jesus' Resurrection in Mark 16.6.
- v. 16: *beheaded*. *Apokephalizō*, like the English 'beheaded', describes what happened. The word *kephalē* is 'head' and the preposition *apo* means 'away from'.
- v. 17: *married*. *Gameō* has a range of meanings: 'to marry', 'to take as a lover/concubine' or 'to have sexual intercourse with'. As we know from elsewhere that Antipas married Herodias, 'marry' seems the best translation.
- v. 18: *lawful*. The word *exestin* means 'permitted' or 'lawful'; but when used in Mark, it means specifically 'permitted by God's law' (Mark 2.24, 26; 3.4; 6.18; 10.2; 12.14).
- v. 19: *grudge*. The verb (*enechō*) has a sense of holding on to something: namely, 'to hold fast on to something' and hence 'to keep a grudge'.
- v. 20: *righteous and holy*. Righteous (*dikaios*) and holy (*hagios*) refer to both virtue under the law ('righteous') and set apart for God ('holy'). Herod thinks John's behaviour and character are admirable.
- v. 20: *protected him*. *Suntēreō* can mean both 'guard' and 'keep safe'. Given Herodias' grudge against John the Baptist, both would be necessary.
- v. 20: *When he heard him, he was greatly perplexed; and yet he liked to listen to him*. This sentence sums up Herod's turmoil perfectly: 'listening (*akouō*) to him, he was much (*polla*) at a loss/perplexed (*aporeō*); and he listened (*akouō*) to him gladly/with pleasure (*ēdeōs*)'.
- v. 21: *opportunity*. Literally, a well-timed (*eukairos*) day (*ēmeras*).
- v. 21: *birthday*. As in English, the word for 'birthday' is linked to birth: *genesis* means birth and a *genesia* is a birthday. It is worth noting that pious Jews considered birthday celebrations to be pagan festivities.
- v. 21: *courtiers, officers and leaders*. The word *mega* means 'great' and a *megistan* was, therefore, a great man (courtier). A *chiliarchos* is, literally, a 'ruler of a thousand' and, therefore, a high-ranking military officer. *Prōtos* ('first' or 'foremost') refers to those at the top of society (leaders). The first and third terms are therefore equivalent to the English phrase 'the great and the good'.
- v. 22: *his daughter Herodias*. Matthew's Gospel and a good number of manuscripts of Mark have here 'the daughter of Herodias' (whom we know, from outside the New Testament, to be called Salome). This seems more likely than that Antipas had an otherwise unknown daughter with the same name as his second wife (though, given the complexity of the Herodian relationships, nothing is impossible).
- vv. 22 and 26: *guests*. As this was a feast, Herod and his guests were reclining at the table; the word used here reflects this: *sunanakeimai* ('recline together'). When the word returns in verse 26, it is slightly different and is just *anakeimai*.

- vv. 22 and 28: *girl*. This story takes an even darker turn, with the use of this word for 'girl' (*korasion*). The same word was used to describe Jairus' daughter only one chapter before. It refers to a girl who is not yet pubescent.
- vv. 23 and 26: *solemnly swore; oaths*. *Omnuō* means 'to swear an oath'. In other words, Herod was bound to do as the girl asked. *Horkos* refers to a solemn invocation, often involving a god to guarantee truth.
- vv. 25 and 27: *immediately*. Mark's often used word, *euthus*, is applied to Salome's going back in and of Antipas' sending orders for John's decapitation. It lends a sense of rushing to the whole episode. Add to that the word *spoudē* ('with haste' or 'with speed') and the hastiness of the decision to execute John is highlighted.
- v. 27: *soldier*. This was not just any soldier. A *spekualtōr* was one of the soldiers from the headquarters (in this case, Herod's palace), so an elite guard.
- v. 28: *platter*. A *pinax* was something sturdy and flat: a platter, a board or a writing tablet. Here, a platter or board seems most likely.
- v. 29: *body*. *Ptōma* refers to something that has fallen – in this instance, a fallen body and hence a corpse.

King Herod heard of it ...

The logic of Mark's narrative is that, although he doesn't say what Herod heard, the most likely thing that he heard was of the mission of the Twelve. One of the sub-themes that runs throughout Mark – first appearing in 1.45, after the leper told everyone what Jesus had done, despite being instructed not to – is the threat to Jesus of his own notoriety. Although some scholars consider this long story a digression, it is much more likely that, as noted above, this is another moment when Mark makes clear that the story of Jesus' life can have only one outcome.

The speculation about Jesus is reported as being threefold: he was John the Baptist, Elijah or another prophet (the phrase 'like one of the prophets' means a descendant of the prophetic line as opposed to any old prophet). Elijah was singled out particularly because of a tradition that he would return before the Day of the Lord. It is interesting to notice that this expectation appears to have been transferred on to John the Baptist too: that he could rise from the dead (a belief shared by some of the people discussing Jesus, and by Herod Antipas himself).

Herod's assumption that Jesus is John the Baptist raised from the dead is the first clue, supported by more detail later in this passage, that Herod is haunted by what he did.

Herod Antipas, Herodias and Salome

The story of the family of Herod Antipas and their marriages is worthy of a soap opera. Indeed, the report in Mark's Gospel does not even come close to the gruesome details of what really went on.

Herod Antipas (along with his brother Herod Archelaus) were the sons of Herod the Great's fourth wife Malthace. Antipas' first wife, Phasaelis, was a Nabataean princess (the Nabataeans were an ancient Arabian people who had a thriving trading empire). He divorced her to marry Herodias. Herodias was the daughter of Aristobulus IV (and a granddaughter of Herod the Great). After Herod the Great executed Aristobulus IV and another son, Alexander, on suspicion of treason, he married Herodias to her half-uncle Herod II (called Herod Philip by Matthew and Mark, but not to be confused with Philip the Tetrarch, another son of Herod the Great). Herodias subsequently divorced Herod II (Philip) and married Herod Antipas, another of her half-uncles.

Herodias' only daughter from her first marriage was Salome. According to the Jewish historian Josephus, she was later married to her great half-uncle Philip the Tetrarch, whom she divorced in AD 34 to marry her cousin Aristobulus of Chalcis.

The imprisonment and execution of John the Baptist

John's imprisonment is recorded not just in the Gospels but also in the writings of the Jewish historian Josephus. Josephus describes the defeat in battle of Herod Antipas by his former father-in-law King Aretas IV of Nabataea, who was furious at the way in which his daughter (Phasaelis) had been treated (*Antiquities of the Jews* 18.5.1). Josephus went on to say that many people saw Antipas' defeat as a punishment from God because of how he had treated John the Baptist. Interestingly, Josephus does not attribute John's arrest to his criticism of the marriage but to Herod Antipas' fear that John would incite the people to rebellion. Josephus says that John was arrested and held in Macherus (a fortress east of the Dead Sea), where he was put to death (*Ant.* 18.5.2).

There are a number of significant differences between Josephus' account and that of Mark's. The two most important are that John's death was at Herod's instigation in Josephus, but at Herodias' in Mark; and that Josephus says John died in Macherus while, from Mark's account, it is often assumed that John was held in Herod's palace at Tiberias. Neither of these pose particular concerns. It is easy to imagine both motivations for John's death being popularly asserted and discussed following his death. And, while we might imagine that John was being held in Tiberias, Mark's Gospel certainly allows for an executioner being sent to Macherus before returning with John's head.

Both Josephus and Mark agree on the judgement of John. Mark calls him 'righteous and holy' and Josephus terms him 'good' (*Ant.* 18.5.2).

Young girl

The use of the word *korasion* ('young girl') so soon after the story of Jairus daughter, gives this story a dark twist. There is no definitive age for a *korasion* but she would have been prepubescent (after which, she would be deemed a woman). The story has been set up as a narrative of desired revenge by Herodias, who felt slighted by John's criticism of her. Here, we meet a young girl, only half a chapter after the story of sorrow at the potential death of another young girl. There, the girl was loved and cherished by her parents; here, a girl of a similar age was sent in, presumably by her mother, to please her stepfather with her dancing while being used as a pawn in Herodias' act of revenge. The contrast between the two stories is striking and shocking.

While there is nothing in the description of the dance to suggest that it was erotic in any way, there is a parallel between Herod Antipas' response – 'Ask me for whatever you wish, and I will give it' – and King Ahasuerus' response to Esther, who pleased him because of her beauty: 'What is your request? It shall be given you, even to the half of my kingdom' (Esth. 5.3). This certainly hints that the dance was not merely childlike and cute.

It may also be worthy of note that, while Herodias asked only for John's head, her daughter asked for it on a platter – embellishing the original request into a truly gory reward (beloved of artists ever since).

The king was greatly distressed

Herod Antipas' dilemma about John the Baptist is expressed beautifully in this story. He had him arrested but didn't want to kill him. When he listened to John, he was confused/perplexed but he heard him with pleasure. He made a promise that forced him to kill John and then was devastated by the act. This all makes sense of why, in verse 16, he was convinced that Jesus was John come back to life. Herod Antipas was preoccupied by his decision to kill John the Baptist and was therefore convinced that John had come back to haunt him.

John the Baptist's disciples

There are multiple references to John's disciples in the New Testament. Some of them decided to follow Jesus (John 1.35–42), whereas others continued to follow him even after his imprisonment (Matt. 11.2–3). Following the events of the Gospels, in Acts, there are references to people who knew only of John's baptism and not of Jesus' (see Acts 18.25 and 19.1–7). John the Baptist was clearly hugely significant while he was alive, and for a season after he had died too.

Mark 6.30–44: A banquet for 5,000

One of Mark's favourite narrative techniques is to put contrasting stories next to each other (or in close proximity) because, together, they are more expressive than one story alone could be. We noticed in the previous story the shocking contrast of the little girl (Jairus' daughter) who was cherished by her parents and healed by Jesus to great joy, and the little girl (Herodias' daughter) who danced for Herod and his guests and asked for John's head on a platter. This story also contrasts starkly with Herod's banquet. Here, we have two feasts next to each other, both extravagant (though in different ways): Herod's led to death and sorrow; Jesus' to life and joy.

Links backwards

- The contrast between Herod's feast (Mark 6.14–29) and this one is striking in a number of ways: those invited; the extravagance – one of wealth, the other of quantity; the outcome – death for John the Baptist and nourishment of sheep without a shepherd; and so on.

Links forwards

- The feeding of the 4,000 (8.1–10), which is both similar to and different from this feeding. For a chart noting the similarities and differences, see p. 175.
- The Last Supper, where Jesus also took, blessed, broke and gave bread (14.22–25).

Note an additional pattern here

- The feeding of the 5,000 (6.30–44).
  - Boat II (walking on the water) and a conversation about whether the disciples understand (6.45–52).
- The feeding of the 4,000 (8.1–10).
  - Boat III (yeast of the Pharisees and of Herod) and another conversation about whether the disciples understand (8.11–21).

The implication of the repetition is that Mark expects the disciples to have learnt more the second time around.

Interesting words ...

- vv. 30 and 34: *taught; teach*. Exactly the same word (*didaskō*) is used of the disciples teaching as is used of Jesus' teaching the crowd many things.
- v. 31: *deserted place*. The place Jesus took the disciples to is described as a desert or desolate (*erēmos*) place (*topos*). It is not a desert (*erēmos* or *erēmia*, used on their own) because, as we discover later in the story, they sat down on green grass. The implication here is that he took them to a place where no one else was (only the crowd saw them going and got there before them).
- v. 31: *leisure*. The Greek word is *eukairos*, which is more literally 'an opportune time'. It wasn't leisure that they needed but any opportunity to eat at all.
- v. 33: *hurried there on foot*. The verb *suntrechō* is one of Greek's wildly irregular verbs (which means its past tense looks nothing like its present; the aorist (past tense) form used here is *sunedramon*, but it comes from the verb *suntrechō*). It means 'to run together' or 'to run alongside. The addition of *pezei*, 'by foot', adds drama. A vast crowd of people guessed where they were going and ran there together.
- v. 34: *compassion*. The word *splangchnizomai* means literally 'a movement in the bowels' and refers to the emotion one feels towards another. The word is used three times in Mark: here; in 8.2, where Jesus also feels compassion for the crowds before the feeding of the 4,000; and in 9.22, where the father of the boy, who has seizures, begs Jesus to have compassion. The only time in the Gospels the word is used of someone who is not Jesus is in Luke 10.33, where the Good Samaritan feels compassion for the man he passes on the road.
- v. 34: *sheep without a shepherd*. In chapter 5, herders (*boskō*) were mentioned in relation to the pigs. Here, the more usual word for 'shepherd' (*poimēn*) is used for someone who looks after sheep (*probaton*).
- v. 35: *When it grew late*. This is a rare phrase (used twice in this verse) in the New Testament, though it is used elsewhere in Greek literature. *Hora pollē* means literally 'much hour' and allows a vague sense of its growing late, without defining the time of day precisely.
- v. 36: *country and villages*. The words based on 'field' (*agros*) and 'unwalled village' (*kōmē*) indicate that, wherever this was taking place, it was a long way from any cities.
- v. 37: *two hundred denarii*. Two hundred (*diakosioi*) denarii were about two thirds of a labourer's wages for a year.
- vv. 37–38: *bread*. In his parallel account, John goes out of his way to make it clear that the bread available is barley bread (the lowest quality bread possible; see John 6.9), Mark makes no such point here. 'Bread' (*artos*) is the usual word for wheat bread. Likewise, the usual word for 'fish' (*ichthus*) is used.
- vv. 39–40: *sit down*. Slightly incongruously, the word here means to recline at a table (*anaklinō*): the same word used for Herod Antipas' guests in the previous story. The significance is that they are not just to sit down but to sit down and be ready to eat. In verse 40, a different word is used, *anapiptpō*, though this also means 'to recline'.
- vv. 39–40: *groups*. The word for 'group' is *sumposia* (from which we get the

English word 'symposium'). It is repeated here to mean 'group by group'. It was originally used to refer to a drinking party but, over time, came to be used to describe any dinner party or banquet. In verse 40, a different word is used (*prasiai prasiai*), which means 'in companies' or 'in groups'.

- v. 39: *green grass*. For those who live in climates where it rains a lot, saying that the grass (*chortos*) was green (*chlōros*) seems superfluous. In the Middle East, however, it indicates what time of year it is (spring), before the summer sun has scorched the grass brown.
- v. 41: *taking, blessed, broke, gave*. For more on the significance of the four words 'took' (*lambanō*), 'blessed' (*eulogeō*), 'broke' (*kataklaō*) and 'gave' (*didōmi*) in relation to the Last Supper, see 'Took; blessed; broke; gave', on p. 150.
- v. 41: *set before*. *Paratithēmi* means 'to set alongside' or 'place before'.
- v. 42: *filled*. The verb *chortazō* can mean 'to feed in order to fatten' or simply 'to satisfy'.
- v. 43: *baskets*. The word for 'basket' is, intriguingly, *kophinos*, the word from which the English word 'coffin' is derived.
- v. 44: *men*. Matthew has the more direct phrase 'five thousand men, besides women and children' (Matt. 14.21), which has often been commented on. Mark's wording probably means the same, as he uses the word *anēr*, which most commonly means, specifically, 'men'. Matthew allows the possibility of the presence of women and children. Mark doesn't mention them at all, which raises the question of whether this was a male-only gathering.

A desert place

It is interesting, and significant, to notice what Jesus did on the disciples' return from their first big mission. After they had reported back (telling him what they had done and what they had taught, both of which appear to be noteworthy), Jesus took them away to a solitary place. Mark's telling of the pressures on Jesus and the disciples is one that will resonate with many. Such a large number of people were coming and going that no one had any opportunity even to eat. Jesus' recognition that great action and great activity require great rest is one that remains important today. It is also worth noticing that none of them got the rest, as a crowd followed them; but the intention is key, nevertheless.

The exodus narrative and the wilderness wanderings have strong resonances with this story (something that is brought out even more clearly in John's account; see 6.1–15, 22–59), with Jesus' extensive reflections on the bread of life. Even here, however, we find the idea of many people being fed miraculously in the wilderness as an outpouring of God's care.

Wilderness places are often, throughout the Bible, regarded as places for rest and recovery. Probably the most famous of these is illustrated by Elijah's fleeing across the desert after his battle with Jezebel and the prophets of Baal. He fell down exhausted in the desert to be awoken by an angel who urged him to eat. This idea that a wilderness place is not just barren and desolate but can also provide rest and recuperation is important. It raises a question for those of us in need of rest and recuperation, who do not live within easy reach of anything similar to a wilderness, of what could provide the same effect.

For more on the significance of the wilderness in the Bible, see the box, 'Wilderness', on p. 24.

Another biblical resonance

Another story, which it is hard not to think about while reading this one, is that of Elisha feeding 100 people in 2 Kings 4.42–44. In that account, someone came to Elisha bringing food from the first-fruit offering, which included 20 loaves of bread and fresh ears of grain. Elisha commanded that it should be given to the people but his servant objected on the grounds that there was not enough. In verse 43, Elisha insisted: 'for thus says the LORD, "They shall eat and have some left"' (which they did). Jesus is so often thought of in connection with Elijah; it is therefore interesting to see such a clear parallel with the life of Elisha here.

Hurried there on foot

One can imagine the horror of the disciples, who had got into the boat thinking they were getting away from the pressures all around them, only to discover a vast crowd waiting for them when they arrived. As the crowd could run faster than the boat could sail, the site was probably just round the coast from Capernaum. Traditionally, the place has been identified as Tabgha, five miles to the west of Capernaum. Luke's Gospel, however, locates it near Bethsaida, seven miles east of Capernaum. The problem for Mark's account of this location is that he records the disciples going towards Bethsaida in the boat in 6.45. This suggests that the traditional location is more likely, at least in Mark's version.

It should be noted that all the Gospel writers get a little confused regarding geography (though all slightly differently), which means it is difficult to tie down precise locations for these events.

Sheep without a shepherd

Jesus' compassion is something that breathes through these stories. He cares for those whom society largely forgets or ignores and restores them to their places within those communities. It is interesting, therefore, that Jesus also has compassion on this large crowd. His concern for them is as vibrant as for individuals. His solution? Teaching. Unlike in Matthew and

Luke, which provide a good few chapters of the content of Jesus' teaching, Mark does not provide it. We are left to imagine what he says to the crowd that leaves them so enrapt that they stay late listening to him.

The description of the people being like sheep without a shepherd is an easily recognizable theme from the Old Testament. It is used, for example, of the people of God in the wilderness when Joshua was appointed to lead them (Num. 27.17); of Ahab's army after his death (1 Kings 22.17); and by Ezekiel for the people in exile whose leaders had failed them (Ezek. 34.5). In other words, it is much more of a criticism of the leaders than of the people. We have noted, so far, the opposition of the leaders (Pharisees, scribes, Herodians) to Jesus; unsurprisingly, this phrase reveals that Jesus was as critical of them as they were of him.

'You give them bread'

It is hard not to feel sorry for the disciples. The prospect of needing to feed 5,000 people when it is late and in the middle of nowhere would cause few people pleasure. The context, however, suggests that Jesus is testing what they have learnt during their mission of a few verses earlier. There they were sent out to be as Jesus was in the surrounding villages. The question is whether they would be able to. The dynamic is a familiar one. If there is someone around, whom we know can do things, we usually leave it to them. Jesus is challenging them here to join him as partners; but they already have sunk back into passively expecting Jesus to solve all problems (as, indeed, they did in the middle of the storm).

Ultimately, Jesus does solve the issue, but he still insists on their assistance first. Even though their contribution is infinitesimally small, given the size of the challenge, he still requires it. This is an important dynamic. Even though God can do everything, and could do everything alone, God chooses to include us in the action. Even if what we can contribute is as small as the disciples' offering, God still wants it. Our walk with God is not about passivity: waiting for God to solve every problem that crosses our path. We are always involved. When we face challenges in our lives, we should always expect to hear the insistent demand (or its equivalent): 'You give them bread.'

Loaves and fishes

Although John's Gospel identifies the source of the bread as a young boy (John 6.9), Mark gives no indication of where the supplies came from. The implication is that the disciples already had them.

From what we know of food at the time, the loaves would probably have been flatbreads of a similar size to a pitta bread. The fish was most likely preserved. Magdala was known in Greek as Tarichaea (which refers to fish that was preserved by salting and/or drying) and in Aramaic as Migdal Nunayya ('Tower of Fish', which probably indicates the towers used for drying fish). In other words, there was a place around 13 miles south-west of Capernaum that became wealthy because of its fish preservation techniques. It was, therefore, entirely likely that people would carry preserved fish with them for occasions when they needed food.

A banquet

Hints of a banquet are woven through Mark's account here.

- They sit down: *sumposia, sumposia* (see 'Interesting words', vv. 39–40, on p. 147). Over time, in Greek literature, *sumposia* came to refer to a banquet.
- They sit down on the *green* grass. As noted above, this could simply point us to the time of year; but, in the context of Jesus' thinking that the people were like sheep without a shepherd, it calls to mind Psalm 23. There, the psalmist talks of the Lord making him 'lie down in green pastures'. The end of that psalm (vv. 5–6) moves on to mention a banquet.
- After everyone has finished eating, they are 'filled' (v. 42): language, again, that would be used at a banquet.

As a result, the contrast is stark between Herod Antipas' banquet, which led to excess, rash promises and the killing of John the Baptist (which Herod had not wanted to do), and this messianic banquet for thousands of people, fed and satisfied by Jesus' generosity.

Took; blessed; broke; gave

In John's discourse about the feeding of the 5,000 (6.22–59), Jesus makes the eucharistic parallels explicit by talking about the bread of life and encouraging those who are following him to eat his flesh and drink his blood. Mark, by contrast, does what he often does: he shows rather than tells. The four verbs ('took', 'blessed', 'broke', 'gave') are replicated in the institution of the Last Supper (14.22), when Jesus again takes bread, blesses it, breaks it and gives it to his disciples.

The question of what Jesus blessed is sometimes raised. The verb 'to bless' is used here without an object so we are left to guess whether he blessed the bread or God. Many commentators observe that the most obvious conclusion is that he was blessing God, which happened at the start of every meal when the host would say: 'Blessed are you, O Lord our God,

King of the Universe, who brings forth bread from the earth.' It also makes sense of Jesus' lifting his eyes to heaven (v. 41).

Twelve baskets

The baskets were of a large, heavy type (called *kophinos*) designed for carrying substantial loads. This raises the question of why, if they had no food, did they happen to have 12 big baskets with them. There are at least two options:

- The boat they came in had baskets in it for carrying the fish;

Or

- The measurement was notional: there was so much left over that, had they had baskets, it would have filled 12 of them.

Either is possible.

Some commentators make a point of the type of basket referred to here. *Kophinos* was used in Roman texts, in a derogatory way (see Juvenal, *Satires* 3.14), for the typical large basket a Jewish peasant would carry. This is in contrast to the basket mentioned in the feeding of the 4,000, which had no such connotations. Whether this is significant or not is hard to judge.

Mark 6.45–52: Boat II. They did not understand about the loaves

The boat scene that we find here is remarkably similar to the one at the end of Mark 4.35–41. It is so similar that it is easy to get the two confused. It almost seems as though it has been included as a review narrative. The disciples heard everything in private from Jesus but hadn't, in the stilling of the storm, managed to work out who he was and how to respond to him. So they accompanied Jesus and saw more of who he was when he dramatically cast out many demons; healed a woman and a young girl; and provided a banquet, leaving 5,000 people satisfied. We now turn to see how their learning had progressed. They had not made much progress. So, following this, we see more of who Jesus was, with two more healings and another miraculous provision of food, this time for 4,000, rather than 5,000, people.

As with the previous story set in a boat, it is late; but this time, Jesus is not with the disciples. The wind isn't as bad as before but, while they row, Jesus passes them, walking on the water. As in the previous boat account, they are terrified and then astounded when Jesus gets into the boat with them. As before, he calms the wind.

Links backwards

- Jesus' telling of the parable of the sower hangs in the background here (but is even more obvious in the third boat scene), when he talks about those outside listening but not understanding (Mark 4.12).
- The parallels between the stilling of the storm (4.35–41) and the walking on the water are striking.

Links forwards

- The third account set in a boat (8.11–21) is where the themes being explored in this passage reach a climax.

Interesting words ...

- v. 45: *made*. This is a surprisingly strong word. *Anagkazō* means 'to compel' or 'to force'. What we aren't told is why Jesus was so keen that they left.
- v. 45: *the other side*. This is the fourth use of the phrase *to peran* in Mark. See the box, 'To the other side', on p. 111, for more on its significance.
- vv. 45–46: *he dismissed; saying farewell*. *Apoluō* has a strong sense of dismissing or letting go; *apotassō* is a much gentler word meaning 'to bid adieu'. For more on what is going on in these verses, see pp. 153–4.
- v. 46: *pray*. The word *proseuchomai*, which means 'to prostrate oneself', 'to bow down', 'to worship' or 'to pray', when used elsewhere causes discussions among scholars about precisely what is meant by the word. There is no discussion here. All assume Jesus was praying.
- v. 48: *straining*. The verb *basanizō* means more than just straining: it is most commonly used to describe torment or torture. The idea is that this was not just an ordinarily strong wind but one so strong that it tortured the disciples as they rowed against it. Bearing in mind a good number of them were fishermen used to the lake, this was a wind that was close to a storm.
- v. 48: *at the oars*. In the Greek, the word 'oar' isn't really used here: it is read into the text. *Elaunō* means 'to make progress' or 'to drive along'. So they were being tortured during their progress, probably by rowing.
- v. 48: *early in the morning*. The fourth watch (*tetartos phulakē*) refers to around 3–6 a.m. The Romans split the night into four watches: first (6–9 p.m.), second (9 p.m. – 12 a.m.), third (12–3 a.m.) and fourth (3–6 a.m.).
- v. 48: *walking*. The verb *peripateō*, from which we get the English word 'peripatetic', means 'to walk around'.
- v. 48: *pass them by*. One of the conundrums of this passage rests on what

parerchomai is taken to mean. It can mean 'pass by' or simply 'pass' (that is, 'overtake') or 'pass unnoticed' (which seems unlikely if you are walking on the water). For more on this, see p. 155.

- v. 49: *thought. Dokeō* has the sense of 'to think' or 'to suppose'.
- v. 49: *ghost*. A *phantasma* was an apparition or a phantom.
- v. 49: *cried out. Anakrazō* means 'to raise the voice and make a loud noise'. 'Screamed' would be a good word to use here.
- v. 50: *terrified*. By now, in Mark, we are accustomed to the word *phobos* or *phobeō* ('fear' or 'to be afraid'). These words are not used here. Instead, *tarassō* is used, which is much stronger; it means 'disturbed', 'agitated' or 'thrown into complete disorder'.
- v. 50: *take heart. Tharseō* means 'to have courage'.
- v. 50: *It is I*. In John's Gospel, the phrase *egō eimi* has huge theological significance but in Mark less so. It probably just means 'it's me' here.
- v. 50: *do not be afraid*. Here, Jesus tells them not to be afraid (*phobeō*).
- v. 51: *astounded*. This is another of Mark's 'astounded/astonished' words (*existēmi*). For more on this, see the notes on 1.22 and 27 (pp. 41–2).
- v. 52: *hardened. Pōroō* means 'to ossify' or 'to petrify' (it was what happened to those who were gazed upon by Medusa): to cause a stone to form and hence to be insensible.

Immediately he compelled them to go; dismissed the crowd and said farewell

There are several odd features, at the start of this passage, including why Jesus was so insistent that the disciples left quickly; why he then went to dismiss the crowd alone; and finally, when he had done so, whom he said farewell to (v. 46).

There are various theories about what is going on.

- One draws on John 6.14–15. There, after the feeding, the crowd wanted to take Jesus by force and make him king, so he withdrew by himself to avoid this. Some commentators argue that Jesus wanted to get the disciples away lest they tell the crowd about the miracle that had just happened, causing the crowd to try to make him king.
- Connected to this theory, some comment that the 5,000 who were fed were solely men; and, therefore, that they had come together with the aim of being a rebellious force. Jesus wanted the disciples to leave lest they became affected by the spirit of the insurgency of 5,000 gathered men.
- A third option is simply that Jesus, at this point, needed time by himself up a mountain to pray and recuperate. Dismissing everyone so firmly allowed him to do this.

As Mark makes nothing of a possible insurrection here, it seems most likely that the third option was what happened and that verse 46 should begin a new paragraph. Jesus compelled the disciples to leave and dismissed the crowd. Once he'd said farewell to everyone, he went up the mount to pray, as was so important to him.

To Bethsaida ... they came to land at Gennesaret

We have noted already some of the confused geography that appears in Mark's Gospel. There is no more confused geography than in this (and the next) episode. Bethsaida is at the north-east corner of the Sea of Galilee, a little east of the River Jordan; Gennesaret is between Capernaum and Magdala on the north-western side of the lake. Again, various solutions have been proposed:

- Mark got confused and, in line with Luke, the feeding took place near Bethsaida. So they were leaving Bethsaida and heading to Capernaum when the wind blew them off course.
- There were two Bethsaidas: the one we know about and one not recorded anywhere else. This second one is near Capernaum. They were heading there when they were blown off course.
- Jesus sent them to Bethsaida but said that if he didn't arrive, they should head back to Capernaum. They went, waited a few hours and then did as he said but the wind blew them off course.

Various combinations of these theories have been proposed. In my view, two things should be borne in mind: that Mark was not writing his account with a map in front of him, so sometimes the geography gets a little confused, and that the strong wind would have blown the disciples' boat off course (something all theories account for).

There is a similar issue with the timing. The feeding took place, probably late in the afternoon, so it is odd that the disciples are still in the middle of the lake at 3 a.m. The odd geography and timings suggest that we do not have all the details of what the disciples did after the feeding miracle (and that we shouldn't worry about it too much).

He saw that they were straining ... he intended to pass them by

Mark does not explain why it is that Jesus could see how difficult their crossing was while he was up a mountain, and they were in the middle of the lake at night. We are left to presume that the Jesus who felt so much compassion for a crowd he had never met also knew when his followers were in need in the middle of the lake. Having said that, however, the oddest feature of this story is that he discerned that they were in need, went to them, but then appeared to intend to pass them by.

The crucial question (see 'Interesting words', v. 48, on pp. 152–3) is what the verb *parerchomai* means. If it means 'pass them', it would make more sense as that would draw him to their attention. Another option is that we are to read this in the light of the Old Testament tradition. For example, in Exodus 33.18–23 or 1 Kings 19.10–12, when God tells Moses and Elijah, respectively, that he will pass them by and so reveal his glory. Here also, Jesus was revealing his glory; but the disciples, instead of recognizing that, were terrified and assumed he was an apparition instead.

'Take heart, it is I; do not be afraid'

Jesus' statement to the disciples has resonances with the stilling of the storm. The opposite of being timid is to have courage. On the earlier occasion, he expressed surprise at their timidity; now, he exhorts them to have courage. This seems to be the marker of what Jesus is looking for in his followers.

They had not understood about the loaves

These boat scenes reveal to us what Jesus expected the disciples to have begun to learn about his nature. He had power over the wind (and hence the sea, like God at creation); he had power over demons; and most recently, like God in the wilderness, provided manna for his people. They should have begun to make the connections from what they saw; but instead their hearts were hardened. In Exodus 7.3 and subsequent passages, we are told that Pharoah's heart was hardened, as were the hearts of the Pharisees in Mark 10.5. The disciples, whom we imagine to be on the 'inside' after the statement about Jesus' teaching to them in Mark 4.34, were beginning to look as though they might fit better on the outside.

It is worth noting the word 'astounded/astonished' here as well. Until chapter 6, the implication of the astonishment of the crowd is that they were receptive to Jesus and his teaching; but in 6.6, Jesus was amazed at the unbelief of the people of his home town. Here, the disciples were astounded at Jesus. A more negative hint begins to emerge that links astonishment to an inability to comprehend.

Mark 6.53–56: More healings

This is the third brief summary of Jesus' healing ministry. The first was in 1.32–34, the second in 3.7–12. The effect is to remind us that, although the healing of individuals was important and described carefully by Mark to introduce us to something key about the character of Jesus, Mark is at pains to remind us that Jesus also healed large numbers of people wherever he went.

Links backwards

- Two previous summaries of Jesus' healing of many people can be found in Mark 1.32–34 and 3.7–12. Mark's love of 'threes' means he provides three similar scenarios.

Interesting words ...

- v. 53: *when they had crossed over. Diaperaō* is the verb connected to *to peran*, the phrase we are used to seeing that means 'the other side'.
- v. 53: *moored.* Although we are very familiar with Jesus and the disciples travelling by boat, the word for 'moor' occurs only here in the Gospels. *Prosormizō* means 'to bring a ship to anchor' or 'to moor a boat'.
- v. 54: *recognized. Epiginōskō* is a compound verb from *ginōskō* ('to know') and *epi* ('on' or 'upon'), which is used to mean 'to look upon' and hence 'to recognize'.
- v. 55: *rushed about.* On p. 146, see v. 33 for *suntrechō* ('to run together'), which was how the people got to the deserted place before Jesus arrived in the boat. We now have *peritrechō* ('to run about').
- v. 55: *mats.* The plural version of the word is used here that was used for the mat the man was brought on by his four friends in 2.1–12. A *krabattos* can mean a mattress but here is more likely to mean 'pallet' or 'mat'.
- v. 55: *sick.* See the note on 1.32 (p. 49) about the use of *kakōs* ('badly') for someone who was ill.
- v. 56: *village, cities, farms.* The description is of different types of place: a non-walled village (*kōmē*); a city (*polis*); a field (*agros*). In other words, he travelled from open countryside to small villages to the large cities of the region (such as Sepphoris or Tiberias, even though they are not mentioned by name).
- v. 56: *marketplaces.* An *agora* was both the marketplace and where all public events took place.
- v. 56: *fringe of his cloak.* Although not used in Mark's version of the woman who was bleeding, the hem of his garment is used here (it is used in both Matt. 5.20 and Luke 8.44). The *kraspedon* can mean 'edge' but more likely means the

tassels (*tzitzit*) that a Jewish man was required to wear by law; and *himation* refers to his outer garment.

- v. 56: *healed*. There are a range of different words for 'heal' in Greek. This one, *sōzō*, can also mean 'to save'. For more on this, see the box, 'Words for "heal" in Mark's Gospel', on p. 50.

See the discussion on p. 154 for the challenges presented here by Mark's geography.

Gennesaret

The region of Gennesaret was described by Josephus in *Jewish War* (3.10.8) as being especially fertile. Its

> nature is wonderful as well as its beauty; its soil is so fruitful that all sorts of trees can grow upon it ... One may call this place the ambition of nature, where it forces those plants that are naturally enemies to one another to agree together.

The purpose of this summary seems to be a reminder that Jesus did most of his healings in Jewish territory. There is no better place to remind us of this than at Gennesaret, the quintessential heart of Galilee (so much so, that the Sea of Galilee was called by some – including Josephus and Luke – Lake Gennesaret, after the region). After these healings, Jesus healed two Gentiles (a woman's daughter from Tyre, in 7.24–30, and a man from the Decapolis, in 7.31–37).

The tassels on his robe

Jesus' presence was what brought healing to those who were sick. In this story (as in 5.21–34), his clothing became an extension of him. What strikes me, in this passage, is the exhaustion that Jesus must have felt. If he felt the power go out of him when one woman touched his cloak, how exhausting must the touch of the many people described here have been?

Mark 7.1–23: What counted as unclean?

Mark has a clever technique of including something that appears to be an entire digression, which, in reality, sets up the next theme that he will explore. Leading up to this passage, uncleanness/impurity has swirled around the background of the stories about the healing of the man in the tombs, the woman who was bleeding and the girl who was believed to be dead. After this discussion, Jesus went on to heal two more 'unclean' people, so the theme of impurity – and what it really was – is presented to us here.

There are two interlinked, but fundamentally separate, topics explored in this debate.

1 The first topic, addressed to the Pharisees, is about the emphasis they placed on oral law, which, Jesus claimed, took precedence over their observance of Torah.
2 The question asked by the Pharisees about impurity was answered by Jesus but, oddly, addressed to the crowd and then the disciples (v. 14 onwards).

This is another example of Mark's sandwich technique. Jesus was asked about impurity but his critique of the Pharisees' overdependence on oral law was inserted before he answered the original question.

Links backwards and forwards

- We are reminded in this passage of the many conflicts with the Jewish leaders, both before this passage (Mark 2.1–11, 23–28; 3.1–6) and after it (11.27–33; 12.1–12, 13–24; 14.53–65).
- The theme of impurity has already arisen, with the healing of the man from Gerasa (5.1–20), the woman who bled for 12 years (5.25–34) and Jarius' daughter (5.21–24 and 35–43). It will continue after this passage, when Jesus heals the daughter of a woman from Tyre (7.24–30) and a man from the Decapolis (7.31–37), both Gentiles.
- The theme of understanding emerges again in this passage, reminding us of Jesus' teaching in the parable of the sower (4.12); the comment about the disciples' lack of understanding (6.52); and Jesus' question to the disciples in the third boat scene (8.17).

Interesting words …

- v. 1: *gathered around him. Sunagō* means 'to assemble' or 'to gather together' (the noun connected to the verb is *sunagōgē*: 'synagogue').

- vv. 2 and 5: *defiled. Koinos* means 'common' or 'shared' but came to be used in Judaism to refer to anything that was ritually impure. Koinē Greek (otherwise known as New Testament Greek) was called that because it was regarded as 'common', low in quality, by Greek experts.
- v. 3: *thoroughly wash their hands*. Mark uses a phrase here that no one quite understands. Literally, it reads: 'except (*ean mē*) by the fist (*pugmēi*) they wash (*niptō*)'. It appears to be a colloquial phrase that is hard to capture in English. The context suggests thorough washing. So it probably means 'to wash the whole arm from the fist region upwards'.
- v. 3: *observing*. The verb *krateō* means 'to hold fast to', which has a little more depth than just 'observe'.
- v. 3: *tradition. Paradosis* means, literally, 'hand along' or 'hand down'. So a tradition is something that has been handed along.
- v. 4: *wash*. The word for 'to wash' is *baptizō*, which helpfully points to the close connection between baptism and ritual washing. This could be translated as 'immersed themselves': namely, immersing themselves in a ritual cleansing pool (known in Hebrew as a *mikveh*).
- v. 4: *cups, pots, and bronze kettles*. A *potērion* (cup) is a drinking vessel; a *xestēs* (pot) is a jug; and a *chalkion* ('bronze kettle') refers to anything bronze, which, here, might mean a kettle or a cauldron. A good number of ancient manuscripts also add *klinē* (bed) on to the end of this list.
- v. 5: *asked. Eperōtaō* most often means 'to put a formal question to someone'. 'Interrogate' might be closer to the true sense.
- v. 5: *live*. The word *peripateō* ('to walk around') is used here.
- v. 6: *hypocrites*. The word *hupokritēs* comes from Greek theatre. A *hupokritēs* wore a mask and so was a pretender, dissembler or hypocrite.
- v. 6: *far from*. The words are *porrō* ('far' or 'too far') and *apexō* ('to keep away from'). So, literally, the clause reads 'their heart keeps too far away from me'.
- v. 7: *in vain do they worship me. Matēn* means 'to no end' and the word for 'worship' is not the usual *proseuchomai* but *sebomai*: 'to honour', 'to revere', 'to pay homage to'; that is, 'they honour me to no end'.
- v. 7: *teaching human precepts as doctrines*. Literally, 'Teaching (*didaskō*) teachings (*didaskalia*) of human beings (*anthrōpos*) as commandments (*entolē*).'
- v. 9: *fine*. This is an adverb: *kalōs* ('finely' or 'splendidly').
- v. 10: *speaks evil*. This is a compound verb: *kakologeō* 'to speak evil of' or 'to insult'.
- v. 11: *Corban (that is, an offering to God)*. The Hebrew word *qorban* is here put into Greek letters. Mark then needs to explain the word to his Greek-speaking audience and uses the word *dōron*, which means 'gift' or 'offering'. The words 'to God' are not in the Greek. It really reads 'Corban, which means gift'. For more on what Corban means, see '*Qorban* and honouring parents', on p. 162 (I use the Hebrew spelling when discussing *qorban*).
- v. 13: *making void*. The verb *akuroō* means 'to cancel', 'to set aside' or 'to treat as having no effect'.
- v. 14: *listen*. This is the first major section of teaching to be included in Mark since the parable of the sower, so it is worth noting that they both begin in the same way: 'listen' (*akouō*).

- v. 14: *understand*. The verb 'to understand', *suniēmi*, means 'to bring together', 'to perceive' and hence 'to understand'.
- v. 14: *going in; come out*. *Eisporeuomai* and *ekporeuomai* are the words you would use for going in and out of a building, or something similar.
- v. 15: *defile*. This is the verb *koinoō*, which is connected to the adjective *koinos* that we saw in verses 2 and 5.
- v. 17: *the house*. The NRSV translation is a little misleading here. Mention of 'the house' suggests that Jesus and his disciples have returned to Capernaum and to Simon Peter's house. However, the Greek merely says 'a house' and has no such implication.
- v. 17: *asked*. The word used for the disciples asking Jesus (*eperōtaō*) is the same one used for the Pharisees' question in verse 5.
- v. 17: *parable*. This is the usual word for 'parable' (*parabolē*).
- v. 18: *fail to understand*. This is an adjective: *asunetos* ('void of understanding' or 'witless'). It is not a very complementary word.
- v. 19: *sewer*. *Aphedrōn* does not mean 'sewer' (as sewers didn't exist at that time) but 'toilet' or 'latrine'.
- v. 18: *declared ... clean*. *Katharizō*, connected to our word 'cathartic', means 'to make or declare clean'.
- vv. 21–22: has such a number of words that I will list them in the order of the NRSV translation with, in the same brackets, additional meanings when relevant.

  Evil (*kakos*) intentions (*dialogismos*: 'calculation', this is a word connected to finance); fornication (*porneia*: sexual sin of any kind); theft (*klopē*: 'fraud'); murder (*phonos*: 'slaughter'); adultery (*moicheia*); avarice (*pleonexia*: 'greediness', 'assumption', 'advantage' or 'arrogance'); wickedness (*ponēria*: 'baseness' or 'knavery'); deceit (*dolos*: 'bait', 'trickery' or 'cunning'); licentiousness (*aselgeia*: 'wanton violence'); envy (*ophthalmos ponēros*: 'evil before the eyes'); slander (*blasphēmia*: 'profane speech', 'word of evil omen' or 'defamation'); pride (*huperphania*: 'arrogance' or 'contempt'); folly (*aphrosunē*: 'thoughtlessness').

The Pharisees and scribes from Jerusalem

For more on the scribes, see the box on p. 43, and on the Pharisees, see the box on p. 68.

What is unclear is precisely who came from Jerusalem. In Mark 2.23–27, a group of Pharisees were the ones who challenged Jesus' disciples about plucking corn on the sabbath; and, in Mark 3.22–30, a group of scribes, from Jerusalem, accused Jesus of 'having' Beelzebul. This confrontation is clearly a continuation of both conflicts. The question is whether the local Pharisees (2.23–27) have joined with the scribes from Jerusalem (3.22–30) to form a single group or whether this is a different group made up of Pharisees and scribes exclusively from Jerusalem. The fact that that the debate begins with a criticism of the actions of Jesus' disciples, as it does in 2.23–27, suggests that the two groups have now joined forces.

Oral law and Torah

On a certain level, one of Jesus' criticisms of his opponents here is factually correct. The Pharisees believed that when God gave the law to Moses on Mount Sinai, as well as the written Law (which became the Torah), he also gave the oral law. They believed that God did not give Moses everything that later comprised the oral law but provided a framework that allowed later rabbis to interpret it. After the fall of the temple in Jerusalem in AD 70, Rabbinic Judaism (largely, though not entirely) continued onwards from Pharisaism, preserving the tradition of the oral law. It endured down the generations by word of mouth, eventually being written down in the Mishnah, which dates to around the second century AD. Later, further interpretation of the Mishnah was codified as the Talmud in two versions: the Jerusalem Talmud (completed around the fifth century AD) and the Babylonian Talmud (completed around the seventh century AD). Together with the Torah, these collections of oral law are known collectively within Judaism as the Halakah.

The purpose of the oral law is stated, at the beginning of one of the Mishnah's tractates (*Pirkei Abot* 1.1), as putting 'a fence around Torah'. That is, to provide for the fact that the Torah does not offer enough detail to make it possible to follow it in every aspect of life. For example, the Torah says that it is not permitted to work on the sabbath; but precisely what this means is unclear. The Halakah fills in details to prevent people from unintentionally violating the commands of the Torah.

The Pharisees of Jesus' day were very much using the oral law, which had been handed down to them as tradition, to guide their practices of everyday living. It is very clear that the rules about handwashing (and, indeed, the cleansing of implements too) came from the oral law, not the Torah. The only command about handwashing in the Torah is the requirement for priests to wash their hands ceremonially before entering the tent of meeting or offering a sacrifice (see Ex. 30.20–21). Since the Pharisees believed that all Jews were called to keep a similar level of purity to the priesthood, they expanded the 'washing' requirements to everyday life.

The Pharisees would have considered Jesus' criticisms of the oral law to be unfair, since they would argue that it grew out of the Torah and did not replace it. Jesus' point here, however, seems to be that the oral law had grown so far away from the Torah that following some of the oral law's elements placed people in direct contravention with the commands of the Torah. I suspect the Pharisees would have disagreed with this judgement.

All the Jewish people

In explaining the purity practices to his Gentile readers, Mark somewhat overclaims their widespread nature. There is no evidence at all that Jews observed them in this period. It is probable that the practices were becoming more widespread: for example, the *Letter of Aristeas to Philocrates* – a document dated to the third to second centuries BC (which tells the legendary story of the translation of the Hebrew Scriptures into the Greek Septuagint) – claims that the translators washed their hands during prayers 'as is the custom of all the Jews' (*Letter of Aristeas* 305). Nevertheless, to claim, as Mark does, that all Jews did it is an overstatement.

They do not eat anything from the market unless they wash it

The NRSV translation is probably a little misleading here. It isn't entirely clear what is washed when people return from the marketplace. It might be the cups, jugs and pots or it might be themselves. The most obvious answer would be themselves: they would ritually purify themselves because they would not know whom they'd touched while out. If so, this sentence would mean '[Coming] from the marketplace, they do not eat unless they wash.'

Qorban *and honouring parents*

Rather than being an answer to the Pharisees' initial question about impurity, the example that Jesus used here was an illustration to prove his point that they cared more about the oral law than about the Torah.

The concept of *qorban* is a complicated one; but it does seem to have been used extensively in this period. Mishnah *Nedarim* is entirely dedicated to discussing the regulations that governed how to handle vows that then, subsequently, prevented something existing for normal use. In particular, it discusses vows that deny certain people from benefiting from some property, money or food. Interestingly, the word *qorban* appears throughout the tractate alongside another word, *qonam*. It seems that oaths could be sworn about all sorts of things, with some things dedicated to God; other things not. Once the category was invoked, it would mean that a particular person or group would not benefit from the item declared *qorban* or *qonam*. If this were done regarding produce from a field, for example, it would mean that the named people, here the parents of the person concerned, would be unable to eat anything from that field. Simply saying *qorban* (or *qonam*) meant that the vow was binding and couldn't be undone. Mishnah *Nedarim* focuses around how to handle vows that were irresponsibly made or badly thought through; and discussions reflect on the conditions under which someone could be released from their vow.

It is fascinating that Jesus refers directly to a knotty issue that we know, from the Mishnah, was of great concern in this period. The Mishnah is made up of cases studies and the decisions of rabbis about how to handle such cases. One of the live discussions in Mishnah *Nedarim* are the grounds upon which someone could revoke such an oath. Some rabbis said they could be revoked; others said they could not.

It seems from this discussion that Jesus was bringing up a particular case that he knew about. Perhaps he was aware of someone who had done exactly this: they had said *qorban*, which tied them by an oath, and because they had done so their parents were left uncared for. It might have been that one of the rabbis in the group from the Pharisees had ruled that the *qorban* oath could not be revoked, and Jesus knew that and raised it as a 'hot topic' of the day. It might explain what would appear to be his fury at the injustice of it all.

What is unclear is why people declared things to be *qorban* or *qonam*. It makes more sense in the case of Nazirites – those who dedicated themselves to God in a life of holiness and purity (people would probably have done this by declaring *qorban*) – but why anyone else would do it is less clear. It seems to be a custom that grew up and was widely practised; and from *m. Nedarim*, it appears to have had more of a negative motivation than a positive one, with the intention of preventing certain people from benefiting from something.

This is one of those (rare) occasions in the Gospels when the issue being addressed is so topical it is hard to see how or, indeed, whether it has bearing on life today. It is, however, always worth asking ourselves which commonly accepted practices or attitudes affect our ability to care for the vulnerable in the way that Jesus would have wanted. If declaring something *qorban* was to some extent fashionable, it challenges us to ask what customs we have that are similarly fashionable (or so accepted that we no longer notice them) and that have a similar effect.

It's not what goes in that is the problem, but what comes out

In his teaching here, Jesus directly contradicts the teaching in Leviticus 11 and 17, which makes it clear that eating 'unclean' animals will make the eater unclean. Against the backdrop of Jesus' day, this teaching is among his most radical. It might help us to have Matthew's formula from the Sermon on the Mount in our minds: 'You have heard that it was said … But I say to you …' Jesus is specifically and directly changing the teaching of the Torah by what he says here. It is interesting to note that Matthew's parallel account expresses Jesus' view more gently than Mark's does and avoids saying Jesus declared all foods clean.

This issue of dietary requirements continued to be a live issue in early Christian communities. Indeed, it was a major bone of contention between James, Peter and Paul (see, for example, Acts 15.19–20; Gal. 2.11–14).

The stomach and the heart

We gain, through this teaching, an interesting insight into Jewish attitudes towards the stomach and the heart.

The stomach (which was taken to refer to all digestive organs, including the intestines) was the recipient of food and processed it, brought out the nutrients for the body and sent the rest onwards to the toilet. Elsewhere in rabbinic teaching, the stomach was regarded as being a 'poor organ', subservient to the heart, which was a 'rich' organ. The stomach was where emotion was felt (hence the word for Jesus' feeling compassion being *splangchnizō* – a movement of the bowels). The heart, by contrast, was where decisions were made and the will was located (see, for example, Ps. 19.14: 'Let the words of my mouth and the meditation of my heart be acceptable to you, O LORD'). Jesus' point, therefore, resonated with the physiology of the day. Food simply went into the 'poor' organ; what really mattered was what was going on in the 'rich' organ – the heart.

The parable

It is fascinating that the disciples referred to Jesus' teaching about what goes in and comes out of a person as a parable. For people interested in the nature of parables, this challenges definitions that rely on parables being solely narrative in form. This falls closer to a riddle than a story. The significance of Jesus' point in 7.15 ('there is nothing outside a person that by going in can defile, but the things that come out are what defile') is that, like all parables, it requires reflection and refers not just to the particular issue referenced in this discussion.

Are you so witless?

The NRSV makes Jesus' comment to the disciples in verse 18 much less cutting than in the Greek. 'Do you also fail to understand?' is much gentler than 'Are you so witless?' It is worth noting it here because the sentiment is picked up again in 8.11–21. The emphasis on 'understanding' is crucial in this part of Mark. In some ways, though not all, this discussion mirrors the parable of the sower: a parable is told by Jesus to the crowd and the disciples then ask him more about it in private. The theme of the importance of understanding runs through both accounts.

Evil intentions

Although vice lists are common in the epistles (Gal. 5.19–21; 1 Cor. 6.9–10; Rom. 1.29–31; 2 Tim. 3.1–5; Col. 3.5–8 and 1 Peter 2.1), this is the only one in the Gospels (along with the shorter version found in the parallel passage in Matt. 15.19).

The heading indicates that all the immoral behaviours in the list are held under the umbrella of evil calculations that come from the heart. There then follow 12 words: the first six are plural (fornications, thefts, murders, adulteries, avarices, wickednesses) and so refer to actions; the second six are singular and indicate attitudes (deceit, licentiousness, envy, slander, pride, folly). For alternative translations of these words, see 'Interesting words', vv. 21–22, on p. 160.

It is important to recognize that Jesus includes both behaviours and attitudes here. If we are tempted to feel smug because we haven't actually done any of the first six, the second six hit us with full force (and are reminiscent of the Sermon on the Mount): just thinking evil is enough. These intentions, Jesus says, are what we should be really worrying about.

The logic of Jesus' discussion here

One of the key issues is to decide how Jesus' argument works here (though some do consider the two sections, 7.6–13 and 7.14–23, to be entirely separate and not connected at all).

It is possible, however, to view them together. If you do, this is how the argument goes: the Pharisees criticize the disciples for not following their traditions; the Torah commands people to care for their parents; the traditions allow people who have invoked *qorban* not to care for their parents; therefore, the tradition is flawed and the disciples do not need to follow it.

Mark 7.24–30: Jesus healed the daughter of a woman from Tyre

The next two stories are ones in which Jesus heals people who are Gentiles. The first concerns a woman from Tyre, who is therefore a Phoenician; the second Gentile is a man from the Decapolis (the second from there, as the first one was the man from Gerasa).

With Mark's love of threes, it is worth noticing that his story features three young girls: Jairus' daughter, Herodias' daughter and this woman's daughter. Jairus' daughter and this woman's daughter are joined in the use of the same word, *thugatrion* ('little daughter'). Jairus' daughter is also termed a *korasion* ('little girl'), which is the same word used for Herodias' daughter. Three young girls – two are beloved and cherished, while the middle one is sucked into her mother's plan for revenge.

Links backwards

- An earlier story featuring a man from the Decapolis is found in Mark 5.1–20, where Jesus cast out Legion from the man of Gerasa.
- As noted above, this story brings to mind two other stories that feature young girls: Jairus' daughter (5.21–24, 35–43) and Herodias' daughter (6.14–29). There are three consecutive chapters, with a story of a young girl in each.

Links backwards and forwards

- The mention of bread here, located as it is between the feeding of the 5,000 (6.30–44) and the feeding of the 4,000 (8.1–10), reminds us that bread is something that Jesus can supply in large, feast-like quantities.
- This healing is the fourth in the string of healings of individuals that begins with three (the man from Gerasa (5.1–20), the woman who bled for 12 years (5.25–34) and Jairus' daughter (5.21–24, 35–43)); then continues with a chain of two (this one and the deaf man in the Decapolis (7.31–37)); and ends with the healing of the blind man in Bethsaida (8.22–26).

Interesting words ...

- v. 24: *from there he set out and went away*. In Greek, the suffix *then* indicates direction and means 'from'. So *ekeithen* means 'from (*then*) there (*ekei*)'. The stress is on Jesus going somewhere else entirely: 'set out' is translated from *anistēmi* ('arise') and 'went away' from *aperchomai* ('depart').
- v. 25: *little daughter*. The same word (*thugatrion*) is used for Jairus' daughter.
- v. 25: *bowed down*. The verb *prospiptō* is used only three times in Mark: here; in 3.11, to refer to what happened when the unclean spirits saw Jesus; and in 5.33, to describe what the woman who had been bleeding did when Jesus noticed she had touched him.
- v. 26: *Gentile*. Strictly speaking, the word *ellēnis* means someone who participates in Greek culture but who is not necessarily ethnically Greek. There is evidence elsewhere, however, of its being used to refer to 'pagan' women rather than strictly Greek women.
- v. 27: *dogs*. The Greek word *kuranion* means 'little dog' or 'puppy'.
- v. 27: *crumbs*. A *psichion* is a very small piece of food.
- v. 30: *bed*. The word for 'bed' is *klinē*, the usual word for 'bed', as opposed to *krabbaton* ('mattress' or 'pallet'), which we have seen before. It probably refers to a bed that cannot be moved, rather than one that can be carried.

From there

The story has not, yet, moved from Gennesaret. So 'from there' probably means 'from Gennesaret'. The journey to Tyre was around 35 miles and so would have taken from 11 to 12 hours to complete.

Just as when Mark stressed that Jesus and the disciples were going to 'the other side', his strong emphasis here on going away from where they were points to crossing boundaries. This theme becomes very apparent when Jesus crosses geographical, ethnic and gender boundaries to heal the woman's daughter.

Apart from the symbolic significance, Mark does not make clear why Jesus went to Tyre at this point. It is possible that he was attempting to avoid the hostility of the religious leaders following his most recent conflict; but overall, the importance in Mark's account seems to be more symbolic than anything else.

Tyre and Syrophoenicia

Although Tyre and Sidon are often cited together in the Bible, Tyre is 25 miles south of Sidon, on the Mediterranean coast of what is now Lebanon. It is one of the oldest cities in the world (possibly founded as a colony of Sidon in the third millennium BC) and has been inhabited continuously for nearly 5,000 years. By about 1500 BC, it had already established a reputation for the production of 'Tyrian purple', manufactured from murex shellfish and the desired colour of kings, emperors and other people of wealth and importance.

Tyre and Sidon were both in Phoenicia, a network of independent city states, and thrived from maritime trade and the establishment of trade routes. During the Roman period, Tyre was in the Roman province of Syria, hence the term 'Syrophoenician'. It should be said, however, that this is a very unusual term: ethnically the woman was Phoenician; but it is possible that Mark was attempting to distinguish her from the Liby-Phoenicians, who lived in North Africa during this period.

In Matthew's Gospel, the woman is identified as a Canaanite. The term serves as an umbrella description to describe a number of ethnic groupings in Judea, Galilee, Lebanon, Syria and Transjordan. Although the original inhabitants of the Promised Land were Canaanites, so too were the Phoenicians.

Tyre probably had symbolic significance as well. Tyre was condemned passionately by the prophets Isaiah (Isa. 23), Ezekiel (Ezek. 26–28), Amos (Amos 1.9–10) and Zechariah (Zech. 9.2–3) for conceit and greed. A little like the prejudice they had for the Samaritans, a Jewish audience would have known right away that someone from Tyre was not to be trusted.

Uncleanness (again)

The woman who came to ask for Jesus' help was 'unclean' in several ways. In addition to being a woman, she was a Greek speaker and ethnically Syrophoenician; so a Gentile and her daughter would have had an unclean spirit. Hearing this story for the first time, Mark's readers would have known immediately that this was a woman who was an extreme outsider. They might also have thought about her uncleanness and then remembered Jesus' position on impurity espoused in the previous episode.

The parable

Although what Jesus said to the woman is not often counted as a parable, it does fall into that category. This is the only time in the Gospels when someone responded to Jesus 'in parable': that is, extending his original saying by using similar imagery.

In the ancient world, dogs were viewed very differently from the way they are today. In nearly all texts, dogs were regarded with contempt as scavengers. (The only exception to this is the dog in the book of Tobit, which is portrayed as loyal and faithful.) To call someone a dog (whether with the diminutive, 'little dog', or not) was an insult. See, for example, 1 Samuel 17.43, where Goliath asked David whether he (Goliath) was a dog so that David came at him with sticks; or Philippians 3.2, where the Philippians are warned against evil-doers with the phrase 'beware of the dogs'.

Here are a few additional points worth noting.

- The diminutive form of the word 'dog' (*kunarion*) is probably related to the woman's use of the word *thugatrion* rather than to imply cuteness.
- The image is inspired by the feral dogs that would roam the streets, and presumably enter houses too, seeking any small pieces of food that would fall from the table.
- The reference to bread is important. We are between the messianic banquet of the feeding of the 5,000 and that of the feeding of the 4,000. Bread, therefore, has resonances of a banquet spread by God for those he loves.

Was Jesus wrong?

One of the fierce debates that rages about this story is whether Jesus was wrong in his initial attitude to the Gentile woman and allowed himself to be corrected by her. There are people who argue vehemently on all sides of this issue. No help is given by the text itself as to what the correct reading is; ultimately, you will need to decide where you stand on it for yourself.

There are gradations of positions that can be taken. Here are summaries of the two main positions.

1 Jesus was wrong and was corrected by the woman.

   A more intense form of this view describes Jesus as uttering an ethnic slur against the woman. It was the woman's tenacity and bravery that showed him that he was wrong to imagine that the good news was for Jews alone.

   A softer version of this view is that Jesus understood his mission to be for the Jews only and needed his horizons expanding.

2 Jesus was right and offered the woman the chance to express the depth of her faith.

   A more intense form of this view is that Jesus was perfect and it is impossible to imagine a scenario in which he needed to be taught anything.

   A softer version of this is that Jesus' teaching style was to invite people to work things out for themselves and this is a good example of it in practice. His challenging 'parable' was designed to encourage the woman into a demonstration of tenacious faith.

It is worth adding two points here.

- There is no doubt that what Jesus said about dogs was insulting. It isn't possible to explain this away. His opening statement was rude: there is no way round it.
- He had already healed a Gentile (the man from Gerasa) and had just delivered some of his most radical teaching about uncleanness. So to claim that he was focused on a solely Jewish mission is also inaccurate.

There is no easy solution to the conundrum of this passage. What is clear, however, is that this story reveals to a Gentile audience (like us) the radical nature of Jesus' mission and ministry, which moved from a context in which no one would have batted an eyelid at calling a Greek-speaking Phoenician woman 'a dog' to including her, and people like her, in the scope of the good news. We cannot know how the woman felt or what Jesus was thinking; what we can know is that, as a result of this story, we understand more clearly quite how far people had to travel away from one world view to a position in which Gentiles were not dogs under the table but truly valued and welcomed. It may be that this story is more for us, the readers, than anything else (and that the most important words in it are in verse 31: 'Then he returned'). The marker that is placed down here is that Jesus' healings of Gentiles are not aberrations, but a central part of his ministry.

Healing from a distance

Before we leave this passage, it is worth noting that whereas Matthew and Luke both tell the story of the healing of the centurion's servant (Matt. 8.5–13 and Luke 7.1–10), Mark does not. The healing of the Syrophoenician woman's daughter is the only one at a distance that he records. It stands in direct contrast to the preceding healing story in which people touch the tassels of Jesus' robe to be healed. It underlines that, whether in person or far away, Jesus' power to heal is strong. Where faith is tenacious, Jesus' presence can transform no matter who the person is or where they come from.

Mark 7.31–37: Jesus healed a man who was deaf

The second of Jesus' healings in Gentile territory is recorded only in Mark and took place in the Decapolis (for more on the Decapolis, see p. 121). What this account illustrates is that a general term 'Gentile' does not do justice to the peoples surrounding Galilee and Judea who were not Jewish. While both the woman of the previous story and the man in this one were Greek speakers, their ethnicity was completely different. The woman was Phoenician by heritage whereas the people who lived in the Decapolis were of mixed ethnicities: Greek, Roman, Aramaean, Nabataean to mention a few. The good news was not just for one non-Jewish culture but all of them.

Links backwards and forwards

- This healing is the penultimate in the string of healings of individuals that begins with three (the man from Gerasa (Mark 5.1–20), the woman who bled for 12 years (5.25–34) and Jairus' daughter (5.21–24, 35–43)); then continues with a chain of two (the daughter of the woman from Tyre (7.24–30) and this one); and ends with the healing of the blind man in Bethsaida (8.22–26).

Interesting words ...

- v. 31: *in the region of*. Mark uses a colloquial phrase here: *ana meson* ('in the midst') *tōn opiōn* ('of the limits'); that is, 'within the region'.
- v. 32: *deaf*. The word *kōphos* means 'blunt' or 'muted', and so 'noiseless'. It can therefore mean either 'deaf' or 'mute'. As a word connected to speech comes next, we can assume 'deaf' is meant here.
- v. 32: *impediment in his speech*. The word *mogilalon* is what is known as a *hapaxlegomenon* or a word that occurs only once. We are therefore left to

surmise what it means. As *lalos* means 'speech' and *mogis* means 'scarcely' or 'with difficulty', the word probably means that he could barely talk or he talked rarely.

- v. 33: *in private*. See the section titled 'Privately' on p. 172 for the importance of the phrase *kat'idian* ('by himself' or 'in private').
- v. 33: *spat*. The verb *ptuō*means 'to disgorge' or 'to expel from the mouth'.
- v. 34: *sighed*. *Stenazō* is 'to sigh deeply' or 'to groan'.
- v. 34: *ephphatha*. This is another word taken directly from Aramaic and written using Greek letters. It means, as Mark says, 'be opened'. The Greek verb is *dianoigō* ('to lay open' or 'to reveal'). It should be noted that, because Aramaic and Hebrew are so close, *ephphatha* could be from either language. Most scholars assume it is Aramaic because it is the language that would have been understood in the Decapolis. For more on this, see the box, 'Aramaic and Hebrew', on p. 173.
- vv. 34–35: *opened*. The verb *dianoigō* of verse 34 is followed here by *anoigō*, 'opened'.
- v. 35: *released*. The verb *luō* means 'unloosed', 'freed' or 'released'. A word not translated by the NRSV is *desmos* ('bond' or 'fetter'); so the phrase reads 'and the bond on his tongue was loosed'.
- v. 35: *plainly*. *Orthōs* ('straight' or 'correctly') gives context to what *mogilalon* meant in verse 32. The implication is that the deaf man spoke with a slur or stammer.
- v. 36: *ordered*. The word *diastellō* occurs twice in this verse and refers to giving precise orders about something.
- v. 36: *more zealously*. *Perissoteros* means 'even more', 'excessive', 'extravagant' or 'extraordinary'.
- v. 36: *proclaim*. The verb *kērussō* ('proclaim') is used for what they did.
- v. 37: *astounded beyond measure*. One of the usual words for 'astounded' is *ekplēssō* (see the notes on 1.22 and 27, on pp. 41–2) along with *huperperissōs* (connected to *perissoteros*: how they proclaimed), which means 'beyond all measure'.
- v. 37: *well*. *Kalōs* is an adverb that means 'splendidly', 'finely', and so on.
- v. 37: *mute*. Here, a more usual word is used *alalos* 'speechless'.

The route

As Jesus went via Sidon (25 miles north of Tyre) to the Decapolis (which is in the opposite direction to Galilee), we can probably conclude that he was travelling through the region on his way back. The most northerly city in the Decapolis was Damascus, about 53 miles south-east of Sidon. It is possible that this was the place where he healed the deaf man. Alternatively, it might have been Hippos, on the Sea of Galilee. The fact that Mark does not say which of the ten cities it was indicates the importance of its being one of those ten (as opposed to Phoenicia), rather than its strict location.

Privately

There are two healings that take place 'in private', for which the Greek *kat'idian* is used. This one and the healing of the man in Bethsaida (8.22–26). Mark makes no attempt to explain why these three are private whereas the others are public. One possible theory is that these two healings are symbolically connected to Jesus' teaching of the disciples in private (the same phrase is used). These two healings feature enabling someone to listen and to see: the two things the disciples currently seem to be unable to do. It is hard to know whether this is reading too much into the text; but it is interesting, nevertheless.

The healing

Given that other people were healed by simply touching the tassels of Jesus' clothing, the healing here seems to require a very elaborate technique. The only other healings similar to this are the healing of the blind man at Bethsaida (8.22–26) – the only other healing done in private – and, outside Mark, the healing of the man born blind in John's Gospel (9.6).

There are numerous elements to this healing:

- Touch
  Although most of Jesus' healings involved touch, this one included touching the specific parts of the body to be healed (ears and tongue). In this instance, this seems to be important.

- Spit
  There is evidence from other ancient texts that saliva was believed to have healing properties. One of the most interesting, relevant stories is recounted by Tacitus in his *Histories* 4.81. It tells the story of a blind man who approached the Emperor Vespasian, while he was staying in Alexandra. The blind man begged the emperor 'to moisten his cheeks and his eyes with his spittle' (it is told alongside a story of a man with a 'useless hand' who begged Vespasian to trample on it by way of healing). After consulting doctors, who agreed that such a course of action might heal the suppliants, Vespasian did as he was asked and healed both people.

- Sigh/groan
  It could be significant that Jesus sighed/groaned before the healing as that could indicate that his spirit was being breathed out on to the man (though it is worth also noting that this is not said explicitly in the text).

- Look up to heaven
  This is strongly reminiscent of the feeding of the 5,000, where Jesus looked up to heaven and blessed the bread. It implies that prayer is important in this healing.

- Spoke
  The touching, spit, sighing, and so on are all preludes to Jesus' prayer (looking up to heaven) and command in Aramaic ('*Ephphatha*, be opened').

Mark does not explain why all these details are provided for this story. One possibility is that it stresses that it wasn't the touch, the spit or the sigh that healed the man, but the prayer and the command from Jesus.

Aramaic and Hebrew

Aramaic and Hebrew are sister languages; they have the same script and many words in common. They are sufficiently different, however, to mean that you cannot easily understand one if you know only the other.

The ancient language of the Aramaean tribes (a Semitic people), Aramaic was also the common tongue of the Ancient Near East. It was already in widespread use by the tenth century BC. It was the official language of the Assyrian Empire and continued to be used by the Babylonian and Persian Empires, all of which conquered Israel and the land surrounding it in different ways and at different times.

In territories populated with people of very mixed ethnic backgrounds, Aramaic was the language that could be spoken and understood by everyone. As a result, it is not surprising that Jesus would have spoken Aramaic to someone from the Decapolis, with a full expectation of being understood.

Hebrew, by contrast, was the religious language of Jewish texts and hence temple worship. Whereas Aramaic would have been widely understood, Hebrew would not have been.

Tell no one

It is odd that the man from Gerasa was explicitly told to go and tell what God had done for him while this man, and the crowd around him, were told specifically and strictly by Jesus not to tell anyone what had happened (not that it made any difference). No explanation is given for the difference; we are left to speculate without any great success on what it signified.

Mark 8.1–10: A banquet for 4,000

Although Mark doesn't explain why he tells another story of the feeding of thousands, there are enough clues in the text for us to guess, especially by the time we get to 8.11–21. Mark is at pains, both times, to stress that Jesus was moved with pity for the crowds, which was why he fed them. It is also clear that the disciples are meant to be understanding who Jesus was and what he had come to do from his actions. The repetition, with a few enhancements, seems to be saying, 'Are you there yet? Have you understood yet?'

The location of the feeding is not clear but since Jesus was in the Decapolis immediately before this account and went at the end to Dalmanutha (which is thought to have been on the western shores of Galilee near Magdala), it seems likely that this feeding took place in Gentile territory. If we are meant to see echoes of the messianic banquet in these feedings, then this is significant. Gentiles, too, are welcomed to God's glorious banquet.

Links backwards and forwards

- It is worth reading this feeding alongside its parallel in Mark 6.30–44 and also the stories that follow: the feeding of the 5,000 led straight on to the second boat scene (Boat II), in which the disciples' lack of understanding was stressed; in the same way, this story leads on to the third boat scene (Boat III) in 8.11–21, where the disciples' lack of understanding is raised again.

Interesting words …

- v. 1: *again a great crowd*. Mark recalls the first feeding of thousands with the phrase: 'In those (*ekeinos*) days (*hēmera*), there being a great crowd (*pollos ochlos*) again (*palin*) and not having (*echō*) anything (*ti*) they might eat (*esthiō*)', which is a hugely irregular verb that becomes *phagō* in the past tense; this verb is used again in verse 3.
- v. 2: *compassion*. Just as in 6.34, Jesus felt compassion (*splangchnizō*) for the crowd. For more on the verb, see the note on p. 146.
- v. 3: *hungry*. The adjective *nēstis* means 'fasting' or 'not eating'.
- v. 3: *from a great distance*. The adverb *makrothen* has the *then* suffix to mean 'from' and *makros* 'long', 'far' or 'remote'. It is a word often used to refer to Gentile lands.
- v. 4: *how can one … ?* The disciples' response is in the future tense: 'From where (*pothen*) will someone (*tis*) be able (*dunamai*) … ?'
- v. 4: *the desert*. In the feeding of the 5,000, the crowd was described as being in an *erēmos topos* ('isolated place'); now they are in an *erēmia* ('wilderness' or 'desert').

- v. 6: *sit down*. The same word is used here as in 6.40 (*anapiptpō*), as there it can also mean 'recline at a meal'.
- v. 6: *ground*. No grass is described here: the word is *gēs* ('land' or 'soil').
- vv. 6, 7: *took; giving thanks; broke; gave; blessing*. The same words are used as in 6.40, with a few small differences. This time Jesus did not bless, he gave thanks (*eucharisteō*). The word for 'broke' is the simpler *klaō* as opposed to *kataklaō* in 6.41; but 'gave' is the same word: *didōmi*. Jesus did bless (*eulogeō*); but he blessed the fish and not the bread.
- v. 6: *distribute*. Slightly surprisingly, the NRSV chose to translate the same verb differently here. In 6.41, *paratithēmi* was translated 'set before', here it is translated 'distribute'.
- v. 7: *few small fish*. The word used for 'small fish' is *ichthudion* and that for 'few' is *oligos*. The use of the diminutive seeks to stress that these are not substantial, large fish but the small ones that got caught in the net alongside the more sought-after large fish.
- v. 8: *filled*. As in 6.42, they were satisfied (*chortazō*) when they had eaten.
- v. 8: *baskets*. A different word is used for baskets from that in 6.43. Here, the word for 'basket' is *spuris*, which denotes a large basket, though probably not as large as the type of basket known as *kophinos*, used in 6.43.
- v. 9: *four thousand*. Unlike in 6.44, the word *anēr* is not used. It is just 4,000, for which we understand 'people'.

Similarities and differences

It is worth noting the similarities and differences between the feeding of the 5,000 and the feeding of the 4,000.

	Feeding of the 5,000	**Feeding of the 4,000**
There was a great crowd	6.34	8.1
Jesus had compassion on them	6.34	8.2
Jesus taught the crowd	6.34	No teaching
How long they were there	6.35 ('late on the same day')	8.2 ('after three days')
Who identifies that the crowd were hungry	6.35–36 (the disciples)	8.2 (Jesus)
Where they were	6.34 (an isolated place)	8.4 (wilderness)
How many loaves	6.38 (five)	8.5 (seven)
How many fish	6.38 (two)	8.7 (a few small fish)
Where do they recline	6.39 (green grass)	8.6 (ground)

	Feeding of the 5,000	Feeding of the 4,000
Actions with the bread	6.41 (blesses, breaks and gives)	8.6 (gives thanks, breaks and gives)
Actions with the fish	6.41 (divided)	8.7 (blessed and distributes)
All satisfied after the meal	6.42	8.8
Leftovers	6.43 (12 baskets, *kophinos*)	8.8 (seven baskets, *spuris*)
Number fed	6.44 (5,000 *men*)	8.9 (4,000 *people*)

Compassion

The reason why Jesus felt compassion for the crowd is different in this feeding than in the previous one. There, it was because they were like a sheep without a shepherd; here, it is because they have not eaten recently. This may be significant if we are to take them as a Gentile crowd. The Jews could expect to have a shepherd – that was what their leaders should have been doing – but the Gentiles could not. They have not been nourished at all and are in dire need of food (whether actual or metaphorical).

Feeding in the desert

The disciples protested Jesus' desire to feed the crowd. While this was understandable the previous time (6.37), it is much less understandable now. Later in this chapter, Jesus' conversation with the disciples brings this exchange to mind, when he asks them if they don't remember (8.18). As we will see there, one of the keys to understanding is the ability to remember and make connections.

Some point out, in defence of the disciples, that while the time before they were just in an isolated place, now they are in the wilderness proper. This prompts us to wonder where that might have been. The Decapolis bordered the Arabian desert to the east. Although a long journey, it is possible that this could have been in mind. Having said that, at the end of the feeding, Jesus and the disciples got into a boat. This implies that the 'desert' was somewhat closer than that.

One of the key Jewish philosophical modes of argument is a technique known 'as from the lesser to the greater' (in Hebrew it is called *Qal waHomer*). In other words, if this is true in this small instance how much more can it be true in a larger one. It lies behind the logic of a lot of the parables. It is possible that the repetition of the feeding miracle is a worked example of *Qal waHomer*. If Jesus could feed a Jewish crowd in an isolated place, how much more could he feed a Gentile crowd in an actual desert? Jesus appears to expect the disciples to have made that connection.

Was seven important?

There is much discussion of the use of the number seven here for the number of loaves as well as the number of baskets of leftovers. Twelve, in the previous feeding, is easy to identify as a significant number (12 tribes of Israel, 12 disciples, and so on). Many theories have been proposed, including the seven deacons appointed in Acts (6.1–6), the seven Noahide commandments (Gen. 9.4–7) and the seven nations of Canaan (Deut. 7.1); but none of them seems to fit particularly well. Probably the best explanation is that, like 12, seven was seen to be a perfect number.

Giving thanks

In the feeding of the 5,000, Jesus took the bread, blessed, broke it and gave it. Here, he took it, gave thanks, broke and gave it (though in the next verse he blessed the fish). For those who are alert to the actions of Jesus at the Last Supper, it is worth noting that, then, Jesus took, blessed, broke and gave, and then gave thanks over the cup. In this feeding, but not the previous one, all the actions are present, though in a slightly different order. One of Mark's narrative techniques is to trail significant events (especially the Crucifixion) so that, when they happen, they make sense in the narrative. This seems to be another of those occasions. Twice, the Last Supper is trailed; and, in this one, Jesus' key actions (taking, blessing, giving thanks, breaking and giving) all appear.

Satisfied

As with the feeding of the 5,000, after they had been fed the crowd were 'filled' or 'satisfied'. This is even more significant here than in the previous feeding. Here, they had been hungry for three days but, after Jesus' miraculous generosity, were completely satisfied. In fact, the reference to their being satisfied is hugely important. With the feeding of the 5,000, the people needed to be satisfied because they were like sheep without a shepherd to guide them to pasture (though they had had a shepherd in the past); the Gentiles were utterly famished, as they had never had a shepherd to guide them. That they were satisfied indicates that Jesus' mission, which included healing someone from Tyre and someone from the Decapolis, meant that Gentiles of all types were welcome in the kingdom and would be satisfied within it as much as their Jewish neighbours.

Dalmanutha

The name Dalmanutha does not appear anywhere else, so it is not obvious where it was. The fact that Jesus was met out of the boat by Pharisees (who would not have travelled to Gentile territory) suggests that he had returned to the Jewish side, Galilee. In Matthew's Gospel, the place is said to be Magadan (also unknown) or, in some manuscripts, Magdala. It is assumed therefore that Jesus went back to somewhere around Magdala, but precisely where is unclear.

Mark 8.11–21: Boat III. 'Do you not remember?'

The final conversation in a boat reveals quite how little the disciples had learnt. They had been present for countless healings and exorcisms and two miraculous feedings but still they did not understand who Jesus was.

Various English translations separate the discussion with the Pharisees about a sign from the conversation between Jesus and the disciples during this third boat scene; but I think it is better to read the two episodes together.

In this journey in a boat, we encounter a stark reality. The disciples – whom we believed from 4.34 to be 'insiders' because Jesus was explaining everything to them in parables – now find themselves classed as outsiders (see the 'Links' box).

Links backwards

- Although often overlooked because nothing dramatic happens beyond the conversation with Jesus, this story draws together a number of threads that Mark has laid down from the parable of the sower onwards. Lying behind this passage is
  - the description of outsiders 4.12;
  - the two previous scenes in a boat (4.35–41 and 6.45–52);
  - and two miraculous feedings (6.30–44 and 8.1–10).

  Surely the disciples would understand what was going on now?

Links forwards

- Also important is the question from 4.41: 'Who then is this?' It will be partially answered by Peter in Caesarea Philippi (8.29) and by God at the Transfiguration (9.2–7).

Interesting words ...

- v. 11: *argue*. The verb *suzeteō* means 'to examine together', 'to search' and, therefore, 'to dispute'.
- v. 11: *asking*. *Zeteō* means 'to ask', 'request' or 'demand'. So this sentence could be translated quite gently as 'They began to examine together with him,

requesting a sign' or much more aggressively as 'They began to dispute with him, demanding a sign'. Given the role of the authorities thus far, the second option seems more likely.

- v. 11: *sign. Sēmeion* is a 'sign' or a 'signal'. It can refer to a signal from, for example, flags or, in Greek literature, a sign from the gods. Here, they are clearly asking for a sign from God, and one wonders what sign would have satisfied them. The disciples also ask Jesus for a sign in 13.4.
- v. 11: *testing*. The verb *peirazō* can mean 'to tempt', 'to test' or 'to try a person' and is the same word used in the temptation stories.
- v. 12: *sighed deeply in his spirit. Anastenazō* refers to 'sighing deeply', 'groaning' or 'bemoaning'. The verb *stenazō* was used when Jesus healed the deaf man; this is a stronger form of the same verb. The usual word for 'spirit' (*pneuma*) is used here.
- v. 12: *Truly I tell you*. This characteristic opening (*amēn legō humin*) to a saying by Jesus occurs once early on in Mark and then with increasing frequency towards the end (3.28; 8.12; 9.1, 41; 10.15, 29; 11.23; 12.43; 13.30; 14.18, 25, 30). For more on the phrase, see the note on 3.28 (p. 85).
- v. 12: *no sign will be given*. The construction used here is a Hebrew one and is hard to put into English. It reads literally, 'If a sign will be given to this generation', to which we need to add the implied 'May God do to me if ...' In other words, it is a vow that no sign will be given.
- v. 13: *left them*. The word is a strong one. *Aphiēmi* does mean 'leave', but it also means 'abandon'. The implication is that Jesus has given up on the Pharisees at this point.
- v. 13: *the other side*. This is the fifth and final use of *to peran* ('the other side') in Mark. See 'The other side', on p. 180, for discussion about its use here; and see the box, 'To the other side', on p. 111, for its significance in the Gospel.
- v. 14: *forgotten. Eplanthanomai* means 'neglect' or 'forget' but can have the sense of 'forget wilfully'.
- v. 14: *they had only*. More literally, the phrase reads 'except (*ei mē*) one (*hena*) bread (*artos*)'.
- v. 15: *cautioned. Diastellō* has more of the sense of 'command'. A sign of Jesus' abandoning the Pharisees is that he now commands the disciples to beware of them. This is an order, not just good advice.
- v. 15: *watch out – beware*. The two verbs *horaō* and *blepō* mean almost the same thing ('look', 'watch', 'see'). This provides an emphasis: 'take great care to watch out for'.
- vv. 16–17: *said; talking*. The NRSV translates the same verb differently each time: the first instance as 'said' and the second as 'talking'. The verb *dialogizomai* means 'to reason thoroughly', 'to discuss' or 'to converse', so it implies more than just talking.
- vv. 17–18: the list of words Jesus asks the disciples are all significant (and will be discussed further below). I will list them all with alternative translations, if there are any:
  'perceive' (*noeō*: 'apprehend' or 'reflect'); 'understand' (*suniēmi*: 'perceive'); 'hearts' (*kardia*); 'hardened' (*pōroō*: 'ossify' or 'petrify'); 'eyes' (*ophthalmos*); 'see' (*blepō*); 'ear' (*ous*), 'hear' (*akouō*); 'remember' (*mnēmoneuō*: 'call to mind').

- vv. 19–20: *baskets*. The two types of basket referred to here are *kophinos* (for the feeding of the 5,000) and *spuris* (for the feeding of the 4,000).
- v. 21: *understand*. The verb *suniēmi* is used again here.

Left the Pharisees

Jesus' abandonment of the Pharisees is significant here. They had already decided to plot his downfall in 3.6; but it seems that Jesus had not given up hope on them, until now. His leaving them, followed by stern commands to the disciples to beware of them, indicates that this was a crucial moment. Jesus recognized that there was nothing he could do or say to them as a group that would persuade them of who he was or what he had come to proclaim.

The addition of 'groaned/sighed deeply in his spirit' gives a sense of the strength of his feeling. It is one of those occasions on which we get a glimpse of Jesus' emotion. He was deeply frustrated and grieved by the Pharisees' attitude. The significance of groaning in his spirit is not entirely clear. It could refer to 'sighing on the inside' while not allowing his emotions to show; or it could be a sign of how deeply his frustration was felt, right down to his inner core.

A sign

The reason for Jesus' frustration is not hard to find. The request coming immediately after his second feeding, the feeding of the 4,000, indicates how far apart he and the Pharisees were. It is clear that the Pharisees would not consider any of Jesus' miracles to be a sign. Unlike John's Gospel, Mark's account does not describe miracles as signs. What the Pharisees were looking for was something like a thunderclap or a voice from heaven (ironically, similar events happened at Jesus' baptism, at his Transfiguration and at his Crucifixion). The real issue was that nothing would have been good enough for the Pharisees. They all knew that to be the case, which was why Jesus abandoned them.

The other side

As we saw above (p. 111), going to the other side is crucial in Mark's account. Each time our expectation of the disciples is raised. Will they understand this time? Will a different perspective allow them to see and comprehend who Jesus really was? Each time the answer has been 'no'. This is the last occurrence of the phrase in Mark. Will this time be any different? Given how Mark has set this up, we all know the answer.

The yeast of the Pharisees

The *zumē* ('yeast' or 'leaven') refers to a sourdough method of making bread (now very popular again). The *zumē* is the live culture that is kept, fed and then introduced into flour to make a loaf.

Mark does not say exactly what the leaven of the Pharisees was, though Matthew identifies it as their teaching (Matt. 16.11) and Luke as their hypocrisy (Luke 12.1). The reference to the leaven of Herod loops us back to Herod's banquet before both feeding miracles: a banquet that ended sordidly, with the dance of a young girl that led to the death of John the Baptist. The influence, whether of the Pharisees or Herod, brought the opposite of good news into the world.

In a way, this commandment is reminiscent of the parable of the woman with the yeast: a small amount goes a long way. The kingdom is like this. If you introduce a small amount of live culture into a large quantity, it spreads no matter how much flour it is put in.

In the same way, but in contrast, the 'culture' of the Pharisees and Herod did the same thing. This is why the disciples were to be wary of them.

Jesus' warning rings in our ears today. There are some cultures or attitudes that will grow to affect the whole. The kingdom is certainly like this; you should, however, be acutely aware of other places, situations or attitudes that grow similarly but with negative effect.

One loaf

Mark allows us a moment of humour in this exchange. The disciples, it seems, had learnt nothing at all. They had just collected seven baskets of leftover food from the feeding of the 4,000 and didn't think to bring any of it with them. Also, despite witnessing two miraculous feedings for which they needed five loaves and seven loaves respectively, they had only one loaf with them. Not only did they not understand who Jesus was, they hadn't even learnt to bring food with them in case Jesus' teaching went on for a while.

Add to this the fact that they were arguing about it in a boat that was no more than 27 feet long, it didn't take any supernatural powers on Jesus' part to work out what they were talking about.

Five key questions

The crux of this third journey in the boat comes not after anything miraculous, as in the previous two boat journeys, but in what Jesus says to the disciples about their attitude. The important feature of this is that it brings to mind what Jesus said about outsiders before the first journey in a boat, in the middle of the parable of the sower. Speaking there, he quoted Isaiah

6.9–10, that everything was said in parables to outsiders. In the table, I compare the two sets of words.

Mark 4.11–12	Mark 8.17–18
for those outside, everything comes in parables; in order that 'they may indeed look (*blepō*), but not perceive (*horaō*), and may indeed listen (*akouō*), but not understand (*suniēmi*); so that they may not turn again and be forgiven.'	Do you still not perceive (*noeō*) or understand (*suniēmi*)? Are your hearts hardened? Do you have eyes, and fail to see (*blepō*)? Do you have ears, and fail to hear (*akouō*)? And do you not remember?

Obviously, the quotation from Isaiah is not a direct one, and not all words are the same. The similarities, however, are such that it is hard not to conclude that Jesus was effectively saying that, by their responses, the disciples had identified themselves as outsiders; and not just that: the phrase 'Are your hearts hardened?' calls to mind the Pharisees, whose hearts were declared to be hard in Mark 3.5. This raises the question of whether the disciples had already been affected by the leaven of the Pharisees.

This, of course, is not the first time the disciples' hearts have been described as hard (it happened after the walking on the water in 6.52). Their responses have moved them from the category of insiders to potential outsiders.

Insiders and outsiders

The theme of insiders and outsiders that was introduced as far back as 3.13 now emerges with full force.

Mark has carefully set up this theme, which he has clearly repeatedly reversed. Jesus' family thought they were insiders but turned out to be outsiders because of their response to Jesus. The Pharisees were, in their own estimation, the ultimate insiders but they have just been abandoned by Jesus.

But there were, of course, some legitimate insiders: the disciples and, even more importantly, the inner group of the Twelve. To them were given the secrets of the kingdom of God. It now turns out that the insiders were not necessarily inside after all. Like the outsiders, they neither perceived nor understood; like the Pharisees, their hearts were hardened.

Over the course of the past few chapters, however, there have been people who have seen, recognized and responded to Jesus; people who were commended for their faith and responses. These were a man who lived among the tombs, possessed by demons; a man who thought his daughter had died; a woman who had bled continuously for 12 years; a woman from Phoenicia whose daughter was possessed; and a deaf man from the Decapolis. All these were outsiders in one way or another (by virtue of being impure, female or Gentile, or a combination of the three). It turns out that these outsiders were more inside than the insiders were.

Mark leaves us with this powerful reflection as his story continues.

'Do you not remember?'

In Jesus' list of questions to the disciples, the new question (which does not pick up resonances we have seen already) is the one of whether the disciples remember or not. To help them, Jesus rehearses the details, first, of the feeding of the 5,000 and then of the 4,000. Part of the skill of discipleship, it seems, is the ability to recall and rehearse what has happened, which enables them (and us) to perceive, understand and respond.

We are left at the end of this passage with the disciples in a sorry state, transferred by their own responses to the category of outsiders. All is not lost, however. Jesus' specific question to them about whether they can see and whether they can hear reminds us, the readers, of the healing of the deaf man in the Decapolis and points forward to the healing of the blind man at Bethsaida. Not being able to hear or see is not a problem within the economy of Jesus, for either them or us.

We are left at the end of this encounter with Jesus' question hanging in our ears: 'Don't you understand yet?' The 'yet' is important. Not yet ... but maybe soon.

Mark 8.22—10.53: On Seeing and Not Seeing – the Challenge of Following Jesus

The next section of Mark is bookended with two healings of blind men. The first one is a healing in stages and takes place in Bethsaida; the second features someone whose name is Bartimaeus and takes place in Jericho. Between these two, we have more concentrated teaching than we have encountered so far in Mark; the teaching is littered with examples of the ways in which the disciples do not understand who Jesus is or what he has come to do. The two blind men, once healed by Jesus, could see far better than the disciples, who, though spending extensive time in his presence, seemed unable to see beyond their own fixed expectations and desires.

As in the previous section, we have numerous repetitions, with the implication that the disciples should have learnt something along the way. Over and over again, we see that they have not.

Patterns in 8.22—10.53

Before looking forwards, we need to look backwards. One of the reasons why it is so hard to decide on a structure for Mark is that some stories fit in two different patterns. The healing of the man from Bethsaida completes the previous pattern while, at the same time, starting the next one.

The three scenes in a boat (4.35–41; 6.45–52; 8.11–21) have stitched between them, first, three healings (5.1–20; 5.21–24, 35–43; 5.25–34); then two (7.24–30, 31–37); and now one (8.22–26): all are healings of outsiders who responded to Jesus. The last two healings of a deaf man and a blind man are on either side of Jesus' question to the disciples about whether they can see and hear.

The Bethsaida healing then moves us into a different section, which is bookended with this first healing of a blind man (8.22–26) and then with the second at Jericho (10.46–52). In between these two healings, we encounter Jesus' most focused and most challenging teaching about the cost of following the way of the cross, both for him and for his disciples. In particular, there are three predictions of his death (in keeping with Mark's love of threes) at 8.31–9.1; 9.30-32; and 10.32-34. An illustration of how much the disciples do not understand is that, after the first prediction, Peter rebukes Jesus for saying that he will die; after the second prediction, the disciples dispute who is the greatest; and after the third prediction, James and John ask to sit at Jesus' right and left hands.

The theme of seeing and not seeing runs throughout this whole section.

Mark 8.22–26: Jesus healed a blind man I (in Bethsaida)

The healing of the man who cannot see picks up one of Jesus' questions from the boat in the previous story. The disciples currently cannot see, and neither can the man from Bethsaida; but Jesus is able to heal him, even if in two stages. This prepares us for the next encounter between Jesus and Peter, who declares Jesus to be the Messiah but then tells him that he isn't to die. Peter's sight has cleared a little but still has a long way to go.

As this section centres so much on physical disability as a metaphor for spiritual disability, it is important to note that we need to think carefully about how this metaphor is used today. It is important not to elide the two. Some of the most insightful people I have ever known are people who cannot see or hear physically. Even here, Bartimaeus 'sees' who Jesus is ('Son of David') in a way that no one else does.

Links backwards

- This passage looks back to healing of the deaf man (Mark 7.31–37) and links to Jesus' conversation with the disciples about whether they can see and hear.

Links forwards

- It also looks forwards to the healing of Bartimaeus, who was blind (Mark 10.46–52), framing this section of Jesus' teaching.

Interesting words ...

- v. 22: *a blind man. Tuphlos* can mean 'something that is dark or dim' or (concerning a person) 'blind'.
- v. 23: *village*. An unwalled village (*kōmē*) as opposed to a fortified town (see the comment on 1.38, on p. 51).

- v. 23: *put saliva on his eyes*. More literally, 'spitting (*ptuō*) into his eyes (*omma*)'. On other occasions, the word for 'eye' has been *ophthalmos*. Interestingly, this word (*omma*) is a more poetic form often used (in Greek mythology) for the eye of the gods.
- v. 24: *looked up*. The verb here (*anablepō*) is a play on words; it can mean both 'look up' and 'see again'. It is clear that both are meant.
- v. 24: *I can see people*. The whole phrase is worth including here. The man says, 'I see (*blepō*) people (*anthrōpos*) that I see (*horaō*) walking (*peripateō*) like trees (*dendron*).'
- v. 25: *eyes*. Mark switches the word for 'eye' and here uses *ophthalmos*.
- v. 25: *look intently*. This is another version of the verb *blepō*: *diablepō*, which means 'to stare with eyes wide open'.
- v. 25: *his sight was restored*. The Greek simply says, 'he/it was restored' (*apokathisēmi*).
- v. 25: *he saw everything clearly*. Here, we have another variation of *blepō*: *emblepō* ('to look at'). 'He looked at (*emblepō*) everything (*hapas*: 'the whole' or 'the entirety') clearly (*tēlaugōs*: 'plainly').

Bethsaida

Crossing to 'the other side' here makes sense if Dalmanutha is taken to be near Magdala. Bethsaida is on the north-eastern shore of the Sea of Galilee, so the journey would involve crossing to the top corner of the lake.

What is odd is that Mark describes Bethsaida as an unwalled village (*kōmē*), whereas it was probably a fortified town. Philip, in whose tetrarchy Bethsaida was located (see below for more on Philip), had turned the 'village' into a fortified city in AD 30 and renamed it Bethsaida-Julias, after the daughter of Caesar Augustus. This raises the question of when this healing happened and whether Mark was remembering it as it was before AD 30.

Philip the Tetrarch

Philip was the son of Herod the Great's fifth wife, Cleopatra of Jerusalem. On Herod's death, the kingdom was split between Archelaus (called an 'ethnarch', which means 'ruler of the people'), who inherited half the kingdom, and Herod Antipas and Philip, each of whom was a 'tetrarch' ('ruler of a fourth'), as they got a quarter each. Philip's territory stretched from the north-eastern corner of Galilee (taking in Bethsaida and Caesarea Philippi) north to Mount Hermon (in modern Syria) and east as far as the Arabian desert.

He married Salome, the daughter of Herodias (see the box, 'Herod Antipas, Herodias and Salome', on p. 143).

Unlike his half-brothers, Herod Antipas and Herod Archelaus, he did not carry the family name: he was not known as 'Herod Philip' in any contemporary literature.

He ruled until his death in around AD 34.

A healing in private

In many ways, this healing is similar to the healing of the deaf man in 7.31–37: Jesus was begged by the man's friends to heal him; he used touch and spit in the healing; and the healing happened in private. As with the two feedings, it seems as though Mark is repeating details for the sake of emphasis. The element of privacy is odd, as most of the other healings are not done privately. As a result, they are reminiscent of Jesus teaching the disciples in private. Which leaves the question hanging in the air: will the disciples – who have been taught in private, but who cannot hear or see – be healed as these two men were?

Spit (again)

As noted above (on p. 172), the use of spit in Jesus' miracles was rare, though much more common elsewhere in the ancient world.

On eyes and seeing

This healing makes much of the words for 'eye' (*omma* and *ophthalmos*) and for seeing (*blepō, horaō, anablepō, diablepō* and *emblepō*). The use of the poetic word for eye, as well as the more prosaic one, emphasizes over and over again that this healing is about seeing generally, as well as the man's physical ability to see.

This point is emphasized by the only need for a double healing in Jesus' ministry. The man can see a little but needs a second healing to enable him to see clearly.

Many of Jesus' healings are simply about the healing; this one is about more than that. It is, of course, important that the man is healed but – coming as it does so soon after Jesus' engagement with the disciples, who are declared to 'have eyes to see but cannot see' – clearly, it has two foci: the man himself and the disciples.

Given that the man was healed enough the first time to see but not completely, we are now ready for Jesus' conversation with Peter at Caesarea Philippi.

Mark 8.27–33: 'Who do you say that I am?' And Jesus prophesied about his death the first time

We now reach one of the key climactic moments in the Gospel in which a number of threads in Mark come together (see 'Links backwards' and 'Links forwards' below). The question of who Jesus is, asked by the disciples after the stilling of the storm, now becomes Jesus' own question to the disciples. Have they understood yet? Are they able to say who he is? As with the man healed from blindness in the previous passage, Peter responds with a partial picture: Jesus is the Messiah; but Peter is horrified at the thought that Jesus would die.

This is one of those passages in Mark in which many themes are brought together and interlinked.

Links backwards

- The Pharisees and the Herodians have been plotting to destroy Jesus (Mark 3.6); Jesus now acknowledges the conflict and predicts his own death.
- The first boat scene, during the stilling of the storm, was when the disciples asked, 'Who then is this?' (4.35–41). Jesus now asks them the question: 'Who do you say that I am?'
- The third boat scene was the one in which the disciples were declared to have eyes to see but could not see (8.11–21). Peter understood some, but not all, of who Jesus was.
- The double healing of the blind man at Bethsaida (8.22–26). Peter saw something of Jesus, but nothing clearly.

Links forwards

- The Transfiguration: God declares who Jesus is (9.2–7), further answering the question of who he is.
- Prophecies of death and resurrection: Jesus declares who he is and what he will do (9.30–32; 10.32–34).
- The Crucifixion: the centurion declares who Jesus is (15.39).

Interesting words …

- v. 29: *Messiah*. The Greek word *christos* ('anointed') translates the Hebrew word 'messiah' directly. The use of 'Jesus Christ' as a phrase is a constant reminder that we are talking about Jesus who is the Messiah. It is worth reminding ourselves that Mark told us about this in 1.1: 'the good news of Jesus Christ'. This is the first time in his Gospel that any of the characters have picked up the word.

- vv. 30 and 32–33: *sternly ordered. Epitimaō* means 'to rebuke' or 'to give a warning that implies a threat'. The same word is used for how Peter rebukes Jesus in verse 32 as for how Jesus rebukes the disciples in verse 30. It is then used again for Jesus' rebuke of Peter in verse 33 (there was a lot of rebuking going on!).
- v. 31: *suffering*. The verb *paschō* means 'to experience something' or 'to suffer it'.
- v. 31: *rejected. Apodokimazō* doesn't just mean 'to reject' but also gives the reason for the rejection. Jesus will be rejected as unworthy or be considered as not genuine.
- v. 31: *rise*. The verb *anistēmi* has a wide range of meanings from 'make' to 'stand up'; to 'wake from sleep', 'rouse' or 'raise'. There are two words used for Jesus' Resurrection: this one and *egeirō*.
- v. 32: *openly*. The adverb *parrēsiai* can mean 'outspoken', 'frank' or 'boldly'.
- v. 32: *took aside*. Although 'to take aside' is probably the right translation, the verb *proslambanō* actually means 'to take hold of' or 'to grasp'. This may communicate some of Peter's horror.
- v. 33: *turning*. Intriguingly, the verb *epistrephō* can mean 'to change one's views/ways' (which Jesus didn't do here) or simply 'to turn around'.
- v. 33: *get behind me*. In an intriguing echo of his first call to Peter (where he said 'Here, behind (*opisō*) me', Jesus says here, 'Go away (*hupagō*) behind (*opisō*) me (*egō*).' This could mean one of two things: either 'fall in line behind me as a disciple should be' or 'go away from me' (similar to what Jesus said to the devil in Matthew 4.10).
- v. 33: *Satan*. This is a Hebrew word and means 'accuser'.
- v. 33: *setting your mind. Phroneō* means 'to ponder', 'to hold a view' or 'to think about'.

Who do people/you say that I am?

It is said that the best teaching occurs through asking questions. This is certainly a view with which Jesus agreed. Although he did teach (as he does in 8.34—9.1), he was just as likely to ask questions to encourage people to understand what he was saying. One of the striking features of this passage is that this question echoed the disciples' question from 4.34: 'Who then is this?' Four chapters later, Jesus turned the question back on them: 'Who do you say that I am?'

Caesarea Philippi

Caesarea Philippi was in the territory of Philip the Tetrarch, 25 miles north of Bethsaida (hence inland from the Sea of Galilee). It was previously a small village called Paneas, dedicated to the Greek god Pan. However, when Philip became the tetrarch, he expanded it and renamed it after Caesar and himself (in other words, 'Caesar's city of Philip').

One of the discussions about this passage is whether we should conclude anything from the fact that there had been a shrine to Pan in this city and then, after it was renamed, one to the emperor. It was also a centre of Ba'al worship. Nothing is made of this in the account. In fact, Jesus is explicitly shown not to be in the city but in the surrounding villages. Nevertheless, acknowledging Jesus' messiahship in a place so full of the worship of other gods is striking.

It should not be confused with Caesarea Maritima (today, known just as Caesarea) on the Mediterranean coast, an important port in the Roman era.

John the Baptist, Elijah, one of the prophets

The first response to Jesus' question cites common views of who Jesus might have been.

- John the Baptist. We saw, in 6.17–29, Herod's fear that Jesus was John, back from the dead. This view obviously took hold and is cited to Jesus here. It certainly fits with the impression we have, from the Jewish historian Josephus, that John the Baptist was well known in this period.
- Elijah. There was widespread speculation at this time about the return of Elijah. In 2 Kings, he did not die but was taken up to heaven in a whirlwind (2 Kings 2.11). This, therefore, provided grounds for an expectation that he might return at some point. This belief was exacerbated by Malachi 4.5–6, which reads: 'Lo, I will send you the prophet Elijah before the great and terrible day of the LORD comes. He will turn the hearts of parents to their children and the hearts of children to their parents, so that I will not come and strike the land with a curse.' Given the content of Jesus' teaching, it is not unreasonable for people to see him as the returned Elijah.
- One of the prophets. The vaguest answer of all suggests that Jesus was either one of the prophets of old returned or a new prophet in their tradition.

The point about all these answers is that they are all a little bit true. Like John the Baptist, Jesus had come to call people to repentance. Like Elijah, he had come to turn the hearts of those he taught. Like the prophets, he had come to proclaim God's message. These are not wrong answers but nor are they entirely right. Jesus is all these things and more.

'You are the Messiah'

One of the important features of Mark's story of Jesus is that Jesus himself never says that he is the Messiah. He simply waits for the disciples to work it out. This is one of those many occasions in Mark where we have an advantage over the disciples. We are told in 1.1 who Jesus is ('The beginning of the good news of Jesus Christ') but the disciples have not been told. The question is, given the varying beliefs about who the Messiah was in Judaism of this period, could they reasonably have been expected to recognize Jesus as the Messiah? See the box, 'The Messiah', below.

The Messiah

The word 'messiah' simply means 'anointed one' in Hebrew. In Greek, it is translated as *christos* ('Christ').

However, the Hebrew word was never used in the Old Testament to refer to someone in the future who would come to save God's people. The word itself occurs only twice: once to refer to Cyrus, the Persian King (Isa. 45.1) and once to refer to the whole people of Israel (Hab. 3.13).

Although the word 'messiah' doesn't really occur in the Old Testament, and certainly not to refer to a future saviour, people are described as being anointed, most notably kings, prophets and priests (see, for example, 1 Kings 19.15–16; Ex. 29.7). The important feature, however, is that their role was always in the present, never as a future, expected saviour.

It is in Jewish texts, outside of the Bible, that we can begin to see a growth in expectation about a 'messiah'. The problem is that there was no single view about the kind of person who would be the Messiah. When the word is used as a title, it refers to different types of people: sometimes to a king like David, sometimes to a priest and sometimes to an angel who would act on God's behalf. Although there was no one view about who the Messiah would be, there was a good level of agreement that the Messiah would intervene in the world, save God's people from their enemies and establish a kingdom of justice and righteousness, such as Isaiah looked forward to in his prophecies.

When Peter said that Jesus was the Messiah, it would make sense that this is what he had in mind. No wonder he was so opposed to the idea that Jesus would be rejected and die. He was waiting for Jesus to rule gloriously, not to die, rejected by the Jewish leaders.

In Matthew's parallel account, Jesus declared that God revealed to Peter that Jesus was the Messiah ('For flesh and blood has not revealed this to you, but my Father in heaven' (Matt. 16.17)); but Mark does not say this. The implication of how Mark tells his story here is that the disciples, for whom Peter was a spokesperson here, accompanied Jesus through his ministry and saw his healings, his exorcisms and other miracles. They also had everything explained to them in private, and so, therefore, should have been able to work out for themselves who he was.

He began to teach them

Given how little teaching has been recorded in Mark's Gospel at this point (what Jesus said has been described but very little of it captured), it is significant that Jesus began to teach about his own death and Resurrection. As noted above, Jesus taught three times about his upcoming death: here, and in 9.30–32 and 10.32–34. We have, therefore, moved from simply recognizing who Jesus was to understanding what that meant about what he had come to do.

In Mark's characteristic fashion, he has trailed (albeit subtly to this point) the dark shadow of the cross. The increasing conflict with the authorities, which began at 3.6, with the decision to destroy Jesus, has been lurking in the background, with occasional additional scuffles breaking out since then. The moment that Jesus abandoned the Pharisees in 8.13 marked a watershed. These three predictions of his death indicated that Jesus was fully aware of how this whole situation would end (and then begin again with the Resurrection).

The pressure on the disciples has stepped up a level. Until this point, the question had simply been whether they could work out who he was; from now on, they also need to understand what this would mean for him and for them.

Son of Man and the first prophecy of death and resurrection

For more on the Son of Man, see the box on p. 61; for a chart comparing the content of the three prophecies, see p. 213; and for more on the significance of elders, chief priests and scribes, see the boxes on pp. 261, 258 and 43.

Jesus' prophecies about his death become more detailed as they go on. This is the simplest of all: he will undergo suffering, be rejected, be killed and will rise again.

After three days

Each of Jesus' prophecies about his death state that he will rise after three days. The Resurrection took place on the morning of the third day – but not after three days: it was only two and a half days.

Some see this as an argument that the latter number was in reality what Jesus said (otherwise, it would have been changed to fit what happened).

The most likely explanation is that Jewish custom was to treat a part day as a whole day, and so 'on the third day' becomes the same as 'after three days' (especially when the day begins in the evening). Thus, Friday before sundown is day one; Friday sundown to Saturday sundown is day two; and Saturday sundown marks the start of day three.

A suffering messiah

There is extensive discussion among scholars about whether someone at the time of Jesus would reasonably have expected a messiah to suffer. It is very difficult to find any writings that point to this explicitly; not least because it is clear that the *Targum Isaiah* 52.13—53.12 (the most likely passage from the Old Testament to indicate suffering) is understood to refer to the whole of Israel. In other words, it was taken to refer to the experience of the whole people of God, not just one person. Any expectations about what a messiah would do, therefore, would focus on saving the people from their oppressors, not on suffering and dying. It is not surprising that Peter was so taken aback by Jesus' teaching.

A Targum

Targums were ancient Aramaic paraphrases of the Hebrew Scriptures. They are particularly interesting to scholars as they provide a window into how certain passages were understood at the time of Jesus.

The *Targum Isaiah*, sometimes known as the *Targum Jonathan on Isaiah* after Jonathan ben Uzziel to whom the paraphrase was attributed, is thought to date to the first century BC.

The issue seems to be not so much Peter's surprise but that he rebuked Jesus (8.32), in the way Jesus rebuked the disciples in verse 30 and then Peter in verse 33.

Rebuking in Mark

The verb *epitimaō* occurs nine times in Mark and its use is interesting. In 1.25, 3.12, 9.25, Jesus rebukes the unclean spirits; in 4.39, he rebukes the wind and the waves. Following this passage, in 10.13, he rebukes the disciples for trying to stop children from coming to him; and in 10.48, the crowd rebukes Bartimaeus for calling out. The word is normally used, therefore, of those who have authority over those who do not. For Peter to rebuke Jesus is an act of considerable rudeness and indicates that he was trying to exercise authority over him.

'Get behind me, Satan!'

Jesus' response to Peter seems harsh but does make sense. The Satan figure in the Old Testament was one that asked questions, posed possibilities and by doing so affected action (for example, Satan persuaded God to test Job; see Job 1.6–12). As we see in the Garden of Gethsemane, Jesus did not embrace death lightly. It was a source of torment and fear. Peter's suggestion, therefore, that it could be avoided was very much the kind of proposition Satan would pose. Peter's motivations were based, Jesus claimed, on a human understanding of the world (probably the desire to evict the Romans) rather than an understanding of God's plan.

The words for 'rise' and 'resurrection' in Mark

In Mark, there are two Greek words used for Jesus' Resurrection: *anistēmi* and *egeirō*. The challenge of the word *anistēmi* is that it is also the regular word for 'get up'. So when Levi got up and followed Jesus (Mark 2.14), *anistēmi* is used. As a result, when Jairus' daughter (5.41) and the boy with the unclean spirit (9.27) are described as getting up or able to stand (using *anistēmi*), it isn't clear how much to read into the statement (for example, it would be equally correct to say 'the boy stood up' or 'the boy rose'). Similarly, when Jesus commands people to get up (see, for example, the healing of the paralytic in 2.11), he uses the word *egeirō*. So that word, too, is hard to translate properly.

It is nevertheless helpful to see the different words used for 'resurrection/rise' when used specifically of Jesus' Resurrection. In the three predictions, the word *anistēmi* is used throughout. It switches, however, to *egeirō* in 16.6; but interestingly, it is used in the passive voice: not 'he rose' but 'he was raised'. So the action moves to God.

Mark 8.34—9.1: Take up your cross

So far in Mark, we have begun to get a sense of Jesus' expectations of his disciples: that they should not be timid but have faith (4.40); that they should be courageous (6.50); and that they should be able to perceive, understand and remember, and not have hard hearts (8.17–18). We now begin to see why. The need for all these characteristics is because they must follow Jesus in the way of the cross. The call to suffering is not Jesus' alone, but theirs too.

Links backwards

- This passage looks all the way back to Jesus' call to discipleship: 'Follow me' (Mark 1.17). Those who have heard that call now discover the extent of what they signed up for.
- We also discover, now, why Jesus said what he did to the disciples during the three boat journeys: 'Why are you timid? (4.40); 'Have courage' (6.50); 'Perceive, understand and remember' (8.17–18). All these qualities, and more, will be needed for those who take up their crosses to follow Jesus.

Interesting words ...

- v. 34: *become my followers.* Literally, 'come (*erchomai*) behind (*opisō*) me (*egō*)'. It is important to note that the word *akolouthō* ('follow') isn't used here.
- v. 34: *deny. Aparneomai* means simply 'to say no to'. It does not mean to turn your back on who you are but to say no to the demands that come when you place yourself at the centre of your own life.
- v. 34: *cross.* A *stauros* was a pole, a stake or, in the context of the Romans, a cross. It is a word that gains meaning through Jesus' own death, otherwise the instruction to take up a pole might seem strange.
- v. 35: *life.* The word *psuchē* can be translated as 'soul'. In Hebrew thinking, however, a better translation is often 'life force'; and this seems a good translation here. Although much has been made in literature (see, for example, the Faustus myth) of 'losing your soul', this is not what Jesus is talking about here. He is referring to the whole of your life and what makes you unique.
- v. 35: *save and lose.* 'Save' is translated from *sōzō* and 'lose' from *apollumi*, which can also be translated as 'destroy utterly' or 'kill'. An interesting alternate translation here is 'if anyone wants to save their life, they will destroy it'.
- v. 35: *gospel. Euangelion* refers to 'good tidings' or 'good news', and hence 'gospel'.
- vv. 36–37: the key words here are connected both to business and to crime:
  - 'Profit': the verb *ōpheleō* has a range of meanings: 'to be of use', 'help', 'aid',

'service' or 'benefit to'. It was often used in business to refer to the benefit that is derived from a transaction.
  - 'Gain': *kerdainō* has its roots in business and refers to gaining a profit, winning over or making a trade to one's own advantage.
  - 'Forfeit': Unlike *kerdainō*, *zēmioomai* has a more punitive connotation: 'suffer loss', 'damage' or 'undergo punishment'.
  - 'Give in return': *Antallagma* is another word drawn from business and refers to 'exchange': you give one thing in exchange for another.
- v. 38: *ashamed*. In a world where honour and shame were important, the word *epaischunomai* is significant. It means 'to feel or show shame for something'. It is used both times in this verse.
- 9.1: *Truly I tell you*. This characteristic opening (*amēn legō humin*) to a saying by Jesus occurs once early on in Mark and then with increasing frequency towards the end (3.28; 8.12; 9.1, 41; 10.15, 29; 11.23; 12.43; 13.30; 14.18, 25, 30). For more on the phrase, see the note on 3.28 (p. 85).
- v. 1: *taste*. Here, the word 'taste' is the equivalent of 'take a small amount to test' (*geusomai*) and hence 'to experience'.
- v. 1: *see*. The verb *horaō* can and often does mean 'see'; but it can also mean 'perceive' or 'understand'. This is important here, as you will see below.
- v. 1: *has come*. The verb *erchomai* ('come') is used here in the perfect tense. The key thing is that some will see that the kingdom has come in power.

He called the crowd

This marks a change in Jesus' relationship with the crowd. Previously, a crowd gathered around him, sometimes even pursued him around the lake. Now he calls the people to him deliberately in order to teach them.

What is intriguing is where the crowd has come from. In the previous narrative, we imagine Jesus to be alone with the disciples for the declaration about who he is. It suggests that, at this part of Jesus' ministry, we are to imagine that he is accompanied by a crowd wherever he goes, and the teaching to the disciples alone happens in the midst of the throng.

'Follow me'

The emphasis on following in verse 34 ('If anyone wants to come behind me ... pick up the cross and follow me') now clarifies what the following of Jesus entails: it means being prepared to go where he goes – exactly where he goes. The call to follow Jesus is not something that requires an act of self-identity; in fact, it necessitates quite the opposite. It obliges followers to say no to themselves and be prepared to follow Jesus, even to suffering and death. It seems as though the stakes have suddenly been raised for his disciples, from trying to piece together who Jesus might be to committing to follow him on a path they never expected him to take.

On saving and losing your life

In a Hebrew context (as noted above), the noun *psuchē*, which in the Greek world meant 'soul', means something closer to 'life force': it is what makes you who you are, but which also gives life. The use of it in verses 35–36 indicates the slipperiness of the word, which is used here for who you really are, what you think gives you life (but does not) and true life. Also hovering behind what Jesus says is life in this age or world, and life in the age or world to come. What is a little confusing is that Jesus moves through the different meanings of *psuchē*.

Verse 35 is a riddle and, like Jesus' other parables, is best understood with deep reflection. If you read it carefully phrase by phrase, it can seem a little confusing; but stepping back and taking it as a whole makes it much clearer. Those who cling to what they think constitutes life will ultimately lose, or even destroy, it. Those who are prepared to lay down life for the sake of Jesus and his good news will discover that they have saved it (probably in the age to come). Since *psuchē*, in Hebrew thinking, encompasses the whole of who you are, including your body, the hint here is that the saving will take place in the resurrection from the dead; but it also implies a saving of what really matters now.

This riddle is expanded into verse 36. Those who cling to life are clinging to what can be gained in this world. Even if you owned the entire world but lost who you were in the process, there would be no point to it whatsoever.

Being ashamed of Jesus and his words

Jesus moves here from the general (losing and saving life) to a specific instance in which this might occur in the future. The implication is that there will come a moment when the choice for people to distance themselves from Jesus and his words will be offered. If they do, they will save their lives temporarily but then Jesus will distance himself from them (again, the implication is that this will happen at the moment of judgement when Jesus recognizes his own).

It is worth adding as a rider to this that the disciples, especially Peter, did exactly this at Jesus' Crucifixion and were forgiven. Jesus was offering hardline teaching here; but, in reality, he did understand how difficult it was to do and forgave those who needed forgiveness when they were unable to live up to his expectations.

Some will not taste death

This is one of the most contested verses in the whole of Mark. It appears to say that there would be some in the crowd who would not die before Jesus comes again. Since this has clearly not happened, it causes us to ask whether we have understood the passage correctly or whether Jesus was wrong.

Some commentators suggest that Mark didn't think Jesus was wrong, otherwise he would not have kept the saying in the Gospel. There is quite a strong argument for this. The only question there is whether, when Mark was writing (see the discussion of dates in 'When was it written', on pp. 8–10), he still believed Jesus would return before the entire generation had died out.

Here are some other options.

- Mark 9.1 is to be read closely with 8.38 ('of them the Son of Man will also be ashamed when he comes in the glory of his Father'). If the glory of his Father is seen as the glory that is revealed in the Transfiguration (the next passage), and if we note that this signals that the kingdom of God has come with power already, then almost everyone included in 9.1 would still have been alive.
- The same interpretation could be provided for the Crucifixion, the Resurrection and/or the sending of the Spirit at Pentecost since, in all of these, the kingdom can be seen to come with power.
- A third option places the emphasis not on the event but on the response to the event. Arguably, Jesus' whole ministry has demonstrated that the kingdom of God has come with power: the healings, exorcisms, feedings at the messianic banquet, the Transfiguration, the Crucifixion and the Resurrection – all point to this. Perhaps the load-bearing verb is 'see'. As we noted in the third boat scene, Jesus places a lot of emphasis on seeing and therefore understanding. This whole section of Mark has been exploring this theme. The verb 'see' can also mean 'perceive'. Perhaps the real point is that there will be some who perceive the kingdom has come with power, because it has already if they have eyes to see.

It is this third option that I think is the most likely. Trying to discern which of the other events most encapsulates the kingdom coming with power is tricky.

Mark 9.2–13: 'This is my Son' – the Transfiguration

The description of this passage as the Transfiguration can, if we are not careful, distract us from one of the key elements of the passage in Mark's narrative. Of course, it is important that Peter, James and John are given a glimpse of Jesus as he really is; but the key voice in this passage is God's. The passages around this one explore who Jesus is. Various people of Jesus' day wonder if Jesus is John the Baptist, Elijah or another prophet; Peter declares he is the Christ (though understandably doesn't comprehend what that means); now God speaks.

What he says points us backwards to Jesus' baptism where, as he came up out of the river, Jesus heard God saying that he was his 'Son, the Beloved'. It also points us forwards to the Crucifixion, where the centurion identified him as God's son. It is worth remembering that the disciples were not there at Jesus' baptism and, even if they had been, the voice did not speak to those who were there. This was the first time that they heard God declaring who his Son is.

Who then is this? 'The Christ' is one answer, but 'the beloved Son of God' is equally important.

Links backwards

- The baptism of Jesus, where God spoke to Jesus and said, 'You are my Son, the Beloved; with you I am well pleased' (Mark 1.11).
- Also important here is the disciples' question, 'Who then is this?', at the stilling of the storm (4.41); and Jesus' question to the disciples at Caesarea Philippi, 'Who do you say that I am?' (8.29).

Links forwards

- The Crucifixion, where the centurion says, 'Truly this man was God's Son!' (15.39).

Interesting words ...

- v. 2: *high mountain.* The description of the mountain (*oros*) is simple: *upsēlos* means 'high', 'lofty' or 'tall'.
- v. 2: *apart, by themselves.* This phrase is one that has occurred a few times in Mark so far. *Kat'idian* means 'privately'; it was used when Jesus explained the parables and healed the deaf man in the Decapolis and the blind man in Bethsaida. It is stressed here, with the addition of *monos* ('alone'). This is even more private than other previous private experiences have been.
- v. 2: *transfigured. Metamorpheō* means 'transformed' or 'transfigured'.
- v. 3: *clothes.* Often *himation* refers to an 'outer garment' or 'cloak'; but here, it seems likely to refer to Jesus' clothes in general.
- v. 3: *dazzling white; bleach.* Words are piled up here on top of one another to add emphasis: *stilbō* ('glitter', 'gleam', 'twinkle' or 'shine'), *leukos* ('bright' or 'white'), *lian* ('extremely' or 'very'). The word 'bleach' repeats *leukos*, but this time in verbal form (*leukainō*) 'to make white'.
- v. 3: *one.* A *gnapheus* was a cloth refiner or fuller who would use urine and sunlight to bleach material.
- v. 4: *appeared.* Given the importance of the verb *horaō* in this part of Mark, it is important to note that it is another very irregular verb; and *ōphthē*, which

appears here, is the aorist (past tense) passive form of that verb meaning 'to be seen' or 'to appear'.

- v. 4: *Elijah with Moses*. Two things are odd about this small phrase. Elijah is cited before Moses, though he lived many years later. Mark does not use the word 'and' (*kai*) but 'with' (*sun*).
- v. 4: *talking*. The pleasingly onomatopoeic verb *sullaleō* means 'to converse'.
- v. 5: *dwellings*. The word *skēnē* means 'a tent' or 'a booth'.
- vv. 5–6: *said; say*. The verb *apokrinomai* is used twice here: 'Peter answered. He did not know what to answer.' It indicates that Peter felt a response was necessary but then failed to think of the right words.
- v. 6: *terrified*. We are accustomed to the word 'fear' or 'afraid'. *Ekphobō* is the intense form of the verb, which means 'terrified' or 'very frightened'.
- v. 7: *cloud*. A *nephelē* refers either to a single cloud or a mass of clouds.
- v. 8: *suddenly*. This is not the usual *euthus* but *exepina*, which means 'immediately' or 'suddenly'. The use of a different word when we are so used to *euthus* is worth noticing.
- v. 9: *ordered them*. The verb *diastellō* ('give precise instructions about') is used four times in Mark: when Jesus ordered Jairus and his family to keep others from knowing what had happened (5.43); when he told the friends of the deaf man in the Decapolis to say nothing (7.36); when he warned the disciples about the leaven of the Pharisees (8.15); and here.
- v. 9: *tell*. *Diēgeomai* means more than just 'tell'. It refers to 'describing in detail' or 'telling fully'. The implication of the verb is that vague details might be allowable but precise ones are not.
- v. 9: *Son of Man*. See the box, 'Son of Man', on p. 61 for more detail on what Son (*ho huios*) of Man (*tou anthrōpou*) means.
- v. 10: *kept*. *Krateō* means 'hold on to'. It can be used both of power and of information.
- v. 10: *questioning*. This word, *suzeteō*, has the idea of 'searching' or 'examining' and also of 'arguing' or 'disputing'. This seems likely here, because the disciples were arguing about what rising from the dead meant.
- v. 12: *restore*. *Apokathistēmi* has the sense of 'return' (in terms of property), as well as 'restore'.
- v. 12: *contempt*. *Exoudeneō* is an unusual word that means 'to be ill-treated', 'despised' or 'treated with contempt'.

After six days

Mark's love of the word 'immediately' makes his statement – that the Transfiguration happened after six days – stand out. He doesn't give extended timings very often, so when he does, it is worth noting. One of the important things it does is remind us that this passage is linked closely to the previous passage (Peter's declaration at Caesarea Philippi). We are still hearing who people say Jesus is and now it is God's turn to speak, even if it is six days later.

Theophanies

An important strand that runs through both the Old and New Testaments is that of God's appearance to human beings. These are known technically as 'theophanies' ('theophany' means, literally, 'appearance of God'). In a theophany, sometimes an angel appears; sometimes it isn't clear whether it is an angel or God; and sometimes it is God.

A theophany often took place on the top of a mountain and was accompanied by 'natural phenomena', such as an earthquake, wind, fire, cloud, lightning or shining light. So, for example, when Moses met God in Exodus 3.1–6, the bush that attracted his attention was on fire; when he met God on the top of Mount Sinai (Ex. 19), there were thunder, lightning and thick cloud; when Elijah encountered God on Mount Horeb, there were wind, an earthquake and fire (1 Kings 19.11–18); when Isaiah encountered God in the temple (Isa. 6.1–8), the foundations shook and the temple was filled with smoke. The point made concerning the appearance of God to Elijah at Mount Horeb is important. God was not in the natural phenomena: they heralded his presence.

The other marker of a theophany was that God spoke either to call someone to do something or to reveal something they needed to know.

The presence of cloud and shining clothes in this story, as well as the voice of God speaking, clearly demarcates the event in Mark 9.2–8 as a theophany. If we were tempted to imagine that Jesus was 'just' a human being, a prophet like any other, this passage reveals him to be God.

A high mountain

The location associated with the Transfiguration is Mount Tabor, though some question this as it is only 1,886 feet above sea level (in other words, it's not really a high mountain). Other options include Mount Carmel (1,724 ft – still not very high), Mount Meron (3,926 ft) and Mount Hermon (9,234 ft). Mount Hermon is also quite close to Casarea Philippi.

The point, however, is that Mark doesn't say which mountain it is. The location is much less important than what is revealed there.

Jesus was transfigured

The word *metamorpheō* occurs four times in the New Testament. Here, in Matthew's parallel account (Matt. 17.2) and twice in Paul. When it is used in Paul, it is used of believers and their journey of faith, though it is translated as 'transformed', not 'transfigured': 'And all of us … are being transformed into the same image from one degree of glory to another' (2 Cor. 3.18) and 'be transformed by the renewing of your minds' (Rom. 12.2).

The word means a change of form: physical or spiritual, external or internal. What is clear, here, is that Jesus' transformation was to some extent physical and external – as Peter, James and John could see it – as well as spiritual. This physical change is clearer in Matthew and Luke, as they describe changes to Jesus' face (Matt. 17.2; Luke 9.29).

Revelation or apocalyptic

The word 'apocalypse' or 'apocalyptic' has become, in modern usage, synonymous with disaster or catastrophe. This is largely due to a connection with the book of Revelation (otherwise known as the Apocalypse) which contains visions of calamities striking the earth as a result of the war in heaven between good and evil.

The Greek word, however, means simply 'revelation'. It refers to something being revealed that was previously hidden. Indeed, the book of Revelation may contain catastrophe, but it is named after the revelations it contains. Apocalyptic literature inside and outside the Bible focuses on revealing what is hidden.

By this definition, the Transfiguration is an apocalypse. Jesus' true nature is revealed both visually and audibly. It also points to two other moments of apocalypse in the Gospel: the baptism of Jesus (though there the revelation is kept to Jesus alone) and the Crucifixion (which we will explore further on p. 333).

For many years, in Markan scholarship, much was made of the messianic secret. Indeed, we have noted, as we have proceeded through Mark's account, how often Jesus told people not to tell anyone who he was. This theme of secrecy has to be balanced with these three moments of revelation. Mark is a Gospel of three key moments of revelation as well as the many commands not to tell anyone about what was going on.

Shining, very white clothes

In addition to the features of a theophany noted above, Jesus' clothes are described here as shining brightly. This picks up a tradition about God and, by extension, angels. For example, in Daniel 7.9, God is described as having clothing that is as 'white as snow' and the angel at the Resurrection is also described as wearing white clothing (Mark 16.5). This strand is even more striking in apocalyptic texts outside of the Bible. For example, 1 Enoch 14.19 says: 'And the Great Glory sat on it, and His garment shone more brightly than the sun and was whiter than any snow.' This description, coupled with the signs of a theophany, make crystal clear that Peter, James and John, and we, the readers, are to understand that Jesus' divinity is being revealed.

Scholarly discussions of the Transfiguration often focus on the question of whether what is being revealed is Jesus' pre-existent glory (the glory he had from the dawn of time), his resurrection glory or the glory he will have when he comes again. Most opt for either his resurrection glory or his second-coming glory, or a combination of the two. In my opinion, however, this is the wrong question to ask. This section of Mark is exploring the question of who Jesus is; the Transfiguration gives one more layer of response to this question. He is the person who will die and rise again, and who will return at the end of all time: trying to tie his glory to one moment in time is to miss the point.

Who is this? He is the person who proclaims good news, heals the sick and casts out demons. Who is this? He is the long-awaited Messiah. Who is this? He is God's beloved Son, who is revealed as being divine. Who is this? He is the Son of Man who will die, rise again and come on the clouds of glory. Whose glory do the disciples see? Jesus' glory: the glory that is his at all times and in everything he is and does.

Elijah and Moses

For an event that is so momentous, Mark tells us remarkably little about it. We are left to surmise how Peter, James and John knew that the two figures were Elijah and Moses or what form their appearance took. Peter's suggestion that he make a dwelling for each of them suggests that they appeared corporeally and not in a ghostlike form. The tradition that Elijah ascended bodily to heaven from earth can be found in 2 Kings 2.11; but there was a similar tradition about Moses in post-biblical tradition. In his *Antiquities of the Jews*, the Jewish historian Josephus recounted that Moses, at the end of his life, was covered with a cloud and disappeared (*Ant.* 4.8.48). The idea is that Elijah and Moses lived in heaven with God and the angels in bodily form, and so could appear on earth in a similarly physical way.

It is interesting, but not surprising, that Elijah is mentioned first. He has already been mentioned explicitly in Mark 6.15 and 8.28 (and will be mentioned again in 9.11); and, by implication, in the reference to John the Baptist (1.2–8). Moses, however, has been mentioned only in connection with his writings. Their significance lies probably in the active expectation of a prophet like Moses arising, who would come to lead God's people (see, for example, Peter's speech in Acts 3.22), and in Elijah's being seen as the forerunner of God's glorious intervention in the world to save his people (Mal. 4.5).

Three booths

Peter's suggestion that he erect three booths is often portrayed as his speaking before he thought. In fact, it wasn't that big a leap. The word *skēnē* referred to tents and to the booths that were to be built for the Feast of Tabernacles (Lev. 23.33–42). There was a belief that when God returned to his people, on the Day of the Lord, they would go back to living in tents or booths as they had during the period of the wilderness wanderings. The appearance of Elijah, the forerunner, Moses, the prophet, and the cloud that accompanied God's people in the wilderness would all have suggested to Peter that the long-awaited redemption of God's people had begun. The first job to do would have been to build tents or booths for the leaders of God's people; it was not such a bad idea if, indeed, this was the beginning of the much anticipated world to come.

We should note that it is Mark who gives us the idea that what Peter was saying was daft ('He did not know what to say, for they were terrified'). The reality is that it was only daft once we knew what the Transfiguration meant. While it was possible that this was the start of the long-awaited intervention of God in the world, it was eminently sensible.

'Listen to him!'

God's command to listen to Jesus is reminiscent of Jesus' question to the disciples in the boat scene from the previous chapter: 'Do you have ears, and fail to hear?' (Mark 8.18); the connection is more obvious when you know that 'hear' and 'listen' are both translations of the same word, *akouō*). The disciples have thus far struggled to see, hear and understand. God now commands them to try again. He is revealing to them clearly and unequivocally who Jesus is: they should listen to him and hence come to understand.

Tell no one … until

Until this point in Mark, Jesus' regular command to people not to say anything about what they have seen and heard has been bemusing. We now receive an extra piece of information, which begins to make more sense. There was a time limit on their silence; that is, until Jesus had risen from the dead. After the Resurrection, they could tell all. Indeed, the young man in the tomb very explicitly said to the women that they should 'Go, tell' (16.7). As had just happened, the danger of telling the wrong thing before Jesus had died and risen again was too great. They needed to wait and get the whole picture before telling others about what they had seen.

Elijah must come first

Although the disciples' question makes less sense to us, it was quite topical at the time. In the Judaism of Jesus' day, there was an active expectation that Elijah would return before the Day of the Lord. The presence of Elijah on the mountain, accompanied by Peter's apparent belief that the end times had begun (or, at the very least, were imminent), would naturally lead to this question.

Jesus' response is recognized by most commentators as being a little confusing. Indeed, Matthew's version makes a lot more sense than Mark's:

> 'Elijah is indeed coming and will restore all things; but I tell you that Elijah has already come, and they did not recognize him, but they did to him whatever they pleased. So also the Son of Man is about to suffer at their hands.' Then the disciples understood that he was speaking to them about John the Baptist. (Matt. 17.11–13)

Probably the key to understanding Jesus' response is to recognize, along with Matthew, that he was linking John the Baptist and Elijah. So the Elijah they are all talking about is John the Baptist. As John has been established as the 'coming Elijah' in Mark 1, this seems probable. What follows, then, is Jesus' explanation about the nature of the restoration that they are talking about. The scribal tradition about Elijah coming first to restore all things is true: he has come already (9.13) in the person of John the Baptist; but the restoration is not what they are imagining. It will be marked by the suffering of both John the Baptist and the Messiah. The evidence for this is how John has already been treated.

Mark 9.14–29: The healing of a boy with a spirit

If we take the healing of the blind man at Bethsaida as the start of this section and the healing of Bartimaeus as the end, this healing sits in the middle. This structure seems to make the point that the real lack of sight was in this faithless generation, rather than in those who couldn't see physically.

This account is one of Mark's more vivid stories, told at much greater length and with much more detail than the parallel in either Matthew (17.14–20) or Luke (9.37–43).

Links backwards

- In Mark 1.40, the leper said to Jesus that he could make him clean if he wanted. Here, the father says, 'If you are able' (9.23). Both raise the question of whether Jesus would choose/be able to heal.
- The Twelve had already been commissioned to cast out demons in 3.15 and 6.7. They had authority but not ability here.
- The words used to describe the moment of healing mimic exactly the words used for the healing of Jairus' daughter (5.41). See 'Interesting words', verse 27, below.

Links forwards

- The healing of Bartimaeus (10.46–52), who has faith that Jesus can heal him.
- Jesus' teaching on prayer in 11.24 resonates strongly with this passage, especially when Jesus says that this kind can come out only through prayer.

Interesting words ...

- v. 14: *arguing*. The scribes are arguing (*suzuteō*) with the disciples, just as Jesus, Peter and John had been arguing on the way down the mountain (9.10): the same verb is used.
- v. 15: *overcome with awe*. We are accustomed to Mark's use of the words for 'astonished'. *Ekthambeō* is a variation of *thambeō*, which takes the astonishment to another level. It means something like 'overwhelmed' or 'flabbergasted'. For more on Mark's use of these kinds of words, see the notes on 1.22 and 27 (pp. 41–2).
- v. 17: *unable to speak*. Unusually, the type of spirit is named here: a speechless or mute (*alalos*) spirit (*pneuma*).
- v. 18: *dashes; foams; grinds; becomes rigid*.
  - 'Dashes' is a tricky word to translate. *Rhēgnumi* means 'to break' or 'to shatter'; 'dashes' is probably a good translation.
  - 'Foams' (*aphrizō*) refers to anything that foams. It is used again in verse 20.
  - 'Grinds' (*trizō*) is usually used of sounds made by animals; it means 'shrill cries'. It also refers to similar sounds: creaks, grinding and gnashing. The verb implies a vivid sound from the boy's teeth.
  - 'Becomes rigid': *xērainō* means 'to become hard', 'to become stiff' or 'to become paralysed'.
- v. 18: *could not do so*. *Ischuō* is 'to be strong' or 'to prevail', so the disciples weren't strong enough.
- v. 19: *how much longer ... ?* Although the translation in the NRSV is 'How much longer must I be among you?', the 'must' is not reflected in the Greek. It could read 'How much longer will I be with you?' and the other question could be read as 'How much longer will I endure (*anechomai*) you?'
- v. 20: *convulsions*. This is a particular word (*susparassō*) that refers to being thrown into a fit. See verse 26 for a different form of the verb.
- v. 22: *have pity on us and help us*. The Greek reads 'after having compassion on us (*splangchnizomai*), help [come to the aid of] (*boētheō*) us'. The same word for 'help' is used in verse 24 for 'help my unbelief'.
- v. 23: *able; can be done*. These two words are connected in Greek. 'Able' is translated from *dunamai*, and 'can be done' is the adjective that comes from *dunamai* (*dunatos*). It is hard to find a translation that reflects this; it may be something such as, 'If you can, everything can be done ...'
- vv. 23–24: *believes; believe; unbelief*. The word *pistis* is used in various forms in

these two verses: 'the one believing' and 'I believe' (both *pisteuō*); and 'unbelief' (*apistia*: 'want of faith').

- v. 25: *rebuked.* The word *epitimaō*, used in 8.30–33 for the rebukes between Jesus and Peter, is used here. See the box, 'Rebuking in Mark', on p. 194, for the use of the word 'rebuke'.
- v. 25: *unclean spirit.* The spirit is called 'unclean' (*akathartos*), the usual word for such spirits in Mark before now (see 1.23–27; 3.30; 5.2, 8; 6.7; 7.25).
- v. 25: *speaking and hearing.* The spirit has been described only as *alalos* ('speechless' or 'mute'); it is now also described as 'deaf' (*kōphos*: 'blunt', 'obtuse' or 'muffled'). The Greek says literally that it is a speechless and muffled spirit, which is why, by implication, the boy has those disabilities.
- v. 26: *crying out and convulsing him terribly. Krazō* refers to 'screaming' or 'crying out', and *sparassō* ('convulsing') is a version of *susparassō* (see the note on v. 20). To this is added *polla* ('a lot').
- v. 26: *corpse. Nekros*: 'inanimate thing'.
- v. 27: *took; lifted; stand.* The fact that the NRSV translates the three verbs differently between 5.41 and here makes it hard to see in English, but the same three Greek words are used of the healing of Jairus' daughter: 'took' (*krazō*), 'lifted' (*egeirō*) and 'stand' (*anistēmi*). The fact that the boy was thought to be dead in verse 26 (as Jairus' daughter was) is important here. The verb for 'raise' (from the dead) is the same as 'stand up' (*anistēmi*), so it could mean 'he stood up' and 'he was raised'.

The crowd was overcome with awe

We are used, in Mark, to the crowd being amazed, but this is usually after a healing or some teaching. The fact that they are not just amazed, but overcome with awe or amazement, implies that, to put it crudely, Jesus' Transfiguration has not entirely worn off. There are still signs of brightness, light and glory on him.

The mute and deaf spirit

The symptoms described for the boy suggest to many commentators that he had epilepsy. So much so that the subheadings in some translations describe him like that. The problem is that the other exorcisms in the Gospels are much less easy to pigeonhole and so are usually referred to as 'demon possessions'. The temptation to label this epilepsy also encourages people to attempt to diagnose some of the other spirit-instigated illnesses too, suggesting causes such as schizophrenia or bipolar disorder. This is never helpful, as it suggests a connection between illnesses and demon possession. On balance, it is better to take the conditions simply as they are presented, without attempting a modern diagnosis.

In any case, the spirit here is specifically described as causing speechlessness and deafness, so the epilepsy diagnosis doesn't quite fit. It is also worth noting that the speechless spirit does not speak in this story (unlike the spirits in most of Jesus' other exorcisms), which suggests that not only is it unable to speak but it also causes the boy to be unable to speak.

Faithless generation

Jesus' sweeping categorization raises the question of whom Jesus is talking to. When used elsewhere, the term 'generation' refers to Jesus' contemporaries and there is no reason to think it is different here. The disciples are certainly not excluded from this category (we have seen in the three boat scenes that they too are faithless and lacking in understanding), but it is not limited to them.

Jesus' tone has become increasingly sharp since the scene in the boat when he asked the disciples why they were talking about bread while his focus was on the Pharisees. He has identified the disciples as outsiders and rebuked Peter. Now, he expresses frustration at the faithlessness he sees all around him. The two questions he asks ('How much longer must I be among you?' and 'How much longer must I put up with you?'), along with his prediction of his own death, suggest that Jesus is aware that time is running out, yet no one around him seems to understand the things they should understand before it does.

'If you are able'

This passage is reminiscent of the leper, in 1.40, who expressed uncertainty about whether Jesus would want to help him. Here, the father begs Jesus to have compassion and help him; but his question is about Jesus' ability. This is unsurprising, given the disciples' failed attempt before Jesus arrived. It is important to recognize that the disciples were not wrong to try: they had already been given authority to do exorcisms; they were just unable to help.

Jesus' response in verse 23 should be read as an indignant echo of the man's statement: 'What do you mean, "If you can"?' Although the man's doubt appears rude, it is understandable. He has seen the disciples try and fail to help his son. So a question mark about whether Jesus can do so is not unreasonable. As Jesus points out, however, the real question is the man's faith rather than Jesus' ability: will he demonstrate himself to be part of the faithless generation that were the subject of Jesus' outburst?

The man's reply to Jesus is, in many ways, a perfect response of faith. Faith is not a binary condition: it does not imply that if you do not believe 100 per cent, then you don't believe at all. It is more nuanced than that: belief and unbelief, faith and lack of faith exist side by side. It is the man's reliance on what he does have and his plea for help in an area where he lacks that are crucial. It seems as though, yet again, Mark wants us, the readers, to know that seeing a little bit (the man healed in Bethsaida) and believing as much as we can (the father here) is sufficient for following Jesus, even though the demands of that following (taking up our crosses) will require everything we have.

Was he raised?

The parallels with the healing of Jairus' daughter are striking here.

- A desperate father begs for help for a beloved child.
- The child is thought to have died just before the healing.
- Jesus takes the child's hand, lifts them up and they get up (or are raised).

As with Jairus' daughter, we will never know if this was a bringing back to life or a 'simple' healing. The effect is the same.

Through prayer

The ending of this story leaves us with even more questions than we originally had. Thus far, there has been no mention of prayer in the disciples' healing/exorcisms. Nor does the simple 'through prayer' help us much. Should the disciples have prayed extensively before attempting the healing? Or during it? Was the problem that they tried to heal the boy by relying solely on their own authority (given by Jesus) and not by asking for help from God? It, of course, produces enormous questions for life today too: what does it mean for people suffering ill health? Should we deem that lack of healing indicates lack of adequate prayer?

Before we disappear in a puff of despairing unknowing, it is probably worth noting what we can know from this passage, rather than what we can't. The man's faith, imperfect though it was, along with Jesus' power, was sufficient in this context to heal the boy. The disciples' inability to heal him, the passage implies, was because they relied on their own strength and not on the strength of God. This is another episode in the ongoing saga of the disciples and all they had to learn before Jesus' death. In this context, they needed to learn to rely on God. The fact that they didn't seems to have affected the man's faith too, to the extent that he was uncertain whether Jesus would be able to help.

It is probably ill-advised to attempt to extrapolate from this to all illnesses everywhere and how to deal with them. Discussions about healing are complex and need handling carefully. Healing does happen but when and how it happens is hard to tie down with any certainty. Some positions that attribute lack of healing to sin, lack of faith or insufficient prayer are immensely damaging, and we should avoid them wherever possible.

Indeed, this story is the perfect antidote to such attitudes. The boy's father had lost trust in the disciples and hence in Jesus too; he expressed doubt that Jesus could heal the boy. He acknowledged that his faith was far from perfect, yet healing still took place.

The healing happened when whatever faith the man did have met and entwined with the faith of Jesus. There is something important here. In our journey of faith, our mixed bag of belief and unbelief is met by Jesus' own faith and faithfulness. It is when this happens that we encounter wholeness, though what that wholeness looks like will almost certainly surprise us every time.

Mark 9.30–32: Jesus prophesied about his death a second time

The change in the tone of the Gospel continues with this second prophecy about Jesus' death and Resurrection. While Mark has always had a sense of dynamism, the dynamism has now turned to urgency as the shadow of the cross begins to fall over what remains of Jesus' life and ministry.

Links backwards

- In the stilling of the storm, Jesus asked the disciples why they were so timid (Mark 4.40). The fact that they were too afraid to ask Jesus what he meant when they didn't understand suggested that not much had changed.
- Jesus' first prophecy about his death and Resurrection (8.31–33).

Links forwards

- Jesus' third prophecy about his death and Resurrection (10.32–34).

Interesting words ...

- v. 30: *He did not want anyone to know*. In Greek, the verb 'want' (*thelō*) is followed by 'so that' (*hina*) and a subjunctive (a verbal form expressing wish or desire; here, the subjunctive of *ginōskō*, 'to know'): 'He did not wish so that anyone might know.'
- v. 30: *he was teaching*. This is translated from the verb *didaskō*. Here, it is in the imperfect and, therefore, has the sense of 'he kept on teaching', rather than that he taught them once.
- v. 31: *betrayed*. The verb 'betrayed' (*paradidōmi*) becomes important from now on in the story (see the box, 'Betrayed/handed over', on p. 211). It can mean 'hand over' or 'betray'.

- v. 31: *will kill; after being killed.* The verb used both times here is *apokteinō* ('to slay' or 'to kill').
- v. 31: *rise.* The verb used is one we are now familiar with: *anistēmi.*
- v. 32: *not understand.* The verb *agnoeō* (from which we get 'agnostic') has a range of meanings from 'not to know or perceive', 'to fail to understand' or 'to be ignorant of'.
- v. 32: *afraid to ask.* The usual word for 'fear' appears here (*phobeō*) with *eperōtaō*, 'to enquire' or 'to consult'.

Passing through Galilee

We have had a few events, following Peter's declaration at Caesarea Philippi, for which Mark has not told us where Jesus is. This usually means that, in Mark's mind, they are still where they were. If the Transfiguration took place near Caesarea Philippi (probably on Mount Hermon), then Jesus and the disciples would have returned southwards to the Sea of Galilee on the way to Capernaum, where they arrive in 9.33.

He did not want anyone to know

There were many reasons throughout his ministry why Jesus might not have wanted people to know where he was. But this one adds, perhaps, the greatest urgency to his desire for secrecy: he had too much to tell the disciples before his death. Given Jesus' frustration, which we observed in the previous story, it is somewhat poignant to note that not only did the disciples fail to understand what he was saying, they were too afraid to ask what he was talking about. The theme of timidity that we noted in 4.40 comes to mind here. The disciples were still timid all this time later.

Betrayed/handed over

One of the words that gets obscured in English, but which is very important in the Greek of Mark, is the verb *paradidōmi*. Below are all the verses containing the verb to give a sense of how it is used, even if it is translated unevenly.

> 'Now after John was *arrested*, Jesus came to Galilee ...' (1.14)
>
> 'Judas Iscariot, who *betrayed* him.' (3.19)
>
> 'The Son of Man is to be *betrayed* into human hands, and they will kill him ...' (9.31)
>
> 'See, we are going up to Jerusalem, and the Son of Man will be *handed over* to the chief priests and the scribes.' (10.33)

> 'As for yourselves, beware; for they will *hand you over* to councils ... When they bring you to trial and *hand you over*, do not worry beforehand about what you are to say ... Brother will *betray* brother to death, and a father his child ...' (13.9, 11, 12)
>
> 'Then Judas Iscariot, who was one of the twelve, went to the chief priests in order to *betray* him to them. When they heard it, they were greatly pleased, and promised to give him money. So he began to look for an opportunity to *betray* him.' (14.10–11)
>
> 'Jesus said, "Truly I tell you, one of you will *betray* me, one who is eating with me.' (14.18)
>
> 'For the Son of Man goes as it is written of him, but woe to that one by whom the Son of Man is *betrayed*!' (14.21)
>
> 'He came a third time and said to them, "Are you still sleeping and taking your rest? Enough! The hour has come; the Son of Man is *betrayed* into the hands of sinners. Get up, let us be going. See, my *betrayer* is at hand.' (14.41–42)
>
> 'Now the *betrayer* had given them a sign, saying, "The one I will kiss is the man; arrest him and lead him away under guard."' (14.44)
>
> 'As soon as it was morning, the chief priests held a consultation with the elders and scribes and the whole council. They bound Jesus, led him away, and *handed him over* to Pilate.' (15.1)
>
> 'For he realized that it was out of jealousy that the chief priests had *handed him over*.' (15.10)
>
> 'So Pilate, wishing to satisfy the crowd, released Barabbas for them; and after flogging Jesus, he *handed him over* to be crucified.' (15.15).

In brief, the same word is used for what Judas did, for what the chief priests and Pilate did, and for what will happen to the disciples in future. This gives extra texture to the story ... Jesus kept on being handed over from one person to another.

The content of the prophecies

It is worth noting that every time Jesus prophesies about his death, the details get a little clearer. This becomes apparent when we compare the content of the three prophecies:

Mark 8.31–33	Mark 9.30–32	Mark 10.32–34
Son of Man	Son of Man	Son of Man
Suffer many things and be rejected	Betrayed/handed over into human hands	Betrayed/handed over to the chief priests and scribes
		They will condemn him and betray/ hand him over to the Gentiles
		Mock him, spit upon him and flog him
Be killed	Be killed	They will kill him
After three days, he will rise again.	After being killed, after three days, he will rise again.	After three days, he will rise again.

The common features are that in all three passages, Jesus describes himself as the Son of Man, and being killed and rising again. The closer Jesus comes to the cross, the more details he supplies about the events that will lead him there.

Mark 9.33–37: Who is greatest?

The placement of this story here serves to emphasize the slightly farcical nature of the argument between the disciples. In the context of the increasing urgency of Jesus' teaching and the fact that the disciples didn't understand it (but were too afraid to ask), their discussing who was greatest is at best ironic. Who was best? From what we have seen so far, the answer seems to be, 'None of them.' While Jesus was reflecting on his upcoming suffering and death, they were focusing on status and personal honour.

Links backwards

- The healing of Jairus' daughter (Mark 5.37) and the Transfiguration (9.2–13) both have Jesus taking Peter, James and John to one side. It is natural that some might interpret this as Jesus showing favouritism and indicating that these three disciples were somehow greater than the others.
- Add to this, the disciples' failed exorcism (9.14–29) and the bruised feelings of those who found themselves unable to perform it, and this conversation becomes entirely understandable (if still wrong!).

Links forwards

- Immediately after Jesus' third prediction of his death and Resurrection (10.32–34), James and John ask to sit at his right hand and left hand (10.35–45). As so often in Mark, this was a lesson that needed to be learnt (at least) twice.
- Note also that a second teaching about children occurs in 10.13–16. These two, though similar, have a slightly different focus.

Interesting words ...

- vv. 33–34: *arguing; had argued. Suzeteō* (the word often used for 'argue') is not employed here. Instead, two different words for 'argue' are used. When Jesus asked the disciples about their arguing, the verb is *dialogizomai*, which means 'to balance accounts' and hence 'to consider' or 'to debate'. The second word used was *dialegō*, which is more like 'make a speech' and hence 'debate'.
- v. 34: *silent*. The verb *siōpaō* means 'to be silent' or 'to fall silent'. It is used in Mark 3.4 to describe the Pharisees falling silent when challenged by Jesus; for the wind falling silent in 4.39; and, interestingly, for Jesus' own silence at his trial (14.61). In other words, it is used for silence in the face of a challenge.
- v. 34: *greatest*. The adjective *megas* has a comparative form, *meizōn* ('greater', used here), and superlative, *megistos* ('greatest'). Although technically *meizōn* means 'greater', it can mean 'greatest' when someone is singled out over others.
- v. 35: *first; last*: 'First' (*protos*) is compared with 'last' (*eschatos*) here, as in the first in the queue and the last in the queue.
- v. 35: *servant*. The two key words for 'servant' (*diakonos*) and 'slave' (*doulos*) are often translated interchangeably but are, in fact, very distinct. A servant was free and earned money for their work; a slave was owned and did not. Here, the word used is *diakonos*. In Mark, it occurs only here and in 10.43 and 45. The word *diakonia* ('service' or 'ministry') comes from the same root.
- v. 36: *little child*. The word here is *paidion* ('little child'), as opposed to *pais* ('child'). As with the two other words we have seen used for children in Mark (*korasion*, 'little girl', and *thugatrion*, 'little daughter') *paidion* is neuter.

  It is possible that an Aramaic word play is going on beneath this episode. The Aramaic word *talya* means both 'child' and 'servant'.
- v. 36: *taking it in his arms*. The verb *enangkalizomai* means 'to embrace' or 'to hug' as well as 'take into one's arms'. An *agkalē* was 'a bent arm', so the verb connected to it refers to what you do with your bent arms (hug). The verb is used again in 10.16.
- v. 37: *welcomes. Dechomai* can mean either 'welcome' or 'receive'. 'Welcome' seems more wholehearted than simply receiving.
- v. 37: *the one who sent. Apostellō* means 'to send'. The noun *apostolos* comes from this verb, referring to one who is sent.

Who is greatest?

One social context that helps to shed light on this discussion is the honour/shame culture that existed in the world of Jesus. According to the honour/shame code, it was essential to claim honour for yourself and your family. This was not regarded as pushy or difficult: it was simply expected (hence Jesus' teaching about not taking the highest seat at the table (Luke 14.7–11): taking the place of honour was simply what people did). The corollary of this was that you cast shame on those who failed to claim honour. It was how the culture worked.

We should probably note, though, that when Jesus asked the disciples about it, they fell silent. It might have been a societal norm, but they were clearly embarrassed about it, nevertheless.

Jesus sat down ... and said

We have noticed already that, until chapter 9, there has been very little teaching by Jesus in this Gospel. Here, Jesus teaches at all possible moments, particularly around the prophecies of his own death (see also 8.34–38; 10.42–45).

Also note that sitting indicates that teaching is about to happen (see 4.1–2; 13.3).

There are two elements to Jesus' teaching: how you react yourself (become a servant) and how you welcome someone else (like a child). The two are interlinked but different.

He took a child

The imaginative landscape that we use to envisage the stories in the Gospels has been profoundly influenced by art depicting scenes from Jesus' ministry. So much so that it is easy to forget that children would have been present at most of the events during Jesus' ministry.

Here, Jesus is in a house in Capernaum. Usually, when he is in a house it is Peter's house; and we know that as Peter had a mother-in-law, he also had a wife. It is possible, even probable, that the child was one of Peter's.

What has been hinted at so far in this Gospel now becomes explicit. Our current culture privileges children (to some extent, though others don't). In today's world, children are regarded as cute, adorable, innocent and precious; whereas in the ancient world they had no social status at all. A clue to this is the fact that all words for children were neuter. They were 'non-people' until they became adults. This doesn't mean that someone like Jairus didn't love his daughter dearly: he clearly did. But on a societal level, children were entirely insignificant until they grew up.

The addition of 'in my name' makes clear what Jesus is saying here (and that it is similar to what he says in the parable of the sheep and the goats in Matthew 25). Anyone who welcomes someone of no status in Jesus' name welcomes Jesus and the one who sent him, God. Being a servant involves welcoming those of the lowest social status. This teaching never ceases to be challenging as people of all types and backgrounds, from every society, drift (sometimes rush) towards status and prestige whenever they can.

Mark 9.38–41: Someone else casting out demons

In his placement of stories here, Mark is cleverly showing the ripples that occur when people think they have failed. The disciples failed to cast out a demon; they then engage in a long conversation about comparative importance, which leads to the suggestion that they should stop someone else (not one of them) from casting out demons in Jesus' name. The implication is that this was more than just a matter of principle: it stung too.

This story probably follows on from Jesus' teaching that the disciples should welcome those of no status. The next question is how you should treat those who aren't 'one of us'.

Links backwards and forwards

- The inability of the disciples to cast out a demon (despite receiving Jesus' authority to do so) must be in mind here (Mark 9.14–29).
- This passage also links to Jesus' teaching about receiving those who are of no status (9.33–37; 10.13–16). We don't know who this person was, but he wasn't one of the disciples and so was not welcomed.

Interesting words ...

- v. 38: *casting out. Ekballō* means 'to throw out' or 'to cast out'. It can be used of nets thrown from fishing boats as well as of demons.
- vv. 38–39: *tried to stop*. The word (*kōluō*) is actually 'forbade', 'stopped', 'hindered' or 'restrained'; but in the imperfect, it implies that the disciples kept on forbidding (unsuccessfully), hence 'tried to stop'.
- v. 39: *a deed of power. Dunamis* ('power') is used on its own here.
- v. 39: *speak evil*. 'Speak evil' is simply *kakologeō* (*kakos* means 'evil' or 'bad' and *logeō* means 'speak').
- v. 41: *truly I tell you*. This characteristic opening (*amēn legō humin*) to a saying by Jesus occurs once early on in Mark and then with increasing frequency towards the end (3.28; 8.12; 9.1, 41; 10.15, 29; 11.23; 12.43; 13.30; 14.18, 25, 30). For more on the phrase, see the note on 3.28 (p. 104).

- v. 41: *give to drink; cup*. Two connected words, *potizō* ('to give a drink' or 'to offer a drink') and *potērion* (what you drink from: a 'cup').
- v. 41: *reward*. A *misthos* is 'a wage', 'recompense' or 'a reward'; in other words, it is 'what is due'.

John said

Although I highlighted above that the disciples who couldn't cast out a demon must have been stung by another person doing so, it is worth noting that the person raising the question is John (who had been up the mountain with Jesus). It is the only time in Mark where he appears on his own; soon (10.35–45), however, he and his brother James will ask for special treatment.

'He was not following us'

In a way it doesn't matter who the 'us' is here. It could be Peter, James and John; the Twelve; or even the disciples. The point is that John thinks that the exorcist isn't part of 'us' and so should be stopped. The person may or may not have been a disciple (probably not) but the story is told to reveal more about John than about him.

In terms of a misunderstanding about discipleship, this is extreme. The verb 'following' (*akoloutheō*) is used often in Mark; but John says 'he was not following us', implying that the issue is that the other individual was not one of the disciples. John's slip is telling and significant.

'Do not stop him'

Jesus gives three reasons why they should not stop the other person. They all begin with the word 'for' (*gar*).

- For doing a miracle in Jesus' name means he can't soon speak evil about him.
  It isn't clear whether the use of Jesus' name prevents the person speaking evil (like a kind of talisman) or whether it is more matter of fact: they've used Jesus' name and so would not be believed if they spoke against him right away.

- For whoever is not against us is for us.
  Luke uses both this form of the short proverb (Luke 9.50) and the opposite ('Whoever is not with me is against me' (Luke 11.23)). Mark's version feels much more inclusive and fits well with the theme that he explored, from 3.13 to 8.21, about insiders and outsiders, and who counted as an insider and who as an outsider.

- For whoever gives you a cup of water because you are 'of Christ' will not lose the reward.
  The offering of a cup of water to someone who is 'of Christ' illustrates who can be 'for us'. The smallest of actions can include someone within the bounds of 'not [being] against us'.
  The language of reward, here, picks up the resonance of the parable of the sheep and the goats (Matt. 25.34–39): those who care for the 'little ones' receive a reward.

This passage gathers the threads of insiders and outsiders briefly again. John's question was about someone who behaved like an insider. John, however, thought him an outsider and tried to ensure that he stayed on the outside.

Mark 9.42–50: On stumbling and salt

Although the individual sayings in this section don't fit together as well as they might, this section continues the teaching on discipleship. Having drawn boundaries about who should be welcomed (those with no status; see 9.37) and who should not be excluded (those who don't follow 'us'; see 9.39), Jesus continues now with what to do when Jesus' followers are caused to stumble. The first example (causing the little ones to stumble) could refer either to insiders or outsiders, or both; the ones that follow seem more focused on insiders.

The sayings appear to be linked together by two different catchwords: 'stumble' and 'fire'.

Links backwards

- **The reference to 'little ones' might be suggested by Jesus' teaching on a little child in Mark 9.36–37.**
- **There is also a link to 9.41. There are talks about the reward for those who help followers of Jesus. Here, we move on to the punishment for those who cause them to stumble.**

Interesting words ...

- vv. 42–43, 45 and 47: *stumbling-block; stumble.* The verb *skandalizomai* can mean 'cause to stumble', 'cause to sin' or 'give offence'. The meaning of Jesus' saying is significantly different depending on which is chosen. Most commentators opt for 'cause to stumble', as it is the widest term.

- v. 42: *little ones. Ho mikros* means 'small ones' or 'little ones'. See below for what it might mean here.
- v. 42: *millstone.* A *mulos onikos* is literally a 'millstone of a donkey'; in other words, one that required an animal to turn it rather than one you could turn by hand. It had a hole in the middle, so could be hung around someone's neck.
- v. 43: *hell.* The word 'hell' is the translation of *Gehenna*. For more on this, see the box, 'Gehenna', on p. 221.
- v. 43: *unquenchable. Asbestos* means 'inextinguishable' (after which the fire-resistant mineral is named).
- v. 48: *worm. Skōlēx* refers to worms, the grubs of larvae or insects or, specifically, worms in dung.
- v. 48: *dies.* The usual word for 'die' is *apothnēskō*; but *teleutaō* ('come to an end', 'finish' or 'die') is used here.
- v. 48: *quenched. Sbennumai* refers specifically to fire and means 'to stop burning' or 'to extinguish a fire'.
- vv. 49–50: *salted; salt; lost ... saltiness. Halizō* means 'to be provided with salt' or 'to salt'. The noun connected to it, *halas*, refers to salt, and *analas* is 'to be without salt'.
- v. 50: *be at peace.* The verb *eirēneuō* is 'to keep peace' or 'to live peaceably'.

Caused to stumble

It is interesting that Jesus does not define what the stumbling-block is or looks like. R. T. France, in his commentary, uses an evocative image: that it is someone who causes someone else's 'spiritual shipwreck'; this seems to capture what Jesus had in mind here. The person who does this isn't defined as an insider or an outsider, a follower or not; the point is the effect of their actions.

The use of the same verb (*skandalizō*) in verses 43, 45 and 47 is probably what caused Mark to insert these sayings together here, because the focus changes away from the effect on other people to the effect on yourself. It seems that Jesus held a higher bar for personal self-examination than for judging others. Followers are not encouraged to punish someone who causes one of the little ones to stumble; it is enough for them to know that they would be punished. It is on oneself that preventative action must be taken. This is not an encouragement to judge other people but to keep an eye on one's own actions and inner world.

Little ones

Matthew's version of 9.41 is 'whoever gives even a cup of cold water to one of these little ones in the name of a disciple' (Matt. 10.42). This makes clear that the 'little ones' are followers of Jesus generally, not specifically children. A similar phrase is used in the parable of the sheep and the goats

(Matt. 25.40), where Jesus talks about 'the least of these who are ... my family'. Matthew also uses the phrase 'little ones' in 18.6, 10 and 14. It is probably the case that 'little ones' not only represents all followers, but also especially those who have no social status or agency for themselves, like children.

> ### *Missing verses 9.44 and 9.46*
>
> Those who are alert will notice that verses 44 and 46 are missing from our English translations. This is because although they were present in the manuscripts that set the verse numbering, they contain the same words as verse 48, 'where their worm never dies, and the fire is never quenched'. Manuscripts considered to be more reliable omit them and so they are now left out of most translations.

Millstone

The millstone of a donkey was a very large millstone. A hand millstone would be heavy enough; but one that needed a donkey to turn it would cause certain death if used as Jesus described. This type of punishment, though not common, was known in the ancient world; it would have caused particular horror for a Jewish audience because of the inability to retrieve the body of the victim for burial.

Body parts

Job 31 talks about sins associated with different parts of the body: 'I have made a covenant with my eyes; how then could I look upon a virgin?' (31.1); 'If I have walked with falsehood, and my foot has hurried to deceit' (31.5); 'If my heart has been enticed by a woman' (31.9). Add to this the fact that crimes were punished with the excision of the appropriate body part – cutting off the hand for theft or a slave's foot for running away – then Jesus' point is clear. This passage, therefore, comes close to the Sermon on the Mount in Matthew, where Jesus' high expectations of his followers were laid out. Though slightly more cryptic, they are laid out here too. If a body part causes you to sin, take this very seriously. Punishment will come your way, in the form of *Gehenna*, so it is better if you acknowledge it early and swiftly.

Gehenna

The translation of *Gehenna* as hell is confusing. There are four words used in the Bible that could potentially be translated as 'hell'.

1 *Sheol*. This is a Hebrew word that refers to a place where all those who had died went to. It does not have the idea of punishment associated with it; but some texts imply that those in *Sheol* are cut off from God's presence.
2 *Hades*. In Greek writing and thinking, Hades was the place of shades; it was where those who died went. As with *Sheol*, this was not specifically associated with punishment, though the Harpies (the agents of the punishment of the gods) would carry people to Hades. In the New Testament, *Sheol* is often translated as Hades.
3 *Tartarus*. In Greek writing and thinking, Tartarus was a deep abyss that was located beneath Hades. It was a prison in which the enemies of the gods were kept. This word occurs only in 2 Peter 2.4 in reference to the imprisonment of fallen angels.
4 *Gehenna*. This is the Greek version of the original Hebrew word, *Ge-Hinnom*, or the Valley of Hinnom. The idea of *Gehenna*'s being a rubbish tip that was kept burning continuously – to consume the dead bodies of criminals and the like who were thrown into it – can be traced back to Maimonides, a twelfth-century rabbi; but it is hard to trace earlier references than this. I have looked carefully and, despite many references to it by scholars, I have not yet found any text from the time of Jesus or earlier that refers to *Ge-Hinnom* as a burning rubbish tip. It was thought to be accursed, however; this idea is one that may come from 2 Kings 16.3, which talks about Ahaz sacrificing his son to Molech by making him 'pass through fire'. Josiah later demolished it as a sacrificial place and declared it accursed (2 Kings 23.10). This gives rise to a tradition of burning and of shame and violation.

   At the time of Jesus, a custom was emerging that ascribed punishment after death to those who opposed God. It seems to have come from the very last verse of Isaiah ('they shall go out and look at the dead bodies of the people who have rebelled against me; for their worm shall not die, their fire shall not be quenched, and they shall be an abhorrence to all flesh' (66.24)). Additional examples – such as 1 Enoch 27.2, which talks of an accursed valley where those who spoke against God would be gathered – were also important. It seems as though Jesus was picking up this tradition, along with the idea of burning associated with *Gehenna* (2 Kings 16.3) as a place where those who would be condemned would be gathered.

In short, the theology of hell that requires a devil, with horns and a trident, and eternal torment emerged after the New Testament period, probably in the second century. Passages like this point to the development of the idea; but using 'hell' to describe any of the words above ends up being confusing. It is better to keep *Gehenna* in the translation.

On salt and fire (and quite a bit of confusion)

The final verses seem to have been connected through the use of the word 'fire'; but, in these verses, there are three sayings for which the meaning is not quite clear.

- *Salted with fire*. The connection of salt and fire can probably be traced back to Leviticus 2.13 ('You shall not omit from your grain-offerings the salt of the covenant with your God; with all your offerings you shall offer salt'). The salt was used as a purifying agent. In other words, those who experienced 'fire' (that is, persecution) were purified by it.
- *Salt that loses its saltiness*. This saying is found in Matthew and Luke (Matt. 5.13; Luke 14.34), though the other two sayings are not, and the symbolic meaning of salt changes from purification to flavour. There were two key uses for salt in the ancient world: purification or preservation and seasoning. Mark now moves on to seasoning: salt is important because of the beneficial flavour it brings. It is possible that Mark is sliding deliberately from one use of salt to another here. Once 'salted' (that is, purified) the disciples should not lose their saltiness: namely, their ability to bring flavour into the world.

How does salt lose saltiness?

It is not possible for sodium chloride to lose its 'saltiness'; but the reference implies the salt that would have been used in Galilee and Judea. It was obtained mostly from the Dead Sea, from which water was collected and evaporated. In this case, salt could be leeched from the crystals that were left (often by dissolving them in water), leaving something like gypsum behind, which would be 'unsalty'.

From here, we move to the flavour that a 'salty' disciple can bring. What are the beneficial qualities of saltiness? Jesus says here that it is being 'at peace with one another'. Salt is never used elsewhere as a metaphor for peace; but the message lands well in this context. Rather than focusing on who is greatest (Mark 9.33–37), the disciples should be focusing on being as 'salty' as possible; bringing peace into the world is a very good place to begin.

This short collection of sayings is the closest Mark gets to the Sermon on the Mount. The collection seems to have been gathered by using word association: the teachings move from the subject of sin to *Gehenna* to burning to purification to flavour. The overall impression is clear (even if the transitions made from each saying to the next are not): don't cause those around you to stumble by jockeying for power; aim to bring peace into the world instead.

Mark 10.1–12: On marriage and divorce

In this passage, Jesus' teaching is for the whole crowd again (as it was in 8.34). Since then, his teaching has focused on the disciples. What he gives here is, for a modern reader, some of his most uncomfortable teaching; I think, though, that it is primarily about care for the most vulnerable in society, following on from the theme that was established in 9.33–37.

Links backwards

- Jesus taught the crowd in Mark 8.34. Between then and here, he has taught the disciples about his death and Resurrection (9.30–32); about welcoming the least (9.33–37); about how to treat outsiders (9.38–41); and about stumbling, fire and salt (9.42–49).
- This picks up some of the themes of previous controversies: healing on the sabbath (2.1–12); plucking grain on the sabbath (2.18–22); and ritual purity (7.1–23). In each of these, Jesus took teaching that was widely accepted and turned it on its head.
- It also links back to 9.33–37, in which Jesus talks about the importance of welcoming those of lowest societal value, using a child to make his point.

Links forwards

- Jesus' teaching on children (10.13–16) continues the theme begun in this passage about care for the vulnerable.

Interesting words ...

- v. 1: *left.* As noted previously, the verb *anistēmi* is confusing: it can refer to something momentous, such as resurrection ('rise'), or to an everyday action, such as getting up or setting out. Here, it means 'setting out'.
- v. 1: *beyond.* The word here is *peran*, which we've seen used for 'the other side'. It is now used (without 'the') to mean 'beyond'.
- v. 1: *as was his custom.* The verb *ethō* means 'to be accustomed to' or 'to be in the habit of'. Although 4.1 and 8.34 are the only occasions where the content of Jesus' teaching was revealed, he also taught the crowd in 2.13–17 and 6.34–44 (even though we do not know what he said). Mark's point is that although he hasn't mentioned the content of Jesus' teaching much, this was his custom.
- v. 2: *to test him they asked.* The same verb that was used in the Pharisees' debate with Jesus in 7.5 is used again here: *eperōtaō* ('to put a formal question'). Somewhat intriguingly, not all the manuscripts explain who put the question. It is assumed that the conflict and the use of this verb indicate that it

was the Pharisees. Note that the same verb is used again when the disciples ask Jesus about divorce in verse 10.

- v. 2: *lawful*. The word *exestin* means 'permitted' or 'lawful', but when used in Mark means, specifically, 'permitted by God's law' (Mark 2.24, 26; 3.4; 6.18; 10.2; 12.14).
- v. 4: *certificate*. The word 'Bible' comes from the Greek *biblia* ('books'). Here, this is used in the singular (*biblion*) and is better translated as 'document' or 'certificate'. *Apostasion* refers to the particular type of certificate: the one for divorce.
- v. 5: *hardness of heart*. This single word (*sklērokardia*) is composed of two different words: *sklēros* ('hard', 'stiff' or 'unyielding') and *kardia* ('heart'). This is the only occasion when this word is used for 'hardness of heart'. Usually, when it is referred to (3.5; 6.52; 7.6; 8.17), the word *pōrōsis* is used alongside *kardia* for the same meaning.
- v. 6: *beginning of creation*. The use of *archē* ('beginning') here, alongside *ktisis* ('creation'), surely brings to mind the start of the creation story in Genesis 1.1 ('In the beginning').
- vv. 7 and 9: *joined*. Two different words and images are used for 'join' here: in verse 7, *proskollaō* has the sense of 'to be glued or stuck to', hence the word 'cleave'; and, in verse 9, *suzugnumi* refers to 'yoking together' (as with a pair of oxen).
- v. 9: *separate*. *Chōrizō* means 'to separate' or 'to divide' and was used in various contemporary Greek texts to refer to divorce.
- vv. 11–12: *marries; commits adultery*. The word for 'marry' is *gameō* and can refer either to legal marriage or taking someone as a concubine. 'Commit adultery' is *moichaō*.

To Judea

Concerning this passage, there is considerable debate about where Jesus went. We assume that, at first, he was in Capernaum because that was the last location given for him (9.33). To go to Judea, and then beyond the Jordan, would have required his travelling through Samaria. Many commentators assume that, as a Jew, he would have steered clear of doing so. The usual route was to travel down the east side of the Jordan to avoid Samaria. However, we know from elsewhere that Jesus did travel through Samaria (Luke 9.52; John 4), so his choice shouldn't cause us any level of surprise.

'Beyond the Jordan' refers to Perea (which was probably where John the Baptist preached), which was part of the kingdom of Herod Antipas.

Is it lawful to divorce?

The Pharisees' question to Jesus is an odd one. So far, they have asked him questions that were part of regular rabbinic discussion. This one was not. All rabbis accepted that it was lawful to divorce. The topic of conversation centred on what the grounds for divorce were. It is possible that they had heard that Jesus did not hold the usual rabbinic view on this subject and had come to find out for themselves. Alternatively, their question implied a similar meaning to the one in Matthew's version of this debate, which adds 'for any cause' to the end of the question (19.3).

The rabbis and divorce

The process for divorce within Judaism was (and is) for the man to issue a Gett to his wife. This is the document of divorce mentioned here (it was very rare for a woman to be able to do so; it would only have been possible for the wealthiest of women, such as Herodias).

Its acceptance can be seen across the literature written in this period. Ben Sirach 25.26 counsels: 'If she does not go as you direct, separate her from yourself.' In other words, if a woman doesn't do what you say, divorce her. The Jewish historian Josephus also recounts that he divorced his wife because he did not like her behaviour.

In terms of rabbinic debate, there were two major schools of thought. One was represented by Hillel, who allowed divorce on any grounds, including if a man found someone fairer than his wife or if she spoiled the dinner. The house of Shammai had much stricter rules: it declared that divorce was possible only because of adultery, though this seems to have been the minority view.

Jesus' response, as recorded in Mark, therefore, must have been astonishing. It is only in Matthew's Gospel that an exception of adultery is added (19.9). In Mark, he disallowed it entirely. The reason for Jesus' argument here seems to be to support the needs of women. A world in which a woman could be discarded for being less pretty than someone else or not a good enough cook was harsh and unfair. It was often used as an excuse to care neither for the woman nor for her children after the divorce had taken place.

Jesus' teaching here seems to connect back to the point he was making in the passage about the child. The Christian community should be a place where people with no rights could be supported and welcomed. Casting off a woman because she no longer suited a man did not fit into Jesus' vision of kingdom values.

Hardness of heart

Jesus' response to the Pharisees, interestingly, questioned the Mosaic commands by indicating that they were a concession owing to hardness of heart. Instead, he went back to the story of creation as the basis for his understanding. The law of Moses was, Jesus argued, put in place because of how human beings function. Divorce was not a right but a necessity because of human nature.

Jesus' argument reaches back to what happened before the fall. There, God joined two distinct and different beings as one. Any attempt to separate them was as much an affront to God as to the two who were joined. This was the pre-fall vision of the world; Moses' law provided for post-fall human frailty.

Against her

Another way in which Jesus' teaching was in support of women, and thus countercultural, was that the world of Jesus' day never spoke about a man committing adultery against his wife. The experience was always articulated in the other direction, against the husband. Adding these two words is important. The woman was seen to be an equal partner in the marriage, capable of being sinned against.

'If she divorces her husband'

The addition of this phrase is, in some ways, odd. Josephus wrote in his *Antiquities of the Jews* 15.259:

> But some time afterward, when Salome happened to quarrel with Costobarus, she sent him a bill of divorce and dissolved her marriage with him, though this was not according to the Jewish laws; for with us it is lawful for a husband to do so; but a wife, if she departs from her husband, cannot of herself be married to another, unless her former husband put her away.

However, it was permitted in Greek and Roman society and clearly happened in Jewish society among the wealthiest. This phrase therefore ensured that women couldn't think that their instigating divorce was all right because it was not mentioned.

Reading Jesus' teaching on divorce today

This leaves us with the question of how we relate to Jesus' teaching today. It is passages like these that remind us that the reading of Scripture is not simply about lifting something from the Gospels and applying it to our modern lives as though there can be a simple one-to-one correlation. In my view, these passages lay out principles that we need to reflect on deeply and then see what we can learn today.

I believe this passage says that divorce was provided for a post-fall world. The pre-fall ideal was that two people became one flesh and would never be separated. However, we don't live in that ideal world and, because we don't, a provision was laid down by Moses. But, by the time of Jesus, the provision had been distorted and women had come to be treated as property that could be discarded when men chose.

This must never be allowed. A woman has equal rights with her husband and could have adultery committed against her: she should therefore not be cast off on a whim. For me, what comes out most clearly from this passage is that women are whole people, to be treated with respect and equality. Jesus' message in this passage makes this clear.

If we apply this to life today, it means that not divorcing is the ideal; but when it must happen (and it may, for all sorts of reasons), there is provision for that eventuality. It should not happen on a whim; it should not undermine the well-being of the most vulnerable. The full human dignity of both partners should be upheld at all costs.

Mark 10.13–16: And on children

The placing of this passage, immediately after his teaching on divorce, is important. There, Jesus made it very clear that women were equal partners in marriage and not to be discarded on a whim. Here, other vulnerable people enter the frame. As in 9.33–37, children – who, in wider society, were regarded as being non-people – are placed front and centre.

Links backwards

- The healing of the leper, where Jesus is described as being angry (in Greek but not in English in Mark 1.41).
- Jesus' teaching about welcoming a child (9.33–37).
- In the story about the person performing an exorcism who wasn't one of the disciples, Jesus told them not to stop or prevent him; the same word ('indignant') is used here (9.39).
- Teaching on marriage and divorce, and care for the vulnerable (10.1–12).

Interesting words ...

- v. 13: *little children. Paidion* ('little child') is the diminutive of *pais* ('child'). This word does not tell us how old the children were. Jarius' daughter, who was aged 12, was also called a *paidion*. The clue to their age comes from the fact that Jesus could take them in his arms.
- v. 13: *spoke sternly*. Here, we see the return of the verb *epitimaō* ('rebuke' or 'reprove someone'). It is used elsewhere in Mark (1.25; 3.12; 4.39; 8.30, 32, 33; 9.25; 10.48).
- v. 14: *indignant*. This word is not the same as the one used in 1.41, where the verb *orgizō* occurs. This word is *aganakteō*, which means 'to be incensed', 'to be irate' or 'to be displeased'.
- v. 14: *stop them*. Jesus uses the same word here (*kōluō*) as was used in 9.39, when the disciples tried to stop the person who wasn't one of them from performing exorcisms.
- v. 15: *Truly I tell you*. This characteristic opening (*amēn legō humin*) to a saying by Jesus occurs once early on in Mark and then with increasing frequency towards the end (3.28; 8.12; 9.1, 41; 10.15, 29; 11.23; 12.43; 13.30; 14.18, 25, 30). For more on the phrase, see the note on 3.28 (p. 85).
- v. 15: *receive*. The same word is used in 9.37 for welcoming or receiving (*dechomai*) a child.
- v. 16: *took them up in his arms*. The verb *enangkalizomai* means 'to embrace' or 'to hug' as well as 'take into one's arms'. An *agkalē* is a bent arm, so the verb connected to it refers to what you do with your bent arms (hug). The verb is also used in 9.36.
- v. 16: *blessed*. The usual verb for 'bless' is *eulogeō*. This is a strengthened form of the same verb (*kateulogeō*).

Mark's repetitions

We have already observed how Mark gives similar but different stories throughout his Gospel to illustrate the points the disciples are not getting. The most obvious examples of this are the two feedings, after which the disciples still had not learnt anything. This account illustrates another similar occasion, though with multiple strands.

- In 9.33–37, after the discussion of who was the greatest, Jesus taught that welcoming little children was equal to welcoming him and the one who sent him. The same word for 'welcome/receive' is used here. The disciples had the opportunity here to demonstrate that they had understood his previous teaching, but did not.
- In 9.38–41, they tried to stop someone whom they considered to be an outsider from doing exorcisms: Jesus told them not to. Here, Jesus used the same word to tell them not to stop children being brought to him.

- In the previous passage, Jesus' teaching about divorce made it very clear that his concern was for the most vulnerable in society.

There were three occasions on which the disciples could have learnt and, therefore, not prevented the little children from being brought to Jesus. Yet they still tried to stop them.

The disciples rebuked them

The disciples probably rebuked the people bringing the children because they did not consider them worthy of Jesus' time. There seems to be no reason for them to have come to this view: Jesus had healed Jairus' daughter, the daughter of the woman from Tyre and the son who had a spirit (after the Transfiguration). In all these healings, Jesus showed no sign of considering children beneath his notice: a stance that was reinforced by his teaching about welcoming a child in 9.33–37. The disciples were functioning as gatekeepers out of their own prejudices alone.

Jesus and anger

The example of Jesus' anger that is usually given is the one of his turning over the tables of the money changers in the temple. Two other examples are evident in Mark, however: Jesus' anger when the leper suggested he might not want to heal him (1.41) and his anger at the disciples, here, for turning the children away. These examples are important. Our Victorian image of gentle Jesus, meek and mild, is entirely wrong. He became angry at injustice; he engaged in rigorous debate when challenged; and he rebuked those he thought were wrong.

'Such as these'

The term 'such as these' (in Greek, *toioutos*) indicates a rightful share in the kingdom. The question is, 'Who are "such as these"?' Does the term refer to all children and, therefore, mean that children have an automatic share in the kingdom? This seems unlikely. It is much more likely, especially following Jesus' teaching on divorce, that he is saying the kingdom belongs to all those who are seen as lowly in status, in the way the disciples view the children here. This passage is therefore very like the first beatitude: 'Blessed are the poor in spirit, for theirs is the kingdom of heaven' (Matt. 5.3).

Receiving the kingdom as a child

The problem with the grammar of this sentence is that it could be taken in two ways:

- As a child receives it.
- As they receive a child.

As both are possible, there may be a virtue in seeing it both ways at once. We need both to be like children and to receive children with honour.

The question is what this means. We shouldn't, at this stage, lapse back into a romantic view of how children were perceived in the first century. Commentators often talk about the importance of being 'childlike'. The problem is that there is no evidence that childlikeness was seen as a virtue in this period. It is more likely that receiving the kingdom as a child involved receiving the kingdom as you would if you had nothing: no status and no position in the world. This seems even more probable given that the next story features the opposite of this: a man who had many possessions. The New English Bible's translation of the first beatitude seems to sum it up better than any other: 'How blest are those who know their need of God' (Matt. 5.3, NEB).

Jesus took them in his arms and blessed them

We are not told what those bringing the children to Jesus hoped for. The implication of 'touch', in the context of previous healings, is that they hoped they might brush his cloak or touch him briefly. Jesus demonstrates the generosity of the rules of the kingdom by taking them into an embrace and blessing them. Rather than sending them away, Jesus included them within the circle of his embrace.

Mark 10.17–31: A conversation with someone who had much to lose

The point Jesus was making is amplified by this next story. Moving from those who had nothing in terms of station, position or possessions, we now encounter someone who, Mark tells us, 'had many possessions'.

Links backwards

- This story is a worked example of Jesus' teaching about the cost of discipleship (Mark 8.34—9.1). Although taking up his cross isn't mentioned, the rich man is challenged to follow Jesus truly by giving up what he cared about most.

- **The two stories about receiving children (9.33–37; 10.13–16) stand behind this story. They feature those with no status and nothing to lose in contrast to the man in this account.**

Interesting words ...

- v. 17: *setting out on a journey. Ekporeuō* refers to 'setting out', 'going out' or 'marching forth'; coupled with *hodos* ('road'), it means 'setting out on a journey'.
- v. 17: *ran up. Protrechō* means 'to run towards' or 'run up to' (for those looking at the Greek, *trecho* is a very irregular verb; its past tense is *prosdramon*).
- v. 17: *knelt. Gonupeteō* combines *gonu* ('knee') with *peteō* ('fall down'), so we have 'fall to the knees'.
- vv. 17–18: *good. Agathos* is a common but important word with a wide range of meaning. Here, it clearly means 'morally good'.
- v. 17: *inherit. Klēronomeō* is the usual word for 'inheriting'. For more on this, see 'Inheriting eternal life', on p. 233.
- v. 17: *eternal life.* In Mark, this phrase, *zōē aiōnion*, occurs only here and in 10.30. It means 'life lasting for an age' or 'perpetually'.
- v. 19: *you shall not.* The verbs used for the Commandments are (with alternative translations in brackets): 'murder' (*phoneuō*: 'kill' or 'slaughter'); 'commit adultery' (*moicheuō*: 'be unfaithful'); 'steal' (*kleptō*: 'cheat' or 'seize'); 'bear false witness' (*pesudomartureō*: 'give false testimony'); 'defraud' (*apostereō*: 'cheat' or 'deprive of'); 'honour' (*timaō*: 'revere' or 'hold in esteem').
- v. 20: *kept.* The verb *phulassō* ('keep watch over' or 'guard') can be used in the context of guarding a prisoner.
- v. 21: *looking at.* The implication of *emblepō* is looking long and hard or looking in the face.
- v. 21: *loved.* This is the first time the verb 'love' (*agapaō*) is used in Mark. It comes again two chapters later (in 12.30, 31 and 32, in the discussion about the summary of the law).
- v. 21: *lack. Hustereō* means 'to fall behind' or 'to fall below', 'to be wanting' or 'to fail'.
- v. 21: *treasure. Thēsauros* means 'treasure'. From it, we get our word 'thesaurus', which is a treasure store of synonyms.
- v. 22: *shocked. Stugnazō* means 'to have a gloomy look' or 'to be appalled'. It is sometimes also used to denote anger. A mix of shock, horror and anger seems likely here.
- v. 22: *grieving. Lupeō* refers to being vexed, upset, distressed or in pain.
- v. 22: *possessions.* A *ktēma* is something you own. The rich man had many of them.
- v. 23: *looked around. Periblepō* is a word used in Mark more than elsewhere in the New Testament (3.5, 34; 5.32; 9.8; 10.23; 11.11); outside Mark, it occurs only in Luke 6.10. It has the sense of Jesus taking in the situation.

- vv. 23–24: *hard*. Literally, 'with difficulty' or 'with discomfort'. The first time it is used, it is an adverb: *duskolōs* ('they will enter with difficulty'). The second time, it is an adjective: *duskolos* ('how hard it is').
- v. 23: *wealth*. *Chrēma* refers to 'riches', 'wealth' or 'property'.
- v. 24: *perplexed*. *Thambeō* is one of the words Mark uses for 'amazed' or 'astounded'. The disciples were astounded by what Jesus said here. For more on Mark's different uses of the word 'amazed', see the notes on 1.22 and 27 (pp. 41–2).
- v. 24: *children*. *Teknon* ('child') is the word Jesus used when he spoke to the man who was paralysed in 2.5. It is used here in the plural.
- v. 25: *easier*. The comparative of *eukopos* means 'with less trouble'.
- v. 25: *eye of a needle*. As it sounds: *trumalia* means 'eye' or 'hole' and *rhaphidos* means 'needle'.
- v. 25: *rich*. A rich person was *plousios* ('opulent', 'ample' or 'abundant').
- v. 26: *greatly astounded*. For the different words used throughout Mark to mean 'astounded' or 'astonished', see the notes on 1.22 and 27 (pp. 41–2). The word used here is *ekplēssō*, with *perissōs* ('extraordinarily').
- vv. 26–27: *can; possible*. The Greek picks up the same root here. *Dunamai* means 'to be able' or 'can', and *dunatos* means 'able', 'capable' or 'possible'. Both are connected to *dunamis* ('power').
- v. 29: *Truly I tell you*. This characteristic opening (*amēn legō humin*) to a saying by Jesus occurs once early on in Mark and then with increasing frequency towards the end (3.28; 8.12; 9.1, 41; 10.15, 29; 11.23; 12.43; 13.30; 14.18, 25, 30). For more on the phrase, see the note on 3.28 (p. 85).
- v. 30: *in the age to come*. The word *aiōn* is used twice here: once as a noun – 'the age (*aiōn*) that is coming (*erchomai*)'; and once as an adjective – 'eternal (*aiōnios*: 'of the age') life (*zōē*)'.
- v. 31: *first; last*. This is a slight variation of the phrase at 9.35, including 'many' (*pollos*), but with *protos* and *eschatos*, as before.

Setting off

The reference to Jesus' journey reminds us that Jesus is heading to Judea and Perea (10.1); and we don't know where on that journey this encounter occurs.

Although we know this story as 'the rich young ruler', only Matthew says that he was young (Matt. 19.20–21) and only Luke that he was a ruler (Luke 18.18). Mark simply says that he was rich.

Mark makes it clear that the man was sincere in two ways:

1 He ran and fell to his knees at Jesus' feet. Running and kneeling were not postures that someone of this man's social standing would adopt. In a culture that placed such high emphasis on status, you would not consider lowering your dignity for anything that was not very important.

2 Jesus looked at him and loved him. Jesus' seemingly harsh command came from the love he felt for this person, who was deeply sincere but hampered by wealth.

Good Teacher

The man's way of addressing Jesus, and Jesus' slightly harsh response are fascinating. 'Good Teacher' is not a common form of address, either in the Old Testament or in writings outside the New Testament. As a result, there must be a reason that the man inserted 'good' before the usual 'teacher'.

When we read on and know that he believes himself to have kept all the Commandments, it suggests that he was placing himself and Jesus in the category of 'good' and, by implication, others in the category of 'bad'. Jesus' response reminds him that human beings are not capable of pure, moral 'goodness': that is possible only for God. We can aspire to 'goodness', but achieving it is beyond our capability.

Inheriting eternal life

The phrase 'eternal life' appears only in Mark's Gospel, in this story (at the beginning and the end). At the time of Jesus, not everyone did believe in eternal life. Most notably, the Sadducees did not; but there were numerous others who didn't believe in it either. The Jewish idea of life after death was often expressed as 'the world to come' or 'the age to come', so the frequent use of *aiōn* ('age') makes sense.

The implication of the man's question is that he is not worried about his life in this age. We discover later in the story that he has ample possessions and believes that he obeys all the Commandments. His concern, therefore, is about what is going to happen next. He wants to do everything he can to ensure that he will do as well in the age to come as he has in this one.

The word 'inherit' has, at its heart, the idea of being entitled to something. Someone who inherits property is entitled to that property once the person owning it dies. So this seems to be the rich man's concern: what can he do to ensure that he will be entitled to eternal life when the moment comes? If this appears to be a negative portrayal of him, it is worth reminding ourselves that Jesus loved him for how he was. There was no doubt that he was sincere, even if the expression of that sincerity was a little off.

The Commandments

It is worth paying attention to the Commandments that Jesus cited and those he did not.

Exodus		Mark	
20.1	You shall have no other gods before me		
20.7	You shall not make wrongful use of the name of the LORD		
20.8	Remember the sabbath day, and keep it holy		
20.12	Honour your father and mother		
20.13	You shall not murder	10.19	You shall not murder
20.14	You shall not commit adultery	10.19	You shall not commit adultery
20.15	You shall not steal	10.19	You shall not steal
20.16	You shall not bear false witness	10.19	You shall not bear false witness
20.17	You shall not covet	10.19	You shall not defraud
		10.19	Honour your father and mother

Notice that the Commandments included by Jesus are those that affect how you relate to those around you. They are in the same order as in Exodus, with the exception of 'Honour your father and mother', which has moved to last place, and 'You shall not covet', which is replaced with 'You shall not defraud'.

Some wonder whether the 'do not defraud' has been adapted from 'do not covet' for someone who is wealthy. A rich man is less likely to covet what others have but may well have achieved his wealth fraudulently. Another suggestion is that, since all the other actions are, in modern parlance, easily measurable and covetousness is not, it has been changed into something more closely tied to action. Either way, it is interesting that love of God and keeping the sabbath are not included in the list.

The rich man's response to Jesus' question is not to be read as arrogant (since we are then told that Jesus loved him). All the actions that Jesus listed were what he had done from his youth. This is where the heart of the issue seems to lie. The rich man relied on his own resources and, from that position, was confident that he had done everything he needed to be devout. Jesus' challenge to him was to give up all of that ('go', 'sell', 'give', 'follow') and rely on someone else. This was a challenge too far. The rich man was the very opposite of the person who knew his need of God.

Treasure in heaven

The phrase 'having treasure in heaven' has, for many people, meant that something is kept for them in heaven, which would be retrieved when they died. I would agree with N. T. (Tom) Wright that this is not what is meant. As he puts it:

> When Jesus says, 'You will have treasure in heaven', he doesn't mean that the young man must go to heaven to get it; he means that God will keep it stored up for him until the time when, in the Age to Come, all is revealed. The reason you have money in the bank is not so that you can spend it in the bank but so that you can take it out and spend it somewhere else. The reason you have treasure in heaven, God's storehouse, is so that you can enjoy it in the Age to Come when God brings heaven and earth together at last. (*Mark for Everyone*, SPCK, 2001, p. 135)

We could call this kingdom treasure. Treasure to be spent when the kingdom comes fully at last in the age to come. Hanging in the air is the question of what we really think treasure is.

On camels and eyes of needles

As the conversation between Jesus and the disciples continues, it becomes clear that the rich man is not the only one appalled by what Jesus has said. The disciples are struggling with it too. Mark uses one of his well-used words for 'astounded' to communicate their struggle with what was said.

The analogy of a camel going through the eye of a needle is meant to evoke something impossible. A similar image was used by the rabbis in a later Talmudic text. There, the rabbis maintained that, in dreams, someone saw only 'the thoughts of his heart when he was awake'. An example they gave was that, in a dream, you wouldn't see something impossible like 'a golden palm tree nor an elephant going through the eye of a needle' (*b. Berakoth* 55b). In other words, you couldn't see an impossible thing in your dreams.

Over the years, preachers, recognizing the discomfort evoked by Jesus' saying, have come up with explanations that make it less impossible. One of the most popular is the idea that 'the eye of a needle' is the name for a small gate within the large double gate in a city wall. The small one would allow pedestrians through, without the larger gates being opened. The idea put forward is that a camel, stripped of its load and on its knees, would struggle to get through, but could do so with difficulty. As reassuring as this reinterpretation is, there is one key problem: there is no evidence for it whatsoever. In the words of the late, great Kenneth Bailey: 'There is not the slightest shred of evidence for this identification. This door has not in any language been called the needle's eye' (*Through Peasant Eyes*, Eerdmans, 1983, p. 166).

The point of this teaching is that it refers to something impossible and we, like the disciples, are meant to find it profoundly uncomfortable. Finding ways to make it less so is to miss the point entirely. This is where verse 27 comes in. It is impossible for human beings by themselves, through their own actions, to be saved. This was what the rich man was asking for: a checklist of what he could do, all by himself, to ensure he could inherit eternal life. But what is impossible for human beings is possible for God.

'We have left everything'

Peter's exclamation that they had left everything behind seems heartfelt (though it is worth noting that he appeared still to have a house that they visited in Capernaum). Jesus' response, though, is a little confusing. While it is easy to see how followers of Jesus would receive new family, it is harder to see how they would gain houses or fields (intriguingly placed at opposite ends of Mark's list). The most likely explanation is that property would be shared between followers, as it was at the start of Acts (4.32–37), and therefore, along with a new family, would come houses and fields for the benefit of the community. The 'with persecutions' seems to be an important, realistic addition. In this age, there will be the joys of new community and the sharing of possessions; but, nevertheless, it will come with persecutions. The disciples should not forget the teaching about 'taking up your cross'.

At the end of this passage, we return to the rich man's original question. In the age to come, there will be eternal life; but it is impossible for human beings to achieve by themselves, and it involves much sacrifice and persecution along the way.

The first and the last

The final verse links us back explicitly to Jesus' teaching on greatness and receiving those with no social status. As noted above, this has been a worked example of what this means in practice; and it is entirely uncomfortable (to put it mildly) for those who are first to realize, as the rich man did in this conversation, the extent of what has to be given up to be last. We, like the rich man, need to be able to feel as appalled and distressed as he did. This is the hardest of hard teachings; we are meant to find it difficult.

Mark 10.32–34: Jesus prophesied about his death a third time

See p. 213 for the comparison of Jesus' three prophecies about his death and Resurrection. We are now at the third and most detailed of the prophecies in which Jesus lays out what will happen before his death.

Links backwards

- The first (Mark 8.31–33) and second (9.30–32) prophecies of Jesus' death now culminate in this third and final one.

Links forwards

- The prophecies look forward to everything that will happen between Jesus' arrest and Resurrection (14.43—16.8).

Interesting words ...

- vv. 32–33: *going up*. The word *anabainō* ('to go up' or 'to ascend') would have been used to describe anyone going up to Jerusalem for the festival.
- v. 32: *amazed*. The word *thambeō* ('astounded' or 'astonished'), used in 1.27 and 10.24, is used again here. The context of each suggests that Mark is saying 'astounded with a hint of fear'.
- v. 32: *afraid*. The usual word for 'fear' (*phobeō*) is used here.
- v. 32: *happen*. This is a compound of *bainō*: this time, *sumbainō*. Literally, it means 'go together' and hence 'to come to pass or happen'.
- v. 33: *handed over. Paradidōmi* can mean 'hand over' or 'betray'. For more on the use of this word, see the box, 'Betrayed/handed over', on p. 211.
- v. 33: *Gentiles*. The word *ethnos* refers to a nation or a people. When used in the plural, it means 'foreign people' and, in this context, 'Gentiles'.
- v. 34: *mock; spit; flog*. The specific suffering Jesus will endure will be to be mocked (*empaizō*: 'ridicule' or 'jeer'), spat at (*emptuo*: 'spit on') and flogged (*mastigoō*: 'whipped'). It is interesting that, in Mark 15.15, the word used for 'flog' is different: there, it is *phragelloō*.

On the way to Jerusalem, amazed and afraid

The journey that started at the beginning of the chapter continues here. Only here, the destination is made more explicit. We now know that the goal is Jerusalem: a goal that is emphasized by the use of 'go up'. Pilgrims always went *up* to Jerusalem. When we add to this the first mention of Jerusalem as the place of Jesus' death (10.33), we can see the intensity increasing.

The image painted by Mark is vivid. Jesus was ahead of the rest, the implication is that he was striding with purpose, fixed on Jerusalem. 'They' were behind, according to Mark, astounded; and another group, those following, were afraid. The implication that it was a different group is highlighted by the presence of the small word *de* ('but'), which is often used to introduce a new theme.

We are left, then, with two intriguing questions:

1 Who were the two groups?
2 Why were they astounded/afraid?

Since Jesus takes the Twelve aside in verse 32 for his third and final prediction, it is natural to assume that the first 'they' were the Twelve. The second group, referred to by the wider term 'those who followed', suggests a bigger group of others who accompanied Jesus on the road. We know from elsewhere (15.41) that a group of women had gone with Jesus from Galilee. It seems reasonable to assume that we are being directed to imagine two key groups here: the Twelve and the wider, larger group of disciples.

Usually in Mark, people are astounded/afraid in response to something that Jesus has said or done. Here, they are astounded by his striding ahead. It seems most likely that this is new. Jesus didn't usually walk ahead of them. He tended to walk with them, talking and teaching as he went. His new determination seems to be what they find unnerving.

Third prediction

As noted above, the third prediction inserts an additional step into what will happen. Jesus will be sentenced to death by the Jewish leaders and then handed over to the Gentiles.

At the hands of the Gentiles, he will suffer four things: mocking, being spat at, flogging and death. Of course, all these things did happen at Jesus' death, but this prediction seems to pull strongly on the suffering servant from Isaiah, who spoke of

- insult and spitting: 'I gave my back to those who struck me, and my cheeks to those who pulled out the beard; I did not hide my face from insult and spitting' (Isa. 50.6);
- physical injury: 'he was wounded for our transgressions, crushed for our iniquities; upon him was the punishment that made us whole, and by his bruises we are healed' (Isa. 53.5);
- and death: 'For he was cut off from the land of the living, stricken for the transgression of my people. They made his grave with the wicked and his tomb with the rich' (Isa. 53.8–9).

The final element of the prediction is the same as in the previous two prophecies. See the box, 'After three days', on p. 193, for comment.

Mark 10.35–45: On being the servant of all

Each one of Jesus' Passion predictions is followed by one or more disciples demonstrating how much they don't understand what he is talking about. After the first prediction, Peter rebukes him for talking about death; after the second prediction, the disciples begin discussing who is the greatest. It, therefore, comes as no surprise to find James and John asking Jesus whether they could sit at his right hand and his left in this narrative.

Three times Jesus told them what would occur, and three times they misunderstood. They thought that whatever was about to happen could lend them grandeur and importance. Looking back with the benefit of 2,000 years of hindsight, it is hard to imagine how they got it so wrong. The persistence of their misunderstanding, however, suggests that what they 'knew' was going to happen was so strong it was unshakeable.

Links backwards

- After Jesus' first and second predictions of his death respectively, Peter rebuked him (Mark 8.31–33) and the disciples discussed who the greatest was (9.33–37). This episode continues in a similar vein, with James and John misunderstanding what he said.
- James and John, with Peter, were present at the Transfiguration when Jesus' glory was revealed (9.2–13). Their request here makes one wonder not only where they thought Peter might sit, but also Elijah and Moses too.
- The wording in this passage also picks up the language of 9.35 (when Jesus put a child in the middle of them). Jesus said that those who want to be first must be last and servant of all, a teaching reinforced by the episode with the rich man who couldn't part with his possessions: it led to Jesus' second declaration that the first shall be last (10.31).

Links forwards

- Jesus' prayer in Gethsemane to remove the cup of suffering from him (14.36) resonates with his describing his future suffering as drink from a cup.

Interesting words ...

- v. 35: *came forward. Prosporeuomai* can mean 'draw near' or 'approach'; it can also mean 'attach oneself to'.
- vv. 35 and 38: *ask; asking*. The verb *aiteō* means 'ask' or 'demand'. The tone of the brothers' question, here, hints that it might be closer to 'demand'.
- v. 37: *sit*. The verb for 'sit' (*kathizō*) does mean 'sit', not 'recline'. For the importance of this, see p. 65.
- v. 37: *right; left*. Here, the word for 'right' is *dexios* and for 'left' *aristeros*; but in verse 40, while the same word is used for 'right', the word for 'left' changes to *euōnumos*. There is no noticeable change in meaning between the two words for 'left'.
- v. 37: *glory. Doxa* is the Greek word for 'glory', which is translated from the Hebrew word *kabod*.
- vv. 38–39: *drink the cup. Pinō* refers to 'drink' and *potērion* to 'cup'.
- vv. 38–39: *be baptized with the baptism that I am baptized with*. The verb for 'baptism', *baptizō*, and the noun connected to it, *baptisma*, are used here. Outside the New Testament, the verb means 'to dip', 'to wash' or 'to plunge'.
- v. 41: *be angry*. This is the same verb (*aganakteō*) as the verb used for Jesus' anger when the disciples prevented the children from being brought to him (10.14).
- v. 42: *recognize as their rulers*. More literally this reads: 'Those considered or seeming (*dokeō*) to rule (*archō*)'. It could mean either of these. It would also be interesting to think that Jesus meant 'those who seem to rule' (but in fact do not because God is ruling).
- v. 42: *lord it; are tyrants*. The verb *katakurieuō* means 'to gain complete dominion' or 'to exercise complete dominion' and *kateouxousiazō* means 'to exercise authority over'. The nouns *kurios* ('lord') and *exousia* ('authority') lie under the verbs.
- vv. 43–45: *Servant; slave; serve*. These verses use the nouns *diakonos* ('servant') and *doulos* ('slave'), followed by the verb *diakoneō* ('serve').
- v. 45: *ransom*. The noun *lutron* comes from the verb *lutroō*, which means both 'to free someone by paying a ransom' and, more generally, 'to rescue' or 'to set someone free'. So *lutron* can be the ransom paid or the price for the release.

James and John came forward

In order to understand James and John's actions, we need to remember the previous story. Jesus was walking ahead of the others, we assume with determination and focus, causing the disciples to be astounded/afraid. If James and John 'came forward', they caught him up to ask their question. Given that Jesus had been talking about his own death immediately before, this and their subsequent questions seem even more insensitive.

Sitting at the right and left, 'in your glory'

That the verb used means 'to sit' and not ' to recline' points to the fact that James and John are not thinking of a meal; it therefore suggests that they are thinking of sitting on thrones: one on either side of Jesus. In Ancient Near Eastern thought, it was usually the son or chief advisor who sat at the right hand of the ruler. Although the word for 'left' can also mean 'boding ill' or 'ominous', there is no hint here that it had any negative connotations. After the right-hand position, the left would be the next most desired (though how James and John would decide who sat in which position raises further questions).

James and John – like Peter, after the first prediction of Jesus' death and at his Transfiguration – have completely misunderstood what is going on. They seem to imagine that Jesus' glory will involve thrones and status, not death and suffering. This is a worked example of how people will hear what they want or expect to hear, even if it is not what has been said.

Cup and baptism

Jesus' use of 'cup' and 'baptism' to refer to his suffering and death form an unusual pairing. 'Cup' is used again in 14.36, in the Garden of Gethsemane, when Jesus asks for the cup to be taken from him. Baptism is not used in this way anywhere else: the closest anyone can find is the use of *baptizomai* in contemporary Greek literature to refer to being overwhelmed. Nevertheless, although the analogy and pairing are unusual, the meaning is clear.

It is tempting to look at the tradition about James and John's martyrdoms as evidence that Jesus was correct here. If we do that, then James' death is referenced (in Acts 12.2) at the hands of Herod Antipas; but John's is harder to identify. It requires taking a view on whether the John who was on Patmos at the start of Revelation was the same John as this John; and, if so, whether his reason to be there was exile or not. In this context (of Jesus talking about the cost of discipleship for all his followers), it seems more likely that a general reference is meant to the future deaths of the disciples rather than a specific reference to the deaths of James and John.

'The Gentiles ... But it is not so among you'

The next element of Jesus' teaching directly compares what the Gentiles do with what the disciples should do.

Mark 10.42	You know that among the Gentiles	**Mark 10.43**	But it is not so among you
	those whom they recognize as rulers		whoever wishes to become great
	lord it (or rule) over them		must be your servant
	their great ones	**10.44**	whoever wishes to be first
	tyrants over		must be slave of all

It is interesting that Jesus uses the present tense to hold up the alternate view: 'it is not so among you'. What we have observed of the disciples so far suggests that this is optimistic. What it probably means is that these are the rules of the kingdom and they are functioning whether they know it or not.

The upside-down rules of the kingdom mean that those who want to be great must first, counter-intuitively, become servants and slaves. At its heart, what this means is that, rather than claiming power and authority (as James and John have just done), the disciples should give it up, placing the needs of others above their own. The rules of the kingdom require people to displace themselves and their desires from the centre of their world and, instead, to prioritize everyone else. It remains as hard to do today as it was for the first disciples; but how different our churches and Christian communities would be if we were only a little more successful.

'Not to be served but to serve'

See the box, 'Son of Man', on p. 61.

Jesus ends this section of teaching with a reminder that the rules of the kingdom apply as much to him as to everyone else. This is a 'do as I say, not as I do' scenario. The reason why this economy already exists is because Jesus is already living it out. The Son of Man has come to do precisely this ... not to be served but to serve.

Mark 10.45 is one of the most extensively discussed verses in the whole Gospel and there isn't enough space here to do justice to the breadth of the debate. Two particular issues, however, are worthy of note:

- Commas may seem trivial but they can be quite important. John N. Collins (in *Diakonia*, OUP, 1990) has argued (in my view persuasively) that we should remove the comma after 'serve', in this sentence, so that Jesus came to do one thing not two. In other words, he came to serve in such a way as to give his life as a ransom for many. His service *is* his giving his life. This makes sense of this passage coming straight after the third prediction of his death. The upside-down rules of the kingdom require everyone to serve, and Jesus' own death is a manifestation of his service. The challenge for each of the disciples is to discover what their service looks like – as it is for us.

- Isaiah 53 may lie behind Jesus' teaching here (though some disagree with this and there is extensive discussion about it). Given the link between the third prediction and Isaiah (see p. 238), I generally agree with the view that Isaiah 53 lies behind this saying of Jesus, especially Isaiah 53.10–12. Indeed, it is worth reading Mark 10.32–45 alongside Isaiah 52.13—53.12 to observe the resonances between the two.

Mark 10.46–52: Jesus healed a blind man II (in Jericho)

Having begun in the far north (Bethsaida), we come to the end of this section of Mark by arriving at Jericho. The next part of the story moves to Jerusalem, beginning with the entry into the city and ending with the Resurrection.

We started this section with a blind man regaining his sight and end it in a similar way. In between, as noted above, we have observed a remarkable catalogue of the disciples not 'seeing', sometimes in the crassest ways.

Links backwards

- When Jesus heals Bartimaeus, he uses the same words he used for the woman who was bleeding in Mark 5.34.
- The account of the healing of the blind man at Bethsaida (8.22–26) stands as a bookend with this story here.

Interesting words ...

- v. 46: *blind beggar*. In Mark, the word 'blind' (*tuphlos*) is used only in the story of the blind man at Bethsaida and then here again. The verb *aiteō* means 'to ask'; *prosaiteō* is 'to beg' and a 'beggar' is, therefore, a *prosaitēs*.
- v. 47: *of Nazareth*. Jesus was a very common name in this period, so where he came from was needed as a qualifier. *Nazarēnos* means 'a Nazarene': that is, someone from Nazareth. It is not to be confused with 'Nazarite', which refers to someone who made a vow to God.
- vv. 47–48: *have mercy*. The verb *eleeō* means 'to have mercy' or 'to show mercy'.
- v. 48: *sternly ordered*. The word *epitimaō* ('rebuke' or 'censure') has been used

quite often (see 1.25; 3.12; 4.39; 8.30, 32, 33; 9.25; 10.13); but it does not appear again after this instance.

- v. 48: *he cried out even more loudly*. The verb *krazō* is 'cry out' or 'scream', to which is added *pollos* ('much') and *mallon* ('more').
- v. 49: *stood still*. The verb *histamai* means, generally, 'to stand'. It also means 'to be firm', 'to be established' or 'to stop'. As Jesus was travelling at this point, it must mean he stopped.
- v. 49: *take heart*. The Greek word the crowd said to Bartimaeus is the same as the one Jesus said to the disciples when he walked on the water: *tharseō* ('have courage').
- v. 50: *throwing off his cloak*. *Apoballō* means 'to throw off', and *himation* the 'outer garment' or 'cloak'.
- v. 50: *sprang up*. *Anapēdaō* means 'to jump' or 'to leap up with excitement or fear'.
- v. 51: *My teacher*. Bartimaeus used the Aramaic word *rabbouni* here. In the Gospels, the word is used only here and by Mary at the tomb (John 20.16).
- vv. 51–52: *see again; regained his sight*. The verb *anablepō* (*blepō* ('see') and *ana* ('again')) implies that the blind man had been able to see in the past. It was also used of the man in Bethsaida (8.24) and, interestingly, of Jesus looking up to heaven (6.41; 7.34).
- v. 52: *your faith has made you well*. Jesus uses the same formulation here as he did with the woman who was bleeding in 5.34: 'Your faith (*pistis*) has saved you (*sōzō*).' There are a range of different words for 'heal' in Greek. As we can see here, *sōzō* may also mean 'save'. For more on this, see the box, 'Words for "heal" in Mark's Gospel', on p. 50.
- v. 52: *followed him*. In contrast to the rich man who went away devastated, this man, who had nothing, followed Jesus (*akolouō*) immediately.

Jericho

Jericho is an ancient city, founded around 9000 BC, and is thought to be one of the world's oldest continuously inhabited cities. It is located 846ft below sea level, in an oasis in the middle of the desert. Its temperate climate meant that the Hasmoneans (the descendants of the Maccabees) built their winter palaces there; but they constructed a new city around a mile to the south. So at the time of Jesus, there were two Jerichos: the old city and the new one.

Both Herod the Great and Herod Archelaus had winter palaces in Jericho too. As well as the healing reported here (recorded also in Matt. 20.29–34 and Luke 18.35–43), Luke notes the conversation between Jesus and a tax collector by the name of Zacchaeus. Jericho appears in one other story in Luke as well: the parable of the Good Samaritan (Luke 10.25–37), which features the perilous road from Jerusalem to Jericho. Since Jesus was in Jericho for this narrative and in Jerusalem at the start of chapter 11, we can only assume that he, too, took this road, but in the opposite direction.

Bartimaeus

Mark is the only Gospel writer to name the blind beggar. Indeed, this is the only time that someone who is healed is named in Mark (the only other named person connected to a healing is Jairus, whose daughter was healed). The reference to Simon of Cyrene's sons (Alexander and Rufus) by name in Mark 15.21 implies that they were known to Mark's community, which hints that the same was true of Bartimaeus. The name Bar-Timaeus means 'son of Timaeus' in Aramaic; for those who would not know, Mark translates it into Greek. What is odd here is that Timaeus is a Greek name; so we are given an Aramaic prefix (*bar*: 'son of') with a Greek name. This may suggest that Timaeus himself was known to Mark's community.

Son of David

The only time this title is used in Mark's Gospel is here.

The title was slowly becoming used at the time of Jesus to refer to the Messiah. For more on expectations about the Messiah, see the box, 'The Messiah', on p. 191.

Those whose messianic expectations focused around a descendant of David began to talk about a 'son of David' who would come to save God's people. Texts, such as the *Psalms of Solomon* (which were written around the middle of the first century BC), tell of a son of David who would arise to rule over Israel (*Psalms of Solomon* 17.21).

It is surprising, therefore, to see Bartimaeus asking for healing. The expected Son of David would come to be king, not to heal people. It is thought, therefore, that Bartimaeus' request might have had more to do with an expectation about the Son of David caring for the lowly rather than healing people: David was held up as a protector of righteousness, and part of that would have involved taking care of the poor.

The crowd

At the start of the previous passage, we saw Jesus' determination to go to Jerusalem, with his striding out ahead of those following him. There are hints that his behaviour attracted notice and a larger crowd. Whereas in the previous passage, the people with Jesus were described as those following, they are now portrayed as 'a large crowd' (v. 46). They did not want Jesus to be distracted from his goal by the shouts of an insignificant beggar. The beggar's persistence, however (as so often in Mark), bore fruit and the crowd shifted from rebuking him to encouraging him to go forward.

'What do you want me to do for you?'

In this passage and the previous one, Jesus asks the same question of James and John, and of Bartimaeus. While all respond with a personal request, Bartimaeus' appeal comes out of deep need; James and John, on the other hand, are seeking status. Bartimaeus receives what he requests, while the others do not (or at least not in the form they have in mind).

Bartimaeus then addresses Jesus with a title only otherwise used by Mary in John 20.16. *Rabbouni* is the Aramaic for 'rabbi'. It is a heightened form, so offers greater honour and respect than merely 'rabbi' or, indeed, 'teacher', which was how Jesus was most often addressed by those who came to him.

Jesus declares that Bartimaeus' faith, just like that of the woman who was bleeding, has saved him. Bartimaeus demonstrates the depth of his faith by immediately following Jesus on the way, unlike the rich man who had too much to lose to follow Jesus.

Mark 11.1—16.8:
On the Road to the Cross and Beyond

With Mark 11, we enter the last phase of Jesus' ministry. Chapters 11—13 consist of another section of teaching, this time in Jerusalem; chapters 14—15 include the arrest, trial and Crucifixion; and 16.1–8 covers the story of the Resurrection. The tension (which has been growing slowly since the Pharisees and Herodians decided to destroy Jesus (3.6); and then more rapidly from the end of chapter 8 as Jesus tried, unsuccessfully, to communicate what was going to happen to his disciples) now comes to a head. The shadow of the cross falls fully over the narrative.

Mark gives relatively clear timings for the events of this week (with a couple of confusing references).

- First day (the equivalent of our Sunday): entry into Jerusalem and going into the temple to look around and then leave (11.11).
- Second day (the equivalent of our Monday): cursing the fig tree and cleansing the temple (11.12–19).
- Third day (the equivalent of our Tuesday): noticing the fig tree is withered to its roots, and teaching in various forms (11.20—13.37). There is nothing to indicate that this teaching happened over more than one day.
- The next timing noted is in 14.1, which is said to be two days before the Passover and the Festival of Unleavened Bread. This makes the date 13 Nissan, and the equivalent of our Wednesday, when Judas decided to betray Jesus and the woman anointed him.
- For a discussion of the timing implied by 14.12, see p. 300; but it seems that the Last Supper was prepared on 14 Nissan (the equivalent of our Thursday) and eaten at the start of 15 Nissan (the equivalent of our Friday, beginning at sundown – as all Jewish days did – on Thursday evening).
- If Thursday to Friday is day one and Friday to Saturday is day two, then Sunday morning is on day three: the third day, on which Jesus rose.

Patterns in 11.1—16.8

Mark uses his 'sandwich' technique three times in this section (wrapping one story around another to give more depth of meaning).

- The 'cleansing' of the temple is inserted between the cursing of the fig tree and the discovery that it has withered (11.1–25). For more on the withering of the fig tree and its significance, see p. 259)
- The anointing at Bethany is interleaved between the chief priests and scribes' decision to kill Jesus and Judas' decision to hand him over (14.1–11), contrasting the greatest devotion with the greatest betrayal.
- Peter's denial of Jesus is placed between Jesus' two trials – the first before the Sanhedrin and the second before Pilate (14.53—15.5) – revealing the contrast between Jesus' silence and Peter's frantic denials.

There is also another technique that is obvious in this part of Mark. Two key sections have a psalm running underneath them, adding extra depth to the portrayal.

- Psalm 118 is quoted both during Jesus' entry into Jerusalem (11.1–11) and in the parable of the tenants (12.1–12). As the psalm features a king returning to the temple to be welcomed and blessed by the priests, the attitude of the chief priests stands out starkly here.
- Psalm 22 runs underneath the Crucifixion narrative (in reverse) and prepares us for the statement – by the centurion, who is a representative of all the ends of the earth (Ps. 22.27) – that Jesus is the Son of God.

Mark 11.1–11: Jesus entered Jerusalem

Although in John's Gospel Jesus goes to Jerusalem three times for the Passover (John 2.13; 5.1; 10.22), in Mark this is the first time that he is said to have travelled there. A grand entrance, therefore, makes sense. At the start of Mark 10, Jesus set out from Capernaum and has, at last, arrived.

In the Gospel so far, other than when people were flocking to hear John the Baptist, the mentions of Jerusalem have been negative. Scribes who debated with Jesus came from there (3.22; 7.1); Jesus set out in 10.1 to go there and prophesied (in 10.32–34) that there he would die. Not only that, Galileans were generally disdained by the inhabitants of Jerusalem (see more on this subject on p. 250). As a result, the very name Jerusalem should give readers a sense of foreboding.

Links backwards

- The conflicts between Jesus and those who came from Jerusalem (Mark 3.22; 7.1), and Jesus' prophecy that he would die there (10.32–34), prepare us for the fact that Jesus' time in Jerusalem will be challenging.
- The healing of Bartimaeus (10.46–52), where Jesus was addressed as the 'Son of David', rings in the air here: for the first time, we see Jesus acknowledged as the long-awaited king; and the kingdom of David is welcomed by the crowd.

Links forwards

- The charge against Jesus to Pilate was phrased as his being the 'King of the Jews' (15.2): a statement Pilate then had written and placed above Jesus, on the cross, at his Crucifixion (15.26).

Interesting words …

- v. 1: *approaching*. The verb *engizō* ('come near', 'draw near' or 'approach') appears only three times in Mark. The other two instances indicate that its use here is important (see 'Draw near' below).
- vv. 2, 4–5 and 7: *colt*. The word *pōlos* can refer to the young of any animal; but when the animal is otherwise undefined, it usually refers to an ass or donkey.
- v. 2: *never been ridden*. 'On which no human (*anthrōpos*) had yet sat (*kathizō*).'
- v. 4: *street*. We have not encountered this word before, as most of Jesus' ministry has been in the countryside. An *amphodon* denotes a city street.
- v. 5: *bystanders*. The verb *histēmi* is used: 'those standing there'.
- v. 7: *threw … on*. The verb *epiballō* is formed from *ballō* ('throw') and *epi* ('on').
- v. 8: *spread*. *Strōnnumi* can refer to making a bed but more generally means 'to spread out'.
- v. 8: *leafy branches*. A *stibas* could be a rush (many of which could be spread on a floor) or a leafy branch of some kind. Since Mark says the people had cut them (*koptō*) in the fields, leafy branches seem more likely.
- v. 9: *went ahead; followed*. 'Going ahead' is translated from *proagō*, which more often means 'lead forward' or 'escort'; and 'following' is the usual *akolouō*. The idea is that Jesus is in the middle of the crowd, which is both leading and following.
- vv. 9–10: *Hosanna*. A Hebrew word transliterated into Greek. For more on what it means, see 'Psalm 118', on pp. 252–3.
- vv. 9–10: *Blessed*. In the Beatitudes, the word 'blessed' is translated from *makarios*, which has the sense of 'happy' or 'fortunate'. Here the verb *eulogeō* ('speak well of') is used. The two words are quite different.

- v. 11: *looked around.* The verb *periblepō* is often used in Mark to refer to looking around carefully.
- v. 11: *late. Opse* is an adverb that has a specific meaning: 'after sunset but before dark'. It is used here, in 11.19 and 13.35.

Draw near

The verb *engizō* ('draw near') occurs in

- Mark 1.15: 'The time is fulfilled, and the kingdom of God has come near; repent, and believe in the good news.'
- Mark 14.42: 'Get up, let us be going. See, my betrayer is at hand.'

The significance of its use here is more than that of Jesus and the disciples being close to Jerusalem. A key moment is close; and this verb signals its approach.

Galilee and Jerusalem

In the first century, the inhabitants of Jerusalem regarded Galileans as, at best, second-class citizens. They viewed them as 'less pure' because Galilee was surrounded by Gentile territories. The easy ability to travel to Gentile territories, and for Gentiles to travel to Galilee, meant that Galilean purity was considered compromised. They also thought that Galileans were provincial and unsophisticated (because of the predominance of agriculture in the area) and uneducated (because most rabbis taught in Jerusalem, in the vicinity of the temple). Galilee was also regarded as politically unstable because of the large number of bandits, or political revolutionaries, who hid in the Galilean hills; so it is easy to see why Galileans were regarded with intense suspicion by those from Judea and Jerusalem.

This kind of attitude is illustrated well by Nathanael's question to Philip in John 1.46: 'Can anything good come out of Nazareth?'

Given this, the best a Galilean could hope for would be to be treated with toleration by the people of Jerusalem; but even that did not often happen.

Connections in Bethany and Bethphage

It is easy to imagine that we know everything about Jesus' life and ministry, but stories like this one remind us that we don't. As far as Mark is concerned, this is the first time that Jesus has been to Jerusalem and yet he knew the owner of the colt well enough to arrange to borrow it. There are all sorts of reasons why this might have happened; but it is worth noting here that it reveals what we don't know about Jesus, which, in this instance, are his connections in and around Jerusalem.

Bethany is two miles from Jerusalem, on the slopes of the Mount of Olives. Bethphage no longer exists. Rabbinic literature (*m. Menachot* 11), however, indicates that it was on the boundary of the limit that one could travel on the sabbath day from the temple (2,000 cubits or 0.57 miles). This made it closer to Jerusalem than Bethany. If this is correct, it is odd that Bethphage is mentioned first.

It is worth reminding ourselves that Jesus' route here was from Jericho. It was an arduous climb (laying aside the danger of the route) of 18 miles, ascending 825 feet through the desert.

On donkeys and other symbols

The details that outline the prearrangement for borrowing the colt make it very clear that it is no accident that Jesus began to ride, rather than walk, down the Mount of Olives; otherwise, one could be forgiven for imagining that he was tired after the gruelling climb through the desert from Jericho. This action was deliberate and we, along with the original crowd, are intended to see significance in it.

At this point, Jesus would have been travelling in the middle of a large group of people. We know that a large crowd was following Jesus in Jericho and, since he was going to Jerusalem for the festival, there is no reason to imagine that anyone stopped following him on the way. Not only that, Passover was one of the three principal festivals of Judaism (the other two being Pentecost and Tabernacles), which meant that everyone (who could) travelled to Jerusalem for the festival; and the route from Bethany was the primary route into Jerusalem from the north. As a result, Jesus would have been surrounded by a large throng of people.

The interesting question is what suddenly made them treat Jesus in the way that they did. The first factor was Jesus' decision to ride a donkey. This would have called to mind Zechariah 9.9: 'Rejoice greatly, O daughter Zion! Shout aloud, O daughter Jerusalem! Lo, your king comes to you; triumphant and victorious is he, humble and riding on a donkey, on a colt, the foal of a donkey.' The crowd might also have been reminded of 1 Kings 1.33, which describes Solomon's riding to his coronation on a mule.

Alongside these verses, there is Zechariah 14.4, which identifies the Mount of Olives as the place where the Lord will stand to begin the redemption of Israel ('On that day his feet shall stand on the Mount of Olives, which lies before Jerusalem on the east; and the Mount of Olives shall be split in two from east to west by a very wide valley'). The cumulative symbolism of the remembrance of Solomon's coronation, the expectation that a new king would come riding on a donkey, and that God's redemption would begin on the Mount of Olives signalled to the crowd that this was a moment of huge importance.

This raises the question of whether Jesus' entrance can be seen as 'triumphal', as it is sometimes called. The phrase 'triumphal entry' comes from the idea of the Roman triumphal procession. After a great victory, a general would return to Rome, bringing with him everything that he and his legions had won (both treasure and slaves). The general would ride a white horse as a symbol of his triumph. It is possible that this type of triumphal procession is in mind here; but Jesus' procession would have been a huge subversion of it: a donkey instead of a white horse; a willing crowd rather than unwilling slaves; a triumph on the horizon but not yet won. It would be much more of a 'kingdom triumph' like so much else we have seen: a triumph turned on its head; what you might call an 'un-triumphal triumphal procession'.

The crowd's response

The crowd's response indicates that the people understood the symbolism unfolding before them. Their reaction was to greet Jesus in the way that the crowd had greeted the victorious Maccabees when they entered Jerusalem after they had defeated the Greek Seleucid Empire. See, for example, 1 Maccabees 13.51:

> On the twenty-third day of the second month, in the one hundred seventy-first year, the Jews entered it with praise and palm branches, and with harps and cymbals and stringed instruments, and with hymns and songs, because a great enemy had been crushed and removed from Israel.

The waving of the palm branches and singing of psalms (principally Psalm 118; see below) does suggest that this event was in the crowd's mind.

The spreading of cloaks on the ground, though, comes from another occasion. In 2 Kings 9.13, when Jehu was anointed king of the northern kingdom of Israel, his followers 'hurriedly … all took their cloaks and spread them for him on the bare steps; and they blew the trumpet, and proclaimed, "Jehu is king"'.

All in all, we can conclude that Jesus' deliberate, symbolic actions suggested to the crowd the arrival of the long-awaited king; the people recognized this and responded accordingly.

Psalm 118

The words shouted by the crowd are a quotation from Psalm 118.25–26: 'Save us, we beseech you, O LORD! O LORD, we beseech you, give us success! Blessed is the one who comes in the name of the LORD. We bless you from the house of the LORD.' You will notice that the word 'hosanna' does not appear in it. This is because hosanna was a Hebrew word and Mark has, as so often throughout the Gospel, simply written it in Greek. It is interesting that only this word was kept in Hebrew, whereas the rest of the quote was translated fully into Greek.

This tells us that, during this period, the word 'hosanna' was being used as a cry of praise, maybe even a rallying cry of hope. This is connected to a subtle shift in the meaning of the word from its original usage. *Hoshi'a na* means literally 'save now' and, in its context in Psalm 118, is a cry of supplication by the whole people of God to God to hear them and save them. The word's usage in the Gospels suggests that it had shifted from being simply a prayer to something closer to a statement of confidence: something along the lines of 'We know that you will save us and give praise because of this'.

This shift in meaning can probably be ascribed to the popularity of Psalm 118, around the time of Jesus, as a psalm expressing the hope of Israel's coming salvation by a future Davidic king-like figure. In the Talmud (*b. Pesachim* 119a), Psalm 118.25ff. was used with particular reference to a Davidic king-like figure. If, in Jesus' actions, the crowd saw the promise that he was the king who had come to save them, then it would be natural to sing 'hosanna' – a cry of victorious confidence – as part this psalm.

'Blessed is the coming kingdom of our ancestor David!'

The addition of this phrase into Psalm 118.26 makes the crowd's response to Jesus specifically messianic: it draws together expectations about the long-awaited Messiah with the hope that a descendant of David would come to lead God's people. Since the first time that Jesus was greeted as 'Son of David' was by Bartimaeus, it seems that the title has stuck in the crowd's mind and has shaped their view of Jesus.

He went into the temple

If we read Jesus' entry into Jerusalem with an eye on Psalm 118, then Mark 11.11 becomes more important than it would otherwise. After he entered the city, Jesus went to the temple to look around. Psalm 118 tells of an unnamed king, who had been saved in battle by God (118.5–14) and who comes to the temple to give thanks (118.19–20). Most scholars think that the end of Psalm 118, which includes 'blessed is the one who comes in the name of the LORD', would have been spoken by the priests to welcome the king into the temple. It is therefore poignant that Jesus went into the temple, looked around and was not welcomed at all.

Psalm 118 returns in the parable of the tenants (Mark 12.1–12).

Mark 11.12–25: Jesus cursed the fig tree and then the temple

One of the episodes that people struggle with most in the Gospels is the cursing of the fig tree, which seems petty, vindictive and pointless. Mark's placing of it, however, sheds important light not just on what it meant but what Jesus' actions in the temple meant.

Links backwards and forwards

- Mark 9.29 introduced the theme of praying in complex situations.
- Psalm 118 is introduced, during the entry to Jerusalem, with the words shouted by the crowd. Jesus quotes from it again in the parable of the tenants. The passages between the entry into Jerusalem and that parable can be seen to contain reflections on the temple in the light of the psalm.
- Mark 3.6 spoke of the Pharisees and Herodians seeking for a way to destroy Jesus; in 11.18, a similar phrase is used of the chief priests and scribes.
- If Jesus' actions in the temple are seen as a cursing (like that of cursing the fig tree), then this whole passage resonates with 13.2, in which Jesus says of the temple that not one stone will be left upon another.

Interesting words …

- v. 12: *following day. Epaurion* means 'the following day', 'the next day' or 'tomorrow'.
- v. 13: *season.* Mark uses the word *kairos* ('right time' or fitting time').
- v. 14: *again.* The word 'again' is not used here. Instead, Jesus said, 'into the age' (*eis tōn aiōna*): 'May no one eat fruit from you into the age'; in other words, 'either now or in the age to come'.
- v. 15: *drive out.* The verb *ekballō* is used here, which means 'throw out' or 'cast out'.
- v. 15: *selling and buying. Pōleō* refers to 'doing business' or 'selling' and *agorazō* is 'buying', as in buying at the market.
- v. 15: *money-changers.* A *kollubistēs* was someone who exchanged currency.
- v. 15: *doves.* The only other time a dove/pigeon (*peristera*) is mentioned in Mark is at Jesus' baptism (1.10).
- v. 16: *anything.* The word used here is *skeuos*, which is a 'vessel' or 'implement'. These are not otherwise mentioned and may have had nothing to do with either money changing or selling.
- v. 17: *nations.* The word for nation is *ethnos*, elsewhere translated as 'Gentile'.
- v. 17: *den of robbers. Splēlaion* refers to a 'cave' or 'hideout' and a *lēstēs*

was a 'robber'; it also means a 'bandit' (which, in this context, had political connotations).

- v. 18: *kill.* This is not the word for 'kill' used in Jesus' predictions of his death; rather, it is *apollumi*, the word used in 3.6 for 'destroy him'.
- v. 18: *spellbound. Ekplēssō* is one of Mark's words for 'amazed', which is used also in 1.22; 6.2; 7.37; and 10.26. For more on Mark's use of these verbs, see the notes on 1.22 and 27 (pp. 41–2).
- v. 19: *evening. Opse* is used again here, as in 11.11. It means 'after sunset but before it was dark'.
- vv. 20–21: *withered away to its roots. Xērainō* means 'to dry up' or 'to become parched' and the Greek says *ek* ('from') *rhiza* ('roots'), implying that it dried upwards from the roots.
- v. 23: *Truly I tell you.* This characteristic opening (*amēn legō humin*) to a saying by Jesus occurs once early on in Mark and then with increasing frequency towards the end (3.28; 8.12; 9.1, 41; 10.15, 29; 11.23; 12.43; 13.30; 14.18, 25, 30). For more on the phrase, see the note on 3.28 (p. 85).
- v. 23: *be taken up and thrown.* The verb *hairō* means 'to lift' or 'to pick up'. It is in the passive voice here so means 'to be picked up'. Likewise, *ballō* is also in the passive form, so it is 'to be thrown'.
- v. 23: *doubt. Diakrinō* has a range of meanings, from 'dispute' to 'criticize'; but most likely, here, it is 'doubt' or 'be uncertain'.
- v. 24: *ask for in prayer.* Two verbs are used here: *proseucomai* and *aiteō* ('pray' and 'ask').
- v. 25: *forgive. Aphiēmi* means 'to let go', hence 'to forgive'.
- v. 25: *trespasses.* There are a number of words for 'sin'. Here, *paraptòmata* means 'to take a false step or blunder'. It is often translated as 'trespass'.

Staying at Bethany

The story of the fig tree reveals to us that Jesus and the disciples were staying at Bethany. As with other details in the story, Mark does not expand on why Jesus and the disciples stayed in Bethany and not in Jerusalem itself. It could be because the city was overcrowded, because Jesus feared he would be unsafe or because he had contacts in Bethany (who provided the colt for the entry into Jerusalem). Without any clear information, we are left to guess at the reasons.

One thing is clear: Bethany was outside the limit for walking on the sabbath or feast days (see p. 251). This would explain why Jesus and the disciples went to Gethsemane (roughly half a mile or 2,000 cubits away from the city) after the Last Supper, rather than to Bethany, which exceeded the allowed walking limit.

Fruitful fig trees

In the Old Testament, fig trees, along with vines, symbolized God's blessing and abundance. So much so that one of the visions of the future was that everyone would have vines and fig trees of their own: 'On that day, says the LORD of hosts, you shall invite each other to come under your vine and fig tree' (Zech. 3.10). Conversely, a lack of figs on the fig tree symbolized spiritual aridity: 'When I wanted to gather them, says the LORD, there are no grapes on the vine, nor figs on the fig tree; even the leaves are withered, and what I gave them has passed away from them' (Jer. 8.13).

Also significant is the fact that figs have a very unusual two-year cycle. The following year's crop (the breba crop) grows alongside the current year's crop (the main crop). So a fig tree with just leaves and no figs was one that was not going to bear fruit either in the present year or the next.

The cursing of the fig tree and of the temple

Jesus' cleansing of the temple is often regarded popularly as his objecting to any kind of business taking place within the temple courts. The problem with this view is that both the animal traders and the money changers were essential to the running of the temple. The temple was a large and very busy place. Josephus, in *Against Apion* 2.108, estimated that the total number of priests was about 20,000. While this may be an exaggeration, there were certainly many thousands of priests, who would all have been on duty during a major festival. It is also estimated that, during a festival, between one and two million people would come to the temple. The pure logistics of managing this situation required special arrangements.

The temple tax that was levied on all adult males was paid in Tyrian shekels (pure silver coins that were originally minted in Tyre). In order to pay, people would have to change their denarii (the Roman coinage) into Tyrian shekels. The simplest place to do so was the temple itself. Alongside this, animals had to be checked for purity by a temple official before they were sacrificed; so, in a large and busy temple, the simplest way to present a pure animal that had already been checked by the Levites was to buy one in the temple precincts.

Some people surmise that there was huge corruption in the temple and that this is what Jesus was combating. There is certainly evidence of opposition to the temple from groups, such as the community at Qumran (where the Dead Sea Scrolls were found), based on the behaviour of the priests. The problem is that Mark does not record Jesus' criticizing corruption.

Also important to note was that the temple was not significantly affected by Jesus' actions. It seemed to be functioning without any issue in the days after the 'cleansing', which was evidenced by the widow coming to give her two coins two days later.

Herod the Great's temple

Herod the Great began rebuilding the temple in 20–19 BC. Although the holy place and the holy of holies were completed in around a year and a half, the outer courts took another eight years to build. The entire project, however, took much longer and was only finally finished in AD 63 (seven years before its destruction).

The inner temple building (the holy place and the holy of holies) was constructed at the same size as the one in Solomon's original temple. The outer courts – the court of the women and the court of the Gentiles – were double the size of the originals, however, and covered around 35 acres.

The inner temple building could be entered only by priests, and the holy of holies only by high priests. Outside the building was the (inner) court of the priests, into which Jewish men could enter to bring their sacrifices. The women were not permitted in this area but could enter both outer courts (the court of the Gentiles and the court of the women).

The treasury (where people brought their taxes and gifts for the upkeep of the temple) was in the court of the women. The 13 treasury boxes were located around the treasury's sides. Each box had a large trumpet-shaped funnel on top into which people could put their money.

The court of the Gentiles was the largest and outermost court; it was where the money changers and animal sellers would have been located. The porticos around the edge of this court were where rabbis gathered to teach and debate.

This raises the possibility that Jesus' actions were more symbolic than anything else, which leads us back to the fig tree. If the fig tree was the symbol of God's blessing and abundance, so was the temple. As Jesus said, when he overturned the tables, the temple was meant to be a house of prayer for all nations. The priests at the heart of the temple were meant to welcome the king (Ps. 118); they were also meant to be ready for the great and glorious day when those from all nations would stream to the temple to worship God (Isa. 56.6–8). Instead, Jesus declared that they had become a cave or hideout for *lēstēs*. At the time, this important word was used for politically motivated outlaws who sought to bring about the downfall of the Romans.

Jesus' accusation, then, was that the priests (who should have welcomed him to the temple after his entry into Jerusalem as they should a king) had in fact hijacked the temple for their own advantage and were using it for political gain. Just as the fig tree was not doing what it was created to do (produce fruit), neither was the temple (being a house of prayer for all nations). Jesus' criticism of the priests and all connected to the temple was concerned with far more than simply financial mismanagement. They were not living up to their God-given vocation to be a place of prayer and welcome for all.

The chief priests and scribes

In Mark 3.6, the unlikely collaboration between the Pharisees and the Herodians had occurred so that they could find a way to destroy Jesus. The same phrase is now used of the chief priests and the scribes, and so the tension heightens. Before, Jesus was teaching and healing in the far-off territory of Galilee; now, he was bringing his message to the heart of the temple itself. Before, the scribes from Jerusalem had to travel a long way to be offended by Jesus; now, he was bringing his critique to their very doorstep. So, in a way, the chief priests had no choice but to act.

The high priests/chief priests

The chief priests will be mentioned with increasing regularity from this point onwards, so it is worth adding a note about them here. The challenge of the term 'chief priest' is that there was no such office. One high priest was in office at any one time. The liturgical role of the high priest was to enter the holy of holies once a year, on the Day of Atonement, to sprinkle the blood of the sin offering and burn incense. During the time of Jesus, the high priest was also the leader of the Sanhedrin and therefore, to a certain extent, a leader of the people of Judea. As a result, the chief priests, though not existing formally, might be a very loose description of the 'leading priests' (possibly members of the Sanhedrin; for more on the Sanhedrin, see p. 261), an informal gathering of former high priests or a combination of the two.

An important feature of this era was the dominance of Annas' family among the high priests. Annas was appointed as the first high priest after Herod Archelaus was deposed in AD 6. Annas himself was deposed as high priest in AD 15 after imposing death penalties he had no authority to enforce. Despite this, his influence remained strong because his five sons and one son-in-law were high priests after him. Here is a list of the members of the Annas dynasty, together with their dates as high priests:

- Annas ben Seth (AD 6 – deposed in 15)
- Eleazar ben Ananus (son, AD 16–17)
- Joseph ben Caiaphas, known as Caiaphas (son-in-law, AD 18–36), who had married the daughter of Annas
- Jonathan ben Ananus (son, AD 36–37 and 44)
- Theophilus ben Ananus (son, AD 37–41)
- Matthias ben Ananus (son, AD 43)
- Ananus ben Ananus (son, AD 63)

These dates go way beyond the time of Jesus but illustrate the Annas family influence among the high priests for much of the first century AD. For most of the lifetime of Jesus, Caiaphas, Annas' son-in-law, was high priest. Given the regular references to the 'chief priests', it seems at least possible that it refers to Annas' family, members of which ran the temple between them.

The withering of the fig tree

The location of this story immediately after Jesus' action in the temple tells us as much about the temple as it does about the fig tree. If we take Jesus' actions as a symbolic cursing of the temple then, just as the fig tree had shrivelled up from its roots upwards, so the temple would too. Jesus picks up this theme again in 13.2. It is important to recognize that this is not talking about Israel or the Jews but, specifically, the temple. Jesus considered the temple and its leaders to have failed in their vocation and cursed it. Mark's original readers, who would have been reading the Gospel around the time of the destruction of the temple in AD 70, would probably have made the connection with that event. Once the temple had been cursed, it was only a matter of time before it shrivelled up just like the fig tree had.

On faith, prayer and forgiveness

Jesus goes on from this to teach the disciples, using the fig tree as an example, on how faith in God can achieve the apparently impossible. This implies that his cursing of the fig tree (and the temple) falls into the same category of faith. As it was in 9.42–49, additional teaching is given, probably inspired by catchwords ('faith', 'prayer', 'forgive'). So we start with faith, move to why faith is important in prayer and end with something else that is necessary in prayer – forgiveness.

The idea of a small amount of faith that can move something much larger runs throughout the New Testament. As well as here, it also appears in Matthew 17.20 and Luke 17.6: faith the size of a mustard seed can move a mountain (Matthew) and uproot a mulberry tree (Luke). Paul also talks of faith that can move mountains in 1 Corinthians 13.2; and James writes of the importance of asking in faith without doubt (1.6). It is also reminiscent of Jesus' teaching after his conversation with the rich man: whereas with human beings, things can often seem impossible; with God, anything is possible.

On standing to pray

Interestingly, although kneeling to pray is the posture associated with prayer for many, standing to pray was more common throughout the Bible. For example, Hannah stood to pray to God (1 Sam. 1.26) as did Solomon (1 Kings 8.22). In Luke 18.11, the Pharisee stood while praying in the temple.

Kneeling to pray occurred in extremity; for example, when people fell before Jesus to beg for his help (see Jairus in Mark 5.22) or when Jesus was praying in Gethsemane (14.35).

From faith Jesus goes on to prayer, which – like moving mountains – requires faith that God will act. The implication is that if God can move mountains, God can also answer prayer; the key connection between the two is believing that this is the case.

The final piece of teaching is on the importance of forgiving others before praying to God. The implication is that not forgiving others gets in the way of our ability to have complete faith in God.

We cannot leave this section without commenting on the problem posed for us by Jesus' teaching on prayer. The challenge is that it isn't true or, at least, not true all the time. Many people pray with full faith to God to no effect. What Jesus doesn't teach here, but which is clear elsewhere in the New Testament, is that our prayers need to align with God's will. So 1 John 5.14 states: 'if we ask anything according to his will, he hears us'. Even Jesus, in Gethsemane, includes this in his prayers: 'yet, not what I want, but what you want' (Mark 14.36). Even having this knowledge doesn't help much when we pray for what we sincerely believe to be God's will and our prayers are still not answered. If I am honest, this is teaching I continue to wrestle with; I have no easy answers to the complexity of it.

Mark 11.27–33: 'By what authority are you doing these things?'

In the cleansing of the temple, Jesus brought the conflict between him and the chief priests to the temple itself. It is, therefore, unsurprising that they should now approach to challenge him. This, however, is not a new challenge. The question of his authority has been raised before (see 'Links backwards' below).

Links backwards

- In Mark 1.22, Jesus' first exorcism in a synagogue, we see people wonder about his authority. This theme loops back here.

Links forwards

- In many ways, Jesus responds in kind by questioning the religious leaders' authority in the parable of the tenants (12.1–12).

Interesting words …

- vv. 28–29: *authority. Exousia* is used here.

- vv. 29–30: *answer me*. *Apokrinomai* usually means 'answer' but can, in some instances, mean 'respond to charges' or 'defend yourself'. Jesus' response here has a hint of that.
- v. 31: *argued*. The verb *dialogizomai* has been used a number of times already (2.6, 8; 8.16, 17; 9.33) and means 'to debate' or 'argue'.
- v. 32: *afraid*. The usual word for 'fear', *phobeō*, is used here.

Walking in the temple courts

Herod the Great expanded the size of the temple when he rebuilt it. As a result, there was a lot of space to walk in.

See the box, 'Herod the Great's temple', on p. 257, for more on the temple. For more on chief priests, see p. 258, and the scribes, see p. 43.

The elders and the Sanhedrin

So far, we have encountered the chief priests and the scribes but not the elders (other than a passing mention in Jesus' first prediction of his Passion in 8.31).

The Sanhedrin was the legislative assembly in Israel at the time of Jesus. It was made up of 70 people, plus the Nasi (leader). Until the second century BC, the Nasi had been the high priest; but when confidence in the high priest dropped, the Nasi was drawn from other sources, most commonly from among the descendants of Rabbi Hillel. The Sanhedrin was made up of priests (largely Sadducees), scribes and elders. The elders were lay people from the most noble families.

The Sanhedrin met in the Hall of Hewn Stone, which was on the edge of the inner court of the temple, every day apart from the sabbath day. It adjudicated on legal cases, issued decrees for the smooth running of the country and managed temple operations.

The mention of chief priests, scribes and elders indicates that Jesus was approached by some or all of the Sanhedrin.

The questions

The members of the Sanhedrin asked Jesus two questions:

1. By what authority do you do these things?
2. Who gave this authority to you?

Used as we have become to 'trick' questions being asked of Jesus throughout his ministry, it is important to recognize that these ones were not. The

Sanhedrin was the body that bore authority within Israel, so its members' questions were legitimate. They knew where their authority came from and wished to know where Jesus' came from too.

It is interesting to compare Jesus' responses to those of Gamaliel in Acts 5. During a debate about the earliest Christians, Gamaliel said, 'If this plan or this undertaking is of human origin, it will fail; but if it is of God, you will not be able to overthrow them' (Acts 5.38–9). Jesus makes a distinction about John the Baptist. The Sanhedrin was a legislative body so Jesus' command, 'answer me' or 'give your defence', fitted in with the situation.

Jesus' response flushed out the dilemmas the Sanhedrin faced. John was very popular, so they had no wish to place themselves in opposition to popular opinion; but if they agreed that John's authority came from God, they would have to concede that Jesus' did too. The safest course of action for them was not to answer. Jesus took the same course of action but then told a parable that ended up becoming an answer.

Mark 12.1–12: The parable of the tenants

Although Jesus declined to answer the question from the members of the Sanhedrin about his own authority, he posed a parable in which he challenged their authority or, at least, noted that they were little more than 'tenants' looking after a property for someone else (God). The point of the parable was that they seemed to have forgotten this fact.

Links backwards

- The words 'beloved' and 'son', used in Mark 1.11 and 9.7 of Jesus, are used of the character murdered at the end of this parable.
- Psalm 118 was quoted in Mark 11.9–10 and is quoted again here. It draws attention to the importance of this psalm for understanding why Jesus thought the priests had not done what they should.
- The discussion between Jesus and members of the Sanhedrin about the origins of Jesus' authority underpins this passage (11.27–33).

Interesting words …

- v. 1: *vineyard; fence; wine press; watch-tower*. All these words are common in wine-growing: an *ampelōn* was a cultivated grape field or vineyard; a *phragmos* was a fence or hedge surrounding an area; and a *huplēnion* was a trough or pit dug to press grapes. A *purgos* was a watch-tower: given the importance of vineyards in this period, security was necessary.

- v. 1: *tenants*. Tenant farmers (*geōrgos*) were a key part of Galilean farming; they ran a farm in the absence of the landlord (see the box, 'Absentee landlords', on p. 264).
- v. 1: *went to another country*. The verb *apodēmeō* means 'to be away from home', 'to travel' or 'to go abroad'.
- v. 2: *season*. *Kairos* or 'right time' is used here.
- v. 2: *to collect from them his share of the produce of the vineyard*. This verse reads, 'so that he might receive (*lambanō*) from the tenant farmers (*geōrgos*) out of the fruit (*karpos*) of the vineyard (*ampelōn*)'. It clearly suggests that payment was a portion of fruit but for the first few years there would have been no fruit (see 'Vineyards' below). Thus, what is implied is rent.
- vv. 3–4: *beat; beat over the head*. The words here are *derō* ('beat', 'cudgel' or 'thrash') for 'beat' and *kephaloō* for 'beating over the head'. The verb appears only here (it is a *hapaxlegomenon*: a word occurring only once) and so its meaning is surmised from the context.
- v. 3: *empty-handed*. *Kenos* is simply 'empty'.
- v. 6: *beloved son*. 'Beloved (*agapētos*) son (*hios*)': the same words used by God of Jesus in 1.11 and 9.7.
- v. 7: *heir; inheritance*. *Klēronomos* and *klēronomia* refer respectively to the person who inherits and what they inherit.
- v. 9: *destroy*. The word *apollumi* is exactly the word used for the decision by the chief priests to destroy Jesus.
- v. 10: *cornerstone*. It isn't quite clear exactly what *kephalē gōnias* (literally, 'head of the corner') referred to. It could mean a foundational cornerstone (that is, the load-bearing stone) or a capstone that completes an arch and holds it together. Alternatively, it could be a capital that sits at the top of a building. Most go with cornerstone (I think correctly) but the others are all possible.
- v. 11: *amazing*. *Thaumastos* is the noun derived from *thaumazō* 'to be amazed'.
- v. 12. The Greek is in the opposite order to the NRSV translation: 'They sought (*zēteō*) to arrest (*krateō*: 'seize') and they feared (*phobeō*) the crowd (*ochlos*), for they knew (*ginōskō*) ...'

Vineyards

In the Bible, vineyards are commonly used as an analogy for Israel. One of the most striking of these can be found in Isaiah 5.1–7. This is a poetic passage, possibly a song, which tells the story of an owner's disappointment with a vineyard he planted. Despite the care lavished on it, it produced only wild grapes rather than the cultivated grapes that the owner hoped for. Although the focus of Jesus' parable is those who tend the vineyard, not the grapes. Isaiah's poetic prophecy is so evocative that it must have sprung to mind as soon as Jesus spoke about a vineyard. Isaiah was unambiguous that the vineyard was Israel; so moving the focus from the grapes to those who care for the vineyard makes it clear that Jesus was talking about Israel's leaders.

Absentee landlords

At the heart of this parable lies an absentee landlord. Indeed, he is so important to the parable that it is worth pausing to reflect on this cultural phenomenon, particularly with respect to Galilean farming.

Most people living in Galilee in the first century were poor; the best land, located in the plains that were especially fertile, was owned by wealthy urban dwellers who visited their lands at most a few times a year. They were often experienced by those who worked their land as distant and merciless, visiting only to receive their rent.

The large estates of the wealthy absentee landlords were farmed by tenant farmers and casual day workers. Both groups faced poverty on a regular basis. Tenant farmers were expected to pay rent for their tenancy with the crops they produced; but a bad harvest could drive them into debt. Day labourers were, as their name suggests, hired each day to work. They did not have a steady or reliable income. There is evidence that a good number of the bandits who hid in the hills were those driven there by poverty.

Among the crops most favoured by absentee landlords were grapes. The costs of setting up a vineyard were high; but once the vines started bearing fruit, the returns were significant.

The inheritance will be ours

What the tenants say to each other is odd. If they kill the son of the owner, the vineyard will still belong to the owner. Possibly the best way to understand what they mean is to translate *klēronomia* as 'possession' rather than inheritance. So they would be saying that were they to kill the son, they could take possession of the vineyard. We shouldn't, however, take what the tenants say too seriously. Their role is that of farcical 'baddies'; they are not meant to be seen as logical and strategic.

It is intriguing to notice that our sympathies are meant to lie with the absentee landlord here. Newly planted vineyards would not be expected to produce fruit for at least the first four to five years. The owner is sending his slaves to collect rent even though the vines would not yet have produced grapes of sufficient quality for wine. Perhaps Jesus told this parable in Jerusalem deliberately. In Galilee, he would have struggled to get his audience (primarily made up of tenant farmers and day labourers) to relate to the absentee landlord. The crowd in Jerusalem, on the other hand, would have been made up of people much more likely to be on the landlord's side.

The hearers of the prophecy in Isaiah 5.3–4 are asked to adjudicate what the landlord would do; Jesus does the same here. Those listening are invited to pass sentence on the tenants.

'The stone that the builders rejected'

We have noted already the recurrence of Psalm 118 here, which was first sung during Jesus' entry into Jerusalem (Mark 11.1–11) by the crowd surrounding him. There we noted that the logic of the psalm indicated that the priests would welcome the king into the temple with these words: 'Blessed is the one who comes in the name of the Lord,' but the priests did no such thing. Jesus went, looked around and left, unwelcomed. Here, he cited the same psalm again (Ps. 118.22), this time quoting a verse that seemed to clarify that a grand reversal was taking place.

In Psalm 118, the grand reversal was that the king, who thought he was about to die in battle, was saved and returned to the temple to be blessed. The use of Psalm 118 makes the irony even greater here. The king, Jesus, has returned to the temple but has been ignored and opposed by the priests, rather than blessed by them. The king will be saved, after he has died to save others, and he will become the chief cornerstone. But they, who have not blessed him and will kill him, will be rejected and find the temple torn down around their ears.

Mark 12.13–17: Should we pay taxes?

After being approached by members of the Sanhedrin, Jesus was then confronted by three successive 'interest groups'. The first of these, the Pharisees and Herodians, we are explicitly told were sent by the Sanhedrin; the others may or may not have come of their own volition (given the context, the hint is probably not).

Links backwards

- The unlikely alliance of the Pharisees and Herodians reminds us of their first alliance to destroy Jesus (Mark 3.6). While the Sanhedrin has now joined them in their intent, these two groups first decided to destroy him very early in the Gospel.
- The 'they' mentioned in verse 13 is almost certainly the Sanhedrin picking up the animosity shaped in 11.15–19, 27–33 and 12.1–12.

Interesting words …

- v. 13: *trap*. The verb *agreuō* means 'to hunt' (it is used to describe wild animals tracking their prey) and, by extension, 'to catch in a mistake'.
- v. 14: *sincere; truth*. *Alēthēs* refers to being honest or truthful and *althēia*

means 'truth'. In other words, 'he is true or honest and teaches the way of God truthfully'.

- v. 14: *show no deference; for you do not regard people with partiality*. Two odd phrases are used here, side by side.
  - The first reads, 'You do not concern (*melei*) yourself about anyone.' This can mean 'you don't care about anyone', but in context means 'you do not allow others to affect your view'.
  - The second reads, 'You do not look (*blepō*) into the face (*prosōpos*) of human beings (*anthrōpos*),' which is a colloquial phrase meaning 'you do not show favouritism'.
- v. 14: *lawful*. The verb *exestin* ('permitted') when used elsewhere in Mark has referred to permission under divine law (Mark 2.24, 26; 3.4; 6.18; 10.2).
- v. 14: *taxes*. *Kēnsos* referred to the poll tax (see the box, 'Herod Archelaus and the imposition of a poll tax,' on p. 267).
- v. 15: *hypocrisy*. The *hupokrisis* has the same root as *hupokritēs*, which comes from Greek theatre. A *hupokritēs* wore a mask and so was a pretender, dissembler or hypocrite.
- v. 15: *put to the test*. The verb *peirazō* is used to describe Jesus' temptations by the devil; but translating it as 'test' is probably right here.
- v. 17: *utterly amazed*. Another of Mark's words denoting amazement, *ekthaumazō*, is used here and is a strengthened form of *thaumazō*.

'We know that you are sincere'

This is one of those occasions when Mark is speaking directly to his readers. We understand that the Pharisees and Herodians do not mean what they are saying; Mark reinforces this by telling us that Jesus knows of their hypocrisy. We would agree, however, that Jesus is truthful, isn't swayed by what people say and shows no favouritism. The Pharisees and Herodians mean to set an elaborate trap but, in reality, what they say is absolutely true.

Paying taxes to Caesar

The tax the Pharisees and Herodians were asking about was probably the poll tax that affected Judeans but not Galileans. This makes it interesting that some of this group were Herodians: if they lived in Galilee, they would not have had to pay the tax unless they also had a base in Judea.

Herod Archelaus and the imposition of a poll tax

From Herod the Great's death until AD 6, Herod Archelaus, the brother of Herod Antipas, was the ethnarch of Judea, Samaria and Idumea (a title bestowed on him by the Romans). Archelaus' time as ruler was an unmitigated disaster. In 4 BC, two teachers, named Judas and Matthias, had incited their followers to remove from the temple a golden eagle (mounted by Herod the Great), which was considered sacrilegious because of the prohibition of images. On Archelaus' orders, Judas, Matthias and their followers were burnt alive, after which Archelaus faced an angry mob. In the rioting that followed during Passover, 3,000 Jews were killed. Archelaus then travelled to Rome to be crowned by the emperor. In his absence, the rioting was so intense that Publius Quinctilius Varus, the Roman governor of Syria, intervened; he crucified 2,000 of the rioters.

Things got no better on Archelaus' return and, after ten years, the Samaritans and the Judeans united and sent envoys to Rome begging to be ruled directly by their imperial overlords instead. Archelaus was exiled and a succession of Roman prefects governed Judea in his place. The fifth of these was Pontius Pilate, who was the prefect from AD 26 to 36.

The result of being governed by Rome directly was that a poll tax was imposed on the population. It followed Quirinius' census and sparked a riot led by Judas the Galilean. What the Pharisees and Herodians were trying to do, therefore, was to place Jesus in a position that would lead to trouble. If he said that the Judeans should pay the poll tax, he would alienate the Jewish patriots who were horrified by the tax; if he said not to, he could be reported to the Romans for inciting rebellion.

'Bring me a denarius'

Jesus' request for a denarius is his first clever move. The silver denarius (which was the means of paying the tax) was stamped with the profile of the emperor, which was idolatrous, and the inscription 'Son of the divine Augustus'. Loyal Jews avoided using these coins, except for paying the tax. They used, instead, copper coins that did not contain these features. By showing that he did not have a denarius with him, and that the Pharisees and Herodians did, Jesus revealed their hypocrisy. They were carrying an idolatrous coin, which they should not have done if they truly believed what they declared.

Jesus' second side-step was to say it was possible to give both the emperor and God their dues. His opponents were trying to force him into an either/or position; instead, he responded with a both/and solution. In other words, he was saying that if you believed in God, it did not automatically mean that you were a zealot. You could be devout and live in harmony with the Romans as well.

Mark 12.18–27: Marriage and resurrection

The next group to challenge Jesus were the Sadducees (for more on them, see the box, 'The Sadducees', on p. 269). They brought to him an absurd case study. It demonstrated that you can make any position bizarre if you take it to extremes. It is a technique that some still use today – attempting to undermine an opposing view by pressing it so far that it becomes ridiculous.

The different groups of opponents attempted to undermine Jesus in different ways: the Sanhedrin claimed he had no authority; the Pharisees and Herodians tried to make him declare a political allegiance; and the Sadducees hoped to embarrass him by demonstrating that one of his beliefs was ludicrous.

Links backwards and forwards

- This section consists of a series of controversies, which begins with the chief priests, scribes and elders (Mark 11.27–33); it continues with the Pharisees and Herodians (12.13–17); goes on with the Sadducees here; and ends with the story of an individual scribe asking about the First Commandment (12.28–34).

Interesting words ...

- v. 18: *resurrection.* The noun *anastasis* ('make to stand' or 'make to rise up', hence 'resurrection') comes from the verb *anistēmi*, which occurs throughout the Gospel.
- v. 19: *raise.* The Sadducees' position becomes clear with the use of this verb. *Exanistēmi* ('to procreate' or 'to raise children') is connected to *anistēmi* ('to raise'). So their understanding of 'life after death' was that life continued in the children who came after them.
- vv. 19–21: *children.* The word used is *sperma*, which means 'seed' and, by extension, 'children' or 'offspring'.
- vv. 24 and 27: *wrong.* The verb *planaō* means 'to lead astray' or 'to deceive'. Here, it is in the passive voice: 'to be led astray' or 'to be deceived'. The second time Jesus uses the verb, he adds *polus*, which means 'very' or 'exceedingly'.
- v. 25: *marry nor are given in marriage. Gameō* means 'to marry' (or 'to take a concubine'). It appears here, first, in the active voice ('marry') and then the passive ('be given in marriage'). The implication is that the first is what a man does and the second is what happens to a woman.
- v. 27: *dead.* The word *nekros* refers to a corpse and so can also mean 'dead'; thus, verse 27 could be translated as 'he is God not of corpses but of living people'.

The Sadducees, who say there is no resurrection

Belief in resurrection, or other forms of life after death, was not held by everyone at the time of Jesus. The Pharisees believed in it, but the Sadducees did not. The most explicit reference to resurrection can be found in Daniel 12.1–2:

> But at that time your people shall be delivered, everyone who is found written in the book. Many of those who sleep in the dust of the earth shall awake, some to everlasting life, and some to shame and everlasting contempt.

Other texts contain hints of a belief that, later, were taken to refer to resurrection; but it is only in Daniel that it is fully articulated. Given that the Sadducees used only the Torah as Scripture, it is unsurprising that they had not developed a belief in resurrection. As is clear from their question to Jesus, they believed that life after death existed through the descendants who lived on after them.

The Sadducees

The Sadducees belonged to a form of Judaism that flourished in Judea from the second century BC to the fall of the temple in AD 70. Josephus, who was not supportive of the Sadducees, described them as a sect attractive only to the rich. They were certainly highly influential and made up a good portion of the Sanhedrin.

It is thought by many that their name came from Zadok, who was the first high priest of the first temple in Israel, and that they were made up of members of high-ranking priestly families (though not all priests were Sadducees). They were supporters of the Hasmoneans, the descendants of the Maccabees, and historic rivals of the Pharisees.

It is very difficult to know what they believed because none of their own written texts survive. The only trace we have of their beliefs appears in the Gospels and in Josephus. As neither of these were favourable to the Sadducees, it is hard to be confident about their views; but it seems likely that they used the Torah (though not the rest of the Old Testament) and were sceptical about life after death, angels and free will.

Levirate marriage

The law the Sadducees refer to is known as levirate marriage, from the Latin word for brother-in-law: *levir*. Deuteronomy 25.5–10 lays down a requirement that if a man were to die, his brothers would be obliged to sleep with his wife, provide offspring and then raise them. The story in

Genesis 38.8–10 tells of Onan, who spilled his seed to avoid having to fulfil this requirement, and was killed for having done so. It is hard to tell whether this law was still being observed at the time of Jesus; many scholars think that it was not, making this a fantasy question rather than a real one.

A woman with seven husbands

The story of the woman with seven husbands seems to be a well-worked 'But what about ...' scenario. Some suggest that the idea was drawn from the book of Tobit 7.9–15, which tells the story of the marriage of Tobias and Sarah. Sarah had married seven times before, but each husband had died on their wedding day. Eventually, she married Tobias, son of Tobit, with a happy outcome, thanks to the intervention of the archangel Raphael.

Jesus' response

Jesus' response to the Sadducees is argued in a classic rabbinic way. He maintains two principles:

1. The Sadducees haven't understood Scripture. Jesus cites a different part of the writings of Moses to them, in which God's continuing covenant with Abraham, Isaac and Jacob is given as evidence of God's nature: namely, that it is one of an ongoing, living relationship.
2. They don't understand the power of God. Resurrection life will not be a continuation of this life (with the same rules of marriage). It will be life that will never end: a life already enjoyed by Abraham, Isaac and Jacob.

The key to Jesus' slightly confusing argument may be found at the end of verse 25. When people rise from the dead, they will be like the angels in heaven (in whom, ironically the Sadducees also do not believe). This does not mean that the risen will be sexless (Genesis 6.1–4 makes clear that angels are not sexless), but that they will never die and so will not need to procreate. If they will never die, then levirate marriage will no longer be necessary (as it exists only in cases where people die). New marriages and procreation will not be necessary because no one will die. Jesus' hint here is that the exclusiveness of marriage exists to protect children; when children are not needed, the exclusiveness of marriage will also be unnecessary.

Jesus seemed to be making the point that the Sadducees' vision of life and death was small and disappointing compared with the realities of the God of life. They believed only in keeping the line alive; God believed in raising people from death.

The story about the bush

A fascinating peripheral point of this episode was how Jesus referred to passages from the Old Testament. Jesus' discussion with the Sadducees was many centuries before chapter and verse numbers were inserted into the text, so he referenced Exodus 3.1–12 by calling it 'the story about the bush'. His method was, of course, immensely effective because we know what he was talking about.

Jesus used the Exodus passage because he needed one from the Torah to make his point to those who read no other Scripture.

It is important not to believe that an entire doctrine about resurrection or, indeed, relationships in the resurrection life can be derived from this passage. It is very clearly a philosophical response to a deliberately hard question; such answers do not provide the fullest and most satisfying theologies. This seems to me to fall into the category of a specific answer to a tricky question and should not be extrapolated outwards to refer to all marriages and/or relationships after death. It seems that Jesus specifically answered the question about procreation, not about relationships per se.

Mark 12.28–34: Which Commandment is first?

The fourth in the list of 'hard questions' to Jesus took a different turn. The Sanhedrin, Pharisees and Herodians, and the Sadducees all came with set-piece questions designed to trip Jesus up or shame him publicly. This fourth question was very different in kind. The scribe was given the idea to speak to Jesus because of the debates he saw him having with other people; but his question was far more genuine than the other three.

It is worth noting, given Mark's stereotyping of groups, that although one of the scribes, this scribe came on his own and his response to Jesus was correspondingly more sincere.

Links backwards

- Jesus' conversations with the disciples, in which he looked for 'understanding' from them: Mark 8.21 comes to mind here. Here is someone who does, apparently, understand.
- The previous conversations with Jewish authorities (11.27–33; 12.13–17; 12.18–27) stand in striking contrast to this conversation, which, alone, seems to be an honest exchange.

Interesting words ...

- v. 28: *disputing*. The word *suzēteō* means 'search or examine together' or 'dispute'.
- vv. 28 and 32: *well; truly*. The scribe notices that Jesus answers well (*kalōs*: 'right', 'fair', 'finely' or 'certainly') and repeats this in verse 32, which, more literally, reads 'Certainly, teacher, you spoke out of truth (*alētheia*)'. This contrasts with the Pharisees and Herodians, who were less believable when they said they thought Jesus was *alēthēs*.
- vv. 28–29: *first; one*. *Prōtos*, 'first', as in 'foremost' or 'primary'. When Jesus quotes the Commandment 'the Lord is one', this has been translated from *heis* (the usual word for 'one').
- v. 30: *heart; soul; mind; strength*. The key words here are 'heart' (*kardia*), 'soul' (*psuchē*), 'mind' (*dianoia*: 'thought') and 'strength' (*ichus*: 'might' or 'power'). When the scribe responds in verse 33, his list is similar but shorter, with one different word: 'heart' (*kardia*); 'understanding' (*sunesis*: 'insight') and 'strength' (*ischus*).
- v. 31: *neighbour*. The word for 'neighbour' is *plēsios* ('someone who is near').
- v. 33: *much more important*. *Perissoteros* is simply 'much more'.
- v. 33: *whole burnt-offerings and sacrifices*. The word *holokautoma* ('holocaust') was known in Hebrew as the *Olah*. It involved burning an animal whole and happened twice daily, every day, in the temple. The word *thusia* refers to the other sacrifices that took place.
- v. 34: *wisely*. *Nouechēs* means 'with understanding or wisdom'.

The First Commandment

The word 'first' in Greek, as in English, can mean 'most important' rather than simply the first ever. This is clearly what is meant here.

The discussion about the most important Commandment was widespread in Judaism at the time of Jesus. Possibly the most famous example from this kind of debate is the quote from Rabbi Hillel, recorded in the Talmud: a Gentile approached him and asked him to teach him the whole law while standing on one foot. Hillel responded, 'Do not do to your neighbour what is hateful to you: this is the whole Torah, the rest is commentary' (*b. Shabbat* 31a). Rabbi Akiva also said, '"You shall love your neighbour as yourself" (Leviticus 19:18) – that verse represents the central tenet of the Torah' (*Bereshit Rabbah* 24).

Examples of a summary of the law that are even closer to what Jesus said here can be found in the *Testaments of the Twelve Patriarchs*: for example, *Testament of Issachar* 5.2 says, 'Love the Lord and your neighbour, and have compassion on the poor and feeble.' *Testament of Daniel* 5.3 says, 'Love the Lord with all your life, and another with a sincere heart.'

Jesus' own version stays closer to the original text. He quotes first from what is known in Judaism as the Shema (which is from the Hebrew, 'hear'):

> Hear, O Israel: The LORD is our God, the LORD alone. You shall love the LORD your God with all your heart, and with all your soul, and with all your might. (Deut. 6.4–5)

Jesus then quotes from Leviticus 19.17–18:

> You shall not hate in your heart anyone of your kin; you shall reprove your neighbour, or you will incur guilt yourself. You shall not take vengeance or bear a grudge against any of your people, but you shall love your neighbour as yourself: I am the LORD.

The Shema

Mark's version is different from the Septuagint (LXX) translation (that is, the Greek translation of the Hebrew Bible) and from Matthew. See the table below.

Hebrew – Deuteronomy 6.5	**LXX – Deuteronomy 6.5**	**Mark 12.29**	**Matthew 22.37**	**Luke 10.27**
Heart (*lēb*)	Heart (*kardia*)	Heart (*kardia*)	Heart (*kardia*)	Heart (*kardia*)
Soul (*nephesh*)	Soul (*psuchē*)	Soul (*psuchē*)	Soul (*psuchē*)	Soul (*psuchē*)
Strength (*me'od*)	Strength (*dunamis*)	Mind (*dianoia*)		Strength (*ischus*)
		Strength (*ischus*)	Mind (*dianoia*)	Mind (*dianoia*)

It seems likely that 'mind' has been added to compensate for a change of view of the heart. In Hebrew understanding, the heart was where decisions were made and reasoning happened (see, for example, Ps. 19.14); Greek thought located thinking in the mind. Mark's extra word provides what might have been missing in this shift.

More than all the burnt offerings and sacrifices

The scribe's response resonates with a number of Old Testament verses, such as Hosea 6.6: 'For I desire steadfast love and not sacrifice, the knowledge of God rather than burnt-offerings.' It demonstrates that the scribe was well versed in the Hebrew Scriptures.

Jesus' approval of the scribe reminds us of his earlier conversations with the disciples in which he looked for understanding from them. The scribe demonstrates this in his conversation with Jesus, though he has not followed him, hence he is only near to the kingdom of God.

No one dared to ask him any question

This shouldn't be seen as a triumphalist statement celebrating Jesus' besting of all opponents, not least because it comes after the most eirenic of conversations in this sequence. It is more that Jesus was able to respond so well, no matter what the question, that no one wanted to take him on any more.

Mark 12.35–37: Jesus posed his own question

The last sentence of the previous passage acts as a bridge to this short passage. No longer were there any substantial queues of people waiting to ask questions, so Jesus could now pose his own. His question is best classed as a riddle; the implication is that he was posing a tough question to his opponents, none of whom could answer – to the crowd's delight.

Links backwards

- Jesus used David as a source in his conflict with the Pharisees over the disciples' plucking wheat on the sabbath (Mark 2.25).
- The reference to James and John sitting at the right and left of Jesus (10.35–45) is also brought to mind by the reference to David's sitting at the right hand of God.
- Bartimaeus was the only one to address Jesus as 'Son of David' (10.47–48); that title now resonates here.

Links forwards

- Mark 13.11 relates the prediction about the Holy Spirit speaking when the disciples are brought to trial.

Interesting words ...

- v. 36: *Holy Spirit*. In Mark, the phrase 'Holy (*hagios*) Spirit (*pneuma*)' occurs only here and in 13.11.
- v. 36: *Lord*. The usual word for 'lord' (*kurios*) is used here.

- v. 37: *large crowd*. The crowd (*ochlos*) is described as *polus* ('great' or 'large') here.
- v. 37: *with delight*. They listened (*hēdeōs*) gladly or with enjoyment: just as Herod Antipas had listened to John the Baptist (6.20).

How is the Messiah the Son of David?

For more on the Messiah, see p. 191, and on the Son of David, see p. 245.

The specific linking of the Messiah role with the Son of David was suggested in Nathan's prophecy to David: 'When your days are fulfilled and you lie down with your ancestors, I will raise up your offspring after you, who shall come forth from your body, and I will establish his kingdom' (2 Sam. 7.12). This promise was then later interpreted to mean that a descendant of David would come to save God's people.

Jesus adds to his riddle by quoting from Psalm 110.1. The crux of the quote includes David's sitting at the right hand of God, which means he is to act as his vice-regent. The logic then continues

- that David is the author of the psalm;
- that the first 'LORD' refers to God and the second 'lord' refers to the Messiah;
- that the one called 'LORD' is of superior standing to the one saying 'Lord'.

In other words, David is inferior to the Messiah and so the Messiah should not be seen as the 'son' of David.

Confusingly, Jesus left his riddle hanging so we are not clear about what we are meant to take from it. There are two features that seem likely:

1. Jesus can equal the scribes in philosophical pirouetting (this is probably why the crowd is so delighted).
2. The term 'Son of David' should not limit people's understanding of the Messiah to a purely political, human role. If the Messiah is superior to even God's vice-regent and able to be called 'Lord', then expectations of who he is and what he is coming to do have to be adjusted.

Mark 12.38–44: On scribes, widows and generosity

The end of this particular focus on Jesus' conflict with the scribes (and others) features the contrast between their attitudes and that of a poor widow who arrived at the temple to give a gift she was not obliged to offer.

Links backwards

- The scribes have featured regularly in Mark as Jesus' most common opponents (2.6, 16; 3.22; 7.1, 5; 11.18, 27). This, and the previous passage (12.35–37), are the first times that Jesus has taught against them without their first asking a question.
- Jesus' opening 'beware' recalls his earlier teaching about the leaven of the Pharisees and of the Herodians (8.15).
- The themes of this passage are reminiscent of Jesus' teaching about the first and last (9.35; 10.31). Here, we have the scribes who consider themselves 'first' and the widow who must be deemed by most to be among the 'last'.

Interesting words ...

- v. 38: *long robes*. A *stolē* was a long flowing robe worn for celebratory or festive occasions.
- v. 38: *greeted with respect*. *Aspasmos* refers to a greeting: often an affectionate one, with an embrace.
- v. 38: *market-places*. The *agora* wasn't just the marketplace: it was the public square where debates occurred and goods were sold. The equivalent Latin name is *forum*.
- v. 39: *best seats; places of honour*. The word *prōtokathedria* refers to the first or best seat of honour and *protoklisia* was the first seat (reclined) at the dining table.
- v. 39: *banquets*. *Deipnon* can refer either to a meal or to a banquet.
- v. 40: *devour*. *Katesthiō* means 'to destroy' or 'to consume utterly'.
- vv. 40 and 42: *widows; widow*. *Chēra* ('widow') is used both in Jesus' condemnation and in his commendation of the widow in verse 42. The word is what connects the two.
- v. 40: *for the sake of appearance*. A *prophasis* is 'a pretence' or 'a cover'.
- v. 40: *condemnation*. A *krima* was a 'judgement' or 'condemnation'.
- v. 41: *treasury*. The *gazophylakion* refers to the treasury or offering box.
- v. 42: *small copper coins; penny*. The widow put in two of a specific type of coin, called a *lepton* ('tiny thing'), which is translated by Mark into the Greek word *kodrantēs*. For more on the coins, see the box, 'The small coin: *lepton* and *kodrantēs*', on p. 278.

- v. 43: *Truly I tell you.* This characteristic opening (*amēn legō humin*) to a saying by Jesus occurs once early on in Mark and then with increasing frequency towards the end (3.28; 8.12; 9.1, 41; 10.15, 29; 11.23; 12.43; 13.30; 14.18, 25, 30). For more on the phrase, see the note on 3.28 (p. 85).
- v. 44: *abundance; poverty.* The word for 'to be in abundance' (*perisseuō*) is contrasted with *hysteresis*, which means 'need', 'poverty' or 'lack'.
- v. 44: *all she had to live on.* Literally, this phrase reads, 'her whole (*holos*) life (or living: *bios*)'.

'Beware of the scribes'

Given the scribe who was commended by Jesus in 12.34, it is worth noticing that the group Jesus condemns here are not all scribes; they are those who like to wear long robes, receive ostentatious greetings and sit in the best seats. His critique could very much fall under the rubric 'If the cap fits ...'

There are four features of scribal behaviour that Jesus criticizes:

1. Wearing long, flowing robes. If the identification of scribes as priests is correct, then their long robes would have identified their role in the temple and given them honour. If the people concerned weren't priests, then the wearing of flowing robes was a sign of importance; they were dressing in a way to draw respect from others.
2. Greetings in the *agora*. It is thought that this refers to the practice laid out in the Jerusalem Talmud (*j. Berakoth* 2.1) that states that you should greet someone greater than you. In other words, if you have low status and meet someone of higher status, you should initiate a greeting. Indeed, the Babylonian Talmud notes of Rabbi Yohannan ben Zakkai 'that nobody ever greeted him first, not even the heathen in the street' (*b. Berakoth* 17a), and that this was something notable and unusual.
3. Taking the best seats. The best seat in the synagogue was probably right at the front, next to the Torah, facing the congregation.
4. Places of honour at banquets. During this period, strict protocols existed for dining and at banquets. The most highly honoured person would recline at the right hand of the host or, failing that, they would be as close as possible.

Precisely what the scribes did to devour the houses of the widows Jesus leaves to the imagination. It is possible that, as women could not act for themselves in law and widows were widely seen as the most vulnerable in society, the scribes abused their trust when they should have been looking after their interests. Alternatively, it could refer more generally to abusing women's or widows' hospitality in a context in which it would be difficult to say no.

It isn't clear whether we are to consider the long prayers to be connected to the scribes' abuse of widows or separately. It could mean that they covered for their abuse of the widows by saying long, showy prayers; or that the saying of long showy prayers was a crime in addition to abusing the widows.

The generous widow

Jesus sat down in the treasury to watch the comparative generosity of the worshippers who came through. The treasury was located around the sides of the court of the women. For more on this, see the box, 'Herod the Great's temple', on p. 257.

Jesus holds up the widow's action in contrast to the behaviour of the scribes. Whereas they acted for show and to receive the greatest honour, she did the most she could with the little she had.

She was not obliged to give any money at all. It was men over the age of 20 who needed to pay. Her gift was generous at the outset and made more generous by the fact she gave two coins rather than one.

The small coin: lepton *and* kodrantēs

The word *lepton*, as noted above, means 'tiny thing'. It was the name of the smallest copper coin in circulation in Palestine. It was made from bronze or copper and would have been about the size of a small fingernail. The woman's generosity is noted because she gave two of these coins. She could have kept one back for herself. It is probable that Jesus knew she had given two because the horns (funnels) of the offertory boxes were bronze and so the coins would have clinked as they fell in.

Mark put the word *lepton* into Latin currency for his readers (transliterated into Greek letters): a quadrans (in Greek, *kodrantēs*) was worth one sixty-fourth of a denarius.

Mark 13.1–2: 'Not one stone will be left'

This short, two-verse section is a bridge leading us away from the temple and into the longer discussion between Jesus and Peter, James, John and Andrew about how to identify when events predicted by Jesus will happen. The conversation takes place on the Mount of Olives. These two short verses, however, record what was said as Jesus leaves the temple and so need treating separately. They are significant because they tie at least some of what Jesus is talking about to the destruction of the temple. The question is when, if at all, does he move on to talking about his return? We shall come back to this question later in chapter 13.

Links backwards

- The cursing of the temple in Mark 11.15–19 intimated that the temple would be destroyed. Jesus now confirms this in stark terms.

Interesting words ...

- v. 1: *he came out*. The verb *ekporeuomai* can mean 'come out' or it can mean 'march forth'. That would be too dramatic a translation; but there is a sense, here, of Jesus' quitting the temple. The questions are over.
- v. 1: *what large*. *Potapos* means 'what sort of' and, in an exclamation such as this, 'How great!'
- vv. 1–2: *buildings*. The word *oikodomē* refers to a building or structure.

How great this building is

The comment by the unnamed disciple is a reminder of the splendour of Herod the Great's temple (see p. 257). Josephus states that the stones used in the construction of the temple were each 45 cubits (67 feet) long. A visit to the Temple Mount today (now a holy place in Islam and the site of the Dome of the Rock and the El Aqsa Mosque) reveals some of the stones from Herod's temple still lying where they were left by the Romans in AD 70. They are truly huge and give weight to the disciple's exclamation: 'How great these stones are!'

No stone will be left

The temple was destroyed by Titus, the son of the Emperor Vespasian, and his 48,000 troops, which he brought to suppress the Jewish rebellion. In the summer of AD 70, the Roman forces breached the outer walls of the temple; a soldier threw a piece of burning wood into a building, which led to the entire temple being engulfed in flames. Despite a desperate fight by many Jews to save the temple, the Roman army triumphed, brutally killed many people and looted everything they could find. Once the fire had died down, they also systematically razed the buildings to the ground.

The loot that the army captured was so great (it was said) that the price of gold halved in Syria at the time. The great Colosseum in Rome was built by Vespasian from the wealth that had been looted from the temple and the rest of Jerusalem.

Mark 13.3–37: Keep watch and know the signs

From 11.11 until this passage, the focus of the narrative was in and around the temple. Jesus arrived in 11.11, looked around and left but then returned the next day. From then on, he fielded questions and challenges from the Sanhedrin, the Pharisees and Herodians, and the Sadducees. The action of the whole narrative from 11.20 until chapter 13 took place in a single day, in the temple. In 13.3, Jesus is said to be on the Mount of Olives; never again did he go back to the temple. As far as Mark is concerned, he spent one very focused day in the temple – from the evening of his entrance to the next day – and that is all.

Different scholars split this chapter at different points, depending on their view of whether Jesus was talking about one thing (the destruction of the temple or the second coming) or a combination of both things (the destruction of the temple and the second coming). I see this as one single whole and so have kept it as one section, although I think that Jesus may have had more than one event in mind.

Links backwards and forwards

- In this passage, the stilling of the storm (Mark 4.35–41) and Jesus' walking on the water (6.45–52) resonate with his message to the disciples about navigating a course through stormy times.
- Jesus warned the disciples of the Pharisees, the Herodians and the scribes in 8.15 and 12.38. With a similar tone, he warns the disciples three times in chapter 13 of what will happen to them (13.9, 23, 33)
- Jesus entered the temple from 11.11, then went back out to Bethany. He started out for the temple again in 11.20 and arrived in 11.27. He stays there until 13.3, when he leaves the temple and does not return.

- Jesus told the Sadducees that they had been led astray in 12.24 and 27. In 13.5, he warns the disciples not to be led astray, using the same word.
- In 14.32–42, Jesus tells the disciples to keep awake three times (14.34, 37, 38) while he prays in Gethsemane. Their first chance to practise these skills is not used well.
- The phrase 'the Son of Man coming with the clouds' occurs both here (13.26) and in Jesus' trial (14.62).

Interesting words ...

- vv. 4 and 22: *sign; signs. Sēmeion* is 'a sign' or 'a signal'. It can refer to a signal from, for example, flags or a sign from the gods in Greek literature. The Pharisees asked for a sign (*sēmeion*) in 8.11, which Jesus refused to give; the same word is used here. It is used again in verse 22, with the addition of the word *teras* ('portent' or 'miracle').
- v. 4: *accomplished*. The verb *sunteleō* can be used to refer to a workman completing a job and so means 'completed' or 'accomplished'. In verse 7, Jesus uses the word 'end' (*telos*), which is connected to this verb.
- v. 5: *beware*. Jesus uses the command *blepete* seven times in Mark to issue a warning (four of those seven times are in 13.5, 9, 23, 33). In verse 23, it is translated as 'be alert'. The other three times, Jesus warns about the importance of listening (4.24); and about the yeast of the Pharisees and Herodians (8.15), and the scribes (12.38). In my commentary below, I have opted for 'keep watch'.
- vv. 5 and 22: *lead(s) ... astray*. Jesus told the Sadducees that they had been led astray (*planaō*) in 12.24 and 27; he warns the disciples not to be led astray here. The related verb *apoplanaō* is used in verse 22.
- v. 7: *rumours*. An *akoē* is a 'hearing' or a 'sound' but can mean 'tidings' and hence 'rumours'. The key focus is on things you hear.
- v. 7: *alarmed*. The word *throeō* occurs here, in the parallel passage in Matthew (26.5) and in 2 Thessalonians 2.2, where the Thessalonians are implored not to be alarmed. It means 'to be so alarmed that you cry out'.
- vv. 8 and 10: *nation; nations. Ethnos* often means 'Gentiles' and probably means foreign nations here, as any nation that wasn't Israel was, by definition, a Gentile nation.
- vv. 9, 11 and 12: *hand you over; bring to trial. Agō* means 'lead away' and *paradidōmi* 'hand over'. The word used means to hand Jesus over to death (*paradidōmi*). When it is used in verse 12, it is translated 'betray'. So 'arrest' and 'hand over' seem closer to the intended meaning here. See the box, 'Betrayed/handed over', on p. 211, for the use of *paradidōmi* in Mark.
- v. 9: *councils*. The plural for the word 'Sanhedrin' (*sunedrion*) is used. The meaning is clearly that they are other councils in other places, probably local councils rather than the central one.

- v. 9: *beaten*. The word used for 'beating' in the parable of the tenants (but not concerning Jesus' own death) is used here: *derō*.
- v. 9: *governors and kings*. *Hegemōn* was used of any leaders but could also be used of a Roman emperor. *Basileus* was the usual word for 'king'. The use of both effectively means leaders anywhere in the known world.
- v. 12: *rise*. *Epanistēmi* means specifically 'to rise in rebellion', which is probably meant here.
- v. 13: *endures*. *Hupomenō* does mean 'endure' but it also means 'resist', 'stand firm' or 'persevere', which all seem a little more active, and were probably what Jesus was referring to.
- v. 14: *desolating sacrilege*. A *bdelugma* is an 'abomination' and *erēmōsis* a 'desolation' or 'destruction'. For more on this, see the box, 'The fall of the temple or the second coming?', on p. 284.
- v. 16: *coat*. This is *himation*, which means 'outer garment' or 'cloak'.
- vv. 20, 22 and 27: *elect*. The Greek word *elektos* means 'to hand pick' or 'to choose'.
- v. 27: *ends*. The word for 'ends of the earth' is *akron*, which refers to the extreme limits of something.
- v. 28: *learn*. *Manthanō* ('learn') is the verb from which the noun *mathētēs* ('disciple') comes.
- v. 28: *lesson*. The word *parabolē* is used here: 'parable'.
- v. 28: *tender*. *Apalos* means 'soft to the touch' or 'tender'. Although the branches of a fig tree don't become soft when the sap rises: they become flexible.
- v. 29: *gates*. *Thura* can mean 'door' or 'gate'; but (as the parable in verse 34 refers to a house) 'door' might be better here.
- v. 30: *Truly I tell you*. This characteristic opening (*amēn legō humin*) to a saying by Jesus occurs once early on in Mark and then with increasing frequency towards the end (3.28; 8.12; 9.1, 41; 10.15, 29; 11.23; 12.43; 13.30; 14.18, 25, 30). For more on the phrase, see the note on 3.28 (p. 85).
- vv. 30–31: *pass away*. The verb used to speak of this generation 'not passing away', heaven and earth 'passing away' and Jesus' words 'not passing away' are all versions of *parerchomai* ('cease' or 'pass by').
- v. 33: *keep alert*. Alongside *blepō*, *agrupneō* is used, which means 'be on guard' or 'keep alert'.
- v. 34: *going on a journey*. The word used is an adjective, *apodēmos*; with *anthrōpos* ('person'), it means 'a journeying person' or 'a travelling abroad person'.
- v. 34: *puts his slaves in charge*. More literally, 'gave his slaves (*doulos*) authority (*exousia*)'.
- v. 34: *doorkeeper*. A *thura* is a 'door', so a 'doorkeeper' is a *thurōros*.
- vv. 34–35 and 37: *watch; keep awake*. The verb *gregōreō* is used three times in the next three verses but differently translated. It means 'to stay awake', 'to be alert' or 'to be vigilant'.
- v. 35: *evening; midnight; cockcrow; dawn*. The four words for time refer to different parts of the night: *opse* refers to the part of the evening before it gets dark; *mesonuktion* is the 'middle of the night'; *alektophōnia* means literally 'the sound (*phonia*) of a cock (*alektōr*)'; and *prōi* is 'first light' or 'very early morning'.

Sitting on the Mount of Olives

A number of commentators make the connection between Jesus' actions here and the prophecy of Ezekiel. The prophecy speaks of the glory of God leaving the temple and stopping on the mountain to the east of Jerusalem (the Mount of Olives) before the invasion of the Babylonian army, which destroyed the temple (Ezek. 11.22–23). Ezekiel's prophecy describes the glory of God resting above the wings of the cherubim on top of God's chariot, their ascending from the middle of the city to the mountain in the east, and symbolically leaving the temple to what will befall it. It is hard to know if Mark is hinting at a similar idea. If he is, the symbolism is poignant: Jesus has abandoned the temple to its fate.

Andrew

Usually, the inner circle of the Twelve consisted of Peter, James and John. This is the only occasion when Andrew is mentioned too. It is so unusual that some suggest it gives evidence of a personal recollection by Peter.

As Peter, Andrew, James and John were the first to be called by Jesus, it seems appropriate that they are there with him as he talks about the 'end times'.

'When will this be, and what will be the sign?'

The question the four disciples ask can be split into two:

- When will this be?
- What will the sign be?

Jesus answers the second question slightly more clearly than the first; but there is a timescale that can be traced throughout the chapter.

- 13.5: *Keep watch*: many will lead you astray and you will hear rumours of wars; but it is *not yet* (13. 7). 13.8: all this is only the beginning.
- 13. 9: *Keep watch*: you will go on trial; but it is *not yet*. 13.13: you need to stand firm to the 'end' (which isn't yet).
- 13.14: *But when you see* the abomination of desolation, know that there will be great suffering (13.19); but if anyone says they are the Messiah, don't believe them (13.21) – this is *not yet* the end.
- 13.23: *Keep watch*: I have told you everything.
- 13.24: *But in those days* (after the suffering Jesus points to in 13.19) …
  - 13. 26: *Then* you will see the Son of Man coming in clouds
  - 13.27: *Then* he will send out his angels
  - 13.30: *All these things* must take place before *this generation* passes away.

- 13.32–33: But no one knows precisely when ... so *keep awake* (13.35; and one more time in 13.37), *keep awake*.

One of the frustrating features of this teaching is that we feel none the wiser after all these pointers. Indeed, Jesus seems to be warning the disciples against forecasting when any of these events will take place. The signs all seem to point to its being close but not quite yet. This may indicate the fact that the real key to understanding is not the timescale but the attitude of those waiting (see 'Keep watch, keep alert, keep awake', p. 285).

The fall of the temple or the second coming?

The traditional interpretation of Mark 13 is that the whole chapter is referring to Jesus' second coming. The word that is used for this is the *Parousia*, which is a Greek word meaning 'presence' or 'arrival'. The problem with this view is not only that Jesus says this generation will not pass away until these things have taken place (13.30), but also that there are some parts of this chapter that do seem to point clearly to the destruction of the temple, such as 13.2 and 13.14.

N. T. Wright has argued extensively that we should not see Mark 13 as referring to the *Parousia* at all; rather, the whole chapter refers to the destruction of the temple. The crux of his argument is that the reference to the Son of Man coming in clouds is a direct quote from Daniel 7.13, in which the Son of Man 'came' not to earth but to the Ancient of Days to receive vindication (see, for example, *Jesus and the Victory of God*, SPCK, 1996, pp. 339–68). The quote is used again in 14.62 and that is how it is used there. So the Resurrection was Jesus' moment of vindication by the Ancient of Days in which political powers and rulers fell. The problem with making Mark 13 entirely about the destruction of Jerusalem is that verses such as 13.27, which talks about the angels gathering the elect, don't really fit with it.

A range of other scholars see both the destruction of the temple *and* the second coming lying behind Mark 13. Some split the chapter at verse 24, with 1–23 being about the temple and 24–37 being about the second coming; others split it at verse 32, with everything before being about the destruction and the final section being about the second coming; and yet another group splits it twice and views it as referring to signs on earth (13.1–23, 28–31) and signs in heaven (vv. 24–27, 32–37).

To say that there is little agreement on which events lie behind this passage is a vast understatement. Some of you will already know what you think; others will find the different options disorientating and confusing. My own view is that which event (or events) Jesus' teaching refers to here is less important than that he is teaching us about *how* to wait. If I had to choose, I would opt for the third choice. I see in the passage *both* hints at the destruction of the temple *and* hints about Jesus' second coming; *and*, indeed, hints of other disasters that have occurred since the temple was razed. Chapter 13 moves us dizzyingly, at times, from a specific event that is long past (the destruction of the temple) through other events that look and seem like that event (cataclysmic moments in world history) to the end of all times, which has not yet come. Personally, I am content to see Mark 13 as referring to all three at once: beginning with the destruction, continuing in world events, but not complete until the end of all times.

However, I would say that placing too much emphasis on what the event is distracts our attention from the real focus of what Jesus was teaching the disciples: namely, to live when it feels as though the world is crumbling around you. For me, the key focus of this passage is on the phrases 'keep watch', 'keep alert', 'keep awake'. Our attention should not be solely on what is happening but on how we react when it does happen.

Keep watch, keep alert, keep awake

The three phrases that come throughout this chapter seem to me to be the real focus of what Jesus is talking about here.

The first word – 'beware' or 'keep watch' (*blepō*: 'look around' or 'watch carefully') – stresses the importance of constant vigilance: watch what is happening and make sure you can interpret what you see. Jesus is teaching the disciples what they need to be vigilant about. They need to watch out for false leaders who will lead them astray (13.5); and for the times they will be handed over to trial (13.9). They will also need general alertness (13.23) because they will not know when these things will happen (13.33).

On to *blepō*, in verse 33, is added *agrupneō*: another, similar word for keeping alert. This is then followed at the end of the chapter with *gregōreō*, also with a comparable meaning: 'keep awake' or 'keep alert'. These three words, used eight times altogether, begin to shape what the chapter is about. Until now, Jesus' warnings to the disciples have been about events that were happening around them or people they would encounter; the warnings of chapter 13, however, are all about what would happen after Jesus died. It is very much as though he was preparing them for life without him. So he is encouraging them to develop an attitude of vigilance, care and alertness to enable them to navigate the very complex events that would be coming their way.

It is easy when the world feels overwhelming to withdraw or even to run away. Jesus counsels them, instead, to deep attentiveness: keep watch, keep alert, keep awake.

It is worth adding that this passage looks forward to Jesus' prayer in the Garden of Gethsemane. There, he instructs Peter, James and John to keep awake while he prays, only to return three times to find them sleeping.

Don't be thrown off course

Alongside the attentive attitude that the disciples must adopt, Jesus is also keen that they should not misinterpret what is going on around them. They should not be led astray by leaders who claim to be who they are not (13.6); they should not be knocked off course by wars breaking out around them (13.7); they should not be anxious even when they are arrested and put on trial (13.9) or when conflict breaks out in families (13.12). The image that comes to mind is of the boat journeys that the disciples took in 4.35–41 and 6.45–52. As the storm lashed them, Jesus wanted them not to be timid (4.40), to be courageous (6.50) and to understand (6.52). The lessons they learned there were going to be crucial in the storms ahead. Over and over again, in this chapter, the message of Jesus is 'Be alert, keep watch, stay vigilant: you don't know when it is going to happen; and every time you think the end is happening, it probably isn't. Stay alert anyway and stand firm' (13.13).

Through all this Jesus seemed to be shaping the disciples – and, by extension, we who are reading – to be wise inhabitants of the world. They were not to jump to conclusions but remain alert; they were to steer a course through the storm and remain resilient at all times; they were not to ignore the disasters around them but, equally, not to overreact to them. Chapter 13 could be subtitled 'How to live in a complex and disturbing world'. Jesus' advice is as relevant now as it was then.

Underpinning Jesus' message, confusing though it may be, is the steady beat of a God's-eye view of history. History will be littered (as it has been) with disasters, wars and famines; but God remains in control and the Son of Man will be vindicated and rule over the world. The catastrophes around us are not unexpected. They are birth pangs and need to be treated as such.

Mark's first readers lived in a world that looked as though it was collapsing in on itself. The Christians in Rome were targeted by the Emperor Nero, after the fire in AD 64, to shift the blame from himself. They were killed gruesomely by wild beasts, crucifixions and burnings. Then the Jewish rebellion against Rome began in AD 67, with many different individuals claiming that they could lead the people to victory. The Roman Empire tottered in AD 69 when, in the space of a single year, there were four emperors. Then, however, Vespasian (the general who had been sent to fight against the Jews) was proclaimed emperor: first in Egypt and then, after a massive victory, in Italy. His son, Titus, remained in Judea; he led the Roman army to conquer Jerusalem and destroy the temple. Many people, including me, think that Mark was written at some point during this period.

It would have been very easy for first-century Christians to have imagined that these events were signs that the world was ending. It is here that Jesus' words become important. What was ending was the world as they knew it: the power that had reigned until that point. Political rulers and kingdoms were collapsing but the end of all things was not yet. It was not a time for giving up and waiting for the end to come, but of faithfulness and witness, keeping watch, keeping alert, keeping awake, and of standing firm.

'The desolating sacrilege'

One of the most confusing elements of chapter 13 is that it moves from what seem like quite general scenarios, which could occur at almost any time, to very specific situations that happened in the first century. The Greek phrase translated as the 'desolating sacrilege' in the NRSV, or as the 'abomination of desolation' elsewhere, is a quotation from the book of Daniel. Daniel says three times that, in the temple, there will be an 'abomination that desolates' (9.27; 11.31; 12.11), which was established by the Seleucid ruler Antiochus Epiphanes. It is described in more detail in the book of 1 Maccabees 1.54: 'Now on the fifteenth day of Chislev, in the one hundred and forty-fifth year, they erected a desolating sacrilege on the altar of burnt-offering.' The same Greek phrase used in Mark 13 is used here in 1 Maccabees. The desolating sacrilege was a pagan altar that was built over the altar at the very centre of the temple. Its construction was what triggered the Maccabean revolt, which was finally successful three years later, in 164 BC, when the temple was repurified. The festival of Hanukkah celebrates this victory.

Unfortunately, it isn't as clear what the desolating sacrilege is in Mark. Various ideas have been proposed.

- The moment, in AD 26, when Pontius Pilate sent Roman Soldiers into Jerusalem carrying standards that bore images, which was something Jews considered idolatrous.
- Caligula's order to erect a statue to himself in the temple (AD 39–40).
- The moment when zealots took over the temple during the Jewish war, in AD 68–69. They allowed criminals to wander through the temple courts; and a random person was made high priest.
- When Titus entered the temple to make a Roman sacrifice there in AD 70, before it was utterly destroyed.

It is unlikely to be the first two options, since AD 26 was before Jesus uttered this prophecy and the statue was never erected: it was just proposed. In a way, we can't know which of the last two it was. The point is that Mark's audience is to be ready; and the minute they see the thing that they know is a desolating sacrilege, they should flee. Keeping watch and standing firm is important until the moment arises when disaster is most definitely coming. Then fleeing quickly is what is needed.

From this distance, we can't know what the event was. But Mark was confident that his readers would know it when they saw it (hence his side note, 'let the reader understand').

It is possible that Jesus was saying that the disciples had to learn the tools of discernment. Given that no one can agree which specific historical event his comments referred to, it might be that it was symbolic. It was something so great, so appalling that things could not go on as they were. Perhaps Jesus was saying that the disciples would need to be skilled in adjudicating between those events that were terrifying but not the end, and the one event that would tip everything over the edge and mean that things would never be the same again. He warned that people would rise up, making false claims about leadership; but that would not be the time to run. They would hear about wars; but that would not be the time to run. They would be arrested and tried; but it would still not be the time to run. Families would turn on one another; but the time to flee would still not have come. But when the tipping point came – a moment so great that things could never be the same again – then that would be the moment to run.

Woe to those who are pregnant or breastfeeding

Jesus expressed deep compassion for the people who would need to flee when the time came. The word 'woe' (*ouai* in Greek) is an exclamation of pain. Jesus grieved here for those who would suffer most.

A swift flight, when the world is crumbling around you, is difficult for anyone; but for those with young babies it becomes even more perilous. It is hard to read this and not think about the many young families around the world who have been forced to flee their homes when war or another disaster strikes. How dreadful it is for them. Jesus knew that and uttered the word of lament used in mourning: *ouai*.

Suffering of a kind unlike anything before

The stories of the siege of Jerusalem that we read in Josephus make clear that the experience (described in detail in books 5–6 of *Jewish War*) was truly awful. The example given on p. 287 of what it was like when the zealots took over the temple gives a flavour of the lawlessness inside the city during the siege. There was infighting, murder and even cannibalism. Outside the city it was just as bad: the Romans crucified so many people that they ran out of wood.

Again, Mark may have been alluding to these events. Alternatively, he may have been using symbolic language (drawn from Daniel 12.1) about how awful things would be before the end.

Cut short the days

The elect mentioned here are God's covenant people; but it isn't clear whether we are to take them as Jewish Christians or righteous Jews. When the word is used in texts outside the Bible (see, for example, 1 Enoch 1.1), it refers to the righteous few. This seems to be likely here: that the elect were not specifically Christians, but anyone who, in these difficult times, was deemed to be righteous.

The idea of God hastening the time or cutting short the days does occur in other texts, but exactly what it means here isn't really clear. The cutting short of days means some survive (though not all) and probably refers to the fact that, even in the worst scenarios where there are death and destruction, God is still in control and can shorten the days of anguish and pain. It rather begs the question of why, therefore, he can't shorten them altogether so that this distress and misery don't happen at all. The answer from Mark 13 would be that in times of collapse, when world regimes fall, suffering is inevitable. God simply makes it as short as possible.

'Son of Man coming in clouds'

The word 'but' (*alla*) that begins verse 24 leads some people to think that Jesus has now moved on from the subject of the destruction of Jerusalem to the second coming. Others, however, argue that the destruction is still in view until after the lesson of the fig tree (13.28–31); this finishes a section that began in 11.12–14, when Jesus cursed the fig tree before cursing the temple.

Whichever event is being referred to here, the key thing is to recognize that the language used in verse 24 is a classic sign of a theophany (revelation of God), just as when, at the baptism, the heavens were 'torn apart' (1.9–11) or at the Transfiguration, when a cloud descended (9.2–8). Earthly signs, such as the sun and the moon being darkened or the stars falling from heaven, were indications that God was about to appear. Here, it is the Son of Man; now the identity of the Son of Man is truly revealed. The whole earth can see who he is. As N. T. Wright argues, the verb 'coming' may not refer to the Son of Man coming to earth but going to the Ancient of Days to receive the vindication and authority due to him. Once he has received these, he would then be able to gather his own to him (see, for example, *Jesus and the Victory of God*, SPCK, 1996, pp. 284 and 288).

The fig tree

It does seem as though Mark is reminding us of the fig tree from 11.12–13 in this parable. This time, however, he is doing so with a different point, which accords with his message throughout this chapter: 'Learn how to interpret what is going on around you because there will come a moment when this becomes vital.' Fig trees were some of the few deciduous plants in Israel. Their branches did not become soft when the sap rose; instead, they became flexible, which signalled that leaves were coming.

'This generation will not pass away'

The strongest argument for this chapter referring to the destruction of Jerusalem can be found in verse 30. A biblical generation was around 40 years, which would take us from the time of Jesus to AD 70 and the destruction of Jerusalem. The verse poses much more of a problem for those who want to argue that this passage is solely about the second coming. If it is, then Jesus was wrong here.

If, as I suspect, the chapter refers to all those time periods in which cataclysms occur, including the destruction, then we can view this verse as noting that all these things did take place before the disciples' generation passed away. But, not only that, other catastrophes would then happen again and again, and would continue to do so until the end of all times. Through it all, Jesus, the Son of Man, would remain vindicated and ruling over the whole earth.

Keep watch

As noted above, the real crux of chapter 13 is not which event it describes but how Jesus' followers are to behave when something like it occurs. To ensure that this point is as clear as possible, Jesus repeats it one more time at the end. You never know when this kind of event will happen, so you need to hone the skills you will need when it does. Be alert, keep watch and be ready to act when you need to but don't be thrown off course; learn to recognize the signs and, whatever you do, stay awake.

Chapter 13 is one of the hardest chapters to understand in the whole of the Gospel, possibly even in the whole New Testament. I can't pretend that I comprehend it all, even after 30 plus years of trying. But from the chapter, I have learnt the importance of acquiring skills that we will need when disaster strikes: of not panicking when things happen all around us but are not the ultimate disaster; of recognizing what *is* an ultimate disaster and then acting swiftly; and, most importantly of all, of remembering that the Son of Man has been vindicated and rules supreme so that, no matter what happens, we can know this to be the case. Beyond that, I will continue to wrestle with the chapter and look forward to what else can be learnt along the way.

Mark 14.1–2: The plot to kill Jesus picked up pace

After an extensive period of discussion, debate and teaching (11.27—13.37), we now return to the main narrative. This is the beginning of Mark's Passion narrative, which is made clear with the timing given as two days before the Passover. Until now, events have either happened immediately or after a number of days. This is the first time that the time has been given before a key date. It indicates that our attention is now focused forwards.

Links backwards

- Mark 3.6 and 11.18 spoke of, first, the Pharisees and Herodians and then the chief priests and scribes deciding to kill Jesus, which was reaffirmed after he told the parable of the tenants (12.12). This short, two-verse passage reminds us, after Jesus' long teaching about future woes, that his opponents have not forgotten their grudge.
- The three predictions of Jesus' death (8.31—9.1; 9.30–32; 10.32–34) are also important here, as we are now expecting their completion.

Links forwards

- After the anointing of Jesus in the next passage, Judas agrees to betray him (14.10–11). Here, we have one of Mark's favourite framing or sandwich techniques; he embeds Jesus' anointing between sections of the narrative about the chief priests plotting Jesus' death.

Interesting words ...

- v. 1: *Unleavened Bread*. The feast is known simply as *azumos*: that is, 'no yeast' or 'unleavened'.
- v. 1: *by stealth*. *Dolos* means 'trickery', 'cunning' or 'stealth'. In other words, the chief priests and scribes wanted to find a solution by underhand means, which they did, in 14.10–11, when Judas comes to see them.
- v. 2: *festival*. An *eortē* is a 'feast', 'festival' or 'holiday'. The ancient world had holidays only for religious feasts.
- v. 2: *riot*. *Thorubos* means 'a clamour', 'an uproar' or 'unrest'. These were common during the festivals.

Passover and Unleavened Bread

The feast of Passover commemorated the night when the angel of the Lord killed the firstborn of the Egyptians but passed over the houses of the people of God. It is celebrated for a full day from sundown to sundown on 15 Nissan. The Festival of Unleavened Bread continues from Passover for seven days (15–21 Nissan) and commemorates the people's rapid exit from Egypt in which they ate bread without yeast.

If 14.1 is identified as two days before Passover, this means it is 13 Nissan and, for us, the Wednesday of Holy Week.

Jewish months

The Jewish calendar consists of 12 lunar months, each lasting 29 or 30 days. As this calendar is a lunar one, it does not always sync up with the Western solar calendar.

The first month of the year, corresponding to September or October is Tishrei; Nissan is the seventh month of the year corresponding to April or May.

Riot

It is hard to know how many people came to Jerusalem for the Passover. Josephus' figure (three million) is thought by many to be a vast exaggeration. A twentieth-century scholar, J. Jeremias estimated that there may have been about 180,000, which may be on the low side. Given, however, that the usual population was around 30,000, the point is that it swelled to around six times its size. Many people would have had to camp just outside the city, which hints at the possibilities for unrest.

It was not unreasonable for the chief priests to fear a riot during the Passover. There was one in 4 BC when, just after Herod died, Roman soldiers brought in standards that had on them images deemed to be idolatrous. The swollen size of the population, alongside a large number of zealots coming in from the north, gave good reason for the authorities to be afraid.

Mark 14.3–9: The anointing of Jesus

Jesus' impending death is made even more clear in Mark through the telling of a story in which he is anointed. In case we are in any doubt about its significance, Jesus explicitly identifies that the woman has anointed his body for burial (14.8). This act of tender care towards Jesus, stitched between the two accounts of plots to kill him, is striking.

Links backwards

- This is another, albeit implicit, prediction of Jesus' death to add to the others from Mark 8.31—9.1; 9.30–32; and 10.32–34.
- The other person in Mark whom Jesus commended so warmly was the woman, with her two small coins, in the temple (12.41–44). The action of both women demonstrated profound generosity.

Links forwards

- When the women go to the tomb to anoint Jesus after his death (16.1), this story hangs clearly in the background. Given that he has risen from the dead by the time they arrive, Jesus' body would never have been anointed had it not been for this unnamed woman in Bethany.

Interesting words ...

- v. 3: *sat at the table.* As with previous descriptions of meals, the word is simply 'reclined' (*katakeimai*).
- v. 3: *an alabaster jar of very costly ointment of nard.* An *alabastros* was a jar for perfume oil, sometimes (but not always) made of alabaster; in Greek, the rest of the phrase reads 'of ointment (*muron*) of nard (*nardos*) unadulterated (*pistikēs*: 'genuine') very expensive (*polutelēs*)'.
- v. 3: *broke open. Suntribō* means 'to smash' or 'to shatter'.
- v. 4. *in anger.* The verb *aganakteō* occurs three times in Mark: once when Jesus was angry with the disciples for not letting the children come to him (10.14); once when the disciples were cross with James and John (10.41); and here.
- v. 4: *wasted.* The word *apōleia* refers to 'destruction', 'waste' or 'squander'.
- v. 5: *three hundred denarii.* A *dēnarion* was a standard silver Roman coin. *Triakosioi* is 'three hundred'.
- v. 5: *scolded. Embrimaomai* means 'to speak sternly', 'to rebuke fiercely' or 'to exhibit irritation'. The verb is in the imperfect, which implies that the scolding went on for some time.
- v. 6: *good.* The word *kalos* can mean 'good', but it is a slightly anodyne translation. 'Beautiful', 'fine' or 'noble' might be better here.
- v. 6: *service.* The word used is *ergos* ('work' or 'deed') and not, as you might expect, *diakonia* ('service').
- v. 8: *anointed.* The verb is connected to the noun *muros* ('ointment') and is *murizō*.
- v. 8: *burial. Entaphiasmos* refers to the particular step of laying a body out or anointing it to prepare it for burial.
- v. 9: *truly I tell you.* This characteristic opening (*amēn legō humin*) to a saying by Jesus occurs once early on in Mark and then with increasing frequency

towards the end (3.28; 8.12; 9.1, 41; 10.15, 29; 11.23; 12.43; 13.30; 14.18, 25, 30). For more on the phrase, see the note on 3.28 (p. 85).

- v. 9: *remembrance.* A *mnemosunon* was a 'memorial' or 'memory'.

Simon the leper

One can't help feeling doubly sorry for Simon, given the ascription by which he is known here. He can no longer be a leper, otherwise (given the dangers of infection) he would not have been able to host a dinner (see the box, 'Leprosy', p. 56, for more on this subject). So he did have leprosy at one point (one reason to feel sorry for him) but no longer does, presumably because he had been healed by Jesus. None the less, he is still remembered as someone who had it (the second reason to feel sorry for him). Never being allowed to forget something that marked you out from everyone else is a particular burden.

Four different accounts of anointing

Jesus is anointed in each of the Gospels, but each account is slightly different. See the table below.

Reference	**Matthew 26.6–13**	**Mark 14.3–9**	**Luke 7.36–50**	**John 12.1–9**
Where it happened	Bethany	Bethany	Galilee	Bethany
Host for the meal	Simon the leper	Simon the leper	Simon the Pharisee	Lazarus
Identity of the woman	A woman	A woman	A woman of the city	Mary of Bethany
Body part anointed	Head	Head	Feet	Feet
Objection to the anointing came from	The disciples	Someone	Simon	Judas
Significance of the anointing	Burial	Burial	Knowledge of her need for forgiveness	Burial

Here are the key differences between these accounts:

- The timings in the Gospels. Mark and Matthew place the anointing in the last week of Jesus' life; John a little before that; and Luke during Jesus' Galilean ministry.
- The body part anointed. In Mark and Matthew, Jesus' head is anointed; in Luke and John, it is his feet.
- What the act symbolized. In Mark, Matthew and John, the act points to Jesus' burial; in Luke it is an act of generosity born of thanksgiving.

In Christian tradition, Mary of Bethany has been conflated with Mary Magdalene, probably because Mary Magdalene is mentioned in Luke 8.2, the passage immediately following the Lukan account of the anointing. This conflation, first suggested by Ephraem in the fourth century, was what gave rise to the tradition of Mary of Magdala being a prostitute (since it was assumed that the sin referred to by Luke was prostitution). This conflation is rightly rejected today as being not only unhelpful but untrue; but the question remains, what, if any, connection exists between the accounts?

It seems likely that Luke's account is different from all the rest and represents a second anointing that happened much earlier in Jesus' ministry. This may also be true of John's Gospel; but it is closer to Mark and Matthew's description, so it is harder to be clear on that.

Anointing of the head versus the feet

Anointing the head with oil is well known in the Old Testament as a sign of blessing on the recipient (see, for example, 'you anoint my head with oil; my cup overflows' (Ps. 23.5)). Psalm 133.2 ('It is like the precious oil on the head, running down upon the beard') suggests that anointing can be with a large amount of oil.

It is harder to see what the purpose of anointing the feet was. There is no evidence anywhere else that this was done. We know of the importance of washing feet (see John 13). It is possible that, after washing, oil was used for fragrance; but this is not mentioned anywhere.

A woman

The name of the woman who anointed Jesus is not given by Mark, which is ironic as Jesus promises that what she has done will be told in remembrance of her – but not so much that her name will be remembered.

In a way, however, this seems to be the import of what Jesus is talking about. Just as seeking status and honour are not at the heart of discipleship, so being honoured by name is not important either. What is remembered is what she did; and what she did was valued by Jesus.

An alabaster jar of pure nard

The container for the ointment is called an *alabastros* in Greek, which simply means a 'container for perfume'. Many of these jars or pots were made from alabaster because their opaque quality preserved the scent well; not all were, however.

The jar contained spikenard oil, which is made from a plant that grows only in the foothills of the Himalayas (in China, Tibet and Nepal). The distance it was carried over the trading routes made it extremely expensive.

Mark's is the only account that says that she smashed the bottle. The usual way to open a jar was to break the seal on the top or open it at its narrow neck. The fact that the woman smashed it meant that she intended to use it all right from the start: it was an act as generous as the widow's giving of her two remaining coins.

The cost of the perfume

Three hundred denarii would have been approximately a full year's wages for a day labourer. As a result, those who are cross with the woman are not wrong that the perfume cost a lot of money. The question then arises of where she got the perfume from. It is highly likely that it was a gift. Alabaster perfume jars were often given to brides at their betrothals or weddings; or it could have been an heirloom. Mark does not say where this jar came from; but the way in which the story is told suggests that it was not only valuable for the money it was worth.

'She has done what she could'

Jesus' response about the woman provides us with a further, implicit prediction of his death. It is not at all clear that the woman understood that she was anointing Jesus for burial. Whether she did or not does not seem important: Jesus understood her actions in this way and that was sufficient.

It is worth noting that nard had a very strong smell. The woman's pouring out an entire bottle on Jesus would have meant that his clothes and hair would have still smelled of it two days later, at his Crucifixion.

Mark 14.10–11: A betrayal planned

The two verses at the start of the chapter indicated that the chief priests had decided to wait until after the festival to arrest Jesus. This intention changed when Judas went to them of his own volition to betray Jesus. Mark gives no hint about why they decided to bring the timetable forward. Betrayed or not, the crowd could have become volatile at the news of Jesus' arrest. It might have been possible that the chief priests thought, with Judas' betrayal, the tide of popular opinion was turning, which would protect them. As we see, this was in fact the case; but they might still have been wiser to wait until after the festival.

> ***Links backwards***
>
> - The three predictions of Jesus' death (Mark 8.31—9.1; 9.30–32; 10.32–34) give texture to this short story.
> - The episode that precedes the anointing story sets up the context for this one (14.1–2).

Interesting words ...

- vv. 10–11: *betray*. The word *paradidōmi* 'hand over' is used here. See the box 'Betrayed/handed over', on p. 211, for more on *paradidōmi* in Mark.
- v. 11: *were greatly pleased*. *Chairō* means 'to rejoice'.
- v. 11: *money*. The word here denotes not just 'money' but 'silver coins' (*argurion*); see 'Silver coins' on p. 298.
- v. 11: *opportunity*. *Eukairōs* was 'a favourable time', which was a blend of two words: 'a good (*eu*) right time (*kairos*)'.

Why did Judas betray Jesus?

One of the features of Mark's narrative is that he does not often tell us why people acted or reacted in certain ways. The story of Judas is no different. We are simply presented with the fact that Judas went to the chief priests to betray Jesus. Matthew's account gives a subtle hint about his motivation. Both accounts relate Judas' decision to betray Jesus after the anointing of Jesus' feet by the woman. Mark makes no explicit connection between the two episodes; but Matthew adds the small word 'then'. In other words, what happened at the anointing persuaded Judas to betray Jesus.

Luke and John go much further. Both state that Satan entered Judas (Luke 22.3; John 13.2), to which John adds an explicit note that Judas was specifically upset by the woman's extravagance (in John, she is called Mary of Bethany).

> ***Iscariot***
>
> Some scholars wonder whether the root of Judas' alienation from the Twelve can be discerned from his name. The name Iscariot seems to come from the Hebrew for 'man of Kerioth'. Kerioth was one of the leading cities of Moab, east of the Dead Sea. During the time of Jesus, it was in the territory of Judea, in the southern Hebron hills. If so, the significance is that Judas would have been the only disciple who came from Judea and not Galilee; it may have contributed to his disaffection with Jesus.

Silver coins

The money that Judas is promised by the chief priests is *argurion* – namely, silver coins. There were two types of coin that were made from silver at the time of Jesus: the denarius (the common Roman currency) and the Tyrian shekel. The Tyrian shekel weighed around 14 grams and was pure silver. The shekels were minted in Tyre (hence their name). They were the currency with which men over the age of 20 paid the temple tax. Given that the chief priests would have had very easy access to the temple tax money, it is likely that Judas was paid in these coins. This detail seems hugely significant, given Jesus' critique of the temple. The chief priests had gone so vastly astray that they used temple money, given to enhance the worship of God, to kill his only Son.

Mark 14.12–26: The Last Supper – a meal that looked backwards and forwards

If we take Mark's account of the Last Supper as a Passover meal (see the box, 'The timing of the Last Supper', on p. 300), then Jesus' last meal with his friends looked both backwards and forwards. It referred backwards to the moment when God freed his people from slavery in Egypt; and forwards to Jesus' death, which would free humanity for ever from sin, and onwards to the culmination of all freedoms in the kingdom of God. It also looked backwards to the many other meals the disciples had shared with Jesus (most notably the feedings of thousands) and forwards to the Christian gatherings after his death, which would repeatedly commemorate this moment.

Links backwards

- The feeding of the 5,000 (Mark 6.30–44) and of the 4,000 (8.1–10) are in the background of this Passover meal, especially regarding the actions of taking, blessing, giving thanks, breaking and giving.
- Just as Jesus had made preparations, on the Mount of Olives, to acquire a donkey (11.1–3), he had also made preparations for the location of this meal.

Links forwards

- In Mark, the link forwards is to the moment of Jesus' death at the Crucifixion (15.37); but, for the first time, the links now point beyond the Gospel to the life of the community after Jesus' death and Resurrection.

Interesting words ...

- v. 12: *sacrificed. Thuō* can mean either 'sacrifice' or 'slaughter'.
- v. 12: *Passover*. The *Pascha* referred to the whole festival or the meal that commemorated it.
- v. 13: *jar*. A *keramion* was a clay vessel: either a jar or a pot.
- v. 14: *owner of the house*. An *oikodespotēs* was a 'master of a household' or, in some of Jesus' parables, a 'landowner'.
- v. 14: *guest room*. A *kataluma* referred to a room or space (in a smaller house) where guests could stay. It is the word used in Luke's account of Jesus' birth: 'laid him in a manger, because there was no place for them in the *kataluma*' (Luke 2.7).
- v. 15: *a large room upstairs. Anagaion* refers to anything raised above the ground. It is possible that this 'room' was on the roof. Mark tells us that it was *mega* ('large' or 'great').
- v. 18: *taken their places*. As was usual for descriptions of seating for meals, the word used is *anakeimai*.
- vv. 18 and 25: *Truly I tell you*. This characteristic opening (*amēn legō humin*) to a saying by Jesus occurs once early on in Mark and then with increasing frequency towards the end (3.28; 8.12; 9.1, 41; 10.15, 29; 11.23; 12.43; 13.30; 14.18, 25, 30). For more on the phrase, see the note on 3.28 (p. 85).
- vv. 18 and 21: *betray; betrayed*. The verb *paradidōmi* ('hand over') is used. See the box, 'Betrayed/handed over', on p. 211, for Mark's use of *paradidōmi*.
- v. 19: *Surely, not I?* In Greek, it is possible to ask questions in a way that prompts either a 'yes' or 'no' answer. Questions beginning with *ou* or *ouk* prompt the answer 'yes' while those beginning with *mē* prompt the answer 'no'. This question, *mēti egō*, prompts Jesus to say 'no'.
- v. 21: *woe*. The word *ouai* means 'a cry of sorrow' or 'a cry of pain'.
- v. 22: *took; blessing; broke; gave; giving thanks*. As with the feeding of the

5,000 and 4,000, the key actions of Jesus were that he 'took' (*lambanō*), 'blessed' (*eulogeō*), 'broke' (*klaō*), 'gave' (*didōmi*) and then 'gave thanks' (*eucharisteō*).

- vv. 22–23: *bread; cup*. Two very common words are used *artos* ('bread') and *potērion* ('cup').
- v. 26: *sung the hymn*. The verb *humneō* means 'to sing praises', specifically psalms from the Scriptures.

On the first day of Unleavened Bread

As the Feast of Unleavened Bread followed on immediately from the Passover, Mark appears to be slightly confused here. He is probably referring to the whole feast under the label of Unleavened Bread. His next statement ('when the Passover lamb is sacrificed') makes it clear that it was immediately before the start of the festival (see the box, 'The timing of the Last Supper', below). As 15 Nissan begins during the evening of 14 Nissan, this is probably what Mark is saying here. It means that the anointing of Jesus took place on the Wednesday (13 Nissan) and these events on the Thursday (14 Nissan, leading into 15 Nissan).

The timing of the Last Supper

There is a disagreement between John's Gospel and Matthew, Mark and Luke's Gospels about whether Jesus' last meal with his disciples was a Passover meal or not. The key issue is that Passover lambs were killed on 14 Nissan and the Passover meal celebrated that evening at sundown (the start of 15 Nissan). Mark is clear that the meal is a Passover meal (14.12), with the Last Supper occurring after dusk on 15 Nissan. John, however, describes Jesus' dying on 14 Nissan, along with the Passover lambs. This makes his meal (John 13) happen on 13 Nissan and have no Passover resonances at all. Significantly, it is much easier to believe that the Sanhedrin met, had a trial and visited Pilate on the day *before* the full feast of Passover than on the first day of this major festival, which would have been the case if the Last Supper were the Passover meal.

There are some who think that the meal described in Matthew, Mark and Luke is not a Passover meal because there is no mention of a Passover lamb or bitter herbs, which both form essential parts of it. Instead, they maintain that it was an important but ordinary Jewish meal, which involved the breaking of bread and sharing of a cup; then, later, Christians imbued the meal with Passover resonances for theological reasons. I would argue that Passover resonances are so deeply important to the story that it is hard to remove them without fundamentally changing the narrative. It isn't an easy problem to solve, but it is worth thinking about in depth.

The sacrificing of the Passover lamb

One of the most hectic days in the life of the temple was 14 Nissan. One-year-old male lambs would be brought and slaughtered. Priests would catch the blood in bowls and sprinkle it on the altar. The lambs' intestines and fat were removed to be burnt on the altar itself and the carcasses taken home to be roasted on a spit for the Passover meal that evening. Josephus estimated that around 250,000 lambs were killed on 14 Nissan; while he is known for exaggerating numbers, it is worth reflecting on the noise, smell and hubbub in the temple that this ritual would have caused.

Two disciples

Whereas Luke identifies the two disciples that Jesus sent as Peter and John (Luke 22.8), Mark implies that a different pair went ahead to prepare the Passover and were joined later by Jesus and the Twelve (14.17). Traditional Christian artwork implies that the only people present at the Last Supper were Jesus and the Twelve; but this is problematic for a number of reasons. Mark makes clear that the room that Jesus had booked was *mega* ('large'), which implies the presence of a group greater in size than just 13 people. More importantly, we learn in all the Gospels that there were a significant number of women in Jerusalem who had followed Jesus from Galilee (including Jesus' own mother; see Mark 15.40).

Jesus had reconstituted his family to include those who followed him (Mark 3.33), not just his biological family. Passover was fundamentally a family meal; therefore, it would have been odd in the extreme for Jesus to exclude people who had specifically followed him from Galilee.

A man carrying a water jar

Jesus' identification of how to find the house where the upper room was may seem somewhat vague. In a city with a population that had expanded by a minimum of six times its usual size (30,000 to 180,000, though quite probably more than this), there would surely have been many people carrying water jars. The unusual feature, which would guarantee his immediate identification, was that the person carrying the water jar was a man. Fetching water was women's work, so he would have stood out significantly.

Just as with the description about the collection of the donkey's colt, we are left no clues as to whose house this was, how Jesus knew them or how he had reserved a large guest room at a time when all space in the city was at an absolute premium. It reminds us, one more time, about how much we do not know about Jesus, his movements and his followers.

It is worth remembering that part of the preparations for the Passover meal would have entailed going to the temple to sacrifice a lamb.

The prediction of betrayal

The prediction of betrayal in Mark's Gospel keeps the identity of the betrayer a mystery to the Twelve; but not to us, as Judas' identity was revealed in the previous passage. In John's Gospel, Judas' role is highlighted when Jesus hands Judas a morsel of bread (John 13.13); but in Mark, Jesus' reference to someone dipping bread into the same bowl is simply another way of saying it is someone in the room.

Mark's version makes more sense of what happened because, if the disciples had known who the betrayer was, it is hard to imagine that they would not have stopped him.

He took bread ... he took a cup

It is widely thought that the blessing Jesus gave over the bread would have been a Jewish prayer of thanksgiving. The Mishnah tractate *b. Berakoth* 6.1 gives it as 'Blessed are you, O Lord our God, king of the universe, who brings forth bread from the earth.'

It is worth noting that Mark's institution of the Last Supper narrative is so short that various details with which we are familiar are omitted: in particular, 'for you' after 'This is my body' (which is found in Luke 22.19 and 1 Cor. 11.24), and 'Do this in remembrance of me' (also in Luke 22.19 and 1 Cor. 11.25).

What would have been startling to the disciples, however, was when Jesus reinterpreted the bread as his body and identified the cup as his blood. Since he was present with them at the table, it must have been a confusing statement. We can only assume that they began to understand the significance of what Jesus said much later, after his death and Resurrection.

The order of the Passover meal

The order of the Passover meal is described in *m. Pesachim* 10. As the Mishnah was written down at the end of the second century AD, it is very difficult to know whether what it describes was the custom in the first century. While we can't be confident about exactly what the order of the Passover meal would have been, it may well have been as described here.

The feast began with the pouring of the first cup of wine. Over this cup, the host blessed God for the wine and the day. This was followed by an entrée, described by the Mishnah as seasoned lettuce. Then the tables were brought forward, and the food was served but not eaten. This was when the second cup of wine was drunk and the first Hallel psalm (Ps. 113) was sung. The main meal, including the lamb, was then eaten, along with the unleavened bread (which the host blessed) and bitter herbs. During the meal, the question about the Exodus ('What makes this night different from other nights?') was asked and answered. Following this, grace was said over the third cup of wine; then the rest of the Hallel psalms (114–118) were sung between that and the taking of a fourth cup of wine. It is impossible to know whether the cup that Jesus shared with the disciples was one of these cups or an additional one.

The clues to aid them in their reflection come from what Jesus said about his blood: that it was 'my blood of the covenant which is poured out for many'. The reference to covenant, especially in the context of a Passover meal, would have brought to mind Exodus 24.8 ('Moses took the blood and dashed it on the people, and said, "See the blood of the covenant that the LORD has made with you in accordance with all these words"') alongside the idea of pouring out blood as a sacrifice. Nevertheless, it must have taken them a good while to process this, as the thought of drinking any blood, let alone Jesus', would have been abhorrent to Jesus' followers.

Jesus' final comment drew the disciples' eyes to the far horizon. This was his final earthly meal; his next would be when the kingdom finally came and the messianic banquet was laid out for all.

Sang a hymn

The reference to singing a hymn was almost certainly to singing the Hallel psalms (Ps. 113–118), which occurred at the end of the Passover meal. If the disciples reached Psalm 118, the singing of it would have been poignant, given the crowd's use of it on the way into the city (Mark 11.9–10) and Jesus' further use of it during his confrontation with the chief priests (12.10).

Mark 14.26–31: A denial denied

As we have seen at numerous points throughout the Gospel, Mark likes to bookend important stories with two similar events or, indeed, to split a story in two and place a different story in between. The technique here makes Peter's denial much closer to Judas' betrayal than in the other Gospels. Peter is going to let Jesus down, just as Judas did. The key difference is that Judas plans his betrayal here, whereas Peter blithely denies that his disavowal of Jesus could ever happen.

It is also worth noting that there are three predictions of failure: of the one who will betray Jesus, of all the disciples, and of Peter; each one of them comes true.

Links backwards and forwards

- Peter's vehement rejection of the idea that he would deny Jesus recalls Jesus' teaching that the first will be last (Mark 10.31). Those utterly confident of themselves will be the first to fall.
- Peter's declaration that he would die with Jesus also brings to mind James and John's acceptance that they would drink from the same cup as Jesus (10.35–45).
- Placing Judas' planned betrayal (14.10–11) and the prophecy of Peter's denial (14.26–31) around the Last Supper (14.12–25) neatly holds them together, without explicitly stating that all the disciples, particularly Peter, betrayed Jesus.
  - Judas' predicted betrayal (14.18–21) is fulfilled in 14.43–50.
  - The disciples' predicted falling away (14.26–28) is fulfilled in 14.50.
  - Peter's predicted betrayal (14.30–31) occurs at the end of this chapter, in 14.66–72.

Interesting words ...

- vv. 27 and 29: *deserters*. The verb *skandalizomai* ('to stumble' or 'to fall away') was last used in 9.42, 43, 45 and 47. Its connection is obscured by the different translation. The seriousness of stumbling is clear there; here, Jesus says they will all do so.
- v. 27: *scattered*. The verb *diaskorpizō* ('spread' or 'scatter') can be used of 'seed' or 'sheep'.
- v. 28: *I am raised up*. When talking about resurrection, Mark usually uses *anistēmi*; but, here, *egeirō* is used instead, which means 'to awaken' or 'to arise'. See the box, 'The words for "rise" and "resurrection" in Mark', on p. 194.
- v. 28: *go before*. *Proagō* means 'to proceed' or 'to go ahead of'.
- v. 30: *Truly I tell you*. This characteristic opening (*amēn legō humin*) to a saying by Jesus occurs once early on in Mark and then with increasing frequency towards the end (3.28; 8.12; 9.1, 41; 10.15, 29; 11.23; 12.43; 13.30; 14.18, 25, 30). For more on the phrase, see the note on 3.28 (p. 85).
- v. 30: *this day, this very night*. The timescale is emphasized with the repetition of 'today' (*sēmeron*), 'on this (*houtos*) night (*nuktos*)'.
- v. 30: *crows*. The verb *phoneō* means 'to (make a) sound' (as in 'to sound the Last Post'). The English word here for the type of sound (a cock crow) is the choice of the translators.
- v. 30: *deny*. *Aparneomai* means 'to claim no knowledge of' or 'to claim no relationship with'.
- v. 31: *vehemently*. *Ekperissōs* refers to saying something with great emphasis.

'You will all become deserters'; 'I will go before you'

Jesus' imagery of a herd of sheep scattered and without a shepherd captures perfectly what happened to the disciples. In fear and horror at Jesus' arrest, they all fled, like a herd of sheep would if a predator were in their midst. It is, therefore, restorative to have the matching prediction that Jesus would go ahead of them after his Resurrection. In the ancient world, shepherds went ahead, leading – not following – their flock to safety and pasture. They will be scattered but, after that, the shepherd will lead them once more.

A cock will crow twice

The reference to a cock crowing does not give a fixed time: cocks crow when they choose as light dawns (even sometimes before dawn). Rather, the point is that, before daybreak, Peter will have done what he swears, here, he would never do.

'Even though I must die with you'

Like James and John, Peter does not seem to be afraid to die with Jesus. It is possible that his courage failed him at the last minute. It may be, on the other hand, that he thought he was signing up to a different kind of death, such as fighting shoulder to shoulder with Jesus against the Roman enemy, rather than accepting death on a cross, apparently crushed by imperial force.

Mark 14.32–42: Jesus' prayer in Gethsemane

The conversation about Peter and the disciples' stumbling or falling away happened between the guest room and Gethsemane. Once Jesus arrives at Gethsemane, the full weight of what is about to happen becomes clear. Various themes from earlier in the Gospel are drawn together in this passage: the predictions of Jesus' death, his teaching on prayer and his urging the disciples to keep awake are particularly important.

Links backwards and forwards

- Jesus took Peter, James and John with him on three previous occasions: to the healing of Jairus' daughter (Mark 5.37); to the Transfiguration (9.2); and spoke to them privately, along with Andrew, on the Mount of Olives (13.3).

- **Jesus' predictions of his own death hang in the air in this passage (8.31—9.1; 9.30–32; 10.32–34).**
- **Jesus' prayer here is a helpful counterpoint to his teaching in 11.20–25, which implies that you can ask anything and it will be done. Here, it is clear that prayer has to accord with God's will.**
- **Jesus' command to the disciples to keep awake (14.34) recalls chapter 13, with a sense of foreboding. If keeping watch was key for navigating a world catastrophe that was on the horizon, their first attempt at doing so does not go well.**

Interesting words …

- v. 32: *place*. The word *chorion* refers to a field or a plot of land.
- v. 32: *sit*. This is the word 'sit' (*kathizō*), not 'recline' as it often is.
- v. 33: *be distressed and agitated*. Slightly surprisingly, the word used here is *ekthambeō*, which is used in 9.15 to describe the crowd's reaction to seeing Jesus after the Transfiguration; it is also used to describe the emotional state of the women when they saw the young man in the empty tomb (16.5–6). The verb can mean 'astounded' too; but the idea here is one of being so overwhelmed that it causes distress. We know that distress is meant because of the other word used, *adēmoneō*, which means 'to be upset', 'to be troubled' or 'to be distressed'. It might be better to translate this phrase as 'he began to be overwhelmed and distressed'.
- v. 34: *I am deeply grieved*. The phrase in Greek is 'My soul/life force (*psuchē*) is very troubled (*perilupos*: 'extremely sad')'. Whereas we saw Jesus moved with anger, frustration and compassion earlier in the Gospel, this is the first time we see his distress.
- vv. 34 and 37–38: *keep awake*. One of the words that was so key to chapter 13 is used here: *gregoreō* ('keep awake' or 'keep alert'). Its importance is stressed by Jesus saying it three times.
- v. 36: *Abba*. The Aramaic word for 'father', here, is transliterated into Greek.
- v. 36: *cup*. In Mark, the word *potērion* is used both for actual cups (for example, in 7.4; 14.23) and for metaphorical cups (that is, facing a difficult task; for example, see 10.38–39) as here.
- v. 37: *Simon*. Peter hasn't been called 'Simon' since 3.16, when Jesus gave him the name Peter. Calling him Simon, here, suggests that Jesus is addressing the man Peter was before he began to follow Jesus. Even though he had yet to deny Jesus, he was unable to stay awake when Jesus needed him most.
- v. 37: *could you*. Usually the word used for 'to be able' is *dunamai*; but here, it is *ischuo* 'to be strong enough'. It could read: 'Were you not strong enough to stay awake?'
- v. 38: *trial*. *Peirasmos* ('trial' or 'examination') is the word for Jesus' temptations in the Gospels.
- v. 38: *willing*. *Prothumos* means 'more eager', 'more ready' or 'more zealous'.

Jesus' point (again, referring to the disciples' vehement expressions in the previous passage) is that their spirits are zealous but their flesh (*sarx*) is weak.

- vv. 41–42: *betrayed; betrayer*. As before, *paradidōmi* ('hand over') is used here. See the box, 'Betrayed/handed over', on p. 211 for Mark's use of the verb.
- v. 42: *get up*. This is the same word (*egeirō*) that Jesus used of his being raised up (14.28). It means 'get up', 'awaken', 'rouse' or 'rise'.

Gethsemane

Throughout this week, Jesus and the Twelve had been lodging somewhere in Bethany. It would be too far to return to once Passover had begun, since they were limited to a walk of 2,000 cubits, about 0.5 miles. Gethsemane's precise location is unknown but there has been no dispute about its traditional location: on the western slope of the Mount of Olives, just across the Kidron Valley from Jerusalem. The implication of Jesus' taking the disciples there is that it was within the allowed distance but was quieter than staying in the city itself.

The name of the area is thought to have come from the Aramaic *Gat-Smane*, which means 'olive press'. Thus, it would have been the place where the olives from the Mount of Olives would have been brought to be pressed. As this was Jesus' time of great 'pressing', it seems apt that he should have gone there.

Peter, James and John

Mark does not say why Jesus took just Peter, James and John with him; but he had done so before: at the healing of Jairus' daughter (5.37); at the Transfiguration (9.2); and to talk to them privately, with Andrew, on the Mount of Olives (13.3). Perhaps it was because it was his usual practice to take his 'inner circle' with him; or it could have been because all three had declared clearly and definitively that they would suffer with him, and Jesus was taking them at their word.

Keep watch

Following hot on the heels of chapter 13, Jesus' command to the disciples to keep awake seems particularly important. As we saw in that chapter, the repeated refrain was 'keep watch, keep alert, keep awake': this was how the disciples would cope with the catastrophe that was heading their way. Here, they had their first opportunity to demonstrate that they understood Jesus' message ... but they fell asleep three times.

This situation is even more striking if they thought they were about to fight shoulder to shoulder with Jesus against the Roman army (necessitating the bringing of a sword; see 14.47). If this was the scenario they had imagined, then they should have been standing guard, ready for action. Instead, they fell asleep three times.

'Abba, Father ... remove this cup'

Other than his cry from the cross, this is the only occasion when the words of a prayer of Jesus are recorded in Mark. From 1.35 and 6.46, we know that he prayed but not what he said.

Much has been made over the years of Jesus' addressing God as *Abba*. Although God was sometimes referred to as 'the Father' or described as the Father of the whole people – 'Yet, O LORD, you are our Father; we are the clay, and you are our potter; we are all the work of your hand' (Isa. 64.8) – what is new here is his addressing God as 'my Father' directly (something Jesus also encouraged his followers to do in the Lord's Prayer; see Matt. 6.9–13; Luke 11.2–4).

In the past, it has often been claimed that *Abba* means 'Daddy', but most scholars today would argue that it does not. In Western culture, intimate relationships are often informal as opposed to other relationships that are distant and formal. In Jesus' day relationships could certainly be intimate but would never be informal (this would go against honouring one's father and mother). As a result, we should view *Abba* as an intimate but formal term of address: 'My Father'.

One of the most important features of Jesus' prayer is that he brought his anxiety and sorrow to God; nevertheless, he understood that, ultimately, God's will must be done. In contrast to Jesus' teaching on prayer in 11.20–25, this makes clear that God won't necessarily answer any old prayer; he responds only to those prayers that accord with his will.

'The spirit ... is willing, but the flesh is weak'

Jesus' response to the disciples' sleep is very understanding. He recognizes that they would have liked to stay awake; indeed, the word *prothumos* even suggests that they were eager or zealous to do so. Their bodies just let them down.

Sinners

It is striking that Jesus described those arresting him as 'sinners'. In 2.15–16, sinners are described, along with tax collectors (see p. 65), as outcasts. The chief priests, whose soldiers had come to arrest Jesus, would be the first to avoid the company of sinners. For Jesus to now describe them as sinners meant that the rules of the upside-down kingdom were truly in full force.

Mark 14.43–51: Jesus' arrest

The action that carries us forward to the point of Jesus' death now begins to pick up pace. As soon as Jesus had announced that his betrayer was at hand, Judas arrived and chaos ensued. Mark's account, in particular, gives a sense of the confusion and terror of the scene.

Links backwards

- Judas' arrival was apparently foreseen by Jesus in Mark 14.42. It isn't clear whether it was because he could see lights in the distance or because he was in such control of the situation that he knew what was about to happen.
- Jesus predicted that the disciples would all desert him (11.27), which became true here.

Links forwards

- It is only much later that we discover that not everyone left Jesus alone. After Jesus' death, we find out that his female disciples had remained and stayed, even if at a distance (15.40–41).

Interesting words ...

- v. 43: *crowd*. Through the rest of Mark, the crowd (*ochlos*) has been a positive, if slightly passive, group. The people are amazed by Jesus; they flock to hear him and to be healed by him, but they are not at all antagonistic. Here, the term is used much more negatively.
- vv. 43 and 48: *swords and clubs*. A *machaira* was a Roman short sword or dagger; a *xulon* was a piece of wood, but the word could also refer to a club.
- v. 43: *the chief priests, the scribes and the elders*. As in 11.27, the three types of members of the Sanhedrin are mentioned here.
- v. 44: *sign*. This is not the word *semeion* used to describe a sign from heaven but a *susēmon*: a non-verbal signal.
- vv. 44–45: *kiss; kissed*. The verb *phileō* means 'to love' but can also mean 'to kiss'. As we know, Judas has given a non-verbal signal, so we can assume 'kiss' is meant here. Nevertheless, the resonance of *phileō* here is strong. Judas employs a sign of genuine love to betray Jesus. The second time the word appears, it is translated from *kataphileō*, which more explicitly means 'kiss'.
- v. 44: *under guard*. The adverb *asphalōs* means 'safely' or 'securely'.
- v. 47: *drew*. The verb *spaō* refers specifically to drawing a sword; lest there be any doubt, the following word indicates what kind of sword: a *machaira*.
- v. 48: *bandit*. The word *lēstēs* has political overtones, especially in the time of Jesus. It refers to a rebel or revolutionary.

- v. 49: *fulfilled*. The verb *plēroō* means 'to fill' or 'to complete'.
- v. 50: *deserted; fled*. The verb *aphiēmi* means 'to abandon' and *pheugō* 'to flee', 'to escape danger' or 'to take flight'.
- v. 51: *following*. The verb *sunkolouthō* (connected to *akolouthō*) means 'to follow with' or 'accompany'.
- v. 51: *wearing nothing but a linen cloth*. Literally, 'dressed by wrapping (*peribalō*) in a linen cloth (*sindōn*) on a naked body (*gumnos*)'.

A crowd with swords and clubs

Luke says that the crowd that appeared included soldiers from the temple (Luke 22.47, 52); John writes that they came with a cohort and a military tribune (John 18.3), as well as people from the chief priests and Pharisees. Mark, however, just refers to the crowd as armed. This is clearly to indicate the shift in mood: the 'crowd' was no longer amazed and astounded or cheering and supportive (Mark 11.1–11): it was now something altogether darker and more menacing.

A kiss

Given Jesus' notoriety during the preceding week, it is a little surprising that he had to be identified by Judas. However, it was now dark and the crowd had Judas to hand, so absolute identification was clearly sensible. Beyond this, a kiss was unremarkable: it was a usual way of greeting an honoured guest (see Luke 7.45). Judas' use of 'Rabbi' was likewise unremarkable. In Mark, Peter had twice addressed Jesus as 'Rabbi' (9.5; 11.21); and Bartimaeus' had called him *Rabbouni*.

Slave of the high priest

Of all the Gospels, Mark's account gives the fewest details about the severing of the slave's ear. Luke and Matthew indicate that the person who cut off the ear was one of Jesus' disciples (Matt. 26.51; Luke 22.49); John names Peter as the culprit and the slave as Malchus (John 18.10). Were it not for the information in the other Gospels, we might, from Mark's account, imagine the man with the sword to be a bystander. It has the effect of downgrading the event to a casual detail.

This action contributes to the sense of chaos and terror surrounding Jesus' arrest in Mark's Gospel. A crowd arrived fully armed; Jesus was seized; someone was injured; the disciples ran away, as did a young man wearing only a linen cloth. The story seems jumbled and chaotic, which appears to be the point.

A young man in a linen cloth

The character that elicits the most curiosity is the young man in 'a linen cloth on his naked body'. It raises so many questions that it is hard to know where to begin.

Most scholarly discussions focus on the young man's identity. These can be split into three main groups.

1 Characters known to us from elsewhere in the New Testament: John Mark (the author of the Gospel, mentioned in Acts 12.12, 25); the beloved disciple of the fourth Gospel; Lazarus, the brother of Mary and Martha; James, the brother of Jesus and, later, the leader of the Jerusalem Church; the young man from the tomb at the Resurrection (Mark 16.5) and the rich man of Mark 10.17–31.
2 Other characters unknown from the New Testament: an unnamed follower of Jesus or a local person not otherwise mentioned.
3 A character symbolizing the risen Christ or baptismal candidates shedding their baptismal garments.

The key issue that rules out a number of options is the fact that the young man was clothed only in a sheet. Anyone who would otherwise have been at the Last Supper or elsewhere is thereby ruled out. It is hard not to be attracted to the, admittedly, romantic notion that this was the author of the Gospel, providing himself with a small but wry cameo role; his genuinely meant attempt to accompany Jesus ended in failure. This does not explain why he had no clothes on, though, and it remains a tantalizing mystery requiring the use of our imaginations to answer it.

Mark 14.53–65: Jesus' first trial (before the Sanhedrin)

In Mark's Gospel, there are two trials: one before the Sanhedrin and one before Pilate (15.1–15); these are positioned around Peter's trial in the courtyard. We pay a lot of attention to Peter's failure here, but it is worth balancing that with the observation that he tried so hard not to run away. Having said that, Mark's setting of Peter's denial between Jesus' arrest and trial makes Peter's disavowal of Jesus even more stark.

Links backwards

- Two of Jesus' predictions of death noted that he would be rejected by the chief priests, scribes and elders (Mark 8.31) or handed over to them (10.33) and spat on (10.34).

- Jesus' many conflicts with different members of Jewish authorities, whether scribes, Pharisees or, more recently, the Sanhedrin, come to a head in this passage.

Links forwards

- The contrast between Jesus' 'trial' and Peter's 'trial' (14.66–72) is noticeable. Jesus was on trial for his life; Peter only feared that he might be but faced the challenge much less well.
- Peter is said here to be warming himself by the light (see p. 317), this means that he is easily recognized by the slave in the next passage (14.66–72).

Interesting words ...

- v. 53: *took*. The verb *apagō* means 'to lead away'. Along with the verb *paradidōmi*, this emphasized that Jesus, from now on, had lost all control over where he went (though not, of course, over who he was, which later becomes clear).
- v. 54: *courtyard*. An *aulē* was a courtyard. While it could be located at the front of a house, many Roman villas had an *aulē* in the middle, open to the sky. It is not clear whether the high priest's house was built in the Roman style or not. If it was, Peter went right into the centre of the building.
- vv. 54 and 65: *guards*. The word *huperetēs* comes from a Greek ship in which there were two or three levels of rowers. A *hupēretēs* was an 'under-rower' and so a 'servant'. The use of the word indicates that Peter was with no one important.
- v. 54: *fire*. Crucially, Mark does not use the word 'fire' (*pur*) but 'light' (*phōs*). This becomes important in the next story, when Peter is recognized because he is in the light.
- v. 55: *whole council*. The Sanhedrin has been hinted at, until now, by the mention of its different members. Now for the first time, it is named (*sunedrion*). See the box, 'The elders and the Sanhedrin', on p. 261, for more on the Sanhedrin.
- vv. 55–57 and 59: *testimony*. The word *marturia* means 'witness' or 'testimony'. Someone who gave witness to their faith was a *marturos* ('martyr') because they were often killed as a result. 'Giving false witness' is *pseudomartureō*; and 'testify against' is *katamartureō*.
- v. 58: *made with hands*. The adjective *cheiropoiētos* could equally be translated 'handmade'. It is contrasted with *acheropoiētos*: 'not handmade'.
- v. 59: *agree*. The word *isos* means 'equal' or 'consistent'.
- v. 61: *silent*. *Siōpaō* means 'to keep silence'.
- v. 61: *Blessed One*. The adjective *eulogētos* refers to someone or something that is blessed or praised.

- v. 62: *I am. Egō eimi* is used here for Jesus' response when questioned about whether he was the Messiah.
- v. 63: *tore.* The verb *diaressō* refers to ripping one's clothes (often as a sign of penitence or mourning).
- v. 63: *clothes.* This is not the word 'cloak' (*himation*), which we have encountered many times before, but *chitōni* ('tunic'). It is interesting that we have the plural noun here, which may suggest that the high priest had more elaborate dress than most other people.
- v. 64: *decision.* The Greek is closer to 'What does it seem (*phainō*) to you?'
- v. 64: *condemned. Katakrinō* refers to passing a sentence.
- v. 65: *strike.* Literally, 'they took him with slaps' (*rhapisma*, which can refer to a range of actions, including beating, slapping, whipping, and so on).

All the chief priests, elders and scribes

What Mark probably means by 'all' is the whole Sanhedrin (he refers to the whole Sanhedrin in verse 55), gathered together to give a verdict. It may not have been the whole council of 71 members: a quorum for a legislative decision was 23.

The high priest during this period was Caiaphas, the son-in-law of Annas (see the box, 'The high priests/chief priests', on p. 258). Although he isn't named in Mark, both Matthew and John name him. Like most high priests, he was a Sadducee and was the high priest from AD 18 to 37. This was quite a long tenure for high priests at the time, which suggests that he worked well with the Roman governor (Pontius Pilate). He was removed from office by Pilate's successor Vitellius in AD 37.

Testimony

The striking feature of verse 55 is that the trial verdict had already been decided (to put Jesus to death) even if the charge had not yet been formulated. A trial such as this was not in and of itself problematic; but the fact that the verdict had been reached without a charge, that it was happening at night and (if Mark's timings are to be believed) during a festival made the whole thing irregular in the extreme.

Despite this, we should note that there was some attempt to follow procedure: *m. Sanhedrin* 4.5—5.4 describes how a cross-examination should take place for a capital trial. The fact that the witnesses' testimonies didn't agree was probably exposed by the cross-examination process. Although Mark doesn't say so explicitly, the attempt to follow the usual practice of cross-examination shone light on the irregularity of the proceedings.

The presence of false witnesses, ready and willing to testify about Jesus, indicated that the chief priests had been laying a plan of what they would do once Jesus was arrested. The implication is that they had sent out spies to listen to Jesus so they could build a case against him.

'We heard him say …'

The specific charge recorded against Jesus was that he said he would demolish the temple. This was a half-truth. His driving out of money changers threatened the temple and its livelihood; and in 13.2, he did say, as he was leaving the temple, that it would be torn down but not that he would do it. It is quite easy to imagine, however, that someone who overheard Jesus as he left the temple would easily arrive at that conclusion and use it to accuse him.

Jesus was silent

A contrast between Jesus' demeanour and Peter's in the following story was that Jesus was completely silent, until forced to speak, whereas Peter spoke as soon as he was questioned. Jesus' stillness, emphasized by the word *siōpaō* ('to keep silence'), is conspicuous. Even though he had been 'handed over' by Judas and he no longer had any say in what would happen to him, he chose silence as his most active means of resisting what was going on.

'Are you the Messiah?'

It seems the high priest intervened in the trial to bring the charge he had decided to lay at Jesus' door: not the destruction of the temple but Jesus' claim to be the Messiah.

In Matthew and Luke, Jesus' answer to the high priest was much more equivocal: 'You have said so' (Matt. 26.64) or 'You say that I am' (Luke 22.70); but in Mark, Jesus' answer is clear 'I am'.

The verses that Jesus quotes are a combination of Daniel 7.13 and Psalm 110.1.

Mark 14.62	Daniel 7.13–14	Psalm 110.1
'You will see the Son of Man seated at the right hand of the Power' and 'coming with the clouds of heaven'.	I saw one like a human being coming with the clouds of heaven. And he came to the Ancient One and was presented before him. To him was given dominion and glory and kingship.	The LORD says to my lord, 'Sit at my right hand until I make your enemies your footstool.'

Here are a few comments to help what Jesus said make sense.

- The 'Power' was a common alternative description for God.
- Sitting at the right hand of the person with power marked someone out as having immense status.
- Mark 14 appears to imagine a scene shortly after the Son of Man had been given dominion, in Daniel 7.13, and was seated on the throne with God.

In other words, Jesus went straight from agreeing that he was the Messiah – which, as we have seen, was not necessarily a divine claim – to stating that he would be seen sitting at God's right hand on his throne, receiving dominion, glory and kingship. A simple claim to be the Messiah would not have caused so much trouble, even though the high priest and Sanhedrin wouldn't have liked it very much.

Blasphemy

What did Jesus say that was blasphemous? This question was a crucial one in this trial. The high priest seemed to believe that Jesus blasphemed not just with words but also with actions.

What was to happen when someone had been found guilty of blasphemy is explored in *m. Sanhedrin* 7.5. First, the court was to be cleared. Then the eldest of the witnesses was to be asked to repeat exactly what the accused had said. This was not necessary at Jesus' trial, as the court all heard what Jesus himself said, which the high priest deemed to be blasphemous. The Mishnah passage goes on to say that when the judges had heard the report, they were to 'stand on their feet and make a tear in their garments, as an act of mourning for the desecration of the honour of God. And they do not ever fully stitch it back together again.'

The challenge was to identify Jesus' blasphemy. It explicitly states, in *m. Sanhedrin* 7.5, that saying the name of God is blasphemous; but Jesus clearly did not do that. He said 'the Power' instead of 'God' when he quoted the Old Testament. What Jesus said was clearly thought to be close enough to warrant the charge of blasphemy. This suggests, therefore, that it was Jesus' claim to sit at the right hand of God that triggered the accusation. Claiming equal authority with God would be deemed close enough to blasphemy for the judgement.

Some began to spit on him ...

The shocking element of Mark's account here is that the Sanhedrin began to abuse Jesus, which was then continued by the servants or guards. This serves to communicate the level of hatred and/or fear that had built up against him. Rather than being a dispassionate, well-executed trial, this hearing degenerated into a circus of spitting, mocking and beating.

Mark 14.66–72: Peter denied Jesus (Peter's trial)

Mark's placing of this story between Jesus' two trials indicates that we are to view what happens to Peter as his being on trial. Somewhat inevitably, Peter conducted himself much less well than Jesus, even though the stakes were lower. Although we, the readers, have been prepared by Jesus' warning that Peter will deny him, it makes the story no less affecting.

Links backwards

- Jesus warned Peter that he would deny him in Mark 14.26–31. His warning now comes true.
- Peter warmed himself by the light (*phōs*; 14.54), which means it was easier for other people to recognize him.

Links forwards

- In Mark's very short resurrection narrative, the young man in the empty tomb tells the women to 'go, tell his disciples and Peter' (16.7). Special mention is made of Peter to ensure that everyone, including Peter, knows that he had been forgiven.

Interesting words ...

- v. 66: *below*. The simple word *katō* indicates that Jesus' trial is in an upstairs room overlooking the courtyard. Peter is in the courtyard below.
- vv. 66 and 69: *servant-girls; servant-girl*. A *paidiskē* is a 'slave girl'. The use of this word could suggest that she is young (*paidiskē* is a diminutive); but it could simply mean a slave of any age, as slaves were often referred to as children.
- v. 67: *stared*. *Emblepō* means 'to look intently'; it has been used a number of times before in Mark to imply a long, hard stare (see 8.25; 10.21, 27).
- v. 67: *from Nazareth*. *Nazarēnos* refers to being from Nazareth; so Jesus is the one from Nazareth (as opposed to the many other Jesuses there were around at the time).
- vv. 68, 70 and 72: *denied; deny*. The verb *arneomai* means 'to deny', 'to renounce knowledge of' or 'to renounce relationship with'. When the verb is used in verse 70, it is in the imperfect, with the implication that Peter continues denying that he knows Jesus.
- v. 68: *know or understand*. The two verbs used are *oida* ('know', 'comprehend' or 'understand', which is used again in verse 71) and *epistamai* ('be aware of',

'possess information about' or 'have insight into'). The two verbs indicate that Peter is saying he has no idea what the slave girl is talking about. Given the emphasis on understanding throughout the Gospel, we might agree that Peter does not understand.

- v. 68: *forecourt*. The *proaulion* refers to the space before the *aulē*; so the gateway, the entrance, is what is being referred to.
- vv. 69–70: *bystanders*. *Paristēmi* refers to 'standing near'.
- v. 71: *curse; swore an oath*. *Anathemetizō* means 'to curse' or 'bind oneself with a curse', and *omnuō* means 'to swear by something'. Again, the two verbs together give emphasis.
- v. 72: *remembered*. *Anamimenskō* means 'to be reminded' or 'to remember'.

She stared at him

Mark does not tell us where the female slave had encountered Jesus before; but, since Jesus had been teaching in the temple for most of the week, and had clearly been notorious for doing so, she had probably encountered him there.

We are told in 14.54 that Peter was warming himself by the 'light', which means that we are ready for him to be recognized. After the first moment of recognition, Peter moved to the entrance way (where there was much less light) in the hope that, there, he would not be quite so visible.

The cock crowed (the first time)

One of the themes that runs throughout Mark's Gospel is that events happen more than once, in the hope that the disciples might learn an important lesson. The cock crowing here, after Peter's first denial, lends the hope that he might remember what Jesus had said and react differently. But as so often in the Gospel, this did not happen. It was only after the second crow, when it was too late, that he remembered and wept.

Bystanders

The ripple of questions in this story hinted at Peter's greatest fear. The first question (which elicited the first denial) was to him alone. The second question was to those standing near Peter and the third was from the crowd of bystanders. The suggestion of the story is that this ripple of questioning was going to spread among all those who were present, possibly even to the high priest himself; and Peter, in his terror, denied any knowledge of Jesus in an attempt to shut it down.

He cursed and swore an oath

Peter wasn't just producing a string of expletives here. The word indicates that he was calling down curses in his vehemence. The question is whom was he cursing? Some commentators believe that he was cursing himself, but the word used does not imply a reflexive mood; it is therefore probable that he was cursing Jesus. The emotional impact of this is stark: he went from declaring undying love and support for Jesus (14.31) to cursing him in front of strangers. No wonder he broke down and wept when he realized what he had done.

Mark 15.1–15: Jesus' second trial (before Pilate) and the release of Barrabas

Jesus' trial before Pilate was relatively brief; but it was lengthened by the addition of the crowd's request for Pilate to let a prisoner go. Pilate's interest in freeing Jesus was quickly quelled by the crowd's desire for him to release Barabbas. In Mark, his efforts to free Jesus seem at best perfunctory (contrast the description here with Luke 23.18–25 or John 18.38—9.16) and he gave way to their wishes.

Links backwards

- The mention of the crowd here reminds us of the role of the crowd throughout Mark. For most of the Gospel, the people followed Jesus as a benign, amazed group. Now, they have changed nature entirely, calling for Jesus' death.
- This passage looks back both to Jesus' first trial (Mark 14.53–65) and to Peter's denial (14.66–72).

Links forwards

- The board that Pilate suspended on the cross, above Jesus' head, read, 'The King of the Jews' (15.25): the charge Jesus was accused of was the one declared at his Crucifixion.

Interesting words ...

- v. 1: *As soon as it was morning*. The Greek reads 'immediately (*euthus*) in the morning (*prōi*)'.
- v. 1: *consultation*. A *sumboulion* was a council or a decision to harm with

a plot: a conspiracy. It was last used in Mark 3.6, when the Pharisees and Herodians conspired against Jesus.

- v. 1: *handed ... over*. The word used here is the one for Judas' betraying Jesus (*paradidōmi*). See the box, 'Betrayed/handed over', on p. 211, for Mark's use of the verb.
- v. 4: *Have you no answer?* Greek can have double negatives in a way that standard English can't, so Pilate asked: 'Do you not answer nothing?'
- v. 5: *amazed*. Now Pilate was amazed. For more on Mark's use of different words for 'amaze', see the notes on 1.22 and 27 (pp. 41–2). The word used here is *thaumazō* ('wonder' or 'marvel at').
- v. 7: *rebels; insurrection*. Although the word *lēstēs* has been used before in Mark to refer to bandits, this is not the word used here. Mark uses *stasiastēs*, which refers to someone who stirs up sedition. In other words, Barabbas wasn't just a rebel: he was a rebel leader. It is connected to *stasis* ('revolt' or 'rebellion').
- v. 8: *came*. The word *anabainō* is used here; it means 'come up'. This makes sense as Herod's palace, where Pilate would have been staying, was built on a high point in the city.
- v. 8: *according to his custom*. Mark's syntax here is abbreviated. He clearly means to say 'as he always did for them' but says 'as (*kathōs*) he did (*poieō*) for them'.
- v. 10: *jealousy*. *Phthonos* refers to 'envy' or 'malice'. 'Malice' may be a better translation here. It is hard to see what the crowd would be envious of.
- v. 11: *stirred up*. The verb *anaseiō* means 'to incite an uproar'. In Jerusalem, during the festival, this verb had a particular resonance: uproars were often incited.
- v. 14: *asked*. The verb is simply *legō* ('said'); but it is in the imperfect, so probably implies 'kept on saying'.
- v. 15: *satisfy*. Translated more literally, it would say 'wanting (*boulomai*: 'desire' or 'wish') to do enough (*hikanos*: 'adequate' or 'what is sufficient') for the crowd'. It isn't quite 'satisfy'; rather it is closer to 'do enough to mollify them'.
- v. 15: *flogging*. The Latin word *flagellare* is the equivalent of the Greek word *phragelloō*. As its translation suggests, it means 'to beat with a whip'.

Held a consultation

It is not clear exactly what the chief priests, elders and scribes did the next morning. As noted in 'Interesting words' above, a *sumboulion* could be a council or it could mean to hatch a plot. As the sentence of death had apparently been passed the night before by the Sanhedrin, it might seem odd to call another council. However, if the meeting was irregular (as suggested above), then a formal council meeting to ratify the decision would have been required. Equally, they could just have been making a plan about what to do next. Both interpretations work here.

Handed him to Pilate

Pilate's official residence was in Caesarea Maritima, a Roman town about 75 miles north-west of Jerusalem on the Mediterranean coast. However, he would have taken up residence in Jerusalem, probably in Herod's Palace, during the Passover in an attempt to control the crowds.

Pontius Pilate

Pontius Pilate was the fifth governor of Judea (after Herod Archelaus was deposed; see the box, 'Herod Archelaus and the imposition of a poll tax', on p. 267) between approximately AD 26 and 36.

We get only the briefest of impressions of Pilate from Mark's account and not much more from the other Gospels. What we do glean, however, accords with what is known from elsewhere.

Pilate was renowned not only for his brutality but also for his self-preservation. Josephus tells, in his *Antiquities of the Jews* (18.3.2), of Pilate's using money from the temple treasury to build an aqueduct into the city. The inevitable riot that ensued was quelled by his sending troops, dressed as Jews, in among the rioters. The disguised soldiers then turned on the crowd with clubs. Although the date for this event isn't clear, it was probably somewhere between AD 26 and 30). In other words shortly, before the trial of Jesus.

Another account (*Ant.* 18.3.1) from the start of Pilate's time as governor, however, indicates that he was prepared to back down if it worked in his favour. He brought Roman standards into Jerusalem at night, so no one would see them; but when a large group of Jews protested and expressed their willingness to die as a result, he relented and removed the standards.

All this behaviour fits with what we see here. While Pilate didn't think Jesus was guilty, he didn't want to antagonize the Jewish leaders; so he sent Jesus to a gruesome death to preserve his own position.

King of the Jews

The 'blasphemy' that made the high priest rip his clothing was Jesus' claim of sitting at the right hand of God: this would have made no sense at all to Pilate as a crime. So the Sanhedrin translated it into a crime that would make sense to him: they accused Jesus of attempting to rival Caesar – hence the accusation 'King of the Jews'. Pilate's insistence that the crowd called Jesus their king (Mark 15.9, 12) indicates that it was what the Sanhedrin had told him. The obvious response of the crowd would have been to deny that Jesus was their king; but the hint of the memory of Jesus' entry into Jerusalem may have counteracted such a response.

Jesus' answer to Pilate causes considerable discussion. In contrast to his reply of 'I am' to the high priest's question about whether he was the Messiah, he responded to Pilate's query about his kingship with 'You say that I am.' This was neither a straight 'yes' nor a straight 'no'. The implication of it seems to be: 'In a way; but not in the way you are thinking.'

Following Pilate's question, the chief priests began accusing Jesus; but Mark doesn't tell us what they were accusing him of. In a way, Mark's account is right here. It doesn't really matter what the content of the accusation was: the chief priests' vehemence in doing so was what was important.

Pilate's amazement at Jesus' silence gives us an insight into how the word 'amaze' is used earlier in Mark. It implies that he was intrigued and surprised and wasn't quite sure what to make of it.

Pilate's custom to release prisoners

While there might have been a general custom to release prisoners during festivals, there is no evidence, in sources from the period, of a custom of Pilate releasing prisoners during festivals, particularly during the Passover. Neither is there any indication that Mark was aware of such a tradition. Interestingly, Josephus refers to Herod Archelaus releasing prisoners (*Jewish War* 2.4) when asked to do so. Given Pilate's self-interested tendency to act to keep people happy, it is not unlikely that he would have been tempted to do so when asked – especially if he might free an innocent man he did not want to crucify.

Mark's account of Pilate's attempt to release Jesus seems perfunctory. His three questions, however (repeated below), reveal a reasonable attempt by Pilate to let him go, especially since it was probable that Pilate kept on asking for information (see 'Interesting words', v. 14, on p. 319). These were the questions:

- 'Do you want me to release for you the King of the Jews?' (15.9)
- 'Then what do you wish me to do with the man you call the King of the Jews?' (15.12)
- 'Why, what evil has he done?' (15.14)

Pilate pressed the point as far as he could; but then he did what he usually did and opted for self-preservation.

Barabbas

The name 'Barabbas' seems to have been common at the time of Jesus. It is Aramaic and means son of (*bar*) either a teacher (*rabban*) or Abba (which was a well-known personal name during this period). Matthew tells us that Barabbas' forename was Jesus (Matt. 27.16), which introduces into the narrative a slight twist: one Jesus was freed while the other was killed.

Crowd

The return of the crowd at this point, in Mark, is significant. As noted above, the crowd followed Jesus for much of his Galilean ministry, amazed at what he did and taught (2.4, 13; 3.9, 20, 32; 4.1, 36; 5.21, 24, 27, 30, 31; 6.34, 45; 7.14, 17, 33; 8.1, 2, 6, 34, 35; 9.14, 15, 17, 25; 10.1, 46; 11.18, 32; 12.12, 37, 41). It is, of course, unlikely that the same people comprised the crowd in Galilee and in Jerusalem. The crowd, however, is so symbolic in Mark of those who followed Jesus as a large, amorphous group that its role can be seen as independent of its individual members.

It is interesting that the word 'crowd' is not used at Jesus' entry into Jerusalem. Instead, it was just the people who escorted him and followed him there. But then, in 14.43, the 'crowd' became dark and threatening, arriving to arrest Jesus. Here, in verses 8, 11 and 15, it sealed Jesus' fate by calling for his Crucifixion and the release of Barabbas. Its amazement, it seems, had been only skin deep.

After 15.15, the crowd is never seen in the narrative again.

Handed him over

Jesus was handed from Judas to the chief priests; from the chief priests to Pilate; he was then handed over for the final time 'to be crucified'. The chain that began with Judas reached its inevitable conclusion. Jesus was now to be crucified.

Mark 15.16–32: The mocking of Jesus from the courtyard to the cross

One of the key elements of Jesus' Crucifixion is that he was mocked: first at the end of the Sanhedrin trial, then at the end of Pilate's trial and finally on the cross itself.

One of the questions that often emerges is 'Who was responsible for Jesus' death?' Mark seems quite clear that the blame should be apportioned evenly. He makes it obvious that many were involved: Judas, the disciple who handed him over; the Sanhedrin, who were irritated by his criticism and afraid of the crowd's response; Peter, who distanced himself from Jesus at a crucial moment; the crowd, who called for his death; and Pilate, who was swayed by the crowd and acted against his better judgement. No one group or person is held up as more culpable than any other.

Links backwards

- James and John had asked Jesus in Mark 10.35–45 if they could sit at his right and left in his glory. There were two to whom this 'honour' was given but they were not James and John (15.27).
- The mocking of, and spitting on, Jesus was predicted (10.34; 14.65), along with his being flogged (15.15).
- The title 'King of the Jews' was the charge Pilate believed was brought against Jesus (15.2, 9).

Interesting words ...

- v. 16: *soldiers*. A *stratiōtēs* was a professional soldier. In this instance, the soldiers would have worked for the Roman army. Most Roman soldiers in Jerusalem would have been auxiliaries, recruited from Samaria and Syrian-Greek cities.
- v. 16: *courtyard*. This courtyard was not the previous one, which was in the high priest's house. This one was in the Praetorium.
- v. 16: *governor's headquarters*. *Praetorion*, rendered in English 'Praetorium', was the governor's headquarters, which were in Caesarea Maritima. So it is assumed that, while in Jerusalem for the Passover, Pilate made Herod Antipas' Jerusalem palace his headquarters.
- v. 16: *cohort*. The *speira* was a cohort: one tenth of a Roman legion, which was around 600 men.
- vv. 17 and 20: *clothed; stripped*. These words are opposites: *endiduskō* means 'to put on' and *ekduō* 'to take off'.
- vv. 17 and 20: *purple cloak*. *Porphura* refers to the murex shellfish, the purple dye extracted from the creatures and the cloth dyed with it.
- v. 17: *twisting ... thorns into a crown*. *Plekō* means 'to braid' or 'weave'. The word *akinthinos* refers to anything thorny and *stephanos* to a crown; so they 'braided a thorny crown'.
- v. 18: *saluting*. The last time a similar word was used was in 12.38 when Jesus said the scribes liked a 'greeting' in the marketplace. Here, the verb (*aspapazomai*: 'they greeted him') is used in a parody of respectful salutation.
- v. 18: *hail*. The verb *chairō* is the one the Angel Gabriel used to greet Mary in the annunciation (Luke 1.28). It can mean 'hail', 'greetings', 'rejoice' or even 'long live'.
- v. 19: *reed*. A *kalamos* was a thick reed or cane, sometimes a rod.
- v. 19: *spat*. The same word *emptuō* ('spit') is used for what the Sanhedrin did at the end of Jesus' trial.
- v. 19: *homage*. *Proskuneō* means 'giving homage', 'worshipping' or 'praying'.
- vv. 20 and 31: *mocking*. The same word, *empaizō*, is used for what the soldiers did in verse 20 and the chief priests in verse 31, which Jesus predicted in 10.34.
- v. 21: *compelled*. The verb *angareuō* refers to the ability given to Roman soldiers to compel service from passers-by, such as that referred to in Matthew

5.41 ('if anyone forces you to go one mile, go also the second mile'). In this case, the compelled service would have been even more alarming than usual.

- v. 21: *coming in from the country*. The Greek could mean 'arriving, for the first time, from the country' or 'coming back after going to the fields'. The word *agros* can mean either 'countryside' or 'field'.
- v. 23: *wine mixed with myrrh*. *Esmyrnismenos oinos*: 'wine flavoured or mixed with myrrh'. This suggests another mockery: the soldiers were pretending to give 'fine wine' to the 'king'.
- v. 24: *divided*. *Diamerizomai* means 'to parcel out' or 'to distribute'.
- v. 24: *lots*. A *klēros* was a specially marked stick, pebble or shard of pottery that would be thrown for making decisions.
- v. 25: *nine o'clock*. The Greek phrase 'third hour' (*hora tritos*) refers to a particular time of day. For more on times of day in the ancient world, see the box, 'Roman hours', on p. 326.
- v. 26: *inscription of the charge*. An *epigraphē* is an 'inscription' or 'written notice'; the *aitia* is the 'charge' or 'accusation'.
- v. 27: *bandits*. *Lēstēs* is used again here, not the word *stasiastēs* used of Barabbas.
- v. 29: *derided*. The word is *blasphemeō*, 'speak ill about' or 'speak profanely about'.
- v. 29: *Aha!* The word is *oua*, pronounced 'oo-a'.
- vv. 29 and 31: *save*. The word used throughout Mark for Jesus' acts to save and heal people (*sōzō*) is now used to deride him here.
- v. 32: *taunted*. The word used to describe the bandits' tone is *oneidizo*, which means 'to insult'.

They mocked him

The content of the mocking has woven within it a strong strand of irony. The soldiers dressed Jesus as a king; the chief priests mocked him for being the King of Israel, yet not coming down from the cross; and those passing by mocked him for his apparent inability to save himself. All these different kinds of mocking highlight how far any of these people were from gleaning the truth. If they had understood it, they would have known that it was precisely in not coming down from the cross and saving himself that Jesus' true power could be seen. His quiet dignity in the face of brutality marked him out as the King. His dying and not saving himself was what would save the whole world. Those who thought they had the upper hand were, in effect, mocking themselves.

The soldiers

As noted in 'Interesting words', the soldiers to whom Jesus was handed over were unlikely to be Roman citizens. Rather, they were probably auxiliaries drawn from local populations who were opposed to the Jews; so they probably came from Samaria and Syrian-Greek cities. This fact would make their attitude even more vicious to Jews who were about to be crucified.

Dressed him as a king

The soldiers dressed Jesus up as a king. It is unlikely, however, that they had a genuine purple robe to dress him in, as such garments were immensely valuable in the first century. During this period, the colour purple ranged from Tyrian purple (made from murex shellfish from the region of Tyre, which produced a deep indigo) to Turkish red (made from the madder root, found in the region of Lydia in Asia Minor, which produced a much redder shade). Matthew suggests that they used a red soldier's cloak (Matt. 27.28), which would make sense under the circumstances.

The whole scene is close to mimicking a Roman triumph, in which the emperor would have worn a purple robe and a laurel wreath on his head, and would have been greeted by the crowd with *Ave, Caesar, Imperator!* ('Hail, Caesar, Emperor!'). The irony is that Pilate had allowed Jesus' to be condemned for purportedly claiming to rival Caesar's power and then the soldiers 'mocked' Jesus as though he were, in fact, Caesar.

Mark's specific statement that Jesus was reclothed before being led to his Crucifixion has caused comment among scholars. People were usually crucified naked to compound their humiliation. Some wonder whether clothing Jesus for his journey to the cross was a concession by Pilate to Jewish scruples about nudity.

When Jesus arrived at the scene of the Crucifixion, Mark records that he was offered wine mixed with myrrh. Myrrh was not known in this period for its painkilling properties. Instead, it was often added to wine to enhance its flavour, turning ordinary wine into 'fine wine'. It seems likely, therefore, that this act was a continuation of the mockery: 'Fine wine for His Majesty.'

Simon of Cyrene

Victims of crucifixion were usually forced to carry the cross beam (in Latin, the *patibulum*), which would, at the site of crucifixion, be fixed to the upright pole (in Latin, the *palus*). Jesus was unable to carry the beam all the way, which suggests the poor state he was in after the beating. As a rule, Romans preferred condemned men to be in a good state so that their crucifixion would last as long as possible, making it a more effective warning to passers-by. People could take as many as four days to die if they were particularly strong.

Cyrene

Cyrene was a Greek city in the region of Cyrenaica in what is now Libya, north Africa. It was part of the Pentapolis, which were five cities of influence during this period. It was ruled, together with Crete, as a single province. It was well known for its Socratic philosophy and was the home of the Cyrenaics, a Greek school of philosophers.

It had a large Jewish population (around 100,000 Jews settled there in the third century BC), so Simon could have been a Jew who had come to Jerusalem for the Passover. After Jesus' death, Cyrene became a vibrant hub of early Christianity.

It is noticeable that Alexander and Rufus are named in a way that implies they were Christians who were known to Mark's first readers.

The phrase 'coming in from the country [or field]' is intriguing. If Simon were Jewish, he should not have gone outside the 2,000-cubit limit for travel during a sabbath or festival. This might mean that he was not Jewish, and was able to travel as far as he liked, or that he had not been very far outside the city.

Golgotha

The Aramaic for 'skull' was *gulgultā*, of which 'Golgotha' may be a version. Alternatively, the Aramaic *gol goatha* could mean 'mount of execution' and, therefore, be a description rather than a place name. The name Calvary comes from the Latin *calvariae*, which means 'of the skull'. Where this 'Place of the Skull' was is not really known, though many people accept the traditional site (now under the Church of the Holy Sepulchre) as the probable location.

Crucifixions were usually held on thoroughfares to be visible to passers-by (to deter them from suffering the same fate). Mark also implies that this was the case since, in verse 29, he mentions 'those who passed by'.

Roman hours

The Roman day was split into 12 hours, beginning at 6 a.m. and finishing at 6 p.m.; the night was likewise split into 12 hours, with four watches of three hours each.

The lengths of hours depended on the time of year. In winter, the hours were closer to 45 minutes; and in summer, they were nearer to 75. The point was that they were evenly split throughout the hours of daylight.

The third hour (around 9 a.m.) was when legal proceedings would often begin; the sixth hour (noon) was associated with a break (lunch and a siesta for the wealthy); and the ninth hour, mid afternoon, was when Romans often went to the baths; the twelfth hour was the end of the day.

Mark carefully records Jesus' Crucifixion using Roman time periods. His account begins at the third hour, with darkness coming at the sixth hour and Jesus dying at the ninth hour. Joseph of Arimathea came to bury the body once it was evening, which implies he arrived at the twelfth hour.

(Note that John's timing disagrees with Mark's, not just on the day (which, in John, is the day before the Passover) but also on the hour: John says noon was when the Crucifixion began.)

They crucified him

As is so often the case, the stripped-back detail of Mark's description adds to its pathos. There were numerous different ways of crucifying people: head down or up; impaled on a stake; or hung from a crossbeam, fastened with nails or ropes. Mark gives almost no details beyond the fact that Simon carried the 'cross', the implication being that this is crucifixion by attachment to a crossbeam. It is John's Gospel that supplies the information, so important in Christian tradition, that Jesus was nailed to the cross (John 20.25).

The plaque, which John says was fixed to the cross (19.19), is just described as an inscription in Mark, and he doesn't give its position. There is evidence that the Romans made plaques to hang round the victims' necks, identifying their crimes for passers-by. It is possible that Mark has this in mind here.

One on his right and one on his left

The two crucified with Jesus are described as 'bandits', *lēstēs*. Since the word used for Barabbas was so different (*stasiastēs*: 'someone who stirs up a rebellion'), it isn't clear whether they were associated with him. It could be that Barabbas was the rebel leader and they the simple 'followers'; alternatively, they might have had no connection to him at all.

Whoever they were, they received the 'reward' requested five chapters before by James and John (10.35–45), who, ironically, did not even stay to observe the 'prize' that they seemed to want so much.

Mockery

Three groups of people mocked Jesus while he hung on the cross.

1. Passers-by. Presumably these were people walking along the road who saw Jesus on the cross, as the Romans intended them to.

   It is interesting that the word used for what they were doing is *blasphemeō*. When used of God, it refers to speaking profanely of sacred things; but when used regarding people, it is to insult or slander. The question is whether Mark is hinting that while they thought they were insulting a human being, they were really blaspheming God.

   Their mockery cites the charge against Jesus by false witnesses at his trial, which implies that the charge was common knowledge in Jerusalem.
2. Chief priests and the scribes. The reference to the Messiah by the chief priests and scribes implies that they viewed the Messiah's role as that of saving the nation (to be King of Israel). That Jesus could not even save himself was taken as evidence that his being the Messiah was proved ridiculous.

   It is worth noting that 'King of Israel' is a phrase the leaders would have been much more likely to use than 'King of the Jews'. That other title certainly seems like a line fed to the Romans by way of a charge.
3. Those crucified with him. We aren't told what those being crucified said, unlike in Luke's Gospel, and are left simply with the statement that they insulted him.

The verbs describing the mockery of the three groups are all in the imperfect (a tense that suggests continuous action), so the implication is that it went on for some time. According to Mark's careful timings, there were at least three hours for this to take place.

Mark 15.33–39: Jesus' death ... the moment of revelation

These six verses, to some extent, seem to be the moment we have been waiting for from the beginning of the Gospel. In them, the arc of Mark's story, begun at Jesus' baptism, reaches fruition and all is revealed at last.

Links backwards and forwards

- The question posed by the disciples in Mark 4.41 ('Who then is this?') is finally and definitively answered here by the centurion.

- Jesus' predictions in 8.31—9.1; 9.30–32 and 10.32–34 converge in this passage, with the hint to us, the readers, that this is not the end of the story: the Resurrection is still to come.
- Jesus' baptism (1.9–11) and Transfiguration (9.2–7) now meet in this passage, with a revelation of a significantly different, yet strikingly similar, kind.
- The references to expectations about Elijah's return (6.15; 8.28; 9.11–13) are highlighted again at Jesus' death.

Interesting words ...

- v. 33: *noon; three o'clock*. 'Sixth hour' (*hora hektos*) and 'ninth hour' (*hora enatos*). For an explanation of the times, see the box, 'Roman hours', on p. 326.
- v. 34: *cried*. Elsewhere in the Gospel, Mark uses the word *krazō* for 'cry'; but here, he uses the word *boaō*, which is more like a 'roar' or 'howl'.
- vv. 34 and 37: *a loud voice; a loud cry*. Jesus gave two loud (*megas*) sounds (*phonē*) from the cross. *Phonē* most often means the sound of a voice, hence a 'cry'.
- v. 34: *Eloi, Eloi, lema sabachthani*. Jesus quotes Psalm 22.1 in Aramaic here. The mishearing of what Jesus said was dependent on how his words sounded (and on the witnesses not hearing very distinctly). It was not based on the way it is written: *Eloi* ('my God') and *lian* (Elijah) are not very similar.
- v. 36: *a sponge with sour wine*. *Spongos* was a 'sponge' (or referred to any spongy substance) and *oxos* was 'poor wine' or 'vinegar'.
- v. 36: *stick*. The same word (*kalamos*) is used for the reed with which the soldiers struck Jesus in 15.19.
- vv. 37 and 39: *breathed his last*. The verb *ekpneō* means simply 'breathe out' or 'expire'.
- v. 38: *curtain*. The *katapetasma* was a 'curtain' or 'veil'. The word was in general use, so 'of the temple' was added to identify which one. While we assume that it was the veil separating the holy of holies from the holy place, it might in fact have been any curtain in the temple.
- v. 38: *torn*. *Schizō* is used only one other time in Mark: for the tearing apart of the heavens at Jesus' baptism (1.10).
- v. 38: *from top to bottom*. *Anōthen* ('from top' or 'from above') to *katō* ('downwards' or 'below').
- v. 39: *Truly*. The centurion doesn't use Jesus' word *amēn*, which is Aramaic or Hebrew, but *alēthōs* ('actually', 'in truth', 'in reality').
- v. 39: *God's Son*. No 'the' is used here (*hios theou*). For more on this, see 'God's Son', on p. 334.

Darkness

In the Old Testament, darkness is often associated with God's judgement. For example, Isaiah 13.9–10 says, 'See, the day of the LORD comes ... the stars of the heavens and their constellations will not give their light; the sun will be dark at its rising, and the moon will not shed its light.' (For similar descriptions, see also Joel 2.10; 3.14–15; Amos 5.18–20.) Equally in Greek and Roman tradition, darkness occurred when great men died. For example, in the *Alexander Romance*, which relates legends about Alexander the Great (written around the second century AD), it says that the sky became dark when he died.

Since no one at the Crucifixion understood the significance of the darkness (or at least not in a way that is recorded), it was clearly something designed to indicate to us, the readers, that a momentous event was taking place. God's judgement was being revealed, and a great man was about to die.

A loud cry

Jesus' silence throughout his trial and mockery makes his loud cries all the more noticeable. The first included the quotation from Psalm 22 and the second happened immediately before his death. The verb 'cry' or 'shout out', together with the loud sound (see 'Interesting words', vv. 34 and 37, on p. 329), stresses the shift from his absolute silence to his anguished cries. Before was the time for silence and stillness; now is the time for a loud shout (accompanied by the tearing of the temple veil; see 'The curtain of the temple', on p. 332). The world will never be the same again and Jesus' cry heralds as much.

Jesus' first cry is the first verse of Psalm 22, cited in Aramaic ('*Eloi, Eloi, lema sabachthani*'), which is unusual enough to deserve comment. Although Aramaic was the everyday language of Galilee and Judea in this period, the Scriptures were still largely read in Hebrew. The exceptions were the Targums: these were translations and paraphrases of the Hebrew Scriptures into Aramaic for those who did not know Hebrew (though Jesus' quotation is not the same as that in the existing *Targum of Psalms* that we still have). It appears, therefore, that Jesus was translating the Scriptures into his heart language or mother tongue at a time of great stress and distress. It seems crucially important that Jesus used the Scriptures as a source of solace (much as many people do today) and that, when doing so, he put them into the language he knew best.

Psalm 22 and Mark's Crucifixion account

Verse 1 is not the only verse from Psalm 22 cited in Mark's Crucifixion account. Two other verses were also alluded to earlier in the story: verses 7 and 18.

- Mark 15.24 – 'divided his clothes among them, casting lots to decide what each should take' – recalls Psalm 22.18: 'They divide my clothes among themselves, and for my clothing they cast lots.'
- Mark 15.29 – 'Those who passed by derided him, shaking their heads and saying ...' – is reminiscent of Psalm 22.7: 'All who see me mock at me; they make mouths at me, they shake their heads.'
- That Mark 15.34 quotes verse 1 of Psalm 22 points to the citing of the psalm in reverse, from the end to the beginning.
- One of the important features of Hebrew thinking and citing of the Scriptures is that, when the first word or verse of something is quoted, the whole is often intended. So, for example, the names of the books of the Hebrew Scriptures are the first word (in Hebrew) of that book. So if I were to refer to *Bereshit*, I would be indicating the book called Genesis in English Bibles by using the first word it contains.
- Jesus' quotation of the first verse of Psalm 22 undoubtedly speaks of his deep desolation and feeling of abandonment. But those of us who are reading this account have the advantage of distance (and the knowledge of the Resurrection). We can also see that Psalm 22 ends hopefully, with the idea that 'All the ends of the earth shall remember and turn to the LORD' (22.27) and that 'Posterity will serve him; future generations will be told about the Lord, and proclaim his deliverance to a people yet unborn, saying that he has done it' (22.30–31).
- In other words, reading Psalm 22, woven backwards through the Crucifixion account, shines the merest glimmer of hope on the scene of desolation before us. Psalm 22.1 is not the end of the story any more than Jesus' death was. It, therefore, comes as much less of a surprise when the centurion, a representative of those from the ends of the earth, declared who Jesus was.

'He is calling for Elijah'

It is hard to see how Jesus' words in Aramaic caused people to think he was calling for Elijah: the sound is entirely different, which probably explains why Matthew changed the first two words into Hebrew – *Eli, Eli* – before continuing with the Aramaic (Matt. 27.46).

There was a widespread expectation that Elijah would return before God's intervention in the world (see Mark 6.15; 8.28; 9.11–13), which was inspired by Elijah's ascent into heaven in a whirlwind (meaning that he could descend again at any moment) and Malachi's prophecy: 'Lo, I will send you the prophet Elijah before the great and terrible day of the Lord comes' (Mal. 4.5). This implies that, while the bystanders had sided with the chief priests, they were entirely open to one last miracle. And until the moment of Jesus' death, there was the hope that, just maybe, Elijah would return to kickstart God's climactic intervention in the world.

In verse 23, the mention of wine flavoured with myrrh was probably a continuation of the parody of kingship, with the soldiers providing 'fancy wine' for the 'king'. The wine might also have been offered out of a genuine curiosity about whether Elijah would return. The 'poor wine' was cheap, probably on hand to sustain the soldiers watching the Crucifixion, and would have been thirst quenching. It was offered less from compassion for a dying man than from curiosity and in the hope of witnessing one last 'miracle'.

Breathed his last

The Greek euphemism for death is very similar to our own. The word 'expire' comes from Latin *exspirare* ('to breathe out'), which would be a direct translation of *ekpneō*. The Greek verb is connected to *pneuma* ('spirit' or 'breath') and does have the hint of the spirit leaving the body, with the breath.

Both John 19.30, 'It is finished,' and Luke 23.46, 'Father, into your hands I commend my spirit,' supply Jesus' final words. Mark, as he has done throughout the Gospel, adopts the policy of 'show, not tell'. If anything, his stark, simple description is even more affecting than the longer accounts of the other Gospels.

The curtain of the temple

The curtain of the temple separated the holy of holies from the holy place. The holy of holies was the innermost sanctuary of the temple and was where God would descend, from time to time, in Old Testament tradition (see Isaiah 6.1–13). Only the high priest was allowed to enter the holy of holies and, even then, only once a year, on the Day of Atonement. The curtain symbolized the separation between God and humanity, keeping each safe from the other (God's purity safe from humanity's impurity, and humanity from the overwhelming nature of God's presence).

When the temple veil was torn in two from top to bottom, it symbolized God's own action: he was tearing apart for ever the boundary between God and humanity as he had done at Jesus' baptism, when he tore the heavens open. Jesus' death meant that God was no longer to be kept safe behind a barrier: God was on the loose in the world.

Various commentators discuss whether the tearing of the temple veil was symbolic of Jesus' critique of the temple. They surmise that the rending of the veil was a sign that the temple would be destroyed. This seems to me to be an unnecessary reading. Jesus had already declared the temple not fit for purpose and that it would be destroyed, just like the fig tree. It does not need to be reconfirmed. Much more important was that the barrier between God and the world was ripped apart. At last, God could come close to us. The first thing that happened, then, was that someone who should have been the very last person to do so (the centurion who nailed Jesus to the cross) came close, saw, perceived, understood and declared that Jesus was truly God's Son.

Three moments of revelation in Mark

See the box, 'Revelation or apocalyptic', on p. 202, for more on this; also consult the commentary on Jesus' baptism, pp. 25ff, and the Transfiguration, pp. 198ff.

Over the years, much has been made of the theme of the 'messianic secret' in Mark's Gospel. It is certainly true that Jesus' command to people not to tell anyone who he was stands out as being very odd. However, we need to balance this with three moments of revelation: three moments when something crucial was revealed about who Jesus was.

The first of these revelations was at Jesus' baptism, when the heavens were torn apart and God's voice was heard (probably just by Jesus): 'You are my Son, the Beloved; with you I am well pleased' (Mark 1.9–11).

The second was the Transfiguration. Nothing was torn apart here; but, on the top of a mountain, a cloud descended (as it had done on Mount Sinai, when the law was given) and God's voice was heard again: 'This is my Son, the Beloved; listen to him' (9.7)

The Crucifixion marks the third and final moment of revelation. This time the curtain in the temple was torn in two (using the same verb as the tearing apart of the heavens at the baptism). Again, a voice was heard declaring that Jesus was God's Son; only this time, the voice was not God's but a centurion's. Someone representing the 'ends of the earth' was now able to see and recognize what was going on, because God was on the loose. Those who had, until now, been kept away at a safe distance could draw near and declare who this person, Jesus, was.

The question posed by the disciples all the way back in 4.41 – 'Who then is this?' – receives its definitive answer: 'Truly this man was God's Son.'

Centurion

A centurion, as the title suggests, was the captain of a century (80 soldiers and 20 support staff). Here, the centurion's century was probably in charge of the crucifixions. Mark does not tell us what it was that made the centurion so sure that Jesus was God's Son. According to Mark's narrative, the most likely explanation was that the temple curtain had been torn in two. His confession shouldn't be tied to a specific thing that Jesus said or did: the world was now different and the centurion spoke, possibly even without thinking.

God's Son

One of the challenges of what the centurion said is that the phrase *huios theou* in Greek has no definite article (the word 'the'), nor should it have with this construction. So it could mean 'the Son of the God', 'the Son of a god', 'a son of the God' or 'a son of a god'. All are possible and we are left to work out which is most likely. It seems obvious to me, when you read the centurion's words alongside the baptism and Transfiguration accounts, that Mark means us to read 'the Son of the God'; but you may wish to disagree.

Mark 15.40–41: Not quite alone ... the women were there

Ever since 14.50–51 – when all the disciples fled (as Jesus had foretold) and the young man, whose naked, desperate retreat emphasized the chaos and despair of Jesus' arrest – we have imagined Jesus to be alone. This sense was accentuated by Jesus' cry of despair from the cross. Here, we have the one whose first act in ministry was to call others to join him left deeply and utterly alone, even by God.

As with the night before the dawn, it is always darkest before the first glimmers of light begin to shine. So it was at the Crucifixion. Jesus' cry in 15.34 was one of utter despair and hopelessness; but then, immediately, there were glimmers of light. The curtain in the temple was torn in two: God broke into the world. The centurion saw and understood that Jesus was God's Son, the only human to do so in the Gospel. And now we discover that Jesus was not alone. His female followers had not left. There were, in fact, glimmers of light as there always are even when we struggle to see them.

Links backwards

- This story makes us think back to Mark 14.50–51, when we believed that the disciples had all fled. The Twelve may have done so, but not everyone had left.

Interesting words ...

- v. 40: *looking on. Theōreō* refers to 'looking', 'perceiving' or 'observing'. This is an important word that is repeated twice more in 15.47, when the two Marys saw where Jesus' tomb was and when they saw that the stone had been rolled away. The overall impression is of the women watching carefully.
- v. 41: *follow*. The verb *akoloutheō* is the usual word for 'follow' in Mark. Here, it is in the imperfect: 'they kept on following'. This introduces the idea of the women's faithfulness.
- v. 41: *provided. Diakoneō* is the verb used to describe the angels waiting on Jesus after his temptations in the wilderness. It means 'to serve' or 'to minister to'.
- v. 41: *many other women*. The feminine plural is used here for 'many' (*polus*) and 'other' (*allos*).
- v. 41: *come up with. Sunanabainō* means 'to go up with'.

Followed

Mark has left it until now to record the significant place of women among Jesus' followers. It is easy to imagine (and certainly many artists through the centuries imagined) that those following Jesus were solely men. Mark's language here is significant. These women – some named, others not – followed Jesus, just as the male disciples did.

They even came up to Jerusalem with Jesus for the festival. So we need to go back through our mental imagery and ensure that we have included these women in the crowd. They laboured up the valley from Jericho to Jerusalem; they were among those accompanying Jesus into Jerusalem; they were with those gathered around him when he cursed the temple and during his conflicts with the leaders; and they were probably at the Last Supper too.

These women were there all along and we need to make sure that we have not forgotten their presence, which has happened for so long throughout church history.

Mary the Magdalene, Mary the mother of James the younger and Joses, and Salome

Although most of the women who were at the Crucifixion are not named, three of them are and they are worth noting.

1 Mary the Magdalene. This is the first time she is mentioned in Mark, though Luke 8.2 mentions her earlier in his account and notes that seven demons had gone out of her. Most scholars think that 'the Magdalene'

refers to the town Magdala, on the Sea of Galilee. In the Talmud, it is called Migdal Nunayya, which means 'Tower of Fishes' and may refer to the fish drying process that was essential for preserving fish in this period. A few think that Jesus may have surnamed Mary 'Magdala' ('tower'), likening her to a tower, in parallel with Peter's being named 'rock'.

2 Mary the mother of James the younger and Joses. This Mary is mentioned again in 15.47, where she is just Mary the mother of Joses, and again in 16.1, where she is identified as the mother of James. These suggest that both James and Joses were well known in the early Church and so mentioning her makes it easier to locate her. It is most likely that the James mentioned was James, the son of Alphaeus.
3 Salome. She is mentioned only here and in 16.1. Matthew's parallel account implies that Salome was the mother of James and John (Matt. 27.56), which would seem to make sense from her role elsewhere.

There is a sense that these women, along with others who are unnamed, were very faithful to Jesus and gave him ongoing support.

Mark 15.42–47: Jesus' burial

After Jesus' death, Mark, somewhat surprisingly, introduces us to people we did not know were present until now. The first group were Jesus' female followers; the second was an individual, Joseph of Arimathea, who was a member of the Sanhedrin. Following the pattern that Mark has set up so often, people in groups react to Jesus in entirely predictable ways; but on their own, they behave differently, and none more so than Joseph of Arimathea.

Links backwards

- The mention of Joseph recalls all the previous passages in which the Sanhedrin was mentioned either directly or indirectly (Mark 11.27; 12.12; 14.53–65; 15.1).
- In parallel with the verses about the scribe who came to ask Jesus a question (12.28–34), this passage shows that not all members of the Sanhedrin were entirely opposed to Jesus.

Interesting words …

- v. 42: *evening*. *Opsios* refers to a time that is late but before dark.
- v. 42: *day of Preparation*. *Paraskeuē* refers to any kind of preparation. Here,

it clearly refers to the preparation day before the sabbath of a Passover. The sabbath of a Passover would have even greater significance than other sabbaths, even if Passover had already started, as it had here.

- v. 43: *respected member of the council*. The word 'respected' is translated from *euschēmōn*, which means 'honoured' or 'of high standing'; it probably also means 'wealthy'. The specific word for 'council' that Mark uses here is *bouleutēs*, which is also found only in Luke 23.50 (also regarding Joseph). He does not use the word *sunedrion* as previously.
- v. 43: *waiting expectantly*. *Prosdechomai* means 'to wait for', 'to welcome' or 'to receive'.
- v. 43: *boldly*. *Tolmaō*, used as a participle here, means 'having been courageous'.
- v. 44: *wondered*. For more on Mark's use of the different words for 'amaze', see the notes on 1.22 and 27 (pp. 41–2). Here, Pilate was amazed (*thaumazo*) that Jesus had died so soon. The translation 'wondered' slightly obscures this sense.
- v. 45: *body*. A *ptōma* refers specifically to a 'fallen body', hence a corpse.
- v. 46: *linen cloth*. A *sindōn* is the same word used for the cloth covering the body of the young man in Gethsemane.
- v. 46: *tomb*. A *mnēmeion* was a 'grave' or a 'monument for the dead'. The word is used previously in Mark to refer to the place where the man from Gerasa, who was possessed by Legion, lived.
- v. 46: *rolled a stone*. *Proskuliō* means 'to roll to' and is the opposite of *apokuliō* ('roll away' or 'roll back') mentioned in 16.3 and 4. A *lithos* was specifically a 'dressed' stone: in other words, a stone that had been shaped to fit the entrance.
- v. 46: *door*. *Thura* means 'door'. Hewn tombs have doorways cut into the rock to allow entrance.
- v. 47: *saw*. The same word is used in 15.40 for 'looking on': *theōreō*.

Evening

Deuteronomy 21.22–23 makes clear that someone who had been executed had to be buried on the same day:

> When someone is convicted of a crime punishable by death and is executed, and you hang him on a tree, his corpse must not remain all night upon the tree; you shall bury him that same day, for anyone hung on a tree is under God's curse.

The timing is a little difficult. If evening had come, it was already the next day: the sabbath during Passover. So it must have been late in the day, but not so late that it was dark and therefore the next day.

Joseph of Arimathea

It is odd that Mark introduces a different word for council here (though all commentators think that it refers to the same entity: the Sanhedrin). Perhaps the change of word serves to distance Joseph a little from the actions of the Sanhedrin related in the previous chapter.

The town of Arimathea isn't mentioned, apart from in connection with Joseph here. It is thought to have been the town of Ramathaim-zophim, which was the birthplace of Samuel (1 Sam. 1.1); it was about 20 miles north-west of Jerusalem.

None of the Gospels states whether Joseph was at Jesus' trial or not, though both Matthew and John say that he was already a disciple (Matt. 27.57; John 19.38). This may be what Mark's cryptic phrase, 'waiting expectantly for the kingdom of God', means. It could also mean, however, that he was more open than others because he was actively waiting for God's kingdom.

Pilate granted the body to Joseph

Pilate's willingness to give Joseph the body suggests that he was clear that Jesus was innocent. He would have been much less likely to allow the body of a rebel to be taken, even by someone as eminent as Joseph.

Rock-hewn tomb

Burial in a rock-hewn tomb was very common in this period. Large numbers of similar tombs have been found around Jerusalem. On entry into the tomb, there would have been a ledge, also hewn out of rock, on which the dead body was laid. The body would have been wrapped and anointed to mask the stench of decomposition. After a year or so, the bones would be collected and placed in an ossuary in a niche in the wall. The ledge would then be available for the next body. It was vital, therefore, that Jesus' tomb was a new one (mentioned in Matt. 27.60, Luke 23.53 and John 19.42 but not Mark), otherwise there could have been doubt over whether he had truly risen from the grave.

John's Gospel tells us that Nicodemus, who helped Joseph to bury Jesus, provided a large quantity (about 100 pounds) of the myrrh and aloes needed to anoint a body. Mark implies that Jesus was buried in such a rush that he was washed and wrapped in a shroud but not anointed (for more on this, see 'Interesting words', 16.1, below).

Joseph's act of tender devotion here is striking. It raises a number of unanswerable questions, however; not least whether he was present at Jesus' trial and sentencing, and how he reacted if he was there. The hint in the narrative is that he was and that he was so uncomfortable with the proceedings that he attempted to compensate by ensuring a respectful burial for Jesus.

Mark 16.1–8: 'He has been raised; he is not here'

Mark's resurrection account is odd. Whereas all the other Gospels have an encounter with Jesus by the tomb, followed by another encounter somewhere else (in John, there is more than one other encounter), Mark leaves us with the women having fled, saying nothing to anyone. And there are no resurrection appearances at all.

The somewhat pleasing twist, though, is that we know the women did eventually tell someone about what they saw. If they hadn't, we wouldn't be reading about their saying nothing. The ending is not really the ending, and that seems to be the point.

Links backwards

- Each time Jesus predicted his death, he also predicted that he would rise again (Mark 8.31—9.1; 9.30–32; 10.32–34). The moment long foreseen has now come true.

Links forwards

- In a way, the links forwards are the whole point of this story. How will the story end? That is for the reader to determine …

Interesting words …

- v. 1: *bought spices. Agoraō* means 'to buy in the market'. The women would, of course, not have had spices ready because they had come from Galilee. The word *aroma* refers to generally aromatic spices, not specific ones; the usual ones, though, were myrrh, aloes, frankincense and nard.
- v. 1: *anoint.* The verb *aleiphō* means 'to daub with oil'. It was also used of oiling an athlete before the games. It is not a specific word for anointing after death.
- v. 2: *very early … when the sun had risen.* Mark was very precise about the timings: 'It was very (*lian*: 'exceedingly') early morning (*prōi*) but after the sun (*helios*) had risen (*anatellō*).' This would have been around 6.30 a.m.
- vv. 3–4: *roll away; rolled back. Apokuliō*, the opposite of *proskuliō*, which is what Joseph did to the stone in 15.46.
- v. 4: *looked up; saw. Anablepō* means 'to look up'. *Theōreō* ('look at' or 'observe') is the word that has been used throughout this section for the action of the women (they watched the Crucifixion, saw the location of the tomb (15.40, 47) and then saw that the stone had been rolled away).
- v. 5: *young man.* A *neaniskos* is a usual word for a 'young man'. It described the young man in Gethsemane who ran away (14.51); but apart from the use of the same word here, there is nothing to suggest a connection between them.

- v. 5: *robe*. Ironically, the last time a *stole* (long, flowing robe) was mentioned by Mark, it was a criticism of the scribes who liked to wear them. Here, the young man wears a similarly flowing robe.
- vv. 5–6: *alarmed. Ekthambeō* is one of Mark's favourite 'amazed' words. Here, it means 'flabbergasted' or 'overwhelmed', either with wonder or fear. See the notes on 1.22 and 27 (pp. 41–2) for more on Mark's use of these words.
- v. 6: *raised*. The verb *egeirō* is used here, rather than *anistēmi*, which could have been. On words for 'resurrection', see the box, 'The words for "rise" and "resurrection" in Mark', on p. 194.
- v. 7: *go; going ahead. Upagō* is 'go away' and *proagō* is 'go before'. The connection between the command to the women to go and the instruction that Jesus would go before them seems crucial.
- v. 7: *see*. Throughout this section, the verb *theōreō* has been used for the women 'looking'. This time, the verb changes and is *horaō*, which has more of the sense of 'perceive' than 'look at'.
- v. 8: *terror and amazement*. The word *tromos* means 'shaking' or 'trembling from fear'; and *ekstasis* can mean a 'trance' or refer to general bewilderment.
- v. 8: *for they were afraid*. The Gospel ends with two words: 'they were afraid (*phobeomai*) for (*gar*)'. While this seems oddly truncated, it is grammatically correct. *Gar* is a word that must come second in a sentence; when there are only two words, it must, inevitably, come last.

Bought spices ... so that they might anoint

Mark does not tell us why the women were bringing the aromatic spices to anoint Jesus' body. There are two reasons why we might think they should not be doing so.

- Joseph apparently had time to locate a linen shroud for Jesus' body, as well as a tomb. The rituals of washing the body and anointing it with the aromatic spices (usually myrrh, aloes, frankincense and nard) to cover the smell of the body's decomposition were very important. John tells us that it was done for Jesus, so it is surprising to discover the women thought it necessary to go to the tomb. The best explanation is that they had observed the ritual and thought it too rushed for a full anointing, so they decided to complete it the next morning.
- Women did not engage in death rituals for a man. This was done by men. Women would be employed to be ritual mourners for a man; but the washing, anointing and binding the body would have been done by men for men. It seems that the women had decided that the men, who had fled, would not be coming back and so that, unusually, they needed to do this ritual themselves.

The stone had been rolled back

It is worth reminding ourselves that, after his Resurrection, Jesus did not need the stone to be rolled back to leave the tomb. As we see from John 20.19, Jesus' resurrection body was able to pass through locked doors (and, we assume, stones blocking entrances). The stone was rolled away so that witnesses could see the empty tomb. The women who had observed (*theōreō*) everything, needed to see one last thing for their testimony – that the tomb was empty.

A young man wearing a white robe

The iconography passed down to us from historical depictions causes many of us to think that the key characteristic of angels is their wings. This is not always the case in biblical texts. The real identifier is a white robe, such as the young man is wearing here. As we saw in Jesus' Transfiguration, the factor that highlighted his divine status was his white clothing. This was also true of angels, who spent time in the presence of God. The young man's flowing white robes immediately signify that he is an angel.

'Don't be alarmed'

Angels regularly tell those to whom they appear not to be afraid (*phobos*). Here, the angel goes one step further. *Ekthambeō* implies an emotional overload. Clearly, the women were far more than afraid. It turns out that the angel's words didn't have any impact: the women ran off anyway.

'He has been raised'

As noted above, there are two words for 'rise' in the Gospels: *anistēmi*, which is used in the Passion predictions (8.31; 9.9, 31; 10.34), and *egeirō*, which is used in 14.28 and here. There is no discernible difference between the two verbs. The key, though, is that *egeirō* is used in the passive voice, 'be raised' (not in the active, 'rise'). This lays the groundwork for much of Paul's language about the God who raised Jesus from the dead.

'Go, tell'

The importance of this short phrase is huge in Mark. As we have noted throughout the Gospel, Jesus repeatedly told people not to tell anyone about what had happened. Here, for the first time, we have the positive command 'Go, tell'. The moment had come. The disciples now had everything they needed to see and perceive, hear and comprehend, understand and remember. Now was the moment to tell, to proclaim the good news about who

Jesus was (and is). Unfortunately, as with the male disciples, the women ran away, afraid; but the moment was here. The question was, what would happen next?

'... and Peter'

Although this mention of Peter is brief, it is hugely important. Just as in John's Gospel, Jesus symbolically forgave Peter for his denial (John 21.15–19), the same happened here. Peter was singled out for special mention. The women were to tell the disciples and the one who probably thought he was no longer a disciple because he had denied Jesus. It is a small, passing but vastly significant point. They were, above all, to let Peter know the news. His last action regarding Jesus was not to be his denial.

Galilee

Going ahead of the disciples to Galilee implies that everyone was going back to the start and beginning all over again. This time, though, the disciples knew so much more than they did at first.

They were afraid for ...

Although it seems odd to end the entire Gospel with the word 'for' (as we noted above, in 'Interesting words'), the rules of Greek grammar dictate that the word *gar* must appear second in a sentence. By definition, in a two-word sentence, it will come last. It is fascinating that in the Greek translation (Septuagint) of Genesis, the same construction can be found with reference to Sarah. Genesis 18.15 states that Sarah laughed when told by the angels that she would conceive; but she denied that she had laughed: 'she was afraid for'. Someone who knew this passage might remember it; they might also remember another occasion when God had worked something inconceivable in the world to which the first response had been fear.

Of course, the subsequent responses were very different. Sarah reacted with fear and later with joy at the birth of her child Isaac (whose name means 'laughter'). Maybe the same would be true for the women (we might then remember that we are reading this with hindsight and so know that they did, after all, tell someone).

Was that it?

There is no doubt that this is the oddest ending of any book of the Bible. It just stops. No grand flourish, no moving ending; just the intimation of the sound of the women's footsteps as they fade into the distance.

Odd as it may be, I join most commentators today in believing that this is the intended ending. It is almost impossible to read it and not ask yourself, 'Is this it?' The answer, of course, is no. It most definitely is not it. Reading today, we know that for 2,000 years, people have taken the angel at his word and gone to tell of all that Jesus was and did. Mark's Gospel continues today to challenge each one of us, the readers, to 'go, tell'. We have seen and heard, understood and remembered all that Jesus was and did. Now the moment has come. How will the story end? How will the beginning of the good news of Jesus Christ continue? The ending hands the story over to you and to me.

Mark's Gospel has introduced us, over 16 brisk chapters, to Jesus the Messiah, the Son of God. We have followed in his footsteps as he healed the sick, cast out demons, taught and proclaimed the good news of the kingdom. We have observed, with unease, the growing opposition to Jesus. We have rolled our eyes, however affectionately, at the disciples' inability to comprehend what was really going on. We have heard and pondered Jesus' teaching about the cost of following him. We have watched his being betrayed and abandoned, and his trials, suffering and death. We have heard the centurion answer the disciples' question from the stilling of the storm: 'Who then is this?' And now the moment has come: Jesus has risen from the dead as he said he would. The women have run away, and the baton has been handed over to us. We, who have been silent characters throughout the whole story, are now thrust centre stage. We hear the echo of Jesus' voice in our ears: 'Who do you say that I am? Now go, tell.' Just as Jesus told the man from Gerasa to 'tell them how much the Lord has done for you, and what mercy he has shown you', so we are called to do the same.

We have read the beginning of the good news of Jesus Christ: now is the time to turn the page and let the story continue.

Epilogue: Alternative Endings

The ending of Mark has, through the years, been considered so odd that alternative endings have been provided to make up for it. As I do not consider them to be part of the original, I won't examine them in as much detail as the rest of the Gospel; but it is worth looking at them briefly.

What happened?

Those who think that Mark did not intend the Gospel to end where it does have theories about what happened to the actual ending. Here are the two most significant arguments.

- Mark became ill or was martyred before finishing the Gospel and so left it as it was.
  The problem with this idea is that sudden though it is, the current ending of 16.8 is not so abrupt that it ends in the middle of a story. For this theory to be persuasive, the ending would have to occur in the middle of the story, not with the women running away.

- There was another ending that was lost and never found again.
  As most early manuscripts were on scrolls, only later moving to codices (that is, pages), it is harder to imagine the loss of the end of a scroll than the loss of a page.

On the whole, the arguments for the 'loss' of a proper ending are not strong enough to be completely persuasive. Nevertheless, copyists over the years were so convinced that 16.8 was not intended to be the final ending that they supplied others. There are two and a half in all.

Since not all translations include the endings, I will replicate them here.

Alternative ending I: The shorter ending

And all that had been commanded them they told briefly to those around Peter. And afterward Jesus himself sent out through them, from east to west, the sacred and imperishable proclamation of eternal salvation.

This ending has no verse numbers in any of the manuscripts and is included in only a very few manuscripts as the ending to Mark. In all but one of the manuscripts where it occurs (which largely date to between the seventh and ninth centuries), the text then continues with the longer ending.

It gives a summary of what happened, which basically contradicts 16.7–8 but explains how the message was then proclaimed. It is clearly not by Mark, given the change in language, especially at the end. Even in English, it is easy to see that the 'the sacred and imperishable proclamation of eternal salvation' is not the kind of language Mark would have used.

Alternative ending II: Mark 16.9–20: The longer ending

Now after he rose early on the first day of the week, he appeared first to Mary Magdalene, from whom he had cast out seven demons.
[10] She went out and told those who had been with him, while they were mourning and weeping.
[11] But when they heard that he was alive and had been seen by her, they would not believe it.

[12] After this he appeared in another form to two of them, as they were walking into the country.
[13] And they went back and told the rest, but they did not believe them.

[14] Later he appeared to the eleven themselves as they were sitting at the table; and he upbraided them for their lack of faith and stubbornness, because they had not believed those who saw him after he had risen.
[15] And he said to them, 'Go into all the world and proclaim the good news to the whole creation.
[16] The one who believes and is baptized will be saved; but the one who does not believe will be condemned.
[17] And these signs will accompany those who believe: by using my name they will cast out demons; they will speak in new tongues;
[18] they will pick up snakes in their hands, and if they drink any deadly thing, it will not hurt them; they will lay their hands on the sick, and they will recover.'

[19] So then the Lord Jesus, after he had spoken to them, was taken up into heaven and sat down at the right hand of God.
[20] And they went out and proclaimed the good news everywhere, while the Lord worked with them and confirmed the message by the signs that accompanied it.

Alternative ending IIb: The Freer Logion

One manuscript contains the following after verse 14, in addition to the rest, as an attempt to soften the criticism of the disciples:

And they excused themselves, saying, 'This age of lawlessness and unbelief is under Satan, who does not allow the truth and power of God to prevail over the unclean things of the spirits. Therefore, reveal thy righteousness now' – thus they spoke to Christ. And Christ replied to them, 'The term of years of Satan's power has been fulfilled, but other terrible things draw near. And for those who have sinned I was handed over to death, that they may return to the truth and sin no more, in order that they may inherit the spiritual and incorruptible glory of righteousness that is in heaven.'

Manuscripts

Although verses 9–20 appear in around 95 per cent of the manuscripts that now exist of Mark's Gospel, the two oldest ones, and some other key ones, do not contain these verses. Nor were they known to some of the Early Church Fathers, such as Clement of Alexandria and Origen.

Vocabulary and grammar

In the space of 12 verses, the longer ending contains 15 words that do not appear anywhere else in Mark. Alongside those are other words that are used differently from those in the Gospel proper.

The transition is odd as well. The three women from 16.1–8 disappear completely, leaving only Mary Magdalene as the focus of the story. Also, Jesus never appears in Galilee as the angel promised: he appears only in Jerusalem.

A Summary

Verses 9–20 are a synopsis of some of the other accounts about the Resurrection:

- Verses 9–10 summarize material about Mary Magdalene in John 20.11–18 and Luke 8.2.
- Verses 12–13 summarize the events on the road to Emmaus described in Luke 24.13–35.
- Verses 15–20 summarize the Ascension narrative in Luke 24.50–53 and Acts 1.6–11.

It's as if someone has decided to produce a précis of the key elements of the Resurrection and post-resurrection narratives and have added them in here.

All in all, verses 9–20 simply do not fit with the rest of Mark; neither, indeed, does the short summary nor the insertion of verses, after verse 14, from the Freer Logion.

We are left, therefore, with the conclusion that either 16.8 is the ending as Mark intended it or that there was another ending, which has been lost almost from the start. We might as well, therefore, treat 16.8 as the ending and make of it as much as we can.

Index of Bible References

Old Testament

Genesis
1.1 16, 224
2.24 226
6.1–4 270
9.4–7 177
13.2 63
18.15 342
22.2 29
38.8–10 269

Exodus
3.1–6 201
3.1–12 271
4.22 29
7.3 155
19 201
20.1–17 234
23.20 21
24.8 303
29.7 191
30.20–21 161
33.18–23 155
34.21 74

Leviticus
2.13 222
11 163
15.25 127
15.29 127
17 163
19.17–18 273
19.18 272
23.33–42 204

Numbers
27.17 149

Deuteronomy
6.4–5 95, 273
6.5 273
7.1 177
17.6 138
19.15 138
21.22–23 337
23.25 74
25.5–10 269

1 Samuel
1.1 338
1.26 259
17.43 168
21.1–9 74

2 Samuel
6.1–23 114
7.12 275

1 Kings
1.33 251
8.22 259
19.10–12 155
19.11–18 201
19.15–16 191
22.17 149

2 Kings
1 87
1 87
1.8 24
2.11 190, 203
4.42–44 148
4.43 148
9.13 252

9.13 252
16.3 221
23.10 221

Esther

5.3 144
9.31 71

Job

1.6–12 194
31.1 220
31.5 220
31.9 220

Psalms

2 29
2.7 29–30
19.14 164, 273
22 248
22.1 330
22.27 248
23 150
23.5 295
23.5–6 150
41.4 59
82.6 29
89.26–28 29
110.1 275, 314
113 302
113–118 303
114–118 303
118 248, 252–4, 257, 262, 265, 303
118.5–14 253
118.19–20 253
118.22 265
118.25–26 252
118.26 253
133.2 295

Isaiah

5.3–4 264
6.1–8 201
6.1–13 332
6.8 99
6.9–10 99
11.2 28
11.6 21
13.9–10 330
23 167
40 24
40.3 21
42.1 28–9
45.1 191
50.6 238
53 243
53.5 238
53.8–9 238
53.10–12 243
56.6–8 257
61.1 28
64.8 308
66.24 221

Jeremiah

8.13 256
9.17–18 131
12.6 136

Ezekiel

11.22–23 283
26–28 167
34.5 149

Daniel

7 61
7.9 202
7.13 315
7.13–14 61, 314
9.27 287
11.31 287
12.1 288
12.1 288
12.1–2 269
12.11 287

Hosea

1.2 16
6.6 273

Joel

2.10 330
2.28 25
3.14–15 330

Amos
1.9–10 167
5.18–20 330

Jonah
1 112

Habakkuk
3.13 191

Zechariah
3.10 256
8.19 71
9.2–3 167
9.9 251
14.4 251

Malachi
3.1 21
4 20
4.5 203, 332
4.5–6 19, 190

New Testament

Matthew
3.1–23 15
4.17 34
5.3 229–30
5.13 222
5.14–16 101
5.20 156
5.41 324
5–7 95
6.9–13 308
8.5–13 170
8.20 48
8.25 112
8.28–34 118
8.29 119
9.18 130
9.21 128
10.1 83
10.2–4 65
10.8 83
10.10 139
10.42 219
11.2–3 144
11.18–19 70
12.11–12 76
12.22–32 89
12.31–32 90
13.18 92
13.55 136
14.6 141
14.21 147
15.19 165
16.11 181
16.17 192
17.2 201–2
17.11–13 205
17.14–20 205
17.20 259
18.6 220
18.10 220
18.14 220
19.3 225
19.9 225
22.15–22 77
22.37 273
25.34–39 218
25.40 220
26.51 310
26.64 314
27.16 321
27.28 325
27.56 336
27.57 338
27.60 338

Mark
1 44, 205
1.1 1, 16–19, 34, 191, 343
1.1–15 15, 17, 19, 21, 23, 25, 27, 29, 31, 33
1.2 21–2

1.2–8	16, 19–20, 140, 203
1.2–13	32
1.3	22
1.4	21–2, 25
1.5	21
1.7–8	25
1.8	16, 19, 25
1.9	26
1.9–11	3, 5, 16, 19–20, 25, 109, 289, 333
1.9–13	32
1.10	26, 254
1.11	29, 199, 262
1.12–13	16, 19, 30, 51, 84
1.12–15	51
1.13	16, 19
1.14	32, 140, 211
1.14–15	16, 19, 31, 51
1.15	13, 16, 19, 32, 34, 52, 77, 92, 101, 104, 122, 250
1.16	20, 77
1.16–20	64, 82–3, 137
1.16–39	37, 39, 43, 45, 49, 51
1.18	37
1.20	37
1.21–28	117
1.22	46, 117, 125, 133, 153, 206, 260, 337, 340
1.23–27	207
1.24	116
1.25	112, 194
1.27	46, 117, 125, 133, 153, 206, 237, 337, 340
1.29	37
1.29–31	37, 48, 76, 86, 123
1.30	37
1.32	49, 86
1.32–34	49, 54, 79, 156
1.33	51
1.34	49–50
1.35	51, 128, 308
1.35–39	51
1.36	37, 51
1.38	51, 185
1.38–39	52
1.40	55, 77–8, 205, 208
1.40–45	53–4, 56, 77–8
1.41	55, 76, 227, 229
1.43–45	5
1.44–45	121
1.45	55, 142
2.1–12	54, 64, 70, 77, 156
2.6	261
2.7	60
2.8	261
2.11	194
2.12	46
2.13	64
2.13–17	54, 64, 70, 77, 82–3, 137
2.14	64, 194
2.15	65
2.15–16	308
2.15–17	66
2.18	70
2.18–22	54, 64, 70, 72
2.18–28	77
2.19	70
2.19–20	72
2.21	70, 72
2.22	72
2.23	104
2.23–27	160–1
2.23–28	54, 64, 70
2.24	141, 224, 266
2.25	274
2.26	141, 224, 266
2.28	61
3	44, 133
3.1–6	48, 54, 64, 70, 77
3.2	50
3.4	141, 214, 224, 266
3.5	76, 182, 224
3.6	53, 76, 135, 180, 188, 192, 254, 258, 265, 291
3.7	79
3.7–12	49, 53, 78, 156
3.8	79
3.9	79
3.9–11	79
3.10	50, 79, 128
3.11	43, 79, 123, 166

3.11–12 5
3.12 53–4, 79, 194
3.13 128, 182
3.13–19 81–2
3.13–20 137
3.14 83, 122
3.14–15 82
3.15 44, 83, 205
3.16 37
3.16–19 65
3.17 83
3.19 211
3.20–21 81, 86
3.20–35 133, 136
3.21 46, 91
3.22 44, 248
3.22–27 88
3.22–30 81, 160
3.23 30, 95
3.23–26 97
3.23–27 106
3.26 30
3.27 97
3.29 90
3.30 90, 207
3.31 86, 91
3.31–35 81, 84, 86
3.33 301
3.35 86
4 82, 95, 106
4.1 94, 103
4.1–2 94, 215
4.1–9 92, 97
4.1–20 81, 92, 100, 164
4.4–8 96
4.9 94
4.10 82, 94, 110
4.10–12 97, 102
4.10–13 92, 97
4.10–20 92
4.11 94, 97, 101, 104, 107
4.11–12 182
4.12 94, 99, 101, 103, 152, 178
4.13 94, 98
4.14 92
4.14–20 92
4.15 30, 84, 95
4.17 95
4.19 90, 95
4.20 95
4.21 101–2, 110
4.21–32 101
4.22 101–2
4.24 101, 103, 110
4.25 103
4.26 101, 104, 110
4.26–27 104
4.27 104
4.28 104
4.29 104
4.30 101, 105, 110
4.32 105–6
4.33 107
4.33–34 106
4.34 98, 107, 109, 155, 178
4.35 109–11, 114
4.35–41 6, 107–9, 120, 151–2, 178, 184, 188, 280, 286
4.36 110
4.37 110
4.38 110
4.39 110, 194, 214
4.40 110, 113, 210–11, 286
4.40–41 131
4.41 12, 110, 112–13, 133, 178, 199, 328, 333, 343
5 44
5.1 111
5.1–20 5–6, 44, 108, 114, 118, 120, 166, 169–70, 184
5.2 207
5.6 116
5.7 116
5.7–8 118
5.8 207
5.9 116
5.11 116
5.13 116
5.14 116
5.15 116, 120
5.17 117
5.19 343

5.20 46, 117
5.21 111, 123
5.21–24 6, 108, 166, 170, 184
5.21–34 157
5.21–43 123
5.22 123, 259
5.23 50, 132
5.24–34 80, 108
5.25–34 6, 166, 170, 184
5.28 50
5.29 50
5.33 166
5.34 50, 132, 243
5.35–43 6, 108, 166, 170, 184
5.36 132
5.37 40, 83, 213, 305, 307
5.38 125
5.39 125
5.40–42 125
5.41 8, 125, 132, 194, 205, 207
5.42 46, 125–6
5.43 5, 54, 125
6.1 133
6.1–6 133–4
6.2 46, 133
6.3 133
6.4 133–4
6.5 50, 133–4
6.6 46, 134, 138, 155
6.7 44, 82, 138, 205, 207
6.8 138
6.9–10 182
6.12 138
6.13 44, 50, 138
6.14–29 20, 108, 140, 145, 166
6.15 203
6.16 144
6.17–29 190
6.18 141, 224, 266
6.20 275
6.22 142
6.23 142
6.25 142
6.26 142
6.27 142
6.28 142
6.29 71, 140, 142
6.30–33 51
6.30–44 2, 6, 108, 145, 166, 174, 178
6.34 174
6.37 176
6.39 147
6.39–40 150
6.40 147
6.41 147, 151, 176
6.42 147, 150, 176
6.43 147, 176
6.44 147, 176
6.45 111, 148, 152
6.45–46 152
6.45–52 6, 107–10, 145, 151, 178, 184, 280, 286
6.46 51, 152–4, 308
6.48 152
6.49 153
6.50 153, 286
6.51 46, 153
6.52 153, 182, 224, 286
6.53 111
6.53–56 49, 156
6.56 50, 128–29
7 44
7.1 248
7.1–23 108
7.2 159–60
7.3 159
7.3–4 8, 162
7.4 159
7.5 159–60
7.6 159, 224
7.6–13 165
7.7 159
7.9 159
7.10 159
7.11 8, 159
7.13 159
7.14 159–60
7.14–23 165
7.15 160, 164
7.17 160
7.18 160, 164
7.19 160
7.21–22 160, 165
7.24–25 79

7.24–30 6, 44, 108, 123, 157, 165, 169–70, 184
7.25 207
7.31 169
7.31–37 6, 108, 157, 166, 170, 184–5, 187
7.34 8, 132
7.36 5, 54, 122
7.37 46
8 112, 247
8.1 174
8.1–10 2, 6, 108, 145, 166, 174, 178
8.2 174
8.3 174
8.4 174
8.6 176
8.7 176
8.8 176
8.9 176
8.11 178
8.11–21 6, 107–10, 145, 152, 164, 174, 178, 184, 188
8.13 111, 192
8.15 280
8.16 261
8.17 224, 261
8.17–18 182
8.18 176, 204
8.19–20 180
8.21 98, 180, 271
8.22–26 2, 6, 108, 166, 170, 172, 184–5, 188, 243
8.23 186
8.24 186
8.25 186
8.27–30 109, 133
8.27–33 188
8.28 203
8.29 12, 121, 178, 188, 199, 343
8.30 5, 54, 193
8.30–33 207
8.31 61, 261, 311, 341
8.31–33 210, 213, 237, 239
8.32 193
8.33 30, 84, 193
8.34–38 215
8.35 197
8.36 197
8.38 198
9 44, 112
9.1 198
9.2 40, 305, 307
9.2–3 83
9.2–7 5, 109, 133, 178, 188
9.2–8 201, 289
9.2–13 198, 213, 239
9.5 310
9.7 26, 30, 262, 333
9.9 5, 341
9.10 206
9.11 203
9.13 205
9.14 206
9.14–29 44, 137, 205, 213
9.15 46, 206
9.17 206
9.18 206
9.19 206
9.20 206
9.22 206
9.23 205–6, 208
9.23–24 206
9.24 206
9.25 194
9.26 206
9.27 125, 194
9.29 254
9.30 210
9.30–32 6, 185, 188, 192, 210, 213, 237, 291, 293, 297
9.31 210–11, 341
9.32 211
9.33 211, 224, 261
9.33–34 214
9.33–37 2, 213, 222, 227, 229, 239
9.34 214
9.35 82, 214, 239
9.36 214
9.36–37 218
9.37 214, 218
9.39 218, 227

9.41	217–18
9.42	219
9.42–43	218
9.42–49	259
9.42–50	101, 218
9.43	219
9.44	220
9.45	218–19
9.46	220
9.47	218–19
9.48	219–20
9.49–50	219
9.50	219
10	248
10.1	32, 248
10.1–12	227
10.2	141, 224, 266
10.2–12	226
10.5	155
10.13	194
10.13–16	214, 227
10.14	240, 293
10.16	214
10.17	90
10.17–31	230, 311
10.19	234
10.24	46, 237
10.26	46
10.27	236
10.30	90
10.31	239
10.32	82, 237–8
10.32–33	237
10.32–34	6, 185, 188, 192, 210, 213–14, 237, 248, 291, 293, 297
10.32–45	243
10.33	211, 237, 311
10.34	237, 311, 341
10.35	240
10.35–45	2, 214, 217, 239, 274, 327
10.37	240
10.38	240
10.38–39	240
10.40	240
10.41	240, 293
10.42	240, 242
10.42–45	215
10.43	214, 242
10.43–45	240
10.44	242
10.45	214, 240, 242
10.46	125, 243, 245
10.46–52	2, 6, 184–5, 206, 243
10.47	243
10.47–48	243, 274
10.48	194, 243
10.52	50, 129
11	247
11.1–11	248, 265, 310
11.1–25	248
11.9–10	262, 303
11.11	82, 250, 253, 280
11.12–13	289
11.12–14	289
11.12–25	254
11.14	90
11.15–19	265, 279
11.18	46, 254, 291
11.19	250
11.20	280
11.20–25	308
11.21	310
11.24	206
11.27	280, 309, 336
11.27–33	260, 262, 265, 268, 271
11.28–29	260
11.29–30	261
11.31	261
11–13	247
12	78
12.1–12	248, 253, 260, 262, 265
12.10	303
12.12	291, 336
12.13–17	77, 265, 268, 271
12.14	141, 224
12.18	268
12.18–27	268, 271
12.19	268
12.19–21	268
12.24	268
12.25	268
12.27	268

12.28	272
12.28–34	268, 271, 336
12.29	272–3
12.30	272
12.31	272
12.32	272
12.33	272
12.34	272
12.35–37	274
12.36	274
12.37	275
12.38	280
12.41–44	278, 293, 296
13	9, 280, 285–7, 289–90, 307
13.1–2	279
13.2	254, 259, 314
13.3	83, 215, 280, 305, 307
13.3–37	280
13.5	283, 285
13.6	286
13.7	283, 286
13.8	283
13.9	212, 280, 283, 285–6
13.11	212, 274
13.12	212, 286
13.13	283, 286
13.14	9, 283
13.19	283
13.21	283
13.23	280, 283, 285
13.24	283, 289
13.26	283
13.27	283
13.28–31	289
13.30	283, 290
13.33	280, 285
13.35	250
14	315
14.1	292
14.1–2	291, 297
14.1–11	248
14.3	296
14.3–9	292
14.8	292
14.10–11	212, 291, 297
14.11	297
14.12	300
14.12–26	298
14.17	82, 301
14.18	212
14.21	212
14.22	150
14.22–23	300
14.22–25	145
14.26	300
14.26–31	303
14.28	307, 341
14.31	318
14.32	83
14.32–42	51, 305
14.33	40
14.35	259
14.36	8, 132, 239, 241, 260
14.37	37
14.41–42	212, 307
14.42	250, 307, 309
14.43	309
14.43–51	309
14.44	212, 309
14.44–45	309
14.47	308–9
14.48	309
14.49	310
14.50	310
14.50–51	334
14.51	310
14.53	312
14.53–65	311, 318, 336
14.54	312, 317
14.55	312–13
14.55–57	312
14.58	312
14.59	312
14.61	214, 312
14.62	313–14
14.63	313
14.64	313
14.65	312–13
14.66–72	312, 318
14–15	247
15.1	212, 318, 336
15.1–15	311, 318
15.9	320–1
15.10	212
15.12	320–1

15.14 321
15.15 212, 237
15.20 125
15.21 245, 324, 326
15.23 324, 332
15.24 324
15.25 318, 324
15.26 324
15.27 324
15.29 324, 326
15.31 324
15.32 324
15.33–39 328
15.33–41 20
15.34 132, 334
15.37–39 5
15.39 26, 109, 133, 188, 199
15.40 301, 335, 337
15.40–41 82, 309, 334
15.41 30, 238, 335
15.42–47 336
15.46 140
15.47 91, 335–6
16.1 293, 336
16.1–8 32, 346
16.3 337
16.4 335, 337
16.5 202, 311, 340
16.5–6 340
16.6 141, 194, 340
16.7 5, 121, 204, 340
16.7–8 345
16.8 17, 340, 344, 347
16.9 345
16.9–20 346–7
16.10 345
16.11 345
16.12 345
16.13 345
16.14 345, 347
16.15 345
16.16 345
16.17 345
16.18 345
16.19 345
16.20 345

Luke

1.5–25 114
2.34–35 60
2.42 126
3.1–20 15
3.21–22 134
4.1–13 134
4.14–30 134
4.22 136
6.12–16 83
6.17–49 95
6.38 103
7.1–10 170
7.45 310
8.2 295, 335, 346
8.44 156
8.55 130
9.3 139
9.29 202
9.37–43 205
9.50 217
9.52 224
9.58 48
10.1 39
10.1–23 84
10.27 273
11.2–4 308
11.23 217
12.1 181
12.8–10 90
13.15 76
14.5 76
14.7–11 215
14.34 222
16.1–9 89
17.6 259
18.11 259
18.12 71
20.20–26 77
22.3 297
22.8 301
22.19 302
22.47 310
22.49 310
22.52 310
22.70 314
23.18–25 318
23.46 332

23.50 337
23.53 338
24.13–35 346
24.50–53 346

John
1.35–42 144
1.39 37
1.44 37
1.45 136
1.46 250
2.4 45
2.13 248
4 224
5.1 248
6.1–15 147
6.9 149
6.14 21
6.14–15 153
6.22–59 147, 150
9.3 59
9.6 172
10.22 248
13 295, 300
13.2 297
13.13 302
18.3 310
18.10 310
19.19 327
19.30 332
19.38 338
19.39–40 340
19.42 338
20.11–18 346
20.16 38, 246
20.19 341
20.25 327
21.15–19 342

Acts
1.6–11 346
3.22 203
4.32–37 236
5 262
5.38–39 262
6.1–6 177
12 33
12.2 241
12.12 8, 311
12.25 311
13.15 126
15.19–20 163
18.25 144
19.4 23
19.5 23
22.3 38

Romans
1.1 32
1.29–31 164
3.23 69
8.15 91
12.2 201
15.16 32
16.7 39

1 Corinthians
6.9–10 164
9.5 136
11.24 302
11.25 302
11.29–30 59
13.2 259

2 Corinthians
3.18 201
11.7 32

Galatians
1.19 136
2.11–14 163
4.6 91
5.19–21 164

Philippians
3.2 168

Colossians
3.5–8 164
4.14 127

1 Thessalonians
2.2 32
2.8 32
2.9 32

2 Timothy
3.1–5 164

James
1.6 259

1 Peter
2.1 164
4.17 32

2 Peter
2.4 221

1 John
5.14 260